UNITED STATES FISCAL POLICY
1945–1959

UNITED STATES FISCAL POLICY 1945–1959

ITS CONTRIBUTION TO
ECONOMIC STABILITY

BY

A. E. HOLMANS

Assistant in Political Economy,
University of Glasgow

OXFORD UNIVERSITY PRESS
1961

Oxford University Press, Amen House, London E.C.4

GLASGOW NEW YORK TORONTO MELBOURNE WELLINGTON
BOMBAY CALCUTTA MADRAS KARACHI KUALA LUMPUR
CAPE TOWN IBADAN NAIROBI ACCRA

PRINTED AND BOUND IN ENGLAND BY
HAZELL WATSON AND VINEY LTD
AYLESBURY AND SLOUGH

PREFACE

THIS book was originally written in the form of a thesis for the degree of Doctor of Philosophy of Oxford University. I wish to acknowledge my indebtedness to the Warden and Fellows of Nuffield College whose award to me of a Studentship gave me the opportunity for research, and to the English-Speaking Union of the United States, whose award gave me the privilege of spending the academic year 1957–8 in the United States as English-Speaking Union Fellow at Yale University.

I wish to thank, for their assistance and encouragement, my University Supervisor, Mr. P. P. Streeten, and my College Supervisors, Mr. J. S. Fforde and Sir Donald MacDougall. Professors T. Wilson and A. K. Cairncross at the University of Glasgow and Dr. Gerhard Colm of the National Planning Association, Washington, D.C., read the manuscript of the revised version in whole or in part and made numerous useful criticisms for which I am most grateful. I also wish to thank Professor J. R. Hicks and the staff of the Oxford University Press for their advice on making the necessary changes from the original form of this work.

I must thank all those in the United States who gave so generously of their time and trouble to answer my many questions, notably Mr. George M. Humphrey, Dr. Arthur F. Burns, Senator Paul H. Douglas, Representatives Richard Bolling and Stuyvesant Wainwright, and members of the staffs of the U.S. Treasury and the Board of Governors of the Federal Reserve System. I wish to thank particularly Professor J. P. Miller of Yale University, who did so much to help me to get the most out of my year in the United States. And no list of acknowledgements would be complete without an expression of gratitude to the countless hospitable Americans whose comments on matters political and economic helped me greatly in putting into their proper context events and opinions that I had hitherto studied from afar.

I wish to thank for their kindness and helpfulness the staffs of the libraries of Nuffield College, Rhodes House, and the Institute of Statistics, Oxford, the Sterling Memorial Library at Yale, and the American Library, London. In view of suggestions made in the United States in 1959 and 1960 that the facilities of the American

Library might appropriately be reduced, I would particularly like to draw attention to how valuable its resources proved to me in the preparation of the thesis that formed the basis of this book.

While those whose assistance I acknowledge above contributed much to this book, they are in no way responsible for any errors that it may contain or for any of the expressions of opinion; the responsibility for all errors and all expressions of opinion is, of course, mine alone.

A. E. H.

University of Glasgow.
September 1960

TABLE OF CONTENTS

Contents

LIST OF TABLES

INTRODUCTION

BY the end of the Second World War the maintenance of full employment was generally accepted in the United Kingdom as the primary object of national economic policy. Both political parties shared this view, which was to be found in most of the writing about post-war economic problems. The principal danger to full employment in Britain was seen to be events abroad, not a failure of internal economic policy. The external event most feared was a depression in the United States. Fears of another American slump cast a long shadow over the debates on international economic policy in 1944–5. There were few expressions of confidence in the ability of the United States to prevent another slump or to confine it to moderate depth and duration.

These fears could not be regarded as baseless, as being merely a by-product of a Leftward trend in the British climate of opinion. In the negotiations about the principles which were to govern international economic relations in the post-war world the American negotiators appeared to attach considerably less importance to the maintenance of full employment than did their British opposite numbers.[1] This obviously reflected the state of opinion in the United States, where there was strong evidence of the existence of a vocal and politically powerful section of opinion which professed a rooted objection on grounds of principle to the measures which nearly all economists had come to accept as the most appropriate for dealing with unemployment. In this respect the United States stood almost alone; in Britain and the Commonwealth countries full employment was the goal of policy, uninhibited by objections to the use of anti-deflationary fiscal policy on the ground that it was incompatible with 'free enterprise' and 'capitalism'. Although in American eyes it may have appeared 'impertinent' to assume that the United States was ignorant of the need to maintain economic stability and indifferent to it,[2] the structure of political opinion in the United States at the end of the War gave solid ground for concern. There is no

---

[1] R. N. Gardner, *Sterling-Dollar Diplomacy* (Oxford, 1956), pp. 272–80, 290, 376.
[2] C. Wilcox, *A Charter for World Trade* (New York, 1949), pp. 33–4; cited in Gardner, op. cit., p. 272, fn. 1.

need to emphasize the gravity of the consequences for the rest of the world of an American slump in the first post-war decade; even in ensuing years, when it had become clear that the rest of the world's resistance to the effects of American fluctuations had become greater than it had been in 1949, the maintenance of high and rising income and output in the United States remained indispensable if a liberal, multilateral system of world trade was to work successfully.

Does the success of the United States in avoiding a slump in the fifteen years after the end of World War II demonstrate that foreign fears were unjustified and based on too pessimistic an estimate of the ability and willingness of the United States to learn from experience and of the willingness of the American electorate to put up with unemployment? Or is it attributable to extraneous causes which have maintained aggregate demand at a level that has been consistently high enough to make it unnecessary to use those anti-deflationary policies which were objected to on principle? It is the purpose of this book to cast some light on this question, through an examination of American fiscal policies in the years between 1945 and 1959. For at the end of the War economists, both in the United States and elsewhere, looked to fiscal policy as the principal technique for controlling aggregate demand. Whether the United States could prevent a slump was thus largely a question of whether she was able and willing to use fiscal policy in a sufficiently powerful anti-deflationary way should the need arise.

Looking back from 1960 on the preceding one-and-a-half decades, it is clear that economic circumstances have been very different from what was expected at the end of the War. Not deflation but inflation was the problem more often than not, and instead of a slump there have been three recessions, all mild compared with previous recessions such as those of 1920–1 and 1937–8. In these circumstances the control of inflation was added to the control of deflation as a problem of economic policy, with the further problem of the correct timing of changes in the direction of policy. The measures taken to deal with inflation in 1946–8, 1950–3, 1955–7, and in 1959 are analysed, together with alternative policies which might have been pursued, and the economic and political reasons which accounted for the choice of policy. The measures taken to deal with the recessions of 1949, 1954, and 1958 are analysed in order to assess the role of economic policy, especially of fiscal policy, in holding these declines within narrow bounds. The question which it is attempted to answer is whether public economic policies form an important part of the explanation of the mildness of the post-war recessions relative to those of earlier years, or whether the explanation lies in extraneous developments unrelated to economic policy. Has the apparent success of the United States in maintaining economic stability really been achieved by a run of luck, leaving the vital questions about the ability and willingness of the United States to pursue an effective stabilization policy still unanswered?

It is argued in this book that although in each of the recessions the element of luck was in favour of stability, capable management of national economic policy was never a negligible factor. Understanding of the economics of counter-cyclical fiscal policy among men in American public life grew during the period, with important consequences in the policies pursued in the recessions of 1954 and 1958. But some support for political views about the proper functions of the Federal government which would place serious obstacles in the way of a drastic anti-deflationary policy still existed in the United States in 1960, so that the doubts and fears expressed in 1945 have not been disposed of altogether.

Although this book approaches the problem of economic stability in the United States in terms of fiscal policy, attention is also addressed to the other techniques used for controlling the economy and to the inter-relations between them and fiscal policy. The increasing importance attached to monetary policy after 1951 requires a discussion of the reasons for the change in its importance relative to fiscal policy. The inter-relations between monetary policy and fiscal policy were becoming increasingly clear by the end of the 1950's, especially the connection between the ability of the Federal Reserve System to conduct a restrictive monetary policy and the change in the size and structure of the National Debt. For these reasons, an adequate account of the use made of fiscal policy to maintain economic stability requires an extensive discussion of the use that was made or might have been made of monetary policy and direct controls.

No satisfactory account of the fiscal measures taken and the reasons why they were taken could be given without bringing the political situation into the analysis. The measures which members of the Administration and Members of Congress are willing to support depends on numerous factors apart from the economic situation. The structure of political power, the opinions of men in political life, the climate of opinion, and the historical background which underlies the structure of politics and the climate of opinion in the United States have to be brought into any discussion of American fiscal policy. This necessarily leads to criticism of the political views of numerous people and groups who have taken part in the process out of which has issued the fiscal policy pursued in the United States between 1945 and 1959. The basis of criticism should be stated explicitly. The writer has tried to keep to a minimum the use of value judgements in criticizing the conduct of affairs in another country, but regards the following judgements as reasonable. Firstly, that national economic policy should be directed to achieving maximum real income, full employment, and price stability (not necessarily in that order) to the greatest extent possible without offending against personal liberty and social justice. Secondly, whether or not a particular measure or policy will contribute to these economic ends or not and whether or not it will lead to infringements of liberty or justice is an empirical question, to be settled, insofar as it can be settled at all, by evidence and analysis and not by appeals to faith or doctrine. In all countries economic problems are not approached in a solely empirical attitude; the attitudes of many people are influenced by principles and doctrines, treating empirical evidence and analysis as at best irrelevant and at worst irreverent. Numerous examples will be met with in the discussion of American fiscal policy. It is a subject which rouses emotions of a type unique to the United States; it is impossible for a foreigner to enter into these emotions; he can observe them and their causes and consequences, but he cannot be expected to sympathize; *tout comprendre* is not *tout pardonner* in this instance. Such is the role of the United States in the world today that its policies and the processes which give rise to those policies are bound to become the subject of critical analysis by foreigners who lack some of the fundamental presuppositions of important groups in the American community, and are therefore liable to come to conclusions which some members of that community would reject, not because available evidence has been overlooked or the logic of the analysis is defective, but because of principles and doctrines to which they adhere.

CHAPTER I

THE INSTITUTIONAL BACKGROUND TO AMERICAN FISCAL POLICIES

THE obstacles to the development of a stabilizing fiscal policy in the United States have been twofold: in the realm of political opinions and in the institutions through which fiscal policy has to be conducted. The development of political opinions can be treated in terms of an historical narrative, as we go along; but it is necessary to have some familiarity with the institutions before the narrative can be understood. Accordingly, a preliminary survey of those aspects of the American political and administrative institutions which are relevant to the conduct of fiscal policy will be given in this chapter, and some conclusions suggested about the extent to which those institutions help or hinder the conduct of a stabilizing fiscal policy.

STATE AND LOCAL FINANCE

It must first be observed that the magnitudes of Federal revenues and expenditures, with which this book is mainly concerned, are much less preponderant relative to the revenues and expenditures of the state and local government than are the revenues and expenditures of the central Government of the United Kingdom relative to those of local authorities. Although the ratio of Federal revenues and expenditures relative to those of state and local governments was substantially greater in 1947 and 1957 than it was in 1937, 1927, or 1907, the economic impact of the fiscal activities of the state and local governments in the years between 1945 and 1960 was far from negligible. Table 1 on the following page compares the total revenues and expenditures of the Federal government with those of the state and local governments and with the gross national product.

The expenditures of the state and local governments are beyond the control of the Federal government except for the influence it can exercise through the medium of its grants-in-aid[1] or through monetary policy. The extent to which state and local governments can

---

[1] Federal grants-in-aid in 1957 amounted to $4·1 billion out of a total state and local government revenue of $37·8 billion.

TABLE 1

Receipts and Expenditures of Federal, State, and Local Governments

	Federal		State and Local		G.N.P. at
	Receipts	*Expenditure*	*Receipts*	*Expenditure*	*Factor Cost*
1947	43·3	31·1	15·5	14·4	215·4
1949	39·1	41·6	19·6	20·2	236·3
1953	70·3	77·7	27·4	27·1	334·8
1957	82·5	79·6	37·8	39·0	404·0

Amounts in $ billion at current prices.

Receipts and expenditures are defined according to the concepts used in the U.S. national income accounts, hence the totals differ from those shown in the 'conventional' or 'administrative' budget and in the 'cash' budget.

Source: Department of Commerce, *U.S. Income and Output* (Washington, 1959) and *Survey of Current Business*, July 1959, Tables I–17, III–1, and III–2.

G.N.P. at Factor Cost equals Table I–17 line 1 *minus* line 4 *plus* line 7.

administer their own finances to contribute to the maintenance of economic stability is small. During the Great Depression the severe declines in local revenues and consequent defaults and inability to borrow led to the financial operations of the state and local governments having an economically perverse effect.[1] The trend away from reliance on the property tax has done something to reduce the danger of a catastrophic fall in state and local revenues, but apart from this most of the features of the finances of state and local governments which gave rise to 'perverse flexibility' in the 1930's still remain, notably the strict legal and constitutional limits to indebtedness and tax rates by which many states, cities, and other local governments are bound.

The trend of state and local expenditures since the end of the War has been one of steady rise.[2] The principal factors responsible have been the rapid increase in population and shifts in its distribution, rising educational standards, and the need for roads adequate for an ever-increasing volume of traffic. The need was aggravated by the small amount of civil construction undertaken during the war. The social costs of holding down state and local government expenditure in order to reduce aggregate demand would thus have been high, even had it been administratively possible. Proposals have been made that state and local governments should accumulate a su.plus

[1] See A. H. Hansen and H. S. Perloff, *State and Local Finance in the National Economy* (New York, 1944), Chapters 1–4.

[2] Purchases of goods and services by state and local governments, measured at constant (1954) prices were $15·8 billion in 1946 and $32·3 billion in 1957. Dept. of Commerce, *U.S. Income and Output* (Washington, 1959), Table I–2.

in times when incomes and employment are high and disburse it when revenues decline.[1] Only a few states have adopted the system, even in principle,[2] and its effect has been slight owing to the need for greater expenditures. A significant part of the revenue and expenditure of the public sector of the American economy is thus not subject to central control for general economic policy, except insofar as state and local government borrowing is affected by monetary policy.[3]

THE FEDERAL BUDGET: PREPARATION BY THE ADMINISTRATION

The Budget is submitted by the President to the Congress in January in each year. The Budget proper is concerned with the estimates of expenditure and requests for appropriations, which are set out in very great detail. The accompanying Budget Message is devoted mainly to a discussion of the various items of expenditure, but contains some reference to taxation and fiscal policy generally. Details of proposed changes in taxation are sometimes included in the Budget Message[4] and sometimes sent up to the Congress in a separate Message.

The preparation of the estimates of expenditures and requests for appropriations is the responsibility of the Bureau of the Budget, one of the agencies constituting the Executive Office of the President and responsible directly to him.[5] The Bureau receives estimates from the various departments, investigates them in order to examine their justification, and relates them to the revenue estimates. About June (in the year preceding the submission of the Budget) a tentative decision is taken as to the maximum expenditure to be allowed to each agency.[6] Important disputes between the 'spending' agencies and the Bureau of the Budget are referred to the President for final settlement. Since 1948 defence expenditure has given rise to many

[1] Hansen and Perloff, op. cit., Chapters 5–8.

[2] Several states adopted the system when wartime limits on expenditures and booming revenues provided a substantial surplus, which it was desired to retain for post-war expenditures.

[3] The restrictive monetary policy in effect in 1956–7 gave rise to complaint from state and local governments about the cost and difficulty of selling their bond issues.

[4] Details of tax changes proposed by the Administration were included in the Budget Message in 1954, but not in 1951.

[5] For a detailed study of the preparation of the Federal Budget, see A. Smithies, *The Budgetary Process in the United States* (New York, 1955).

[6] Smithies, op. cit., pp. 110–1.

intractable problems in the preparation of the Budget, with the commands of the three Services sometimes unable to agree on a total expenditure which the Budget Bureau would approve.

While the work of the Bureau of the Budget in preparing the estimates of expenditure is similar to that of the Treasury in Britain, it is not responsible for taxation or for general economic policy. Taxation, including the detailed work on any proposed changes, is the responsibility of the U.S. Treasury, which is also responsible for the management of the National Debt. Within the Administration proper, the analysis of the economic situation and outlook is the function of the Council of Economic Advisers, which is part of the Executive Office of the President. Both the Federal Reserve System and the Department of Commerce have large staffs employed in the collection and analysis of economic statistics, and the Department of Health, Education, and Welfare and the Department of Agriculture have staffs which make analyses of economic problems related to the work of their Departments. The Board of Governors of the Federal Reserve System's Division of Research and Statistics has a strong staff of economic analysts, which can if necessary be brought to bear on economic problems outside the domain of monetary policy proper.

Responsibility within the Executive branch of the Government for fiscal policy is thus divided. The Bureau of the Budget is responsible for the expenditure side of the Budget and the Treasury for the revenue side, with economic analysis the responsibility of neither. The extent to which a co-ordinated policy is achieved despite the division of responsibility depends on the personalities concerned; in particular it depends upon the President, unless one of the members of the Cabinet concerned with economic policy is a sufficiently dominant personality to be able to achieve the co-ordination. During the Second World War there was established in the Bureau of the Budget a Fiscal Division, staffed by distinguished economists, which was responsible for analysing the economic situation and the application to it of the Budget. If the Senate version of the Employment Act had been passed,[1] a reorganized and strengthened Bureau of the Budget and its Fiscal Division would have become the agency responsible for fiscal policy. But the economic work of the Fiscal Division was assumed by the Council of Economic Advisers and the division of responsibility continued.

[1] See p. 39 infra.

THE FEDERAL BUDGET: CONGRESSIONAL ACTION

The proposed appropriations which are contained in the Budget are only recommendations to the Congress, as are any tax changes proposed. The Congress regards itself as an independent determiner of public policy, and as a rule behaves like one, in a way that the House of Commons does not. The Administration therefore has to convince a majority of Congress of the soundness of the particular measures it proposes.

Although the Budget includes estimates both of expenditures and of appropriations,[1] the Congress enacts appropriations for the given fiscal year, not the expenditures to be made in that year. An appropriation empowers the Government to incur obligations to pay money; when a contract is made for the purchase of goods, the full amount of the contract is normally 'obligated' and hence drawn from the amount of 'obligational authority' provided by the appropriation Act. In many cases not all the expenditure will be made in the year in which the obligation is incurred; the supply of the goods contracted for may be spread over a long period, payments being made on account and when the goods are delivered. Thus a change in appropriations in a given year will not result in a change of equal magnitude in expenditures in that year if the appropriation is for goods which will not all be delivered in the fiscal year, which is common with appropriations for defence, foreign aid, and civil public investment. In any year a substantial part of the expenditure will be to pay off 'obligations' incurred in previous years.

This is not the only limitation on the power of the Congress to control expenditures in a given year by varying appropriations for that year. Some expenditures are required by permanent law, so that the appropriation is a matter of routine. Examples are ex-servicemen's pensions and other benefits, and grants-in-aid to state and local governments. The amount of the expenditures under these heads is determined by the formulae set up by the Acts establishing the programmes, and the exact amount is in most cases beyond the control of either the Administration or the Congress by means short of amending the original Act. It is true that all Federal expenditures, including those that are fixed by permanent law, are based ultimately on Congressional authority, and that the action of the Congress in

---

[1] Appropriations are the most important form of obligational authority. The others are contract authorizations and authority to expend from debt receipts.

passing or rejecting legislation to set up public services has a direct effect on the level of Federal expenditure. But the amount of reduction in expenditure that can be achieved through the annual appropriation process, the chief legislative instrument for the variation of public expenditure in the short period, is very limited.

There are no such inhibitions to Congressional authority over taxation. When tax rates are raised the increase may be for an indefinite period (as in 1950) or scheduled by the Act to expire on a specified date (as in 1951). It is clearly easier to maintain a tax increase of the former type, since no positive action is called for and only enough votes to sustain a veto are required.

Appropriation bills and tax bills are considered separately, the former by the Appropriations Committee first in the House of Representatives and then in the Senate, and the latter by the Ways and Means Committee in the House and the Finance Committee in the Senate. Consideration of tax and appropriation bills proceeds simultaneously, with no formal and hardly any informal co-ordination between the two. The fact that expenditures and taxation are considered by different committees is of special importance in that it is rare for action by one of the Committees to be overruled on the Floor. In the House of Representatives, tax bills are debated under a 'closed rule', that is to say, no amendments may be moved except amendments proposed by the Committee and a single amendment to recommit the bill (i.e. to return it to the Committee for further consideration); and in the Senate, approval on the Floor of amendments rejected by the Finance Committee is rare if matters of substance are involved. Appropriation bills may be amended, but it is rare for the version finally passed by House or Senate to differ much from recommendation of the Appropriations Committee.

The first stage of the consideration of a tax bill or an appropriation bill by a Congressional Committee is the hearings. The principle of the hearings is the gathering of information for the guidance of Members of Congress about the merits of the legislation being considered. The hearings are important, and often time-consuming; the Committees are customarily very accommodating in giving an opportunity to 'testify' to anyone who wants to, so that practically every organization interested can 'put in its two cents' worth'. In hearings on a tax bill the Secretary of the Treasury is by custom the first witness, and the major business organizations such as the National Association of Manufacturers and the U.S. Chamber of Commerce, the trade unions, and the farm organizations such as the Farm Bureau Federation, the National Grange, and the National Farmers Union are always heard. If there is any likelihood of changes in excise taxation the various organizations of butchers, bakers, and candlestick makers send representatives to give evidence or make written representations. A major hearing before the Ways and Means Committee is fairly formal and a considerable amount of the discussion is devoted to the economic consequences of the tax changes being considered. At the other extreme are hearings before a subcommittee of the Senate Appropriations Committee,[1] where the atmosphere is informal, and attention tends to be concentrated on matters of detail, to the virtual exclusion of consideration of the impact that the budget is to make on the economy as a whole. The way in which the Congress considers appropriations is designed to facilitate the scrutiny of details. While detailed examination of requests by the Executive for funds has historically been a legislative function of great importance, its contribution to the formulation of fiscal policy proper is small.

An attempt was made in the Legislative Reorganization Act of 1946 to provide a more adequate mechanism for co-ordinating the handling of taxation and expediture by the Congress. A Budget Committee was set up in each House, to be composed of the members of the Ways and Means Committee and Appropriations Committee in the House of Representatives and the members of the Finance Committee and Appropriations Committee in the Senate. The Budget Committees were to draw up a 'legislative budget' for the guidance of the Appropriations Committees, taking note of what tax changes (if any) were proposed by the Ways and Means Committee. The attempt was a failure, principally because the power of decision still rested with the Appropriations Committees, who carried on just as they had done before.[2] In 1950 appropriations were presented in one 'Omnibus' bill instead of the usual series of bills, in the hope that this would lead to a more effective consideration of total expenditure. The change was, however, one of form rather than substance in that the detailed work was still done by subcommittees, and the bill was considered part by part on the Floor in a way which did not differ from the way in which separate bills were formerly

---

[1] Both the House and the Senate Appropriations Committees work through subcommittees, each subcommittee considering a group of appropriations embodied in a separate appropriations bill.

[2] The Republican majority in the 80th Congress used the Budget Committees to make 'economy' gestures. For a discussion of this episode, see pp. 75–6 infra.

considered. The experiment was not repeated in 1951 owing to its inconvenience in that the Senate could not take up any part of the appropriations until the House had completed action on them all, instead of dealing with each separate appropriation bill as soon as the House had passed it.

FLEXIBILITY IN BUDGETARY POLICY

Although the budget and appropriations are on an annual basis there is some scope for flexibility. While no change in tax rates may be made until after the passage of legislation to authorize it, discretionary changes in expenditure are possible. The President may direct that funds appropriated for expenditures other than those which are determined by permanent law be impounded, as in 1949 and 1956 when Presidents Truman and Eisenhower refused to allow the expenditure of funds voted for the purchase of large bombers which they had specifically asked the Congress not to appropriate. By holding down expenditure for 'discretionary' purposes and delaying the letting of contracts the Administration can hold down total expenditure without specific Congressional approval.

An increase in expenditures beyond the amounts appropriated requires Congressional action in the appropriation of additional funds. However, it is possible to accelerate expenditures and spend the funds appropriated for the whole fiscal year before the end of the year, and for the Congress to provide the funds for the remainder of the year by a deficiency or supplemental appropriation.[1] Among the first business to be dealt with in any Session is a deficiency or supplemental appropriation bill to provide funds for purposes for which insufficient funds were voted in the previous Session. If the Appropriations Committees approve, there is no difficulty in providing funds for an increase in expenditure during the current fiscal year. Agencies such as the Commodity Credit Corporation[2] and the Export-Import Bank, which are financed through 'authority to expend from debt receipts'[3] can increase their expenditures without

---

[1] Although the two are formally distinct, in that a deficiency appropriation is supposed to be for carrying out an existing programme and a supplemental for carrying out a new programme, this distinction of nomenclature is not always adhered to. See G. B. Galloway, *The Legislative Process in Congress* (New York, 1953), pp. 102–3.

[2] The agency which operates the programme for supporting the prices of agricultural commodities.

[3] I.e. authority to borrow from the Treasury out of the proceeds of its sales of securities.

specific Congressional approval provided they are within the limits set by law to their borrowing.

CONCLUSION: THE INSTITUTIONS OF AMERICAN PUBLIC FINANCE DO NOT FACILITATE THE CONDUCT OF A COMPENSATORY FISCAL POLICY

Responsibility for fiscal policy is fragmented within the Congress as well as within the Administration. In the latter it is possible for the President so to apply the central direction as to achieve a cohesive fiscal policy, but in the Congress there is normally no unifying power similar to that which the President can exert. The Committee Chairmen and their senior colleagues are centres of power in their own right, owing their positions to seniority deriving from the support of their local electorates and not to any national party organization. Co-ordination of policy in Congress has to result from personal relationships and skill in negotiation, not from party discipline. A party organization which exercised strong influence over the actions of the Committees could bring about a unified and coherent fiscal policy despite the fragmentation of formal responsibility, but at no time after 1945 did the organization of either party in House or Senate approach the strength needed to do this.

The absence of a strong party organization also makes the success of the Administration in getting Congressional approval of the measures which make up its fiscal policy dependent to a high degree on the personal relationships existing between the President and members of his Administration on one hand and senior Members of Congress on the other. A variety of factors in the political situation will affect these relationships and influence the degree of support in Congress which the President will receive for his policies. Only in circumstances of crisis such as 1933 has it ceased to be the case that 'the President proposes, but the Congress disposes'. During the 80th, 84th, 85th, and 86th Congresses the President faced a majority of the other party in Congress; and during the Administrations of Presidents Roosevelt and Truman many of the seats of power in Congress were held by Democrats whose views on many matters, including those closely related to fiscal policy, were at variance with those of the President.

The division of responsibility for taxation and appropriations between separate Congressional Committees and the absence of a strong party organization makes it unreasonable to look to the

Congress to formulate a coherent compensatory fiscal policy. The Congress has its own source of economic expertise in the Joint Economic Committee,[1] but the Committee can only study and recommend, having no direct responsibility either for taxation or appropriations. The formulation of a fiscal policy is thus of necessity the Administration's responsibility, despite the division of responsibility within it for matters relating to fiscal policy. Because of the working of the 'separation of powers', the passage through Congress of the measures related to fiscal policy in substantially the form in which the Administration recommended them is subject to a considerable, though varying, degree of uncertainty.

Not only is the form in which the Administration's legislative proposals finally reach the Statute Book affected, but also the time taken. For the good conduct of economic policy it is desirable that the time lag between deciding on a policy and putting it into effect should be as short as possible. In this respect the American system has distinct disadvantages. There is no equivalent to the passage by the House of Commons on Budget Day of Ways and Means Resolutions which give authority for the collection of taxes at amended rates for three months pending the passage of the Finance Act. The Chancellor of the Exchequer can announce on the afternoon of Budget Day that the tax on petrol will be increased with effect from six o'clock that evening, whereas the Secretary of the Treasury can only recommend such an increase to the Ways and Means Committee in January or early February, knowing that it may not be enacted until the summer or early autumn. The time lag before a major tax increase can be got through the Congress is usually long; in 1942 and 1951 it was not until October that action was completed on tax increases recommended by the Administration in January.[2] These extremely long lags are only partially offset by the simplicity of the withholding procedure,[3] which permits changes in income tax rates to be put into effect quickly once enacted.

The length of the time lags which American institutions introduce

[1] The Committee was set up pursuant to the Employment Act of 1946 with the title: 'Joint Committee on the Economic Report'. It was renamed 'Joint Economic Committee' in 1956 in recognition of the fact that it regularly extended its purview over a far wider field than the Economic Reports of the President.

[2] The great exception to this generalization was the enactment of tax increases in 1950. See Chapter VIII infra.

[3] 'Withholding' is the American term for deduction at source and P.A.Y.E. For an account of the mechanism see p. 31 infra.

into discretionary changes in fiscal policy adds to the importance of those features of the fiscal system which work automatically to promote economic stability. The difficulties in the way of rapid changes in tax rates and government expenditures, especially the former, in the United States are part of the explanation of the greater prominence given to the 'automatic stabilizers' in the United States than in Britain, where the obstacles to rapid discretionary changes are less important.

The 'automatic stabilizers' or 'built-in stabilizers' are those features of the system of taxation and government expenditure which work to moderate the fall in incomes and expenditures in time of recession and to moderate the increase in time of expansion and inflation. Such effects will follow from any budgetary system in which tax receipts fall when incomes fall and government expenditures fall less than tax receipts, and *mutatis mutandis* when incomes rise. Provided that incomes after tax fall less than incomes before tax, a stabilizing effect will be exerted so long as expenditures are not cut to match the fall in revenues. With a progressive tax structure the proportionate change in tax receipts will be greater than the proportionate change in income before tax, so that the stabilizing effect will be strengthened; similarly, the stabilizing effect will be strengthened if a significant part of total receipts are from a tax on a component of total income that is especially volatile with respect to changes in the level of economic activity. On the expenditure side, the stabilizing effect is strengthened if some government expenditures increase during a recession and decline during periods of boom. The larger the budget relative to 'full employment' G.N.P. the greater will be the effectiveness of the stabilizers, other things being equal.

The principal features of the American fiscal system which contribute to automatic stabilization in the sense described above are the progressivity of personal income tax and the extent of dependence on the corporation profits tax on the tax side, and the transfer payments to persons (notably unemployment compensation) and the subsidies to support the prices of farm products on the expenditure side. The large size of the budget (by pre-1939 standards) after 1945 increased the scope of these stabilizers.

But it is at once apparent that none of the above features of the American fiscal system were adopted because of their efficiency as stabilizers. The large size of the budget in relation to 'full employment' G.N.P. was the result of several causes, of which the most important were the heavy defence expenditure required by the 'Cold War' and the fixed charges that were the legacy of World War II, notably pensions and other benefits for ex-servicemen and interest on the National Debt. The existence of a progressive personal income tax and high rates of corporation profits tax arose from the balance of views about equity in the distribution of the wartime tax burden and the political power of the main economic interest groups. The transfer payments to persons were instituted as a means of relieving hardship, and their usefulness as economic stabilizers discovered afterwards. Likewise the schemes for supporting the price of agricultural products were set up to protect the incomes of farmers rather than to stabilize the economy as a whole, though the schemes have this effect in many instances, since in a free market agricultural prices drop substantially during a recession and farm incomes drop with them. The stabilizing effects of these features of the fiscal system were not appreciated until they had been established for other purposes, but this does not render them any the less useful.

The role of the stabilizers is to provide some insulation of final expenditure from swings in income from production, especially in the case of consumers' expenditure. The stabilizers thus can offset part of the effect of a decline in output, but they cannot bring about an increase in output directly. To prevent final expenditure from falling as much as production will be sufficient to check, in time, a recession which is an inventory recession and no more. But if other elements of demand are declining, the automatic stabilizers will not be sufficient to bring about a recovery sooner than 'natural forces' would do it. The value of the automatic stabilizers lies in reducing the damage done by delay, both in assessing the economic trend and deciding on measures, and in putting them into effect through the due process of politics.

It is reasonable to argue that the working of the American system of government, in particular the relationship between the Administration and the Congress, and the structure of political parties associated with it, give rise to greater obstacles to the conduct of an effective compensatory fiscal policy than do the system of Parliament and Cabinet and the more cohesive party structure that usually (though not always) goes with it. An American President lacks a power possessed by the weakest of Prime Ministers, that of making the passage of important financial legislation a question of confidence.

Good sense, close co-operation, and mutual trust between

responsible men can often make up for drawbacks of formal organization, and it is to this that one must look for the more effective conduct of fiscal policy in the United States rather than to changes in basic institutions, though improvements in procedure may be practicable. There is far more in the question of the separation of Executive and Legislature than its effectiveness or otherwise for the conduct of economic policy. Important political principles are involved, and political institutions that have been long established are not susceptible to rapid change. The assumption by the Government of the United States of the responsibility to promote 'maximum employment, production, and purchasing power' by fiscal (among other) means has led to few changes of significance in American political and administrative institutions. It has been the task of those responsible to achieve this object through institutions not designed for the purpose.

CHAPTER II

THE POLITICAL AND HISTORICAL BACKGROUND: THE TRADITIONAL ORTHODOXY AND ITS CHALLENGE IN THE 1930's BY THE NEW DEAL AND THE 'NEW ECONOMICS'

'THE American Tradition' in economic policy is, as men such as ex-President Hoover continually emphasize, one of private enterprise, 'rugged individualism', and *laissez-faire*. It is true, of course, that the economic activities of government were never quite so negligible as the tradition would assert; in the first half of the nineteenth century state governments undertook such projects as the Barge Canal between Lake Erie and the Hudson river, and the great trans-continental railways were built with the help of huge grants of land from the public domain and of subsidies and pledges of credit from cities and counties that wanted a railway in their area. In addition, the tariff was never merely a source of revenue but was used to promote the prosperity of specific industries. But despite these qualifications of detail, it remains true that the main impetus in the great expansion of the American economy in the nineteenth century came from private entrepreneurs and not from the government.

In this structure of economic organization the seats of power were occupied by businessmen who, in the absence of a hereditary aristocracy such as existed in Britain, became the leaders of the community. Their power and prestige were associated with the ideology of *laissez-faire*. Its principles were not an American monopoly; indeed, they had been formulated mainly by writers in Britain; but it flourished in a more extreme form in the United States than elsewhere.[1] For this the Federal system was in part responsible, for it excluded the Federal government from any direct authority over social conditions, leaving these matters to the states. General legislation similar to that which existed in Britain was impossible in the United States, and the

---

[1] When Mr. Justice Holmes declared that 'the Fourteenth Amendment does not enact Mr. Herbert Spencer's Social Statics' (Lochner v. New York, 198 U.S. 45 (1905)) he was delivering a dissenting opinion.

state legislation varied greatly both in comprehensiveness and in quality of administration.

Just before the turn of the century support grew for policies which required a modification of the extremes of *laissez-faire*. The impoverished farmers of the West and South in their Populist protest looked to government regulation of business to redress their grievances.[1] In the first decade of the twentieth century under President Theodore Roosevelt and reforming state Governors such as LaFollette, with public opinion aroused by the evidence of scandalous conduct in business and government brought to light by the 'muckrakers', an attempt was made to remedy some of the worst excesses to which the extremes of *laissez-faire* had given rise. Federal and state legislation imposed a degree of control over the 'natural monopolies' such as railways; food-and-drug legislation and the inspection of meat provided safeguards for the consumer that the free working of the market had failed to provide; and the hours of work, and in a few instances the wages of women and children, were subjected to regulation. A good start was made in the conservation of natural resources. The Sixteenth Amendment was passed, authorizing the Federal government to levy an income tax.[2]

These measures imposed a degree of restriction on the working of the private enterprise system. Certain practices which were once common were no longer to be tolerated, and in one important area, the conservation of natural resources, the government had had to take over a responsibility that private entrepreneurs had failed to undertake adequately. But with the exception of the grants-in-aid to states for road construction, established in 1916, the measures of the Progressive era did not entail large Federal expenditures. No national system of old-age pensions or assurance against sickness and unemployment such as that established in Britain in 1908 and 1911 had any real prospect of enactment. The American economy was still very much a free enterprise capitalist economy, even if it was not quite so uninhibited as before.

The pressure for radical reforms subsided during the war, and after the post-war alarm at the danger of 'Reds' had waned, the

[1] See R. Hofstadter, *The Age of Reform* (New York, 1955), Chapters 1 (3), 2 (1), and 2 (2); and J. D. Hicks, *The Populist Revolt* (Minneapolis, 1931), Chapter 3.

[2] In 1895 in Pollock *v.* Farmers Loan and Trust Co. (158 U.S. 601) the Supreme Court had ruled that an income tax was unconstitutional, although such a tax had been employed during the Civil War.

United States settled into what President Harding called 'normalcy'. It took its watchword from President Coolidge: 'the business of the United States is business', and the pre-eminence of the business leaders in the community was for the rest of the decade without serious challenge. After recovery from the sharp but short post-war recession, total national income rose until 1929 with only minor interruptions. The average standard of living in the United States was almost certainly the highest yet reached anywhere in the world; when contrasted with less favoured lands, especially Europe, this naturally redounded to the credit of 'the American system of free private enterprise'.

In what had by then come to be known as 'The American System'[1] or 'The American Way' the role of the Government in the economy was strictly limited, being confined to not hampering business more than could possibly be avoided. Its budget was to be kept small and kept balanced. Andrew Mellon, the Secretary of the Treasury from 1921 to 1931 and a supporter of *laissez-faire* carried to an extreme, became a symbol of this approach to public finance. He emphasized the need to retire the national debt and the necessity of not imposing high rates of tax on large incomes.[2] During his tenure of office these policies were put into effect. The series of tax reductions that followed the election of President Harding brought down the maximum rate of income tax[3] from 77 per cent under the Revenue Act of 1918 to 25 per cent under the Revenue Act of 1926; the marginal rate on an income of $100,000 was reduced from 60 per cent to 25 per cent.[4] What Schlesinger[5] calls 'The Golden Age of Business' was thus golden in more senses than one. The American business community enjoyed a low tax rate as well as unrivalled prestige and power.

Although the principle of the balanced budget was subscribed to by supporters of *laissez-faire*, it was part of the intellectual equipment of men who had a broader conception of the proper functions of government than Coolidge and Mellon, both in the United States

---

[1] This twentieth-century use of the term should be distinguished from its use in the first half of the nineteenth century (especially by its chief exponent, Henry Clay), to mean a nearly self-sufficient economy based on a protective tariff.

[2] In his book *Taxation, the Nation's Business* (New York, 1924).

[3] For convenience the 'normal income tax' and the 'surtax' are here taken together and referred to as 'income tax'.

[4] Treasury Department study, printed in House of Representatives, Committee on Ways and Means, *Hearings on H.R. 1* (Washington, 1947), pp. 38–43.

[5] A. M. Schlesinger Jr., *The Age of Roosevelt—The Crisis of the Old Order* (Boston, 1957).

and elsewhere. The idea that the budget might be used to contribute to the stability of the economy by means other than maintaining confidence through sound management (i.e. by retrenchment and meeting expenses out of revenues) was foreign even to men such as Lloyd George and Snowden, who were certainly not adherents of even the British version of *laissez-faire*. When introducing his famous 1909 Budget, Lloyd George mentioned the 'bad trade' of the previous year only as a cause of a decline in revenue, in terms not different from those in which he discussed the effect of increasing sobriety on the yield of the duties on spirits and beer[1]; discussing the proposed insurance against unemployment, he declared: 'You might as well promise to flatten out the Atlantic Ocean'[2] as to propose to control fluctuations in employment. When Snowden's Autumn Budget of 1931 carried out the classical prescription under the most difficult of conditions his critics, with the rarest exceptions, objected to the particular cuts in expenditure and increases in taxation but not to the principle of reducing expenditures and raising tax rates in time of depression. In the United States the view that the national budget ought to be balanced in all circumstances other than war was challenged only by the most unorthodox thinkers, who were few in number and had the status of heretics. Although as Governor of New York Franklin D. Roosevelt had taken the lead in organizing relief services to take care of the hardship caused by the depression, and was a strong supporter of public development of electricity supply, he none the less berated President Hoover in the course of the 1932 election campaign for centralizing power in Washington, extravagance, and failure to balance the budget. In the famous Pittsburgh speech[3] he declared that the budget of the Government resembled that of a family in that neither could live beyond their income for long.

THE DEPRESSION AND THE CHALLENGE TO THE OLD ORDER

The Great Depression dealt the old order a blow from which it never completely recovered. It was an essential point of the doctrine of the self-regulating private enterprise system that the system con-

[1] *House of Commons Debates*, 5th Series, Vol. 4, col. 473–4.
[2] *House of Commons Debates*, 5th Series, Vol. 4, col. 488.
[3] Its text is printed in *The Public Papers and Addresses of Franklin D. Roosevelt* (New York, 1938), Vol. I, pp. 795–810; the remarks on the budget included a qualifying clause in which Roosevelt promised to use deficit financing if starvation or dire need required the expenditure of additional funds.

tained processes which worked with reasonable speed to correct disequilibria and to maintain it at close to full employment. In the three years following the downturn in 1929 all upswings proved to be of short duration and were followed by a fresh downward plunge; although in late 1932 it could be argued that the decline had come to a halt, there were no sure signs that recovery was under way. The automatic processes of adjustment were working extremely slowly or were not working at all.

The measures taken by the Hoover Administration were more vigorous than those taken by any previous Administration to deal with a depression, but they were not enough to check the decline. On the other hand, some of its actions were strictly 'orthodox'. In an attempt to balance the budget the Revenue Act of 1932 provided for drastic increases in the rates and reductions in the individual exemptions of the personal income tax, and imposed excise taxes on a wide variety of goods and services ranging from consumer durables to telephone and telegraph services, chewing gum, and soft drinks. Hoover blocked the efforts by many Democrats and some Republicans in Congress to provide for Federal grants-in-aid to the states for unemployment relief and for additional Federal public works. In February 1933 the Senate Finance Committee held hearings on the economic situation, in the course of which many of the leading figures of the business world gave their views. Almost without exception the one governmental policy that they recommended was reduction in public expenditure.[1] Bernard Baruch advised: 'Balance budgets. Stop spending money we haven't got. Cut government spending—cut as rations are cut during a siege'.[2]

Governor Roosevelt campaigned with a programme of more drastic action. He declared that he believed that the problems facing the country called for 'bold persistent experimentation'.[3] Although in many cases he was far from specific about what experiments ought to be tried, his view that there was much that was wrong in the old order was evident in such remarks as that about 'the forgotten man at the bottom of the economic pyramid'.[4] President Hoover was in a most unfortunate position; his argument that if a Democratic

[1] Senate Finance Committee, *Hearings on Investigation of Economic Problems*, 72nd Cong., 2nd Sess.

[2] Ibid., p. 18.

[3] Speech at Oglethorpe University, 22 May 1932. Printed in *The Public Papers and Addresses of Franklin D. Roosevelt*, Vol. I, p. 646.

[4] Radio broadcast, 7 April 1932. Ibid., Vol. I, p. 625.

Administration were in office the situation would be even worse did not sound convincing when during his own Administration real G.N.P. had fallen by nearly 30 per cent and unemployment had risen from 3 per cent to 23 per cent of the labour force.[1] Although the differences between Hoover and Roosevelt *on specific issues* were not great,[2] Hoover had recourse to identifying his position with that of national patriotism[3]; this was not the first time that the distribution of economic power, income, and prestige that had prevailed in the 1920's was defended by the argument that to attack it would be to 'abandon the principles on which the nation had been built', nor was it the last time.

In his First Inaugural address, President Roosevelt said that the depression had occurred because: 'the rulers of the exchange of mankind's goods have failed through their own stubbornness and their own incompetence and have abdicated'. After declaring that 'The moneychangers have fled from their high seats in the temple of our civilization' he spoke of the need 'to apply social values more noble than those of mere monetary profit'.[4] If that did not mean a rejection of the business leaders who had held sway in the 1920's and their principles, it is hard to see what could.

It is unnecessary here to go into detail about the measures undertaken by the Roosevelt Administration. The measures were many and various and some of them led to substantial increases in government expenditures. Among these was the acutely controversial Works Progress Administration, which undertook mainly short term labour-intensive projects for the purpose of putting men to work and doing it quickly. Its expenditures were substantial, $1,264 million in fiscal 1936 and $1,897 million in fiscal 1937. In some instances there was foundation for the allegations that the value of the work done was disproportionately low, so that the W.P.A. soon became the opposition's stereotype for all New Deal expenditure.

To help finance some of this additional expenditure tax rates were raised several times in the 1930's, especially the taxes on large in-

[1] G.N.P. at 1947 prices was $149·3 billion in 1929 and $107·6 billion in 1932 (Dept. of Commerce, *National Income Supplement to the Survey of Current Business,* 1954, Table 40). The estimates of unemployment, which are less precise than those for the post-war years, are from the *Economic Report of the President,* 1959, Table D–17.

[2] F. B. Freidel, *Franklin D. Roosevelt: The Triumph* (Boston, 1956), p. 323.

[3] Speech at Madison Square Garden, 31 October 1932.

[4] *The Public Papers and Addresses of Franklin D. Roosevelt* (New York, 1938), Vol. II, pp. 11–12.

comes and corporate profits. Some of the tax increases, especially those of 1935, were avowedly of egalitarian inspiration. The grievances of the supporters of the old order were thus increased by high and redistributive taxation associated with the New Deal. This grievance rankled for a long time, as is shown by news items like the following, an Associated Press item from New York dated 11 July 1958, entitled: 'Lawyer Disinherits Sisters Because They Like F.D.R.': 'I leave nothing to my sisters, Hazel and Katherine, as they revere Franklin Delano Roosevelt, and the taxes caused by him have more than equaled their share'.[1]

But even more vigorously attacked than the tax increases were the deficits. The following table shows the total Federal revenues and expenditures and the surplus or deficit for the fiscal years 1929 to 1939:

TABLE 2

Federal Surpluses and Deficits, 1929–39

Fiscal Year	Revenue (Net)	Expenditure (Net)	Surplus or Deficit
1929	4,033	3,299	+ 734
1930	4,178	3,440	+ 738
1931	3,116	3,577	− 462
1932	1,924	4,569	−2,635
1933	2,021	4,623	−2,602
1934	3,064	6,694	−3,630
1935	3,730	6,521	−2,791
1936	4,069	8,493	−4,425
1937	4,979	7,756	−2,777
1938	5,762	6,938	−1,177
1939	5,103	8,965	−3,862

Amounts in $ million, rounded to the nearest million.
Source: Annual Report of the Secretary of the Treasury for the year ending 30 June 1951, Table 2.

In the earlier days of the New Deal there was no sign of any principle underlying the deficit financing other than that the expenditures were urgently needed and that it was just not practicable to raise revenues enough to cover them. When Roosevelt returned to Pittsburgh in the course of the 1936 election campaign he defended the expenditures and the deficits in the following terms: 'we had to balance the budget of the American people before we could balance the budget of the Federal government. . . . We accepted the final responsibility of Government, when all else had failed, to spend

[1] *Denver Post*, 11 July 1958.

money when no one else had money to spend'.[1] When it is recalled that by 1933 many local authorities were in such a financial plight that their school teachers went unpaid for months, the force of the observation that only the Federal government had money to spend is apparent. In 1937, when recovery was still far from complete, the President submitted a budget for fiscal 1938 that would balance if the Congress accepted his recommendations to cut expenditure for relief. The recession of 1937–8 supervened, however, and the budgetary balance was not attained. There can be little doubt that up till 1938 deficit financing was undertaken as an *ad hoc* expedient rather than as a deliberate economic policy.

In 1938 a change can be discerned. By early spring it had become clear that the recession which had begun in the previous autumn was severe and unlikely to be reversed quickly without intervention by the government. Accordingly the President recommended to Congress the appropriation of $3 billion of additional funds for direct expenditure or loan by the government in fiscal 1939. He explained that this was necessary to make good a deficiency of demand: 'today's purchasing power—citizen's income of today—is not sufficient to drive the economy at higher speed. Responsibility of government requires at this time to supplement the normal processes and in so supplementing them make sure that the addition is adequate'.[2] In the Budget Message submitted in January 1940 a counter-cyclical fiscal policy was explicitly discussed and the policy of the Hoover Administration criticized on the ground that its expenditures had been too low.[3]

Deficit financing, adopted at first through sheer force of circumstances and continued with a growing understanding of its economic implications, was an important aspect of the New Deal. It was also the point on which the critics seized most strongly, for it was the most vulnerable. It ran counter to the principles which formed the frame of reference within which practically everyone thought about public finance; and for those unconcerned with the technicalities, it was contrary to the commonsense notions of sound finance that people derive from their experience in house-keeping or business management. Equally important, it lacked the obvious and tangible ad-

[1] *Public Papers and Addresses of Franklin D. Roosevelt*, Vol. V, p. 404.
[2] *Public Papers and Addresses of Franklin D. Roosevelt* (New York, 1941), Vol. VII, p. 230.
[3] *Budget of the United States for the year ending 30 June 1941*, pp. v–vii.

vantages of the specific expenditures; an attack on these could be identified by particular people as a threat to their own well-being, whereas an attack on deficit financing posed no such identifiable threat. These considerations almost certainly underlay the disapproval of deficit financing by numerous people who approved of the specific expenditures. The following table shows the results of a poll, taken in August 1939, on attitudes to some of Roosevelt's policies:

TABLE 3

Poll Data on Approval of Roosevelt's Policies

	Approve (%)	Disapprove (%)	No Opinion (%)
Civilian Conservation Corps	84	8	8
His relief programme	52	38	10
His farm programme	51	33	16
His theory of government borrowing, spending, and lending for prosperity	34	46	20

Source: Elmo Roper, *You and Your Leaders* (Morrow, New York, 1957), pp. 37–8.

Because of its particular political vulnerability deficit spending became a quick and convenient summary of Roosevelt's economic policies, for hostile use, of course. It thus became an object of all the bitterness and resentment that Roosevelt's domestic policies aroused. Although those policies do not now look very radical or outrageous, the tone given to them by the Roosevelt Administration was one of a frontal attack on the structure of economic power, income, and prestige that had held sway in the 1920's, a drive to put down the erstwhile mighty from their seat. In his speech accepting renomination in 1936 he inveighed against the 'economic royalists'[1]; in the course of the campaign he declared that under his first Administration 'the forces of selfishness and lust for power met their match' and that he hoped that it would be said of his second Administration that under it they had met their master.[2] The fall from the peaks of public esteem occupied in the 1920's to the level of being so derided by the President himself was humiliating, and it is not to be wondered at that the New Deal was bitterly resented by many Americans. The events of the 1930's were a traumatic experience for large

[1] *Public Papers and Addresses of Franklin D. Roosevelt*, Vol. V, p. 231. By the phrase he was likening the 'economic tyranny' of big business to the political 'tyranny' of George III and his government.
[2] Speech at Madison Square Garden. Ibid., Vol. V, p. 569.

numbers of businessmen and for the corporate entity known as 'business'[1] and the experience is far from forgotten.

THE ASSOCIATION OF 'THE NEW ECONOMICS' WITH NEW DEAL POLITICS

At the time when Roosevelt's Administration had been driven to a policy of deficit financing by force of circumstances, profound developments in economic theory were taking place that within a decade were to revolutionize the way in which nearly all economists looked at the problem of economic instability and the means of dealing with it. An entirely new analytic apparatus became available to economists, which gave far more adequate answers to the question of why the depression had been so severe and so long lived than did the classical and neo-classical theory, and, equally important, indicated workable remedies. The theory of public finance was completely reoriented within a very short time, and it is hardly an exaggeration to say that what became known as 'the new economics' swept like wildfire through the American academic community in the second half of the 1930's.

In the circumstances of under-employment that prevailed in the United States during the 1930's the policy recommendation of the new analytic technique was that the government should run a substantial deficit. In his famous Open Letter to President Roosevelt, Keynes recommended 'a large volume of loan expenditure under government auspices'.[2] The 'new economics' thus gave a strong analytical basis for the New Deal fiscal policy. If there was any criticism it was that the expenditures and the deficits were not large enough. From this coincidence of the policies recommended by the economists with the policies pursued by the Roosevelt Administration arose the belief that the 'Keynesian' theory of the determination of the national income in the short run and the theory of fiscal policy based on it were not neutral analysis but New Deal party doctrine.

There was some justification for the view that the theory of deficit spending implied a rejection of the old order. A central feature of the orthodox view was that the automatic forces of the private enterprise economy tend to maintain the economy at full employ-

---

[1] For a discussion of the effect of the depression and the New Deal in humiliating business, see T. Cochran, 'Business and the Democratic Tradition' in *Harvard Business Review*, March–April 1956.

[2] 30 December 1933. For the text see American Economic Association, *Readings in Fiscal Policy* (London, 1955), pp. 31–8.

ment or close to it, whereas the distinctive feature of 'Keynesian' economics was that there is no process that will necessarily bring about this result under all circumstances. The whole *raison d'etre* of a compensatory fiscal policy is that there are times when the operations of the private economy will not in themselves maintain economic stability and that as a result government intervention is called for.

Judged by the criterion of profit, there can be no doubt that a compensatory fiscal policy which prevents deep depressions is beneficial to business, since profits are greater under conditions of high income and employment than they are during depressions. On the other hand, it reduces the power of the business community relative to that of the government. The level of employment is no longer dependent on business decisions alone, and if the government is prepared to follow a really vigorous compensatory policy the need to defer to the susceptibilities of the business community in order to avoid the danger of shaking 'business confidence' is much reduced.[1] Since deficit financing is likely in practice to reduce the resistance to increases in government expenditure, it may result in an increase in the size of the public sector, to the detriment of private business. With business decisions no longer all-important for determining the level of economic activity, the prestige of business may decline. There are other drawbacks such as adverse effects (from the business point of view) on industrial discipline which are the result of full employment rather than compensatory fiscal policy as such.[2]

There were thus rational grounds for believing that the power, influence, and prestige of business would be weaker under a regime in which the government intervened by fiscal means to maintain economic stability than they were under the old orthodoxy as it prevailed in the 1920's. These considerations were strongly reinforced by the emotional reaction caused by the association of deficit financing with the New Deal. Because of this association deficit financing became invested in the United States with strong political and emotional overtones, which prevented many Americans who disapproved of Roosevelt and his policies from considering it just from

---

[1] Reduction in private investment caused by the effect of deficit financing on 'confidence' can weaken the stimulus given by a deficit, but if the deficit financing is on a sufficiently large scale any adverse reactions from private demand can be swamped.

[2] See S. S. Alexander, 'Opposition to Deficit Financing for the Prevention of Unemployment' in *Income, Employment and Public Policy, Essays in Honor of Alvin H. Hansen* (New York, 1948).

the technical viewpoint of the desirability of adding to total demand and the magnitude of the transfer problem caused by a rising national debt. It was seen as a sharp break with the country's tradition, which called down upon it attacks phrased in the language of national patriotism.[1] Since compensatory fiscal policy as developed by the end of the decade owed much to theoretical analysis, criticism of it was marked in some instances by a strong whiff of anti-intellectualism, especially in the more extreme business pronouncements on the subject. These features of controversy over compensatory finance as anti-deflationary technique in the 1930's set a pattern which was followed in the next two decades.

THE DIVISION OF OPINION FOR AND AGAINST
THE NEW DEAL

The events of the years between President Roosevelt's Inauguration and his re-election brought about a very significant re-alignment of political groupings.[2] The 1936 election was fought almost entirely[3] on the great domestic issue, the New Deal. That issue appears to have divided the United States more sharply along class lines than had been the case in any previous national election. The vehemence with which large numbers of big business leaders assailed Roosevelt and the New Deal through such organizations as the Liberty League was doubtless partly responsible. The Democrats became the 'poor man's party' and the Republicans the businessman's party to a far greater extent than hitherto, a feature of the structure of American politics that remained important throughout the period covered by this book.

While the Republican platform of 1936 was cautiously 'progressive' in many of its specific proposals, the tone of the campaign was one of an all-out onslaught against 'New Deal socialism' and a return to the *status quo ante* 1933. Roosevelt carried every state except Maine and Vermont, a margin of victory greater than that of any

---

[1] Resort to arguments of patriotism on behalf of the economic *status quo* or *status quo ante* F.D.R. is a common feature of American political argument; sometimes it is merely routine rhetoric for the record, but at others, as in 1936, it is rather the desperate weapon of last resort.

[2] S. Lubell, *The Future of American Politics* (Anchor Ed., New York, 1956), pp. 44–65.

[3] Part of the vote for Lemke (Father Coughlin's candidate) appears to have been inspired by lingering resentments over American entry into World War I (Lubell, op. cit., pp. 151–3). Lemke received just under 2 per cent of the total vote cast.

President since Monroe in 1820. It was a massive vote of confidence in the policy of the New Deal in depression conditions.

The crushing defeat which befell the party that based its campaign on an all-out attack on the New Deal played an important part in the making of the other legacy of the 1930's. The contrast between Hoover's defeat in 1932 and the victory of Roosevelt in 1936 gave the strongest of warnings as to the electoral fate of an Administration that was in office when a depression occurred, and that under depression conditions victory would go to the party which would 'do something', even if the 'something' was attacked as being contrary to The American Tradition. The Republicans had been saddled with the reputation of being the party that had done nothing while the depression had got worse and worse. The potency of this as a source of Democratic votes was very slow to weaken. Among large numbers of Americans the image of the Republicans as 'the party of the full dinner pail' was replaced by that of 'those Hoover years', which in the next two decades was to be as the Cheshire cat which was there to grin at the Republicans whenever fears of depression were aroused.

The elections of 1936 proved to be the high-water mark of support for Roosevelt. In the next four years his support declined, as the elections of 1938 and 1940 showed. There were doubtless many factors responsible for this, including the proposal of the President to 'pack' the Supreme Court, the recession of 1937–8, and the opposition that always builds up against a government long in power. But there is little doubt that a major factor was the opposition of considerable sections of American opinion to intervention in war against Germany on the side of Britain and France.[1] To those who opposed intervention in foreign wars as such or just intervention in this particular war there was a reason for voting Republican strong enough to overcome the economic appeal of Roosevelt.

The alliance between those who objected to Roosevelt's social and economic policy and those who opposed the involvement of the United States once more in war against Germany on the side of Britain was the basis of the anti-New Deal coalition which gained control of Congress in 1938. The informal alliance between Republi-

---

[1] Lubell has produced much evidence to suggest that this opposition came to a considerable extent from ethnic groups sympathetic to Germany and Italy (the German- and Italian-Americans) or hostile to Britain (Irish). See Lubell, op. cit., Chapter VII.

cans and conservative Democrats in Congress was reinforced by the abortive attempt by Roosevelt to secure the defeat of certain conservative Democrats in the primary elections of 1938. The alliance of far Right-wing economics with isolationism (and with the latter's heir and successor, 'go-it-alone') is a feature of the structure of American political opinion which endured throughout the 1940's and '50's. Many of those whose initial hostility to Roosevelt arose from objection to his foreign policy soon came to adopt the views of their new-found allies about social and economic policy. Politicians like Senator Burton K. Wheeler and Governor Phillip LaFollette, and publicists like John T. Flynn, who in the 1930's were critics of Roosevelt's policies from the Left, had before the end of the War become staunch supporters of economic conservatism and foes of 'New-Deal socialism'. As the saying goes, 'war (or in this case the threat of being drawn into it) makes strange bedfellows'.

After the War the frustrations of the 'Cold War' and alarm at the danger of communist activity within the United States went far towards maintaining the mass support won for anti-New Deal economic ideas that had been won by opposition to intervention in the War in 1938–41. There is much evidence to suggest that it was the opponents of intervention against Germany at that time who formed the backbone of the support for Senator Taft in 1949–52. The Republicans who took the most extreme positions in damning 'New Deal (and "Fair Deal") socialism' almost invariably were those who in the 1950's had most to say about the 'loss' of China and took an attitude of *delenda est Carthago* towards the communist countries in general. During the post-war period it was easy and common for those desirous of demonstrating their 'Americanism' to include 'deficit spending' among the objects of their denunciation in such slogans as 'Get the Reds out of the government and the government out of the red'.[1] Such forces as these helped to secure extreme Right-wing views on economic policy the mass support they lacked in 1936.

CONCLUSION: THE LEGACY OF THE 1930'S

The positions taken by the principal economic groups with respect to fiscal policy in the post-war decade reflected their attitude to Roosevelt's economic policies. The staunchest supporters of compensatory fiscal policy as a principle have been the trade unions, whose gains in the 1930's owed much to the active support of the Federal

[1] Lubell, op. cit., p. 160.

government. The most implacable foes have been the business organizations.

The driving force for most of the changes in domestic policy in the 1930's came from the President rather than from the Congress, and in consequence the Presidency came to symbolize the forces of change from the old order and the Congress to symbolize resistance to those changes. The institutional clash became merged with the straight-forward political clash when the anti-Roosevelt coalition gained control of the Congress. As a result issues of more or less government intervention in the economy have at times been debated in terms of the Constitutional question of the proper division of effective control over policy between Executive and Legislature. In a precisely similar way government intervention in the economy has been opposed on grounds of the need to maintain the Federal system of government, though more often than not the dispute has really been not about Federal action versus state action, but Federal action versus no action at all. Large numbers of Roosevelt's opponents in the Press carried on their campaign for many years. During the first half of 1958 there were numerous instances of editorial fulminations against deficits, 'the same discredited New Deal policies' and the like, even if in the same issue the business analyst was referring to a prospective increase in government expenditures as a source of strength.

Throughout the post-war period there were people prominent in the public life of the United States who took positions on issues of fiscal policy that admit of no other interpretation than that they were intent on preventing any further resort to the policies pursued in the 1930's. Examples are the sponsorship by Senators Byrd and Bridges of a Constitutional Amendment to require the Federal budget to be balanced annually except in time of war, and the support given by business organizations to a proposed Constitutional Amendment to limit the maximum rate of Federal tax on personal and corporate income to 25 per cent. That men of the prominence in public life of Byrd and Bridges and an organization of the stature of the National Association of Manufacturers, which includes among its members many of the leading businessmen of the country,[1]

---

[1] NAM's support for the proposed amendment was given by the Chairman of NAM's Taxation Committee in a statement submitted to the Senate Judiciary Committee on 27 April 1954. Senate, Committee on the Judiciary, Subcommittee on Constitutional Amendments, *Hearings on S.J. Res No. 23*, 83rd Cong., 2nd Sess., pp. 215–17.

should support such things is proof of the continued existence in American public life of an extreme Right group that still hankered after a restoration of the *status quo ante* Roosevelt, a position so extreme as not to be supported in public by responsible people outside the United States.

It is the contention of this chapter that the nature of the issues raised by Roosevelt and the New Deal, and the embroiling of compensatory fiscal policy with the passions aroused by those issues, are the reasons why compensatory fiscal policy as an anti-deflationary technique[1] has been opposed so vigorously and so long in the United States. The contrast with the rest of the world is striking; opponents of capitalism in its pre-1929 form proposed stronger remedies than deficit financing (generally socialism) so that the former was left to supporters of private enterprise as a means by which the advantages of private enterprise could be combined with reasonable economic stability. So long as memory of support for or opposition to any of Roosevelt's principal policies has any emotional impact it is likely that there will be opposition in the United States to deficit financing. This legacy of the 1930's was in sharp conflict with the other legacy, the assumption by the government, *de facto*, of an obligation to 'do something' about a depression and the knowledge that failure to 'do something' would almost certainly spell electoral disaster. Not the least of America's post-war economic problems was which of these two legacies would be the stronger and for how long should serious deflation force the issue.

[1] Under inflationary conditions the compensatory policy normally (unless the long-term demand for capital is very low) indicates a surplus, the same policy as the classical principle recommends when there is a large national debt which it is desired to reduce or pay off. Under these conditions the difference between the classical and Keynesian prescriptions is at the most a difference as to the size of the surplus. It is the prescription of the Keynesian fiscal policy under deflationary conditions that differs so sharply from the classical prescription, hence the description of Keynesian economics as 'the theory of deficit spending'.

CHAPTER III

WAR-TIME FISCAL DEVELOPMENTS AND PLANNING FOR THE POST-WAR PERIOD

THE scale of the war effort in the United States, as in Britain, was determined by the real resources available rather then by financial considerations. Controls on the use of scarce materials, notably steel and certain other metals, effectively limited the output of consumers' durable goods and of producers' durable goods for the less essential industries. Building was also limited through the control over essential materials. Rationing was imposed on certain consumer goods in especially short supply.

In such a situation the primary function of tax policy was to help restrain consumers from using their increased purchasing power to bid for the limited supply of civilian goods, and to exercise this restraint in a way which would not so diminish incentives as to damage the war effort, and which was generally regarded as equitable. It was desirable that as far as possible the gap between personal incomes and the amount of civilian goods available should be filled by taxation rather than personal saving, in order to minimize the inflationary potential that would exist at the end of the War if consumers possessed a greatly enlarged stock of liquid assets.

Federal tax rates were raised to unprecedented heights during the War. The levels finally reached were those imposed by the Revenue Act of 1943[1] and the Individual Income Tax Act of 1944. Under these Acts personal incomes were subject to a 'surtax' at rates ranging from 20 per cent to 91 per cent, in addition to a 'normal income tax' of 3 per cent. In 1939 the combined rates of 'surtax' and 'normal income tax' had ranged from 8 per cent to 79 per cent; the top rate was reached in 1939 at an income of $5,000,000; under the 1944 Act it was reached at $200,000. The exemptions allowed to individuals were cut sharply. The exemptions in 1939 were $1,000 for a single person, $2,500 for a married couple, and $400 for each dependent; under the 1944 Act the exemption was set at $500 for each taxpayer,

---

[1] This Act did not become law until 25 February 1944; for a discussion of the circumstances, see p. 34, infra.

with an additional exemption of $500 for each dependent (including his wife); under the 1944 Act these exemptions applied only to the 'surtax'; for the 'normal income tax' only one exemption of $500 was allowed. When account is taken of the rise in prices between 1939 and 1944 the reduction in the exemptions appears even more drastic; if the price index used is the implicit deflator for consumers' expenditure in the Dept. of Commerce's estimates of G.N.P. at constant prices,[1] then the real exemption of a single person was reduced from $1,000 to $360 and that of a married man with two dependent children was reduced from $3,300 to $1,440. In view of the difficulty of measuring changes in real income under war-time conditions, the figures quoted should not be taken too literally, but they give an indication of the reduction in the lower limit of taxable income in real terms caused by legislation and inflation.

The standard rate of tax on corporate profits was raised to 40 per cent (on total profits greater than $50,000) compared with 19 per cent in 1939. In addition corporations were subject to an excess profits tax, which under the Revenue Act of 1943 reached a rate of 95 per cent gross with provision for a post-war refund of 10 per cent of tax paid. Excise tax rates were also raised; but with a few exceptions, of which spirits were the most important, the increases were not large; even on furs and jewellery the rates were only 20 per cent.

An important change was made in the method of the collection of the income tax. A system of taxation at source for wages and salaries was instituted by the Current Tax Payment Act of 1943. Under this procedure, commonly known as 'withholding', tax is deducted, at the lowest bracket rate only,[2] from each wage or salary payment treated as a unit, instead of cumulatively throughout the year as under P.A.Y.E. At the end of the year the taxpayer has to make a return, in which any additional allowances can be claimed, and sends with it the receipt for taxes withheld. People not taxed under the withholding procedure were required to estimate their income for the coming year and pay tax on that estimated income in four instalments. When the actual income is known the final return is made, with appropriate additional payment or refund. Putting income tax payment as near as possible on a current basis was an

[1] Dept. of Commerce, *National Income Supplement to the Survey of Current Business*, 1954, Table 41.
[2] In practice this accounted for nearly all the liability to tax of wage earners because of the width of the bracket, which was $2,000.

important achievement, and for economic stabilization was a valuable legacy from the War.[1]

Despite the increases in tax rates, the revenue raised was less than half of total Federal expenditures during the war years. The following tables show total Federal revenues and expenditures in money terms and as percentages of G.N.P. at factor cost:

TABLE 4

Total Federal Receipts and Expenditures

Calendar Year	Receipts	Expenditures
1939	6,721	8,995
1940	8,641	10,089
1941	15,420	20,539
1942	22,943	56,141
1943	39,258	85,972
1944	41,008	95,585
1945	42,495	84,826

Amounts in $ million.

Source: Dept. of Commerce, *National Income Supplement to the Survey of Current Business*, 1954, Tables 8 and 9.

TABLE 5

Federal Receipts and Expenditures as Percentages of Gross National Product

Calendar Year	G.N.P. at Factor Cost	Receipts (%)	Expenditures (%)
1939	82·2	8·2	10·9
1940	91·0	9·5	11·1
1941	114·6	13·6	17·9
1942	147·5	15·5	38·1
1943	180·0	21·8	47·8
1944	197·9	20·7	48·2
1945	199·1	21·4	42·5

G.N.P. in $ billion at current prices.

G.N.P. at factor cost obtained by subtracting 'indirect business tax' *less* 'subsidies less current surplus of government enterprises' from G.N.P. at market prices.

Source: Dept. of Commerce, *National Income Supplement to the Survey of Current Business*, 1954, Tables 4, 8, and 9.

There was consequently a sharp increase in the National Debt. At the end of 1939 the total amount of debt obligations issued or guaranteed by the Federal government held outside the government investment accounts[2] was $41·1 billion. By the end of 1945 this had

[1] The procedure established by the Current Tax Payment Act has since remained in effect without substantial change.

[2] Principally the Old Age and Survivors Insurance Trust Fund.

risen to $251·6 billion. Its distribution between classes of holders is shown in the following table:

TABLE 6

Ownership of the National Debt, 1939 and 1945

	1939	1945
Federal Reserve Banks	2·5	24·3
Commercial Banks	15·9	90·8
Mutual Savings Banks and Insurance Companies	9·4	34·7
Other Corporations	2·2	22·2
Individuals	10·1	64·1
State and Local Governments	0·4	6·5
Miscellaneous Investors (including Pension Funds)	0·7	9·1
Total	41·1	251·6

Amounts in $ billion at end of year. Detail does not add to totals because of rounding.
Source: Economic Report of the President, 1959, Table D–49.

The fiscal legacy of war finance in the United States can thus be summed up as a tax structure of unprecedented height, based mainly on direct taxes on individuals and corporations; an income tax which applied to all but the lowest of incomes and a considerable part of which was collected currently; and a vastly increased National Debt which under existing circumstances made individuals and firms very liquid.[1]

WARTIME ECONOMIC POLICIES AND POLITICS

The united support of the war effort did not mean an end to political controversy over economic policies. On the contrary, these controversies were long and sometimes bitter, and the way in which they developed cast a shadow over the problem of post-war economic policies. The division between pro- and anti-New Deal remained evident during the War, with many indications of the power possessed by the anti-New Deal coalition. The Administration's tax policies encountered increasingly strong resistance. The Administration rejected a general sales tax on grounds of equity, and hence the tax increases as proposed would have borne very heavily on moderate and large incomes and on profits. This was strongly opposed by business groups and other conservatives as socialistic redistribution

[1] For a full discussion of the relationship of the structure of interest rates of the National Debt and the liquidity of the financial system, see J. S. Fforde, *The Federal Reserve System, 1945–1949* (Oxford, 1954), Chapters 2 and 3.

D

of income under the guise of war finance. They were able to prevent the drastic increases of the type that the Administration wanted, but on the other hand they were not able to force through the sales tax in the teeth of the opposition of the Administration and the trade unions. The result was virtually stalemate.

This was particularly evident in the struggle over the Revenue Act of 1943. The Administration's recommendations for drastic increases in most rates of tax[1] were rejected almost completely by the Congress.[2] President Roosevelt replied with the unprecedented action of vetoing the Revenue Bill,[3] castigating the Congress in extremely sharp language. Senator Barkley, the Democratic majority leader, resigned in protest and moved the motion to override the veto, which was passed by overwhelming majorities. The President had to eat humble pie before Barkley would resume office as majority leader. The episode showed clearly that the dominant Right-wing coalition in the Congress exerted an effective veto over economic measures which the Administration might propose.

This had serious implications for future economic policy because of that majority's attitude to economic policy and to economists, as revealed by certain of its actions in 1943. The Office of Price Administration (O.P.A.) was bitterly attacked for being allegedly 'anti-business', and there was much Congressional complaint because it had several professional economists among its senior personnel. In 1943 Representative Dirksen moved an amendment which was carried by 136 to 116, to the appropriation for the War Agencies in the Executive Office of the President which required that all O.P.A. officials of policy-making rank should have had five years of business experience.[4] It is evident from the debate, which was shot through with references to 'long haired professors' and 'one of the Hansen school of revolutionists',[5] that the amendment was aimed at the economists employed in O.P.A.

[1] For the details, see the statement by Secretary Morgenthau to the Ways and Means Committee on 4 October 1943; the text is printed in the *Annual Report of the Secretary of the Treasury for the year ending 30 June 1944*, p. 384–416. For a discussion of the Administration's policy, see E. D. Allen, 'Treasury Tax Policy in 1943', *American Economic Review*, Vol. XXXIV (1944), pp. 707–34.

[2] See M. Newcomer, 'Congressional Tax Policies in 1943', *American Economic Review*, Vol. XXXIV (1944), pp. 735–56.

[3] The text of the Veto Message is printed in the *Annual Report of the Secretary of the Treasury for the year ending 30 June 1944*, pp. 455–7.

[4] *Congressional Record*, Vol. LXXXIX, p. 6124.

[5] This appelation was applied to the Chairman of the Board of Economic Warfare by Representative Ploeser. *Congressional Record*, Vol. LXXXIX, p. 6106.

Similar forces caused the abolition of the National Resources Planning Board (N.R.P.B.) in 1943 through refusal to appropriate further funds for its operations. In 1942 and 1943 the agency had issued a series of statements setting out what it considered should be the principles governing post-war economic policy.[1] The policies recommended were radical in tone: it should be 'the declared policy' of the United States Government 'to underwrite full employment for the employables' and to 'guarantee, and where necessary underwrite' equal access to security, health, education, and good housing conditions for all.[2] It repeatedly stressed the objective of full employment and the need to use fiscal policy to achieve it. In view of the subsequent controversy over what 'full employment' meant, it is worth noting the definition given to it by Hansen in the pamphlet issued by the N.R.P.B.:

'There will always be, in a society such as ours, a large amount of transitional unemployment . . . in an economy as large as the United States it is probable that at "full employment" there would be at any one time between two and three million unemployed'.[3] This cannot be considered an unduly ambitious formulation of the practical goal of 'full employment' policy.

Although the statements about Federal finance of health and education provided plenty of sources of controversy, it was the statements about the use of fiscal policy that drew the heaviest fire. Senator Taft denounced the N.R.P.B. on the ground that the proposals 'contemplated unlimited deficit financing'[4] and after noting Hansen's connection with the N.R.P.B.'s work cited Hansen's views about the National Debt. Senator Byrd declared that if the N.R.P.B. did the planning for post-war it would present the same kind of policies after the War as Roosevelt had presented before the war. It was this that the majority in the 78th Congress[5] wished to prevent; as deficit financing had been one of the most bitterly criticized of Roose-

---

[1] National Resources Planning Board, *National Resources Development*, Report for 1943, Part I; N.R.P.B., *Post War Agenda*; and A. H. Hansen, *After the War—Full Employment* (written for N.R.P.B.), 1943 edition.

[2] N.R.P.B., *Report for 1943*, Part I, p. 13.

[3] A. H. Hansen (for N.R.P.B.), *After the War—Full Employment* (1943 ed.), p. 3, footnote 1.

[4] *Congressional Record*, Vol. LXXXIX, p. 4924.

[5] The 79th Congress, elected in 1944, contained a larger number of supporters of New Deal policies than did its predecessor, but the change was not large enough to upset the control exercised on most issues by the anti-New Deal coalition.

velt's pre-war policies, its use in dealing with post-war problems was to be avoided if the Congressional conservatives had their way.

PLANNING FOR POST-WAR ECONOMIC PROBLEMS

The serious consequences that might have followed from the strength of the opposition in Congress to deficit financing as a matter of principle are evident when it is recalled that in 1943–4 the general opinion of economists in the United States was that the principal post-war economic problem would be to overcome the deflationary forces that would be set up by the ending of the abnormal expenditures caused by the War. Much of the post-war planning by economists in American government service was directed to this contingency.

Several speeches and articles by senior government economists gave an indication of the general trend of economic thinking in the Federal government. For instance, in April 1944 the *Federal Reserve Bulletin* published an article by E. A. Goldenweiser[1] and E. E. Hagen entitled 'Jobs After the War'[2] in which they tried to estimate the level of real output that would be necessary for full employment after the war. This approach was developed in a speech by Mr. Goldenweiser later in the year;[3] once the problem of transition had been overcome, the United States would be faced by the need to provide employment for 58 million people, 12 million more than had been employed in 1940. To achieve this he advocated reduction in taxes on consumption, increased expenditure for public works and welfare, and low interest rates. In an opinion that echoed the pre-war 'long-run stagnationist' view he said: 'This country will have to adjust itself to $2\frac{1}{2}$ per cent as the return on safe long-term money because the time has come when the returns on pioneering capital can no longer be unlimited as they were in the past'.[4]

On 16 November 1944 Marriner S. Eccles, the Chairman of the Board of Governors of the Federal Reserve System, declared that in his view there was a considerable danger of inflation immediately after the end of the War because of shortages of civilian goods and a swollen consumers' demand, after which there was a danger of a

---

[1] Then Economic Adviser to the Board of Governors of the Federal Reserve System.

[2] *Federal Reserve Bulletin*, Vol. XXX (1944), pp. 424–31.

[3] 'Post War Problems and Policies', a speech to the Annual Agricultural Outlook Conference, Washington, D.C., 14 November 1944. Text printed in *Federal Reserve Bulletin*, Vol. XXXI (1945), pp. 112–22.

[4] Ibid., p. 117.

prolonged deficiency demand.[1] He recommended government welfare expenditure and tax reduction to deal with this.

Further evidence of the extent to which most economists thought in 'Keynesian' terms of the problem of maintaining economic stability is to be seen in the *Postwar Economic Studies* published by the Board of Governors of the Federal Reserve System in 1945-6. In *Public Finance and Full Employment* by R. A. Musgrave and E. D. Domar,[2] the view was taken that deflationary pressures were likely to arise soon after the end of the War and that a budget deficit would therefore be called for. The book presented an outline of the fully developed theory of compensatory fiscal policy. Although this was not a declaration of policy by the Federal Reserve System, the fact that it appeared under the Board's auspices gave it the status at least of reputable economic thinking.

Much thought was given to making the tax structure more efficient for maintaining economic stability. Promotion of economic stability had by then arrived at equal rank with equity and minimum effect on incentives as criteria for the selection of taxes. Three proposals for the reform of the tax structure gained considerable attention after their publication in the middle of 1944;[3] generally known as the 'C.E.D.', 'Ruml-Sonne', and 'Twin Cities' plans, they were not in themselves schemes of fiscal policy, but were intended to promote high levels of economic activity through imposing the minimum restraint on consumption and by designing the individual and corporation income taxes to minimize their effects on incentives. It was estimated that all three proposed tax systems would yield a small surplus at a 'full-employment' level of income, and in all three it was provided that a deficit should be run if incomes fell, instead of raising the rates to try to eliminate it. Here again the impact of 'Keynesian' economics is apparent.

[1] Speech to National Industrial Conference Board; text printed in *Federal Reserve Bulletin*, Vol. XXX (1944), pp. 1156–62.

[2] *Public Finance and Full Employment*, Postwar Economic Studies No. 3, Board of Governors of the Federal Reserve System, Washington, D.C., 1945.

[3] *Postwar Federal Tax Plan for High Employment*, by Research Committee of the Committee for Economic Development, New York; B. Ruml and H. Chr. Sonne, *Fiscal and Monetary Policy* (Washington, D.C.); *The Twin Cities Plan for Postwar Taxes*, by Twin Cities Research Bureau Inc. (St. Paul, Minn.). For discussion and analysis of these plans, see R. A. Musgrave, 'Three Plans for Postwar Taxation', *Federal Reserve Bulletin*, Vol. XXX (1944), pp. 1163–76; and C. Shoup, 'Three Plans for Postwar Taxation', *American Economic Review*, Vol. XXXIV (1944), pp. 757–70.

All the analyses and plans for the post-war period thus far discussed assumed that after the transition from the war-time economy to the peace-time economy the problem would be how to deal with deflation.[1] Econometric analyses tended to this conclusion; but the same conclusion could be inferred from the fact that severe unemployment had persisted until it had been ended by massive military expenditure; it might therefore reasonably be feared that unemployment would return when the expenditure ceased. It was obvious to all that incomes from employment would decline, for there would be less overtime, and men who as a result of the labour shortage had been reclassified into better-paid grades would have to go back to their old grades when the servicemen were demobilized.

Congressional action did not reflect these fears of unemployment; the Colmer and George Committees considered the post-war economic problem, but their conclusions were confined to the need to strengthen private enterprise. The Congress passed the Servicemen's Readjustment Act, commonly known as 'The G.I. Bill of Rights', which made generous provision for the education of ex-servicemen, for pensions, medical benefits, and guarantees for loans for house purchase. But the Administration's proposal for authority to make grants to former war-workers to assist them in moving to other jobs, was disregarded, as was the proposal to provide a national scale of unemployment compensation of $25 a week for twenty-six weeks.

THE FINAL PRODUCT OF THE PLANNING FOR
POST-WAR ECONOMIC PROBLEMS: THE EMPLOYMENT ACT

Although the Employment Act did not become law until February 1946, by which time the passage from the war-time economy to the post-war inflation was well under way, it was the outcome of planning for post-war economic policy. Essentially a declaration, it was similar in purpose to the British, Canadian, and Australian White Papers of 1944 and 1945[2] in which it was declared to be the policy of the governments of those countries to maintain 'high and stable'

[1] For a general account of the analyses and forecasts of post-war developments, see M. Sapir, 'Review of Economic Forecasts for the Transition Period', in *Studies in Income and Wealth*, Vol. XI (New York, 1949), pp. 275–367.

[2] For a comparative discussion of the three White Papers, see D. H. Merry and G. R. Bruns, 'Full Employment, the British, Canadian, and Australian White Papers', *Economic Record*, Vol. XXI (1945–6), pp. 223–33; A. H. Hansen, *Economic Policy and Full Employment* (New York, 1947), Chapters 5, 6, and 7; and S. E. Harris, *Economic Planning* (New York, 1949), Chapter 10.

or 'full' employment. The Employment Act was the last of the quartet because of the American 'separation of powers' which requires an Act of Congress or Joint Resolution to express national policy instead of a statement by the Executive which will suffice in Britain, Canada, and Australia. Unlike the White Papers, the Employment Act was the centre of vigorous controversy. The nature of this controversy throws light on the structure of opinion in the Congress and in the country about policies to maintain economic stability.

The history of the Employment Act has been analysed in detail by Professor Bailey,[1] so that here it is necessary only to draw attention to those aspects which illustrate the divisions of opinion in the Congress and among groups in the country. In his last State of the Union Message[2] President Roosevelt laid much stress of full employment as a primary aim of post-war policy, and hinted at public investment as one of the means to achieve it; he did not, however, recommend the passage of an Act to declare a policy of full employment. The initiative came from Congress, especially from Senator Murray, who prepared several draft bills, the final version being introduced in the spring of 1945 as S.380.

The Murray bill,[3] which was entitled 'The Full Employment Act', provided for a full compensatory fiscal policy. It declared that 'it is the further responsibility of the Federal government to provide such volume of Federal investment and expenditure as may be needed to assure continuing full employment'.[4] The Bureau of the Budget was to prepare a 'national employment and production budget',[5] which was to estimate the magnitudes of the several components of aggregate demand in the next planning period and the addition to demand, if any, that would be required for operation at full employment.

In their report[6] the majority of the Banking and Currency Committee strongly supported the bill. They rejected any inhibitions about deficit financing, saying that the bill 'serves notice that the government will not allow any rigid mathematical formula on balancing of

---

[1] S. K. Bailey, *Congress Makes a Law* (New York, 1950).

[2] Text in *Congressional Record*, Vol. XCI, pp. 68–73, and in *New York Times*, 7 January 1945.

[3] For the text of the bill, see Bailey, op. cit., pp. 243–8.

[4] Section 2(e).

[5] Section 3. The Fiscal Division of the Bureau of the Budget at this time prepared 'The Nation's Economic Budget', *Budget of the United States for the year ending 30 June 1946*, pp. xxiii–vi and Appendix 10, p. 830.

[6] *S. Rept. No. 583*, 79th Cong., 1st Sess.

the Federal budget to interfere with its moral and legal commitment to assure continuing full employment'.[1]

The minority criticized the bill for accepting unlimited deficit financing, and pointed out that prolonged increases in Federal expenditure for anti-deflationary purposes might lead to encroachment on what had hitherto been the responsibility of the private economy or of the state and local governments.[2] The minority remarked: 'This is the so-called compensatory spending theory advanced by Lord Keynes, Stuart Chase, Sir William Beveridge and Mr. Henry Wallace'.[3]

In the course of the bill's passage through the Senate, Taft secured the adoption of his amendment requiring the 'national employment and production budget' to be accompanied by plans for balancing the Federal budget over a 'reasonable' period, 'without interfering with the goal of full employment'.[4] With the insertion of language which might do something to allay fears of unlimited deficit financing, the bill was passed by 71 votes to 10.

In the House the bill received very different treatment. It was referred to the Committee on Expenditures in the Executive Departments,[5] of which the majority of members, including the Chairman, Representative Manasco, were definitely of the Right; assured of a sympathetic hearing, opponents of the bill appeared in force. In their report[6] the Committee proposed a substitute bill which declared the policy to be to maintain 'a high level of employment (including self-employment), production, and purchasing power' by encouraging 'the American system of free competitive enterprise' and 'sound fiscal policy'. A Council of Economic Advisers was to be set up to recommend measures to carry out the declared policy. A guarantee of full employment was rejected on the ground that it could only be achieved by heavy deficit financing, which would destroy private enterprise.[7]

The final version of the bill resembled the House version rather than the Senate version in that the 'national production and employment budget' and the commitment to Federal expenditure to make good any 'deficit' (i.e. deficiency of effective demand) in that

[1] Ibid., p. 12.
[2] *S. Rept. No. 583*, 79th Cong., 1st Sess., Statement of Minority Views, pp. 2–6.
[3] Ibid., p. 4.   [4] *Congressional Record*, Vol. XCI, pp. 9135, 9144.
[5] This Committee had jurisdiction over matters relating to the Bureau of the Budget.
[6] *H. Rept. No. 1334*, 79th Cong., 1st Sess.   [7] Ibid., pp. 6–7.

budget were abandoned. Whereas the Senate version had stated the objective to be 'full' employment, and the House version had said 'high' employment, the word used in the final version was 'maximum' employment. This was apparently regarded as 'splitting the difference' in phraseology, which is a curious piece of semantics and and illustration of the negative emotional charge attaching to 'full employment' in the United States at the end of the War. The final version was passed with the majority of both parties in both House and Senate in support.

In view of the importance of the Employment Act as a landmark in the development of American economic policy, it is worth quoting Section 2, the declaration of policy, in full:

'The Congress declares that it is the continuing policy and responsibility of the Federal government to use all practical means consistent with its needs and obligations and other essential considerations of national policy, with the assistance and co-operation of industry, agriculture, labor, and state and local governments, to coordinate and utilize all its plans, functions, and resources for the purpose of creating and maintaining, in a manner calculated to foster and promote free competitive enterprise and the general welfare, conditions under which there will be afforded useful employment opportunities, including self-employment, for those able, willing, and seeking to work, and to promote maximum employment, production, and purchasing power.'[1]

The declaration is hedged by the proviso about other considerations of national policy, and there is no direct reference to fiscal policy, but the reference to 'all its plans, functions, and resources' must be taken to include the Federal budget.

In the controversies about the Employment Act three main groups of opinion are discernible. First, those who attached great importance to full employment, and were prepared to use deficit financed expenditure without limit if necessary. In this category were the Democratic Left, represented by such men as Senators Wagner and Murray, with a few Left-wing Republican supporters, backed by the trade unions and a variety of 'liberal' groups. Then came the middle group, whose most articulate Congressional spokesman was Senator Taft.[2]

[1] 15 U.S.C. 1021.

[2] See Taft's speeches in the debate (*Congressional Record*, Vol. XCI, pp. 9064–7, 9135, 9137). Taft was clearly influenced by Beveridge's views about the need for controls and centralized planning in order to make a full employment policy work. Such controls were repugnant to Taft's political views.

They regarded budgetary action to promote full employment as desirable and useful, but were concerned lest its operation should lead to an expansion of the activities of the Federal government at the expense of state and local governments and of the private sector. They also feared that the expenditures and deficits might lead to inflation, resulting in the imposition of direct controls. This approach was supported by the Congressional 'moderates' and by the more liberal business groups, such as the Committee for Economic Development. The third group was the irreconcilable Right, whose views are apparent in such statements as '(the full employment policy) simply means that those who work and produce, and consequently pay taxes and buy bonds are to assume the responsibility to support those who fail or refuse to work and produce'.[1] Many of the business organizations took this view; the Ohio State Chamber of Commerce maintained that the Full Employment Act, if passed, 'would be the scaffold on which private enterprise is dropped to its death'.[2]

In all the controversy it seems to have been assumed that an anti-deflationary fiscal policy would mean an increase in expenditure, to be financed by a deficit, and not a deficit-financed tax cut. The probable reason is that in the 1930's, which formed the background of the controversy, the deficits had resulted from increased expenditures and not from tax cuts. Whereas a large and prolonged increase in Federal expenditure might lead the Federal government to undertake activities which hitherto had been left to state and local governments or to the private sector, nothing of the sort could follow from a deficit caused by tax cuts. If an expansion of the activities of the Federal government was considered undesirable on grounds of political principle, then the expansive effect could be achieved, with a rather larger deficit, by means of a tax cut, which could do no harm by increasing government power.

It was also contended that deficit spending could lead to impairment of liberty through causing inflation which had to be dealt with by controls. The problem would only arise if the stimulation were carried to excess, and inflation so caused could be dealt by disinflationary fiscal policy.

But to assert that deficit financing as such, abstracted from an increase in the activities of the Federal government, would menace

[1] Senator Moore of Oklahoma; Congressional Record, Vol. XCI, p. 9074.
[2] House of Representatives, Committee on Expenditures in the Executive Departments, *Hearings on the Full Employment Act*, 1945, p. 389.

private enterprise and individual liberty was merely nonsense. It was the assertion of a doctrine held with bitterness as a result of the tumults of the 1930's. While it is not necessarily the case that all American businessmen held such extreme views as those put forward by the representatives of their organizations, there is little evidence to contradict the view that they did give a reasonable picture of large sections of business opinion.

In contrast to what happened in most other countries, the War was accompanied in the United States by a swing to the Right, with business well on the way towards getting out of the 'dog-house' into which the depression and Roosevelt had driven it, which meant that there was strong opposition to the use of a compensatory fiscal policy as an anti-deflationary weapon. But support for the view that the Federal government should intervene to prevent mass unemployment was still strong enough to get the Employment Act passed despite the business organizations and the Right-wing publicists. Outside the United States only the principle of preventing unemployment had wide public support; criticism of the British White Paper[1] came almost exclusively from those who wanted the abolition of capitalism root-and-branch; there may have been British businessmen who thought as many of their American opposite numbers did, but in the climate of opinion that prevailed in 1944–5 their views had no chance of acceptance and they discreetly held their peace. Whereas abroad the dominant opinion was that full employment must be maintained at all hazards, the United States stood apart in that an influential segment of opinion objected less to unemployment than to the methods that would have to be used to deal with it. The consequences were apparent in the position taken by the United States in the negotiations about the principles that were to govern post-war international economic relations.[2]

Partly because of the controversy it aroused, the Employment Act has been of greater lasting importance than the White Papers. Attacks on the Employment Act from the Right did not cease in 1946. The importance attached by many Americans to the Act as a guide to policy is shown by the proposal that it should be amended to make price stability an explicit goal of economic policy. The Employment Act retained significance as a moral imperative to Administrations and Congresses to take action to check deflationary

[1] Cmd. 6527 of 1944.
[2] See R. N. Gardner, *Sterling Dollar Diplomacy* (Oxford, 1956), pp. 271–80.

trends, despite the existence of sentiment opposed to the measures that would have to be used.

The division of American opinion about anti-deflationary policy that was shown clearly by the controversies over the Employment Act would have been a severe handicap in dealing with the post-war deflation whose expectation formed the background to the debates over the Act. By good fortune the conflict did not have to be resolved forthwith.

CHAPTER IV

POST-WAR RECONVERSION, TAX REDUCTION, AND INFLATION

IN 1945 government economists expected the end of the war to be followed both by rising unemployment as the service men were demobilized and production of munitions was discontinued, and also by rising prices in certain sectors. They believed that shortages of consumer goods, especially durables, during the war had given rise to accumulated demands which consumers would make effective as quickly as they could, drawing on liquid assets accumulated during the War. The reconversion of industrial capacity from the production of military equipment to the production of consumer goods could not be accomplished without some delay, hence it was quite likely that for a time demand for these goods at prevailing prices would exceed supplies. The upward pressure on prices would be aggravated by re-stocking by business, for inventories had been run down and were below the level appropriate to the real income reached by the end of the War. There was thus the prospect of an inflationary spurt, such as had followed World War I, before more fundamental deflationary forces took hold.

Attention was drawn to these possibilities by the reports of the Director of War Mobilization and Reconversion on 30 June 1945[1] and 15 August 1945.[2] In the latter report it was stated that unemployment was expected to reach 5,000,000 within three months of the end of hostilities, and to rise to 8,000,000. In the next report, issued on 1 October,[3] the Director, of OMWR, John W. Snyder, repeated the forecast of 8,000,000 unemployed, which, he said, was likely to be reached in the spring of 1946. He stressed the need to retain price controls and the need for caution in measures to expand demand in

---

[1] The text of the report, entitled 'The Road to Tokyo and Beyond', is printed in the *New York Times*, 1 July 1945.

[2] The text of the report, entitled 'From War to Peace: A Challenge', is printed in the *New York Times*, 16 August 1945.

[3] The text of the report, entitled 'Three Keys to Reconversion', is printed in the *New York Times*, 2 October 1945.

order to keep to a minimum the price increases expected to follow from the shortages.

On 6 September 1945 President Truman transmitted to the Congress a Message on reconversion,[1] in which he recommended 'limited' tax reduction, 'modernization' of the tax structure, the maintenance of price controls, the strengthening of the system of unemployment insurance, and the passage of the Full Employment Act.

Before the Administration made public the details of the tax reduction it would recommend, the House Republicans had got on the record a proposal to reduce the individual income tax and corporation profits tax by 20 per cent of tax liability, and also to repeal the excess profits tax. The prime mover was the senior Republican member of the Ways and Means Committee, Representative Knutson, who proposed it in a statement issued in Washington on 27 August.[2] After the plan had been endorsed by the Minority Leader Representative Martin,[3] Knutson and his next senior colleague on the Ways and Means Committee, Representative Reed, announced that they would fight for it during Committee's discussions on the tax reduction bill.[4]

The Administration's recommendations were presented to the Ways and Means Committee by Secretary Vinson on 1 October.[5] Outlining the forces which might be expected to lead to inflationary pressures in some sectors, he concluded: 'We must therefore at the moment keep up our guards against inflation, not only through price and other direct controls but through taxation'.[6] The changes in taxation recommended by the Treasury were: repeal of the excess profits tax with effect from 1 January 1946, but with provisions for losses incurred in 1946 to be carried back against profits assessed to excess profits tax in previous years; repeal of the 3 per cent 'normal income tax'; and repeal with effect from 1 July 1946 of the increases in excise tax rates enacted by the Revenue Act of 1943. The estimated cost of these reductions in a full year was: excess profits tax, $2,555

[1] Text in *Congressional Record*, Vol. XCI, pp. 8505–16, and in the *New York Times*, 7 September 1945.

[2] Reported in the *New York Times*, 28 August 1945.

[3] In a statement on 20 September; reported in the *New York Times*, 21 September 1945.

[4] Reported in the *New York Times*, 1 October 1945.

[5] The text of the Secretary's statement is printed in the *Annual Report of the Secretary of the Treasury for the year ending 30 June 1946*, pp. 326–32.

[6] Ibid., p. 328.

million; income tax, $2,085 million; excise tax reduction, $1,041 million; total, $5,681 million.[1]

The Secretary advocated the repeal of the excess profits tax on the grounds that its retention would be a serious disincentive to business in that for firms whose 'base' profits were such as to render them liable to excess profits tax it would remove nearly all the profits earned by expansion to meet post-war demand. The reduction of the income tax and the excise taxes was advocated both on grounds of equity and also as the most effective way of maintaining consumer demand. Afterwards at a news conference the Secretary opposed the '20-per-cent-across-the-board' income tax reduction both because it gave too much away and because the relief would be distributed too much in favour of the upper income groups.[2]

Without holding public hearings the Ways and Means Committee quickly reported a bill (H.R. 4309) which differed in many respects from the Treasury's recommendations. The excess profits tax was to be reduced to 60 per cent on profits received in 1946 and repealed with respect to 1947 profits; the corporation profits tax was to be reduced by 4 percentage points; the 'normal income tax' was to be integrated with the surtax and the surtax rates reduced by 4 percentage points,[3] with the proviso that the total reduction should be not less than 10 per cent of tax liability under existing law; the increases in excise tax rates imposed by the Revenue Act of 1943 were to be repealed with effect from 1 July 1946, as the Treasury recommended; and the tax on the use of cars and motor-boats was to be repealed. The purpose of the reduction was stated by the Committee to be 'to provide incentives for business to expand and to increase consumer purchasing power'.[4] The Republican members of the Committee welcomed the bill as a step in the right direction, but regretted that owing to the failure of the Administration to practise sufficient economy it was not possible to provide for larger reductions.[5]

When the bill was debated on 11 October there was wide support for it. Most of its supporters spoke of it as a stimulant to the incentives of business rather than as a means of adding to demand. Nobody described it as a means of 'increasing consumer purchasing

---

[1] Ibid., p. 338, Table A.　　　　[2] *New York Times*, 2 October 1945.
[3] This was the same thing as the Treasury's proposal with an additional reduction of one percentage point in the income tax.
[4] *H. Rept. No. 1106*, 79th Cong., 1st Sess., p. 1.　　　　[5] Ibid., p. 32–3.

power' sufficient to ward off a deficiency of consumption demand. One member[1] opposed it on the ground that it was wrong to 'declare a dividend' when there was still a large deficit; Representative Kean held that there would be no justification for a tax cut in terms of the mere 'black and white figures', but that the 'psychological considerations' (presumably incentives) were more important.[2] There was some criticism of the bill for giving too much relief to corporations and the better-off tax payers.[3] No motion to recommit was offered, and the bill was passed by 343 to 10.

The Senate Finance Committee began hearings on 15 October. The Secretary of the Treasury laid particular stress on the importance of abolishing the excess profits tax forthwith; he said that unless repealed it would have such an effect on incentives of business that production would be held down, adding to unemployment and prolonging shortages. It was not the case, he said, that if the excess profits tax was repealed corresponding amounts of relief must be given to all taxpayers; tax reductions must be selected for their contribution to overcoming the problems of transition to a peace-time economy.[4]

The NAM, the U.S. Chamber of Commerce, and the Council of State Chambers of Commerce advocated more drastic tax reductions, supporting the reduction of '20-per-cent-across-the-board' in the personal income tax and a deeper cut in the corporate profits tax than H.R. 4309 provided. They argued that this would increase the incentive to business to expand output and employment, and that the increase in production achieved would bring shortages to an end and so stop inflation. This last argument was to be heard over and over again in the years of inflation, and is obviously defective in that the increase in production is matched by an increase in income somewhere in the economy, in addition to the increase in demand that is the direct result of the tax cut. The argument only has any validity if the tax rate is so high that entrepreneurs prefer to leave their plant idle. It could not be reasonably contended that this was happening in the United States in 1945. The effect of tax rates on the inducement to invest and innovate may be more important in the middle

---

[1] H. Carl Andersen, Republican, of Minnesota. His remarks on the bill appear in the *Congressional Record*, Vol. XCI, p. 9633.

[2] *Congressional Record*, Vol. XCI, p. 9624.

[3] E.g. by Representative DeLacy; *Congressional Record*, Vol. XCI, p. 9627.

[4] The text of the statement is printed in the *Annual Report of the Secretary of the Treasury for the year ending 30 June 1946*, pp. 332–7.

and long run, but it cannot be held to have much effect on the balance in the short run between aggregate supply and demand in an inflationary situation like that which arose in the United States in 1946.

The C.I.O. and its allies criticized the bill on the ground that the addition to consumption demand was inadequate and that the distribution of the relief was inequitable. The latter point was by far the more heavily stressed. Mr. McAvoy, on behalf of the C.I.O., criticized the bill for giving 'huge windfalls' to large corporations,[1] and assured the Committee that 'the working man . . . will resent the favouritism for the big corporations shown by the House bill'.[2] He presented the C.I.O.'s proposals for doubling the individual exemptions from income tax for single people and married couples, but did not get a sympathetic hearing.

The Finance Committee acceded to the Administration's request that the excess profits tax be repealed with effect from 1 January 1946; the 'normal income tax' was to be repealed and liability to income tax reduced by a further 5 per cent; the corporation profits tax was to remain at existing rates except for corporations with profits below \$60,000; excise tax rates were to remain unchanged. The Committee stated that the repeal of the excess profits tax was necessary to remove an obstacle to reconversion, and that the other reliefs had therefore to be scaled down, because in view of the deficit only limited relief was possible.[3]

The bill was passed by the Senate on 24 October after a brief debate. Apart from O'Mahoney, who held that total demand was strong enough to render unnecessary the reductions other than the repeal of the excess profits tax,[4] no one raised serious objections, and the bill was passed by a voice vote.[5]

The final version of the bill was very similar to the Senate version. The excess profits tax was repealed with effect from 1 January 1946, and excise tax rates left unchanged; the reduction in the personal income tax was the same as in the Senate version. On the corporation profits tax there was a compromise, in that the tax on profits of less than \$25,000 was reduced by 4 percentage points and the standard

---

[1] Senate Finance Committee, *Hearings on H.R. 4309*, 1945, p. 92.
[2] Ibid., p. 101.   [3] *S. Rept. No. 655*, 79th Cong., 1st Sess., pp. 1 and 19.
[4] *Congressional Record*, Vol. XCI, p. 9957.
[5] When a 'voice vote' is taken, the minority is very small; for when demanded by one-quarter of the members a vote by yeas and nays, in which the roll is called and the names of those voting for and against are published, must be taken.

rate on profits above $50,000 was reduced by 2 percentage points; the tax on the use of cars and motor-boats was repealed. The conference report was approved by the House on 30 October by 297 votes to 33 after some protest against its alleged inequity and the dangers of adding to the deficit with consequent risks of inflation. The Senate approved it by a voice vote on 1 November after George had stated that the reduction in revenue was greater than he really approved of, but that it had to be accepted in order to reach a compromise with the House. The Revenue Act of 1945 became law less than two months after the President had recommended a tax reduction.

The effect of the reduction in personal income tax is shown in the following table:

TABLE 7

Effective Rates of Tax under the Revenue Act of 1945 and under Existing Law Rates (%)

Adjusted Gross Income	Single Man		Married, Two Children	
	Existing Law	*Revenue Act 1945*	*Existing Law*	*Revenue Act 1945*
$1,000	11·50	9·50	1·50	nil
$2,000	17·25	14·25	2·25	nil
$3,000	19·50	16·15	9·17	6·33
$5,000	22·10	18·43	15·10	11·78
$10,000	27·55	23·47	22·45	18·62
$50,000	55·89	50·27	53·73	48·22

Source: Tables inserted in *Congressional Record*, Vol. XCI, pp. 10175–6.

The reduction in liabilities to tax on 1946 profits and incomes that resulted from the Revenue Act of 1945 is shown in the following table:

TABLE 8

Reduction of Tax Liability under the Revenue Act of 1945

	Amount of Reduction ($ *million*)
Taxes on Corporate Profits	3,140
Taxes on Personal Incomes	2,645
Use Tax on Cars and Motor-boats	140
	5,925

Source: Annual Report of the Secretary of the Treasury for the year ending 30 June 1946, Exhibit 35, p. 346.

From the remarks both of members of the Administration and of Members of Congress it is evident that a major purpose of the tax reductions made by the Revenue Act of 1945 was to promote expansion in the civilian economy to help offset the deflationary effect of the end of war expenditures. Emphasis was laid on stimulus to the incentives of business rather than on strengthening consumer demand, especially in Congressional statements of tax policy. This emphasis is apparent in the tax reductions enacted; the reduction in excise tax rates recommended by the Treasury was omitted from the final version of the bill, whereas a reduction in the rates of the ordinary corporation profits tax, which the Treasury had not recommended, was included. If a deficiency of consumption demand had been regarded as the main danger, it would have been appropriate to reduce the excise tax rather than the corporation profits tax.

The repeal of the excess profits tax probably was a significant stimulant to business activity. For firms whose profits were high enough to incur liability the excess profits tax established a marginal rate of tax of 85·5 per cent; its repeal reduced the marginal rate to 40 per cent, a reduction large enough to have significant effects. The provision whereby losses incurred in 1946 could be carried back against war-time profits for purposes of liability to excess profits tax also gave an incentive for expansion to firms which had incurred a substantial liability to excess profits tax during the War. If a firm in such a position took a risk in expanding in 1946 and suffered losses as a result, all but 14·5 per cent of the loss would be recoverable from liability to excess profits tax on the profits of previous years; on the other hand, if the firm pursued a cautious policy and 'missed the bus' when profits were to be had, 60 per cent of the profits lost would be its own money. Such a position of 'heads we win, tails we don't lose' would give the maximum inducement to invest and to expand. On the other hand, it is unlikely that the reduction in the ordinary corporation profits tax would have much effect. The effect of the cut from 40 per cent to 38 per cent on the inducement to invest through raising the rate of return could only be very small, and the addition to investible funds was unlikely to be important in many cases, since most firms had ample liquid assets to finance any investment they wished to undertake.

RECONVERSION AND THE ONSET OF INFLATION

During the winter of 1945–6 it became apparent that the transition from a war economy was being achieved with far less trouble than had been expected, and in particular that unemployment was not rising as fast as had been feared. Total unemployment as estimated by the Bureau of the Census never approached the widely quoted figure of 8,000,000; its highest point was 2,700,000 in March 1946, after which it declined fairly steadily. Industrial production, as measured by the Federal Reserve System's seasonally adjusted index, began in May 1946 a sustained rise that lasted until nearly the end of the year.

The most important component of aggregate demand whose expansion was greater than had been expected was undoubtedly consumption. While consumption of durable goods was approximately in accordance with estimates, consumption of non-durable goods and of services, especially the former, was very much greater.[1] According to *Fortune*, sales of consumers' goods late in 1945 'were limited only by the number of people who could get into stores and the durability of sales clerks'.[2] In 1946 both investment in fixed capital and investment in inventories rose rapidly. In consequence the problem on hand very soon became one of a general excess of effective demand.

By the beginning of 1946 the Administration had come to the conclusion that inflation was the immediate problem. The President stressed this in his Budget Message, recommending every effort to hold down government expenditure, including the postponement of all but the most essential public works. Since a tax increase was obviously out of the question, restraint by fiscal means had to be exercised by maintaining existing tax rates while expenditures declined. Setting a lower limit to Federal expenditures were heavy fixed charges arising from the War, such as the interest on the National Debt and the benefits for ex-servicemen provided under the 'G.I. Bill'; in addition there were heavy expenditures abroad through UNRRA; the level of 'peace-time' expenditure for the armed forces was still uncertain, though in December 1945 the Director of the Bureau of the Budget estimated that annual defence expenditure would be of the order of $6–8 billion.[3]

The President tried to accelerate the reduction in government expenditure. On 1 August 1946 he issued a directive to all heads of departments instructing them to hold down their purchases of such

---

[1] See L. R. Klein, 'A Post-Mortem on Transition Predictions of National Product', *Journal of Political Economy*, Vol. LIV (1946), pp. 289–308.

[2] *Fortune*, June 1946, p. 97.

[3] In speech to NAM. Reported in *NAM News*, Vol. XII, No. 54, p. 5.

scarce goods as cars, office equipment, and building materials.[1] On 3 August the President announced that Federal agencies would undertake no new commitments for construction for two months, and that a large amount of construction work would be held over until the last quarter of fiscal 1947.[2] He estimated that these measures would reduce Federal expenditures for construction in fiscal 1947 by $707 million. The Service departments were required to absorb most of the cost of an increase in servicemen's pay by internal economies. The standstill on new construction aroused strong protest and had to be modified. Due largely to the winding-up of wartime commitments, expenditures in fiscal 1947 declined sufficiently to yield a cash surplus of $6·6 billion.

Given the abnormal liquidity in the private sector resulting from the War, there was little opportunity for restraint on demand through monetary policy. Indeed, it required all the effort and ingenuity of the Federal Reserve System to conduct a 'holding operation' to prevent the working of the money and credit system from making the inflation even worse.[3]

The other possible means of restraining the inflation was direct control. In 1945 and early 1946 the Administration strongly advocated the retention of price controls. There was no intention of trying to suppress inflation in the war-time manner, for control over the use of raw materials, nearly all food rationing, petrol rationing, and wage controls were revoked in August 1945. The most that could be done was to slow down the rises in prices and wages and ensure that they took place in an orderly manner. Even this proved impossible. The trade unions, many of which felt that they had been unfairly treated during the War, were anxious to be rid of effective wage limitation, and the business associations, under the leadership of NAM, launched an all-out attack against controls, above all price controls. Their main fear seems to have been that of profits being squeezed between rising wages and fixed prices, a fear that was partly justified by trade union demands, echoed by some members of the Administration such as Secretary Wallace, that wages should be raised without raising prices in order to increase consumer demand. It was common knowledge in the early part of 1946 that the effectiveness of the controls was declining. The controls were extended by a

---

[1] *New York Times*, 2 August 1946. [2] *New York Times*, 4 August 1946.
[3] See J. S. Fforde, *The Federal Reserve System 1945–1949* (Oxford, 1954), Chapters 5–14.

bill passed at the end of June 1946, but in such attenuated form that the President vetoed it; fresh price control legislation passed in August was a failure, for the 'strike' of ranchers led to a shortage of meat and the Administration had to yield. On 11 November the remaining price controls, except those on rice and sugar, were revoked. The suppressed inflation had become open.

Since inflation emerged so shortly after the Revenue Act of 1945 had been passed, question must be raised whether tax reduction at that time was a mistake. Consumption demand was so strong that it would probably have been adequate without the addition resulting from the reduction in personal income tax. The repeal of the excess profits tax was a different matter; its importance was in its effect on the inducement to business to expand and to invest rather than its effect in increasing the funds available for investment or distribution to shareholders. It is impossible to ascertain what would have happened had the excess profits tax not been repealed, since this would require information about what business policies and attitudes would have been in a hypothetical situation. It is also possible to argue that had the excess profits tax been retained, the trade unions would have been more receptive to appeals for moderation in their wage policies, since they considered its repeal was not matched by any corresponding amount of relief for the income groups to which their members belong. The size of the wage claims and the number and duration of strikes in 1946 suggest that the unions were in a militant mood, and it seems doubtful indeed whether their policies would have been significantly different had more heed been paid to their views on tax reduction. Had economic forecasts been more prescient, the policy recommended by the Administration might have inclined less towards 'strengthening purchasing power', but the difference that this would have made to Congressional action is doubtful; the strength of the desire for a reduction in wartime burdens once the War was over should not be underrated.

Although it can be maintained that had tax rates not been reduced in 1945 the subsequent inflation would have been weaker, it is probable that aggregate demand was so great relative to the capacity of the economy to supply that the situation was beyond the control of fiscal measures short of the imposition of tax rates well above those in force during the War. Because of the strength of support in the United States for the principle of free enterprise it was impossible to use the war-time controls to contain demand and release it little by little as the supply situation permitted, as was done in Britain. The backlogs of demand therefore had to be left to work themselves off in a 'free-for-all', subject to such restraint as could be achieved by the combination of constant tax rates and autonomously declining government expenditures. The American economy was less 'empty' than the British economy, so that the inflation resulting from the working-off of backlogs of demand was not disastrously great. Political developments in the autumn of 1946 presaged difficulty in carrying out even the modest fiscal policy outlined above, as will be shown in the next chapter.

CHAPTER V

INFLATION AND THE STRUGGLE OVER
TAX REDUCTION, 1947

THE excess of effective demand that emerged in 1946 sprang from five main sources, all explicable in terms of the economic backwash of the War. Consumers' demand, sustained by large holdings of liquid assets, was very strong, and their expenditures were very high relative to disposable income. There was a serious shortage of houses, partly because of the small numbers built during the War[1] and partly because of the large number of newly-wed ex-servicemen wanting to set up home. Restrictions on investment by industries that were less essential to the war effort had given rise to a backlog to be made good once the restrictions were withdrawn. Inventories had been depleted during the war and by the heavy expenditure by consumers late in 1945, with the result that there was a rush to rebuild them. In addition to these internal sources of demand there was an abnormally heavy demand for American exports. The effects of the war had greatly increased the demand of the European countries for imports from the United States, while seriously impairing their ability to export to her; an abnormally large surplus in the American balance of payments on current account therefore ensued.

These inflationary forces were duly noted in the Economic Report of the President in 1947, the first of the annual Economic Reports required by the Employment Act. These forces were described as 'favourable' factors, as was the existence of a backlog of needed public works.[2] That these inflationary forces should be described as 'favourable' suggests that the newly appointed Council of Economic Advisers was still scanning the economic horizon for the much-bruited post-war depression, counting as 'favourable' any factor that added to total demand and so helped ward off the threat of depression. Certain 'unfavourable' factors were noted, of which the

[1] The number of new non-farm houses started was 356,000 in 1942, 191,000 in 1943, 141,800 in 1944, and 209,300 in 1945. In 1940 and 1941 it was 602,600 and 706,100 respectively. *Economic Report of the President, 1959*, Table D–33.

[2] *Economic Report of the President, January 1947*, printed as H. Doc. No. 49, 80th Cong., 1st Sess., p. 19.

most important was the reduction of real disposable incomes through rising prices. Also cited as causes for concern were the possibility of a decline in business investment due to the working-off of backlogs, and the possibility that uncertainty caused by industrial disputes, which in 1946 had been exceptionally severe, might discourage investment.[1]

The principal danger seen by the Council of Economic Advisers was thus future 'underconsumption' caused by a redistribution of real income away from consumers through rising prices.[2] The existing volume of consumer demand (in money terms) was in excess of that needed to clear the market of consumer goods at current prices and prices had in consequence risen. Since the existing volume of consumer demand was to some extent maintained by running down holdings of liquid assets, it was open to doubt whether the market could be cleared of a growing volume of output at the higher prices. What then happened depended on whether the mechanism whereby prices had risen in response to short supplies was reversible to any extent when supplies improved. A recession could be brought on in this way only if when total consumer demand in money terms was inadequate to clear the market of consumer goods at prevailing prices, this would lead to a drop in output and employment rather than a fall in prices and a consequent swing in the distribution of real income back in favour of consumers. This was probably the reason why the Economic Report recommended 'price and wage adjustments'[3] in a context which suggested that they were to redistribute income away from profits.

In the latter part of 1946 and the first half of 1947 there were recurrent fears that the post-war recession (or 'adjustment') was still in the offing. In December 1946 the editors of *Fortune* in an editorial entitled 'Inflation Over' expressed the opinion that the inflation had 'about spent itself', and that a decline could be expected.[4] Next spring there were further expressions of concern; according to *The Economist*'s American Survey: 'The question is no longer whether the U.S. is going to have a business recession. The question is how

[1] Ibid., p. 20.
[2] 'Compensation of employees' as a percentage of national income declined from 68·0 per cent in 1945 to 65·3 per cent in 1947. Calculated from data in Dept. of Commerce, *National Income Supplement to the Survey of Current Business*, 1954, Table 1.
[3] *Economic Report of the President, January 1947*, pp. 20–1.
[4] *Fortune*, December 1946, pp. 2–3.

long and how deep the readjustment will be'.[1] In September 1946 Wall Street prices had gone down steeply, which could be taken as a sign of impending trouble.

In the spring of 1947 the rise in prices ceased, which at the time could be taken as the beginning of the readjustment. The halt proved to be temporary, for in the third quarter prices began to rise again. The period was described in the *Economic Report of the President* in January 1948 as one of 'hesitation by individual consumers and business, explicable partly by high prices and the expectation of early price reductions'.[2] The index of industrial production declined slightly, resuming its increase only in the last quarter of the year. One of the factors which caused this temporary lull was the cessation of inventory accumulation. Consumers' expenditure did not decline, and house building, business investment in fixed capital, and purchases of goods and services by state and local governments continued to increase; and in the fourth quarter of the year inventory accumulation was resumed. The economic situation late in 1946 and in 1947 was one in which inflationary forces predominated most of the time, but containing elements which might be taken as indicating that the downturn was not far away.

THE POLITICAL SITUATION:
THE REPUBLICAN VICTORY IN THE ELECTIONS IN 1946

Among the opening shots of the campaign was the revival by Representative Knutson and several of his associates of the proposal for a cut in personal income tax liability of '20-per-cent-across-the-board' which they unsuccessfully tried to have included in the Revenue Act of 1945. Knutson said in a statement issued under the auspices of the Republican National Committee: 'The first step is the election of a Republican Congress in November. Then in 1947 income taxes will be reduced by 20 per cent'.[3] Just over a week later a similar pledge was given by Representative Curtis, a colleague of Knutson's on the Ways and Means Committee, who said in a statement that was also distributed by the Republican National Committee: 'They (the Treasury staff) are now thrown into a state of panic by a Republican pledge to cut income taxes 20 per cent for 1947

---

[1] *The Economist*, 24 May 1947, p. 804.
[2] *Economic Report of the President, January 1948*, p. 19.
[3] 11 August 1946. Quoted by the *New York Times*, 12 August 1946.

if the voters elect a Republican Congress in November'.[1] Representatives Knutson and Curtis thus gave pledges to reduce income taxes by a specific amount, without making the reduction conditional on the economic situation being such as to make it safe, or even conditional on a substantial reduction in expenditure. It is open to doubt whether anybody can really commit either party to anything in a Congressional election, but there is no record of any Republican candidate having disassociated himself from these statements about tax reduction. The view that the Republicans had committed themselves to tax reduction was forcefully expressed in February 1947 by the Chairman of the Republican National Committee, B. Carroll Reece. He wrote in a circular letter to Republicans holding public office and to party officials:

'During the campaign of 1946 Republican spokesmen promised definitely and unequivocally that if their party won control of Congress there would be drastic reduction of Federal expenditures and a substantial cut in income taxes, and a start towards the reduction of our monumental National Debt. The American people accepted these promises and elected Republican majorities in both Senate and House of Representatives.'[2]

The Republicans won majorities in both House and Senate; in the Senate the party strengths were 51 Republicans and 45 Democrats; in the House 246 Republicans, 188 Democrats, and 1 American Labor. The election of 1946 resulted in an unmistakable swing to the Right in the composition of the Congress. In the Senate the 'Class of '46', which included Senators Jenner, Bricker, Malone, Ecton, Kem, Martin, Cain, and McCarthy, was to make its reputation in the next decade as including some of the most extreme members of the 'radical Right'[3] in American public life. Similar changes took place in the composition of the House of Representatives. Not only were numerous Left-wing Democrats replaced by Right-wing Republicans, but the liberal Republicans fared badly in the primaries.

Influential Republicans believed that their party owed its victory to a popular revulsion against the New Deal and its supporters. The

---

[1] 19 August 1946. Quoted by the *New York Times*, 20 August 1946.

[2] Quoted by the *New York Times*, 2 February 1947.

[3] This term is to be preferred to such designations as 'extreme conservative' since most holders of these views do not aim to preserve the *status quo* and existing institutions, but to change certain aspects of them in a very radical manner. See D. Bell (Ed.), *The New American Right* (New York, 1955).

following remarks of Representative Martin, Speaker of the House in the 80th Congress, probably represented the views of many of his colleagues: 'It was perfectly obvious that if we were going to get America readjusted to peace, prosperity, and progress, we would have to reduce drastically the squandering of public funds by a bureaucracy that had become overswollen, arrogant, and wasteful. . . . The country wanted the cost of government cut down, the activities of the government cut down, and the tax rate reduced.'[1] One newly elected Republican announced that: 'a new philosophy of government will be initiated, and that is that it is the people's duty and obligation to support the government rather than the New Deal parasitic philosophy of the government supporting the people'.[2]

The attitude expressed above is one of reaction in the strict sense of the word, a reaction against the changes brought about by President Roosevelt and the policies he came to symbolize. That this was the mood of the majority of the 80th Congress is shown by the passage by the Congress in 1947 of the Constitutional Amendment to prevent any future President from holding the office for more than two terms[3]; this was clearly an instance in which the Republicans and the anti-New Deal Democrats wanted to pay off one old score from the 1930's, to inflict a defeat on their old enemy even if it had to be posthumous. This attitude partly explained why in the election campaign the Republicans took a position in favour of a tax cut without any heed of the short-run economic consequences.

TAX REDUCTION: THE OPENING MOVES

Directly the result of the election became known Knutson reiterated the pledge to reduce the personal income tax by 20 per cent.[4] The policy which the Republican leaders in the House of Representatives would follow was announced formally in a statement issued after a meeting of the Republican House of Representatives Steering Committee on 14 November 1946:

'The committee was united in the view that there can be a reduction of 20 per cent across the board in personal income taxes. . . . A report by Republican members of the Appropriations Committee

---

[1] In a radio broadcast on 9 July 1947, the text of which is printed in the Appendix to the *Congressional Record*, Vol. XCIII, p. A3646–8.

[2] Representative Wilson; *Congressional Record*, Vol. XCIII, p. 2720.

[3] This Amendment became part of the Constitution as Amendment XXII in 1951.

[4] Reported in *New York Times*, 7 November 1946.

makes it clear that savings to taxpayers can be achieved while at the same time the current budget can be balanced and payments begun on the national debt.'[1]

There was considerable speculation about what position the Administration would take. Before the election the Secretary of the Treasury, Mr. John W. Snyder, had expressed strong opposition to tax reduction under the circumstances then prevailing,[2] but after the election he declined to comment on the proposed reduction of 20 per cent, preferring to wait and see what bill was actually introduced.[3] The Left-wing Democratic Senator Taylor proposed a crastic increase in the individual exemption from income tax,[4] a form of tax reduction which would give a far larger share of the benefit to the poorer taxpayers than Knutson's plan.

Directly the Congress convened, Knutson introduced his tax reduction bill, which received the designation H.R.1 as a mark of the importance attached to it by the Republican leaders in the House. It provided for a reduction of 20 per cent in liability to personal income tax on all income below $302,000, a reduction of 10½ per cent on that part of income in excess of $302,000, and an additional exemption of $500 for people over the age of 65. The reductions were to apply to the whole of incomes received in 1947. Knutson explained at a press conference that the reason for the smaller reduction in the tax on very large incomes was that such incomes were usually unearned, so that for them tax relief to increase incentives was not needed.[5]

The Administration took the unequivocal position of opposing any tax reduction for the time being. In both the State of the Union Message and the Budget Message the President recommended that the excise taxes which were due to expire on 1 July 1947 should be continued for the whole of fiscal 1948. The Revenue Act of 1943 had provided that the increases in excise taxes imposed by it were to expire six months after the formal ending of the War. The state of war was formally terminated by Presidential proclamation on 1 January 1947, so that unless legislation were passed to set a new expiration date many excise tax rates would be reduced automatically

[1] Quoted by the *New York Times*, 15 November 1946.
[2] At press conferences on 4 September and 9 October, 1946. Reported in the *New York Times*, 5 September and 10 October 1946.
[3] *New York Times*, 12 December 1946.
[4] *New York Times*, 29 November 1946.
[5] *New York Times*, 4 January 1947.

on 1 July 1947. The President's reason for proposing the extension of the excise taxes was twofold: inflation rendered undesirable a tax reduction of $1·5 billion in a full year; and when the economic situation permitted a reduction in excise tax rates it would be preferable to review all excise taxes, not just those whose rates had been increased by the Revenue Act of 1943.[1]

The response of the Republicans to this proposal for the maintenance of excise taxes at existing rates was generally favourable. Senator Taft endorsed it in a speech on 9 January as being necessary to facilitate the reduction of income tax.[2] On 14 January the Republican members of the Ways and Means Committee agreed to support the extension of the excise taxes at existing rates, and on 16 January Representative Grant introduced a bill (H.R.1030) for this purpose. The Ways and Means Committee reported it promptly, without hearings. The bill provided that the excise taxes should be continued at their existing rates without any time limit; the President had recommended their extension for the whole of fiscal 1948, but not in a form of words that unequivocally meant for one year only. The House passed the bill on 29 January by 374 votes to 33. Action in the Senate was equally swift; after two amendments had been inserted to exempt from tax garments trimmed with fur and fares paid for foreign travel, the bill was approved by a voice vote. It was signed by the President on 11 March.

The principal reason why the Congressional Republicans put through so promptly the measure recommended by the President was that it seemed at the time that if a budget deficit was to be avoided income tax and excise tax rates could not both be cut, and the Republicans preferred reduction in the income tax. This reasoning was evident in the speech by Representative Grant introducing the bill:

'If our individuals are to have tax relief and the country is to have a balanced budget, together with a substantial payment on the National Debt, then there seems no alternative to continue these present war excises on so-called luxury items in effect, at least until the Congress has an opportunity to consider the whole budget picture.'[3]

The Republicans' policy amounted to shifting some of the burden

---

[1] *Budget of the United States for the year ending 30 June, 1948*, pp. M.5, M.11
[2] Reported by the *New York Times*, 11 January 1947.
[3] *Congressional Record*, Vol. XCIII, pp. 669.

from direct to indirect taxation, a reform of the tax structure that had for long been supported in conservative circles. Expressed by Representative Dingell in the partisan language of the Left, 'the plan is to penalize the consumer for the high bracket taxpayer'.[1]

The first part of the tax policy recommended by the President, and the only part which required affirmative legislation, was thus enacted by a hostile Congress, not because of agreement with him about general economic policy, but because it favoured the measure for an entirely unrelated reason.

THE ARGUMENTS FOR THE KNUTSON TAX REDUCTION BILL (H.R.1)

Before tracing the course of the tax reduction bill through the Congress to its eventual veto by the President, it is convenient to outline the principal contentions which underlay support for and opposition to the bill. The changes it would make in effective rates of tax are shown in the following table:

TABLE 9

Effective Rates of Tax for a Married Couple with no Dependents

Income before tax ($)	1939	Existing Law (Revenue Act 1945) %	H.R.1 %
1,200	nil	3·2	2·5
2,000	nil	9·5	7·6
3,000	0·3	12·7	10·1
5,000	1·6	16·0	12·8
10,000	4·2	21·9	17·5
50,000	17·7	49·6	39·7
100,000	32·5	63·1	50·5
500,000	60·8	81·5	68·4

Source: Annual Report of the Secretary of the Treasury for the year ending 30 June 1947, p. 223.

The arguments adduced by supporters of H.R.1 fall under three heads: long-term economic advantages; advantages in the immediate economic situation; and general political considerations. The objections fall under two heads: that it was inappropriate in the prevailing economic situation; and that the distribution of the relief was inequitable.

The economic arguments most often adduced in support of the bill were the need to increase the supply of venture capital and to

[1] *Congressional Record*, Vol. XCIII, p. 670.

strengthen through tax reduction the incentives of managers and investors. Introducing the bill in the House of Representatives Knutson declared that it would remove deterrents to managerial effort and the investment of venture capital which constituted a 'serious threat' to prosperity both then and in the future.[1] It was on this ground that the Republicans defended the proportion of the relief given by the bill to the upper income groups. Senator Millikin conceded that the bill would relieve taxpayers in the very high brackets of nearly all the additional taxes that had been imposed since 1939 while leaving those in the lower and middle brackets more heavily taxed than in 1939, but maintained that those responsible for the tax structure developed in the 1930's paid far too little heed to the need for managerial incentives and an adequate supply of venture capital.[2]

Assertions about the need for tax reduction to increase the supply of venture capital or to strengthen incentives are notoriously difficult to prove or to disprove. In view of the very high level of business investment in plant and equipment in 1947,[3] the evidence of a general excess of effective demand, the existence of shortages of materials such as steel that were of special importance for fixed capital investment, and the large quantities of liquid assets possessed by firms, it seems reasonably certain that lack of investible funds was not a serious limitation on investment in 1947. Given the absence of unused resources in the economy a tax reduction could bring real resources into investment only by bidding them away from consumers, which would exacerbate the inflation. This argument refers to the aggregate, however, and because shortage of investible funds does not appear to have been a serious limitation on investment as a whole, it does not follow that this was true for all would-be investors. The adequacy or otherwise of the supply of risk capital of the kind supplied by wealthy individuals to back projects which are too risky for the market cannot be deduced from statistics relating to aggregate investment, and it is hard to think of any statistical evidence which it would be possible to produce which would settle the dispute. But the

---

[1] *Congressional Record*, Vol. XCIII, p. 2721.

[2] Ibid., Vol. XCIII, p. 5732.

[3] A study prepared by the Department of Commerce showed that purchases of producers' durable goods in 1947 formed a higher proportion of G.N.P. than in any year since World War I. The text of the study is printed in House of Representatives, Committee on Ways and Means, *Hearings on H.R.4790*, 1948 (Washington, 1948), pp. 143–53.

arguments presented by the supporters of H.R.1 and similar proposals concerned the finance of investment through the Stock Exchange; it was pointed out that Wall Street prices had slumped, and
that the ratio of bond to equity issues was rather high. Statistics
presented by the Department of Commerce suggested that there
was no visible cause for concern on the latter point[1]; and the fall in
Stock Exchange prices could have many other causes; a post-war
boom had preceded the decline, and it could not be contended that
the supply of venture capital had suddenly diminished in the middle
of 1946.

The arguments about incentives to managerial effort are if anything even more inconclusive. The general tenor of the studies that
have been made in Britain and the United States of the effects of
income tax on incentives in the post-war years is that there is little
evidence to suggest that the income tax has thus far had an appreciable effect in diminishing the amount of effort exerted.[2] None the less,
the existence of such an effect on incentives was often taken as self-
evident truth and stated in the most sweeping terms. According to
Representative Mason, 'every sound economist in the country'
agreed that the rates of income tax had been raised beyond the point
of diminishing returns.[3] The only evidence adduced was that revenues
had risen after each reduction of income tax rates in the 1920's, and
that reductions in the rates of the state income taxes in New York
and Maryland had been followed by increases in revenue.[4] The
analogy between a state income tax whose maximum rate is 7 per
cent and the Federal income tax whose minimum rate is 20 per cent
is obviously uninformative in this instance, and it is probable that
revenues in the 1920's would have risen even more rapidly had tax
rates not been reduced so much. Want of real evidence did not, how-

[1] Equity issues averaged 32 per cent of all issues of corporate securities between
1919 and 1929, the same percentage as in 1947; payments of interest amounted
to only 8 per cent of corporate profits before payment of taxes and interest in
1947 compared with 23 per cent in 1929 and 12 per cent in 1941. House of Representatives, Committee on Ways and Means, *Hearings on H.R.4790*, 1948,
p. 165.

[2] T. H. Sanders, *Effects of Taxation on Executives* (Boston, 1951); G. F. Break,
'Income Taxes and Incentives to Work', *American Economic Review*, Vol. XLVII
(1957), pp. 529–49; Royal Commission on the Taxation of Profits and Income,
2nd Report (Cmd. 9105), para. 149 and Appendix I, Chapters 4 and 5.

[3] *Congressional Record*, Vol. XCIII, p. 2775.

[4] Knutson at his press conference on 3 January 1947. After drawing attention
to the experience of the 1920's, he said that 'history has a habit of repeating itself'. *New York Times*, 4 January 1947.

ever, deter supporters of tax reduction from asserting that the existing rates were having a deleterious effect on incentives with the most
dire consequences for the furture.[1]

In the shorter run, a tax reduction in 1947 would be economically
advantageous only if a deficiency of demand was in prospect, taking
into account the effects of any reductions made in government expenditure. As indicated above, there was widespread belief in 1947
that a recession was in the offing, and this concern was cited as a
ground for tax reduction. In their report[2] the Senate Finance Committee noted that there was uncertainty whether the downturn would
begin sometime in 1947 or in 1948; pointing out that a considerable
time lag must elapse before a tax reduction makes its impact on the
economy, the Committee argued that the reduction should be put
into effect forthwith as a 'hedge against recession and cumulative
deflation'[3] and that if the economy appears in danger of recession
the retirement of a large amount of the national debt in a short time
would aggravate the situation.[4]

This would be a reasonable enough argument given the forecast
of a coming recession and given the decision that action to forestall
the recession should be taken without waiting for evidence of its
onset to become complete, accepting the risk of inflation should the
forecast turn out to be erroneous. Difficulties arise when one considers whether it is likely that the Republican members of the Finance
Committee were really recommending that in order to guard against
deflation the country should run a larger risk of inflation than the
President proposed. In view of their past and subsequent actions it
is hard to believe this, or that they were much influenced by another
argument put forward in their report, that since unemployment was
considerably greater and the average number of hours worked per
week was smaller than in 1944, there was more room for expansion
of real output than the Administration believed.[5] Taken literally this
can only mean approval of measures to add to demand all the time
unemployment is above the lowest point reached in war-time. When
it is noted that of the seven Republican members of Finance Com-

---

[1] John W. Hanes told the Ways and Means Committee that 'industry is finding
it exceedingly difficult to hire good men' because 'The incentive in working and
assuming great responsibility is gone'; by this means 'punitive rates' do 'colossal
damage' to 'our profit-and-loss economy'. House of Representatives, Committee on Ways and Means, *Hearings on H.R.1*, 1947, p. 181.

[2] *S. Rept. No. 173*, 80th Cong., 1st Sess.   [3] Ibid., p. 9.

[4] Ibid., p. 10.   [5] Ibid., p. 7.

mittee[1] Taft and Millikin were the farthest 'Left' by most standards, it is hard to take at its face value the argument about the desirability of a tax cut to prevent a recession that might happen in the future.

Since in so many instances the reduction of the national debt was coupled with tax reduction and reduction of government expenditures as the financial objectives of the Congressional Republicans, it would not be reasonable to interpret the tax reduction in terms of compensatory fiscal policy to deal with threatened deflation. A combination of reduced expenditures and reduced tax rates could be so interpreted if the reduction in expenditure were made for long-term reasons of political principle and the tax cut made to prevent it aggravating a threatened recession. But in such a case reduction of the national debt, i.e. a budget surplus, would be inappropriate. If the prevention of a recession through adding to consumer demand were anything more than a subsidiary purpose of the tax reduction, then it would have been more logical to use a reduction in income tax which gave more of the benefit to the lower and middle income groups or a reduction in excise taxes rather than the tax reduction actually proposed. The explanation was probably that it was common ground among people of all opinions, whether or not they were familiar with the economics of compensatory fiscal policy, that a reduction in tax rates stimulates the economy, whereas the link with the expenditure side of the budget, which is all-important in determining what happens to total demand, was not so widely understood.

It was also argued that tax reduction would damp down the inflationary spiral through raising employees' 'take home pay' without raising costs. It might have such an effect, but it could not be large. The reduction in tax for a married man without children earning $2,000 a year would be $38, making an increase in income after tax of about two per cent. In view of the size of the increase in the cost of living and of the wage increases the unions were claiming, such an increase would in all probability have been swamped. Here again a form of tax reduction which gave more of the benefit to the lower income groups would have been more appropriate if this were a major purpose of the tax reduction. Moreover, any relief achieved in the pressure on costs would have been obtained by adding still more to the excess of demand.

The proposed tax reduction was very often supported on grounds

---

[1] In order of seniority, Millikin, Taft, Butler, Brewster, Bushfield, Hawkes, and Martin.

of political principle and doctrine, and in this way appeared as an expression of the Republican purpose of restoring something of the *status quo ante* Roosevelt. When Knutson first proposed the tax reduction during the 1946 election campaign, he gave the following as one of the reasons for it: 'cut off much of the government's income by reducing taxes and compel the government to retrench, live within its income'.[1] Similar views were expressed on many occasions in 1947, for example by Senator Taft:

'The President's real reason for retaining the taxes is obviously to have more money to spend. The best reason to reduce taxes is to reduce our ideas of the number of dollars the government can properly spend in a year, and thereby reduce inflated ideas of the proper scope of bureaucratic authority'.[2] Such arguments imply that there is no prospect of reduction in government expenditure through Congressional action, either by repealing legislation which entails government expenditure or through reducing appropriations. They also assume, if interpreted literally, that the government cannot borrow to finance that part of expenditures which it deems necessary that cannot be covered by revenues; at this time the statutory limit to the National Debt was $275 billion, whereas the actual debt was about $250 billion, so that the Administration had plenty of leeway.

Another way of looking at it is that the Administration would be forced to choose between taking the lead in reducing expenditures or standing by while the public finances made the inflation still worse. This would obviate any risk of a veto and would spare the Congress and the Republican party the unpopularity that would result from drastic cuts in public services. Judged by the criteria of compensatory fiscal policy, tax reduction for motives of this sort is irresponsible. If it was desired, on grounds of principle, to reduce the role of the government in the economy, this was the worst way of setting about it because of the inflationary side effects that would probably have ensued had such a policy been put into force in 1947.

A further reason for tax reduction of the type provided for by H.R.1 was that it would go some way towards reversing the 'socialistic' New Deal policy of redistributing income through the progressive income tax. Some supporters of the bill saw the issue in such

[1] In the statement of 11 August 1946. Quoted by the *New York Times*, 12 August 1946.

[2] Speech at Columbus, Ohio, to a Republican dinner on 31 July 1947. Text printed in the *New York Times*, 1 August 1947.

terms as the following: 'whether you are going to encourage this free enterprise system to go ahead, and stay with the capitalistic system, or whether we are going to a socialist economy'.[1] The Labour government in Britain, which was alleged to have come to power because Britain's investing classes had been destroyed by progressive taxation,[2] was held up as the fate which awaited the United States if tax rates were not reduced substantially. Here is an example of what Knutson himself stated that his tax reduction bill would do:

'(the bill) puts the ax to punitive taxes designed by alien minds and whizzed through subservient Congresses. . . . For years we Republicans have been warning that the short-haired women and the long-haired men of alien minds in the administrative branch of government were trying to wreck the American way of life and install a hybrid oligarchy at Washington through confiscatory taxation'.[3]

There is little doubt that the main reasons why the Congressional Republicans sought to pass a reduction in income tax of the type provided by H.R.1 were those of political principle and longer-run economic considerations. The origins of the proposal for tax reduction, during the election campaign, indicate that the reasons underlying the bill were unrelated to the immediate economic situation; any advantages it might have in promoting short-run economic stability were incidental and merely subsidiary to the purposes the framers of the bill had in mind.

OPPOSITION TO THE PROPOSED TAX REDUCTION

The opposition to the proposed tax reduction took two forms: the contention that in the existing economic circumstances tax reduction of any sort was undesirable because it would strengthen the inflation; and the contention that the benefits of the proposed tax reduction would be inequitably distributed.

The Administration took the view that tax reduction should be avoided because of the danger of continuing inflation. While the arguments about venture capital and incentives were not denied absolutely, members of the Administration argued that on available evidence the deleterious effects did not appear great enough to justify accepting the harm that substantial tax reduction would do

---

[1] John W. Hanes (a former Assistant Secretary of the Treasury) to Ways and Means Committee. House of Representatives, Committee on Ways and Means, *Hearings on H.R.1*, 1947, p. 187

[2] This was asserted by Senator Millikin; *Congressional Record*, Vol. XCIII, p. 9428.　　　[3] *Congressional Record*, Vol. XCIII, p. 2726.

by exacerbating the inflation. Secretary Snyder told the Senate Finance Committee:

'Under present conditions I do not believe that a tax reduction would bring about any significant increase in production, nor do I believe that a tax reduction at this time is necessary to assure continued high level production. . . . Production is now limited by shortages of labor and materials rather than by lack of venture capital or markets. . . . Inflationary pressures have not subsided. . . . So long as inflationary pressures persist, there is good reason for maintaining high taxes.'[1]

The existence of shortages of important materials, especially steel, was attested by the 'grey markets' for those materials. Average monthly unemployment in 1947 as reported by the Bureau of the Census was 3·6 per cent of the civilian labour force, which was about in line with the war-time estimates of frictional and structural unemployment. The Administration's contention that there were no significant amounts of unemployed resources was sound.

Whereas supporters of the tax reduction often claimed that the inflation was practically over and that a recession was imminent, the Administration disagreed. In the Budget Message the President declared that there was no likelihood of a recession serious enough to require a recasting of the tax policy:

'Should . . . a recession occur, it would be a temporary slump growing out of transition period difficulties and would call for no revision of our budget policy.'[2]

In the course of his discussion with the Senate Finance Committee Secretary Snyder stated quite categorically that there was no recession in sight.[3] Clearly, the economic forecast on which the Administration's fiscal policy was based was that there would be no recession which would require anything more drastic than the automatic stabilizers. This was in accordance with the advice given by the Council of Economic Advisers, though it was the line the Administration would probably have taken anyway.[4] In view of the widely

---

[1] Senate Finance Committee, *Hearings on H.R.1* (1947), p. 14.
[2] *Budget of the United States for the year ending 30 June, 1948*, p. M5.
[3] Senate Finance Committee, *Hearings on H.R.1* (1947), p. 83.
[4] The then Chairman of the Council of Economic Advisers has written that when the Council gave the President this advice on 3 December 1946 'The President expressed gratification that we were in agreement with existing policies, but did not really enter into any discussion of the merits of the issue'. E. G. Nourse, *Economics in the Public Service* (New York, 1953), p. 137.

held fears, whose genuineness there is no reason to doubt, that a recession was in the offing, the Administration was running a considerable risk of deflation, should the recession occur, in order to use the one means available to restrain inflation. If tax rates were cut and the recession did not occur, there would have been no politically available means of exercising any restraint on inflation other than achieving a budget surplus by making drastic cuts in defence, foreign aid, and public services.

In the Administration's view the danger to continued prosperity was the impairment of consumers' purchasing power through rising prices, for which tax reduction was not the remedy. In his Message vetoing H.R.1 the President said that necessary adjustments in prices and incomes should be made by wise policies on the part of business and labour, and not by 'hastily invoking the fiscal policies of the government on a broad scale'.[1] The insistence of the Administration on retaining existing tax rates despite fears of recession and the remarks about the need for readjustments in the private sector rather than the hasty use of fiscal policy should a decline occur do not support the view that the Truman Administration was eager to put reflationary measures into effect at the first sign of a prospective deficiency of demand.

On several occasions the contention that it was necessary to reduce the National Debt was presented by the Administration as an argument quite separate from the contention that a budget surplus, and therefore debt reduction, was needed to check inflation. President Truman himself regarded the achievement of surpluses and the reduction of the National Debt as 'good financing' quite independently of its effect on the level of aggregate demand in the economy. He wrote in his *Memoirs*:

'From June 30 1946 to June 30 1952 we had a net income for the Government of three billions over expenditures. That is what I would consider good financing.

'I had reduced the public debt by 28 billion dollars from the post-war peak. My goal was to bring the total down to 200 billion dollars, but the Congress did not want the political risk of levying the additional taxes to accomplish this.'[2]

---

[1] The text of the Message is printed in the *Annual Report of the Secretary of the Treasury for the year ending 30 June, 1947*, pp. 244–6; and in the *Congressional Record*, Vol. XCIII, pp. 7227–8.

[2] Harry S. Truman, *The Years of Trial and Hope* (London, 1956), p. 40.

In retrospect it appears fortunate that the Congress did not raise taxes enough to accomplish so large a reduction of the debt. During 1947 both the President and the Secretary of the Treasury stressed the need to begin debt retirement then in order to give evidence of determination to retire it,[1] and in order to maintain the 'integrity' of the debt.[2]

As might be expected, this argument was heard a great deal from opponents of the tax reduction in Congress. They took the opportunity to chide the Republicans for abandoning their often reiterated support of 'sound finance', but with very little effect.[3]

The Republican tax policy was also opposed as being inequitable as between income groups. The distribution of relief between income groups, of which the details were not in dispute, is shown in the following table:

TABLE 10
Distribution of Tax Relief under H.R.1

Income Range	Recipients of Taxable Income Within the Range (%)	Tax Relief (%)
Under $2,000	54·7	23·9
$2,000–5,000	41·8	37·8
Over $5,000	3·5	38·3

Source: Calculated from Table E, Senate Finance Committee, *Hearings on H.R.1* (1947), p. 30.

It was also pointed out that whereas the tax reduction provided by H.R.1 would increase the income after tax of a man with an income of $2,500 by 1·2 per cent, the income after tax of a man with an income before tax of $300,000 would be increased by 70·5 per cent.[4] Opponents of the bill held it to be unfair that a man with an income

[1] Secretary of the Treasury to the Senate Finance Committee; Senate Finance Committee, *Hearings on H.R.1* (1947), p. 15. The Secretary did not say whether he meant by this that the whole National Debt should be retired.

[2] President Truman, in his Message vetoing H.R.1, of which the text is printed in the *Congressional Record*, Vol. XCIII, pp. 7227–8, and in the *Annual Report of the Secretary of the Treasury for the year ending 30 June 1947*, pp. 244–6. What exactly was meant by 'the integrity of the debt' was not explained; it is hardly reasonable to suppose that failure to retire some of the debt would give rise to fears of its eventual repudiation.

[3] In 1947–8 only two Republican Members of Congress, Representatives Andersen and Morton, who voted against one or more of the tax reduction bills explained that they did so because they regarded a tax cut which might lead to a deficit as unsound.

[4] Senate Finance Committee, *Hearings on H.R.1* (1947), p. 245.

of $300,000 should get an increase in 'take home pay' of 70·5 per cent,
while the man with an income of $2,500 got an increase of 1·2 per
cent, and that nearly 40 per cent of the tax reduction should go to
under 4 per cent of the taxpayers. As was pointed out at the time,
the comparison of 'take home pay' was unfair because of the high
rates in the upper brackets; if the effective rate on a hypothetical
income were reduced from 95 per cent to 90 per cent the 'take home
pay' would be increased by 100 per cent, whereas a reduction in the
effective rate from 10 per cent to 1 per cent would raise the 'take
home pay' by 10 per cent only. It was also argued that if income tax
liability were reduced by a uniform percentage the ratio of taxes paid
on one income to taxes paid on another would remain the same; the
tax on a taxable income of $50,000 would remain 67 times the tax on
a taxable income of $2,000, so that the same degree of progression
would be maintained. This was just as true as the C.I.O.'s argument
about 'take home pay' and just as inconclusive.

It is indisputable that the type of tax reduction the Congressional
Republicans proposed gave a higher proportion of the relief to the
upper income groups than either of the other forms of tax reduction
that were widely canvassed, an increase in the individual exemption
and a uniform percentage point reduction in each of the bracket
rates. This was the basis of fiery denunciations of the 'Knutson-
NAM bill', 'high income tax relief for the high profiteers', and rewards to the high income groups for their contributions to Republican campaign funds, the Left-wing counterpart to the Right-
wing denunciations of 'socialistic redistribution'.

The Administration opposed the tax reduction on the grounds of
that it was inequitable as well as untimely. In his Message vetoing
H.R.1 President Truman declared that it embodied 'the wrong tax
reduction at the wrong time'.[1]

POLICY ON GOVERNMENT EXPENDITURES IN 1947

The Republicans had been demanding reduction in government
expenditures year in and year out ever since President Roosevelt had
taken office. It had been their claim in 1946 (as in previous years)
that by the elimination of waste, excessive staffs, and functions
which the Federal government ought not to undertake, Federal

[1] The text of the Message is printed in the *Annual Report of the Secretary of
the Treasury for the year ending 30 June 1947*, pp. 244–6; and in the *Congressional Record*, Vol. XCIII, pp. 7227–8.

expenditures could be reduced sufficiently to permit both tax reduction and steady retirement of the national debt. Their efforts to put these views into practice in 1947–8 met with only limited success and aroused storms of controversy.

The following table shows the estimated expenditure by the Federal government in fiscal 1948, as submitted by President Truman in his Budget Message in January 1947; in accordance with later practice, tax refunds are not here treated as an expenditure but deducted from receipts, the latter being shown net of tax refunds.

TABLE 11

Budget Estimates of Expenditures, by Function, Fiscal 1948

Function	Expenditure ($ million)
National Defence	11,256
Veterans' Services and Benefits	7,343
International Affairs and Finance	3,510
Social Welfare, Health, and Security	1,654
Housing and Community Facilities	539
Education and General Research	88
Agriculture and Agricultural Resources . . .	1,381
Natural Resources	1,101
Transportation and Communication	1,530
Finance, Commerce, Industry	426
Labour	118
General Government	1,492
Interest	5,000
Contingencies	25
Total	35,463

Source: Budget of the United States for the year ending 30 June 1948, pp. 1406–9.

With receipts estimated according to existing tax laws this budget showed a surplus of $200 million. The passage of the Act to extend the excise taxes at their existing rates increased the revenue estimate by $1·5 billion, giving an expected surplus of $1·7 billion. The Treasury's estimates of revenue were very conservative indeed, as was shown in the course of the hearings on the tax reduction bill. The estimates presented in the Budget were based on the assumption that total income payments[1] in fiscal 1948 would be $168 billion.[2] At the time Secretary Snyder appeared before the Senate Finance

[1] 'Income Payments' was a series similar to 'Personal Income', which superseded it.

[2] Senate Finance Committee, *Hearings on H.R.1* (1947), p. 43.

Committee the latest available figure was $176 billion; he was closely questioned about the estimates, and the impression from reading the record of the hearings is that the Secretary had an uncomfortable time trying to maintain that the estimate of revenue was reasonable without repudiating his contention that there was no likelihood of a recession in the coming year, the one contingency which might make the income assumption come out right. The conclusion his questioners sought to establish was that there was 'room for' a tax reduction without throwing the budget into deficit; the Treasury's ultra-cautious estimates served to deny this.

The Budget was promptly denounced as being too large. Among the points made was that it was four times as large as that of the last fiscal year before the outbreak of war (1939). This was not a helpful comparison; of the $35·5 billion of estimated expenditure, $27·1 billion was accounted for under the heads of 'national defense', 'veterans' services and benefits', 'interest', and 'international affairs and finance', of which the first three were immune to serious cuts, and even foreign aid was more 'cut-proof' at that time than it became afterwards. In fiscal 1939 expenditure under these four heads was $2,593 million out of a total budget expenditure of $8,959 million. Budget expenditures under the other heads were thus to rise from $6·4 billion in fiscal 1939 to $8·4 billion in the estimate for fiscal 1948. Even when the heavy expenditures in 1939 for relief are allowed for, the comparison does not suggest extravagance in 1948 when the rise in prices since 1939 is taken into consideration.[1]

In accordance with the procedure laid down in the Legislative Reorganization Act the Congress began consideration of the 'Legislative Budget'. The House Budget Committee recommended a cut of $6 billion in expenditure and $5·8 billion in appropriations below the amounts recommended by the Administration, and that the number of Federal civilian employees should be reduced by 500,000.[2] These objectives were stated in round terms only, and in no sense was it a carefully drawn alternative to the Budget submitted by the President. On 17 February the Budget Resolution embodying the recommended cuts was passed by the House. The Senate resolution provided for a reduction in expenditure of $4½ billion, and no

---

[1] The implicit deflator for Federal purchases of goods and services in the Department of Commerce's estimates of G.N.P. at constant prices is 55·1 for 1939 and 100·0 for 1947. Dept. of Commerce, *National Income Supplement to the Survey of Current Business*, 1954, Table 41.

[2] *H. Rept. No. 35*, 80th Cong., 1st Sess.

compromise was reached, partly because of the lack of urgency to
do so, as the consideration of the appropriation bills went forward
in the normal way whether the Budget Resolution was passed or not.
At the most the Legislative Budget would have been for the guidance
of the Appropriations Committees and would not in itself have had
any direct effect on government expenditures. It is difficult to come to
any conclusion other than that the mechanism of the Legislative
Budget was used merely to make a gesture in support of 'economy'
against the Administration.

In the course of the consideration of the appropriations it became
apparent that the cuts which could be achieved would not come to
anything like $6 billion. The reduction in appropriations actually
achieved was $2,765 million,[1] not all of which was a genuine cut in
the funds available to the Administration. Of it $800 million was cut
from the appropriation to the Treasury for tax refunds; as the refunds themselves could not be cut, the cut in the appropriation was
purely 'phoney' and its only result was a deficiency appropriation in
1948. Some real cuts were made; the Bureau of Internal Revenue,
the Coast Guard, and the Bureau of Labor Statistics, among other
agencies, were 'axed'; and the more conservative view of the proper
functions of the Federal government appeared in the cuts made by
the House in funds for soil conservation, Federal power and water
projects, and school lunches. These cuts were extremely controversial; the funds for school lunches were restored by the Senate and
accepted in Conference; and part of the funds for the Departments
of Agriculture and the Interior were later restored. Despite years of
talk about the existence of hordes of 'useless' Federal employees the
Appropriations Committees were unable to find many that could be
eliminated specifically. As a result recourse was had to straight
percentage cuts in appropriations for staff, based not on evidence of
over-staffing in the agencies concerned, but on the general policy of
cutting the Budget. The cuts in expenditure achieved in this way
were too small to have any economic significance. The contrast between the reduction of about $1·8 billion that was actually achieved
and the declarations in favour of a $6 billion cut gave considerable
justification for the jibes about 'how loud is the thunder, how little it
rains'. It was one thing to assail 'Federal spending' in the abstract;

[1] Table presented to the Ways and Means Committee by the Director of the
Bureau of the Budget. House of Representatives, Committee on Ways and Means,
Hearings on H.R.4790 (1948), p. 239.

quite another to make large cuts in defence or services that were important to large numbers of people.

THE PASSAGE THROUGH CONGRESS OF TAX REDUCTION LEGISLATION

The criticisms of the Knutson bill on grounds of equity led to its modification before it was reported out of the Ways and Means Committee. The amendment, sponsored by Representative Kean, provided for a reduction of 30 per cent in the tax on taxable incomes of $1,000 or under, and a reduction of from 30 per cent to 20 per cent on incomes between $1,000 and $1,400 by means of a 'notch'.[1] Apart from this the version of H.R.1 reported by the Way and Means Committee was the same as that originally introduced by Knutson.

When H.R.1 was debated, the motion to recommit provided that the Ways and Means Committee should give the bill further study and not report it out until the appropriation bills had been passed. This motion was rejected by 237 votes to 172 in a division which followed party lines almost exactly, two Republicans voting in favour of the motion and four Democrats against it. On the motion to pass the bill, however, 40 Democrats joined with the Republicans in voting in favour; 32 were from the South[2] and 2 from Maryland. The bill was only one vote short of a two-thirds majority.

The Senate Finance Committee held nine days of hearings on H.R.1 following custom in giving an opportunity to everyone who wanted to be heard. The bill was strongly supported by the business organizations and opposed by the trade unions. The C.I.O. representatives put forward a proposal to increase the individual exemption to $1,000 and to recoup the cost by higher taxes on profits and large incomes; and also, which was more to the point, stated that the C.I.O. would prefer no tax reduction at all to the tax reduction provided for by H.R.1. Many witnesses, including those representing the C.I.O. and the NAM, expressed fears of a coming recession. It would be unreasonable to write off all the expressions of concern

---

[1] A 'notch' is a device for effecting a transition between two rates when those rates are to apply to the whole of taxable income. In this case the provision was for a reduction of tax liability of $67, which was equal to 30 per cent of liability on a taxable income of $1,000 and 20 per cent on a taxable income of $1,400. The need for this device arises only because it is desired to apply the same flat rate to all taxable income instead of a series of separate brackets.

[2] Used here to mean the eleven states of the Confederacy, viz., Alabama, Arkansas, Florida, Georgia, Louisiana, Mississippi, North Carolina, South Carolina, Tennessee, Texas, and Virginia.

about a recession as being merely handy arguments for a tax reduction, and the constant harping on this theme by so many witnesses may account for the emphasis laid on it in the Committee's report.[1] The Finance Committee recommended two amendments to the House version of H.R.1; one reduced the remission of tax on taxable incomes between $79,700 and $302,400 to 15 per cent instead of 20 per cent; the other provided that the tax reduction should come into effect on 1 July 1947 instead of 1 January. The latter would reduce the revenue loss in fiscal 1948 and would eliminate the retroactive tax reduction.[2]

When the bill was debated on the Floor of the Senate, some important divisions of opinion were revealed. Senator George, the senior Democratic member of the Finance Committee said that he approved of tax reduction in the form proposed by the Republicans, but thought that it should be postponed until 1 January 1948.[3] Senator Lucas, the Minority Whip, moved an amendment[4] which was really a substitute bill; it provided for an increase in the individual exemption to $600, a reduction of two percentage points in the rate for each bracket, and the computation of tax liability of married couples under the 'income splitting' system,[5] all to go into

[1] See p. 66 supra.   [2] *S. Rept. No. 173*, 80th Cong., 1st Sess., p. 13.
[3] *Congressional Record*, Vol. XCIII, p. 5738.
[4] The text of the Lucas amendment is printed in the *Congressional Record*, Vol. XCIII, p. 3862.
[5] Under American income tax law, husbands and wives have always been permitted to file separate returns and be taxed accordingly if they have separate sources of income, as when the wife is employed or owns income yielding assets. Under 'income splitting', which is relevant only where the couple file a joint return, the income is treated for tax purposes as belonging half to the husband and half to the wife, with a consequent reduction of total tax paid if the marginal rate in the absence of income splitting is greater than the lowest bracket rate. The problem arose from a discrimination in favour of taxpayers in those states whose law of married women's property rights is regulated by the 'community property' doctrine. Under this doctrine the earnings of a married man and the property acquired out of those earnings are treated as being the product of the joint efforts of man and wife and to belong half to each. When the Federal income tax was introduced in 1913 the community property doctrine was part of the law of seven Western states, and in those states the earnings of married men were recognized as belonging half to the man and half to the wife for tax purposes. With the advent of high progressive rates of income tax the discrimination in favour of the taxpayer in the community property states became substantial enough to induce other states to adopt the community property doctrine. Since an attempt to remove the special treatment had been prevented in 1942 by threat of filibuster by Senators from the 'community property' states, the only way to end the discrimination was to extend the 'income splitting' procedure to all taxpayers.

effect on 1 January 1948. This was an alternative to the Republican tax reduction with the relief apportioned in a way more in harmony with the ideas of equity held by Left-of-Centre Democrats and their supporters.

The Republican reaction to the demands for inclusion of income splitting was to express agreement with the principle but maintain that action should be postponed until 1948, when it was proposed to bring in a tax revision bill.

The voting on the Lucas amendment, which was rejected by 58 votes to 27, gives an idea of the divisions among Democratic Senators on the subject of tax reduction. Twenty-six Democratic votes were cast for the amendment and 10 against. Of the latter, two (George and McCarran) voted in favour of H.R.1 in the final division, indicating that they regarded the type of tax reduction provided for by H.R.1 as superior to that in the Lucas amendment; the remaining eight (Barkley, Byrd, Connally, Ellender, Johnson, McFarland, Robertson, and Tydings) voted against the bill itself, indicating that they opposed tax reduction as such at that time. The bill was passed by 52 votes to 34. Seven Democrats voted for the bill, of whom two (George and McCarran) had previously voted against the Lucas amendment and five (Hoey, O'Conor, O'Daniel, Stewart, and Umstead) had voted or been paired in favour of the amendment.

On 16 June 1947 President Truman vetoed H.R.1, which he described as 'the wrong tax reduction at the wrong time' and stated that 'the time for tax reduction will come when inflationary pressures have ceased and the structure of prices is on a sounder basis than now prevails'.[1] On the following day the voting on the motion to override the veto was 268 votes in favour to 137 against, two votes short of the two-thirds majority. Five Democrats who had voted in favour of the bill voted against the motion to override the veto. Representative Doughton voted against the motion to override despite his having signed the Conference report, explaining that he did so because of the greater uncertainty about expenditures, especially for foreign aid.[2] It is likely that his opposition influenced enough votes to prevent the veto from being overriden in the House.

[1] The text of the veto Message is printed in the *Annual Report of the Secretary of the Treasury for the year ending 30 June 1947*, pp. 244–6; and in the *Congressional Record*, Vol. XCIII, pp. 7227–8.

[2] *Congressional Record*, Vol. XCIII, pp. A3098–9.

THE SECOND ATTEMPT AT TAX REDUCTION: H.R.3950

Shortly after the defeat of the motion to override the veto of H.R.1, Knutson introduced another tax reduction bill, H.R.3950. This was merely the final (i.e. Conference Committee) version of H.R.1[1] except that the tax reductions were scheduled to go into effect on 1 January 1948. Its prospects of passage seemed considerably brighter than those of H.R.1, for while under consideration by the Ways and Means Committee it received the support of three Democratic members, Doughton, Mills, and West. Also encouraging was a statement by Senator Byrd[2] that he would support a tax reduction that went into effect on 1 January 1948 provided the Republicans pressed forward with the reduction of expenditures. This meant two additional votes in the Senate for tax reduction (Byrd's and that of his fellow Virginian and staunch supporter, Robertson) and the support of the Virginia delegation in the House.

The only innovation in the course of consideration of H.R.3950 by the House was in the motion to recommit, which was moved by Representative Forand. In contrast to the motion to recommit H.R.1, it provided for a substitute tax reduction; the individual exemption was to be raised to $600 and the rates to be reduced by three percentage points in each bracket, a programme which strongly resembled the Lucas amendment except that income splitting was omitted. Only fifteen Democrats voted against both the motion to recommit and the passage of the bill, thus demonstrating hostility to all proposed tax reduction at the time. H.R.3950 was passed by 302 votes to 112. Twenty-nine of those who voted in favour had voted against H.R.1; two groups can be discerned among them, the six members from North Carolina[3] whose votes on tax reduction in 1947–8 reflected the position taken by Doughton and whose votes for H.R.3950 were probably accounted for by Doughton's support of it, and five from Virginia.[4] The entire Virginia delegation had voted against H.R.1 and the switch followed Byrd's expression of support for H.R.3950.

---

[1] This was the same as the Senate version except that the 15 per cent reduction of tax liability was to apply to taxable incomes above $136,000 instead of $79,000.

[2] Reported in the *New York Times*, 26 June 1947.

[3] Doughton, Barden, Bonner, Durham, Jones, and Kerr.

[4] Almond, Bland, Gary, Harrison, and Stanley. In view of the power of Senator Byrd in Virginia politics it is almost permissible to use eighteenth-century language and refer to this group as 'the Byrd connection'.

In the Senate an income splitting amendment was again moved and rejected, as was an amendment to increase the individual exemption to $600, which was defeated by 47 votes to 43. Nine Democrats voted against the latter amendment, of whom all but two (Byrd and George) voted against the bill itself. On 14 July the Senate passed the bill by 60 votes to 32. Eleven Democrats voted in favour; they were the seven who had voted for H.R.1, McKellar, who had been absent when H.R.1 was voted on, and three who had voted against it, Byrd, Robertson, and Tydings. The reasons for the switch of Byrd and Robertson are clear from Byrd's statement; it is probable that similar considerations influenced Tydings, particularly the fact that H.R.3950 would not lead to a deficit in the current fiscal year.

The President again vetoed the tax reduction bill, and this time the majority in the House was ample to override his veto, the vote being 299 to 108, with the North Carolina and Virginia delegations both voting to override. Attention then turned to the Senate, where two additional votes were needed to override the veto. It was reported that considerable pressure was put on Langer, who all along had opposed the Knutson bills, to vote to override. Even had this pressure been effective it would not have carried the day, for two Democrats (Umstead and Tydings) and one Republican (Aiken) who had voted for the bill, now voted to sustain the veto, as did Senator Thomas of Utah (Democrat) who had been absent when the bill was passed. With the failure of the Senate to override the veto of H.R.3950 the efforts of the Republicans to enact income tax reduction in 1947 came to an unsuccessful end.

The purpose of the rather lengthy analysis of the voting on the various motions and in particular the changes of position by certain Democrats is to trace the process whereby the bi-partisan majority which in 1948 was able to pass tax reduction despite the President's veto was put together. One of the most important questions in interpreting the votes on tax reduction in 1947 is whether the sponsors of the Forand motion (to recommit H.R.3950) and the Lucas amendment were merely exercising the Opposition's privilege of proposing measures that are superficially popular but which they would not vote for if they were responsible for the government, or whether some or all of those who voted for the Forand motion or the Lucas amendment would have voted for a Republican-sponsored bill containing similar provisions, knowing that it would pass. If the latter was the case, it follows that the reason why the President's opposition to any tax reduction bill succeeded was not that a sufficient number of Members of Congress agreed with him, but that the supporters of tax reduction could not agree sufficiently among themselves on the type of tax reduction that should be passed. The close similarity of the vote of Democratic Senators for the Lucas amendment and their vote for the passage of H.R.4790[1] suggests that the vote for the Lucas amendment was far more than a political gesture.

CONCLUSIONS ON FISCAL POLICY IN 1947

The Administration's fiscal policy in 1947 was based on the assumption that inflation would be the main short-run economic problem, and consisted of maintaining existing tax rates while expenditure declined. It had to achieve this despite the fact that the majority in the Congress for a variety of reasons, mainly political, were intent on cutting tax rates. It emerges from the foregoing analysis of the treatment by Congress of tax measures in 1947 that the Administration owed its success in securing the maintenance of existing tax rates to a concatenation of favourable circumstances. The one piece of affirmative legislation that was required, the extension of excise tax rates, was secured because the Republicans preferred to reduce the income tax rather than the excise taxes. Even more important, to pass the income tax reduction the Republicans had to take the initiative; a result of 'no change' was what the Administration sought, and to achieve this required only enough votes to sustain a veto. The Republican tax reduction bills failed to obtain enough votes to override the veto because it turned out that the type of tax reduction proposed was unacceptable on grounds of equity to Democratic supporters of other kinds of tax reduction. It is obvious how different the outcome would have been had the American income tax been imposed by an annual Finance Act, in which case the Republican majority in the Congress would have been able to offer the President the choice of income tax at rates he considered too low or no income tax at all.

The combination of declining expenditures[2] with constant tax rates resulted in the largest surpluses ever achieved in the United

---

[1] See pp. 94-5 infra.

[2] About $1·8 billion of this was the result of the cuts made by the Congress. Director of the Bureau of the Budget to Ways and Means Committee; House of Representatives, Committee on Ways and Means, *Hearings on H.R.4790* (1948), p. 238–9.

States. The cash surplus in fiscal 1947 was $6·8 billion and in fiscal 1948 was $8·8 billion. The 'conventional' budget surpluses in those years were $754 million and $8,419 million respectively. The reason for the abnormally great difference between the conventional budget and cash surpluses in 1947 was that in 1947 the United States paid into the International Monetary Fund and International Bank her subscription of $2·4 billion in non-interest-bearing notes, which counted as a conventional budget expenditure but did not require an immediate cash payment; similarly in fiscal 1947 $1·8 billion of 'terminal leave bonds', which under existing legislation were not immediately encashable, were issued to demobilized ex-servicemen; this item too counted as a budget expenditure without requiring a cash payment. Legislation passed in 1947 provided that the terminal leave bonds could be encashed forthwith, and in fiscal 1948 bonds worth $1·5 billion were encashed. In the same year $900 million worth of notes that had formed part of the subscription to the I.M.F. and I.B.R.D. were redeemed, making a total cash payment of $2·4 billion in fiscal 1948 which was not accompanied by a corresponding conventional budget expenditure in the same fiscal year.

The economic forecast on which the Administration's tax policy had been based, that there would be no serious recession in 1947 and that inflation would be the main danger, proved to be correct. The 'hesitation' of the spring of 1947 was short lived, and in the second half of the year prices and output rose again. G.N.P. in the fourth quarter of 1947, measured at seasonally adjusted annual rates in constant (1954) prices, was $287·2 billion compared with $280·4 billion in the second quarter,[1] a rise of 2·4 per cent. In the same period the implicit deflator for the estimates of G.N.P. at constant prices rose from 82·0 to 85·3,[2] a rise of 4·1 per cent. Despite the size of the surplus, inflationary pressure was evident, and it is reasonable to suggest that had the surplus been reduced by a tax cut the inflation would have been even worse.

The financial policy of the Congressional Republicans was a facet of their ambition to execute a reversal from the direction in which the economic and social policy of the United States had been proceeding under President Roosevelt. The short-run economic consequences of the Republican financial policy were incidental to the

[1] Department of Commerce, *U.S. Income and Output*, 1959, Table I–5.
[2] Ibid., Table VII–3.

main purpose, and it is reasonably clear that the Congressional leaders did not think about taxation and government expenditures in terms of exerting a stabilizing influence on prices and output. Had they been able to carry out their tax programme in 1947 it would almost certainly have had a de-stabilizing effect. Whether or not this was a price worth paying to achieve the reduction of tax rates and diminution of the redistributive effect of the tax structure is a matter to be determined by the political values of those concerned. That the fiscal policies actually carried out in the United States were in the right direction for economic stability was due quite as much to the inability of the Congressional Republicans to carry out a tax policy based on considerations unrelated to economic stabilization as it was to sound economic judgement in the Administration.

CHAPTER VI

THE REVENUE ACT OF 1948 AND THE
END OF THE POST-WAR INFLATION

IT soon became evident that the defeat of H.R.1 and H.R.3950 did not mean the end of the attempt by the Republican majority in the 80th Congress to force through tax reduction. Less than a month after the end of the first Session, Representative Knutson served notice that the subject would be brought up again as soon as the new Session opened.[1] Nothing came of the suggestion that tax reduction might be taken up during the Special Session called in November 1947 to deal with foreign aid and inflation. The prospect of rising expenditure for foreign aid and the continuation of inflationary pressure did not suggest to Knutson and his colleagues that it might be wise to postpone tax reduction. However, Senator George declared that because of the inflation and the rising expenditure for foreign aid he would support only a 'very moderate' tax reduction, by which he meant an increase in the individual exemption to $600 and provision for 'income splitting'.[2]

Knutson introduced his bill, H.R.4790, directly the new Session of Congress convened. It had five important provisions: the individual exemption was to be raised from $500 to $600; tax liability on taxable incomes of under $1,000 was to be reduced by 30 per cent, on taxable incomes between $1,000 and $1,400 by from 30 per cent to 20 per cent by means of a 'notch',[3] on taxable incomes between $1,400 and $4,000 by 20 per cent and on taxable incomes greater than $4,000 liability was to be reduced by 20 per cent on the first $4,000 and 10 per cent on the rest; married couples were to be permitted to split their incomes for computation of tax liability; an additional exemption of $600 was allowed to the blind and people over the age of 65; and the concept of income splitting was to be applied to the calculation of liability to estate and gift tax. The cost of these reductions was estimated by the Treasury at $6·5 billion in

---

[1] Reported by the *New York Times*, 7 September 1947.
[2] Ibid., 1 December 1947
[3] For the meaning of this term, see p. 77 supra.

a full year,[1] assuming total personal income at $200 billion. The Ways and Means Committee estimated the cost at $7·1 billion, based on an assumed personal income of $212 billion.[2]

H.R.4790 was the 'lowest common denominator' of H.R.1 and H.R.3950 and the Lucas amendment. Testimony about the purely political motives which accounted for the structure of the bill was given by Senator Millikin three years later; discussing how the 'split income' provision got into the income tax law, he said: 'It was deliberately contrived to attract the votes, because we wanted to reduce taxes'.[3] The bill was a political Christmas tree with something for everybody, containing elements of each of the forms of tax reduction that had been canvassed during the previous year. It was obviously intended to secure the support of those who in 1947 had been in favour of tax reduction but had found H.R.1 and H.R.3950 to be too inequitable.

The Administration's reply was outlined by President Truman in the State of the Union Message on 7 January. He recommended a reduction of income tax of $40 for each taxpayer and each of his dependents. To recoup the loss of revenue he proposed that taxes on corporate profits be raised to yield an additional $3·2 billion. The purpose of the reduction was to assist poorer taxpayers who had been squeezed by the increase in the cost of living; because of 'extraordinarily high' profits, corporations could afford to carry a larger share of the tax burden.[4]

The Administration's plan was embodied in a bill introduced by Representative Dingell on 14 January. Under this bill, H.R.4968, the personal income tax would be reduced in the way outlined in the State of the Union Message, and the excess profits tax would be reintroduced. 'Excess profits' were defined as profits greater than 135 per cent of the base established under war-time law, that is to say, the average of 1936–39 profits or 8 per cent of invested capital. A tax of 75 per cent gross was to be levied on excess profits so defined which were earned in the calendar year 1948 or afterwards.

In the budget for fiscal 1949 expenditures were estimated at $39·7 billion and revenue, under existing law, at $44·5 billion. According

[1] *Annual Report of the Secretary of the Treasury for the year ending 30 June 1948*, p. 321.

[2] *H. Rept. No. 1274*, 80th Cong., 2nd. Sess., p. 7.

[3] *Congressional Record*, Vol. XCVII, p. 11731.

[4] The text of the Message is printed in the *Congressional Record*, Vol. XCIV, pp. 34–8, and in the *New York Times*, 8 January 1948.

to this estimate H.R.4790 would replace a surplus of $4·8 billion by a deficit of $1·7 billion. If the Ways and Means Committee's estimate is taken, which was based on a higher total personal income, there would be a surplus of $500 million, plus anything that could be achieved through cutting expenditure.[1] So large a tax reduction would have led to a substantial addition to effective demand. The effect of the Administration's plan was more doubtful. In fiscal 1949 it would cause a drop in revenue, because the tax reduction would go into effect at once through the withholding system, whereas the excess profits tax would produce no revenue until taxes were paid on 1948 profits, that is to say, in 1949.[2] If the accrual of liability to tax caused a corresponding reduction in investment, the result would be deflationary to the extent that any of the increased personal disposable income was saved. But the effect of the excess profits tax was uncertain; it might have had such a bad effect on business expectations that the reduction in investment would have been greater than the liability to tax that accrued; on the other hand it is possible that the tax might have had no effect on investment or distributions of dividends until the payment of it reduced corporate liquidity. The effect of the Administration's plan on aggregate demand was thus very much a matter of conjecture; all that can be said with certainty is that it would have made a smaller addition to demand than H.R.4790.

While the origins of H.R.4790 are plain for all to see, the origins of the President's recommendations are far more obscure. The generally accepted opinion is that the scheme originated in the Council of Economic Advisers.[3] According to the *New York Times*, which gave as its source 'White House advisers' all three members of the Council supported the scheme, but because of the opposition of Dr. Nourse none of the Council appeared before the Joint Committee on the Economic Report or the Senate Finance Committee in its support, although his colleagues wished to do so. The report continues:

'The economic reasoning of the Council was authoritatively reported as follows:

'The Council kept as its No. 1 objective the maintenance of

[1] *H. Rept. No. 1274*, 80th Cong., 2nd. Sess., p. 7.

[2] Under the procedure in effect until the Revenue Act of 1950, taxes on profits earned in a given calendar year were paid in quarterly instalments in the following year, the first instalment being due on 15 March.

[3] *New York Times*, 16 January 1948.

revenue at its present level in order to use fiscal policy to halt inflation. The second objective was to afford relief to the millions of
families in the lowest brackets who were being squeezed by the high
cost of living. While the benefits would be the same in the highest
brackets it would mean most at the bottom of the scale. It was
decided that industry should be taxed more to offset the loss of
revenue, estimated by the President at $3·2 billion, and that industry
could bear the additional burden without injury and that no new
inflationary pressure would be created. . . .

'The figure was set at $40 in joint studies by Treasury, White
House, and Budget Bureau personnel'.[1]

The primary purpose of the recommendation, by this account,
was one of redistribution of the tax burden on grounds of equity,
being related to the control of inflation only in so far as it was intended that the redistribution was to be achieved without exacerbating the inflation. As remarked above, it is very doubtful whether the
redistribution would have turned out to be 'neutral' with respect to
inflation.

It was widely believed that the Secretary of the Treasury was
opposed to the President's recommendation and only supported it
in public out of loyalty to the President.[2] The Republican members
of the Ways and Means Committee made several efforts to draw the
Secretary on this point, but all he would say was that it was the
President's policy. Asked by Representative Doughton whether
there would have been any H.R.4968 had there been no H.R.4790,
Secretary Snyder replied that the question would have to be asked of
the President or Representative Dingell.

One cannot suppose that the President had any real hope that his
proposal for tax revision would be accepted by the Congress. Not
only was increased taxation of profits, especially an excess profits
tax, anathema to conservative Republicans, but the policy was not
worked out in cooperation with the Democratic leaders in the
Congress. The President did not ask Doughton, the senior Democrat
on the Ways and Means Committee, to introduce the bill embodying
his recommendation,[3] and it soon became known that Doughton

[1] Ibid., 23 January 1948.
[2] See Arthur Krock's column in the *New York Times*, 9 January 1948. That
Secretary Snyder was distinctly cool to the principle of an excess profits tax is
apparent from the discussion of the tax in 1950–1.
[3] *New York Times*, 16 January 1948.

was opposed to the President's proposed tax revision.[1] Such was the low esteem in which the President's plan was held by the Democratic leaders in the House that it was not even offered as the substitute in the motion to recommit H.R.4790. In the absence of any attempt by the President to gain the support of the Congressional Democratic leaders for his proposal, it can only be assumed that he had longer term purposes in mind. The redistributive nature of the bill was in close accord with other measures which the President proposed later whose theme was either the redistribution of the tax burden away from small incomes or the finance of higher expenditures for social welfare by higher taxation of profits and large incomes. In this way the tenor of the tax proposals fitted in with the strategy of contrasting the image of a reactionary 'rich man's' Congress with that of a more liberal Administration. The Republicans roundly condemned the President's proposal as a purely political gesture made in the knowledge that it had no chance of success. It was attacked as a mere vote-buying scheme, by which 'High Tax Harry' was making 'a sordid appeal for votes at $40 a head'.[2] It was further charged that if the excess profits tax were enacted businessmen would pass it on to consumers in the form of higher prices.[3] By his proposal the President succeeded in setting the cat among the pigeons, but not in having any impact on the tax legislation passed in 1948.

THE ECONOMIC SITUATION IN EARLY 1948

Nothing in the information available in January 1948 suggested that the situation was anything other than one of continuing inflation. The indices of wholesale and retail prices had risen continuously in the second half of 1947, and there was no slackening of the rate of increase in November and December.[4] The boom in private

---

[1] *New York Times*, 15 January 1948. Doughton said that he would not support a bill which did not provide for income splitting and tax relief 'all along the line'.

[2] *Bridgeport Telegram*, editorial inserted in the Appendix to the *Congressional Record*, Vol. XCIV, p. A500.

[3] The most extreme version of this argument is to be found in a speech by Senator Martin. He claimed that firms would add the tax to their costs of production and raise their prices accordingly, to which wholesalers and retailers would add their usual margins, pyramiding the total to $64·50 a head which the consumer would have to pay. *Congressional Record*, Vol. XCIV, p. A524.

[4] The Consumer 'all items' Price Index rose from 157·1 in June 1947 to 167·0 in December. The Wholesale Price Index (all items) rose from 147·7 to 163·2 in the same period.

fixed capital formation showed no sign of weakening,[1] a factor of major importance, for private investment in producers' durable goods was higher in relation to G.N.P. than at any time between the First and Second World Wars.[2] In 1947 gross private saving fell short of offsetting gross private domestic investment by $7·9 billion,[3] the remainder being offset by the government surplus, mainly that of the Federal government.

It follows from this that unless either private investment were to decline or the private sector's savings were to increase for autonomous reasons, a tax reduction would have had an inflationary effect on total demand unless the marginal propensity to spend for consumption or investment of the recipients of the tax reduction were zero. Since the outlook early in 1948 was for private investment to continue at least at the 1947 levels, a reduction in the government surplus such as H.R.4790 would bring about would be consistent with the avoiding of inflation only if private saving were to increase substantially. This could arise from an increase in personal saving relative to disposable income, an increase in corporate profits as a proportion of national income, or a reduction in the proportion of corporate profits after tax distributed in dividends. The latter two circumstances might well occur as a by-product of a sharp increase in excess demand but could not be relied on to occur autonomously; an increase in personal savings would take place when backlogs of consumers' demand had been met, but the time at which this would occur was as yet uncertain. The report on H.R.4790 by the majority of the Ways and Means Committee[4] laid most stress on the argument that the tax reduction would strengthen the incentives of managers and business investors and thereby led to increased production which would reduce the excess of demand over supply. Such an argument disregards the effect of tax reduction in adding directly to demand, while there was no evidence of the existence of an effect on incentives which would be large enough and swift enough to offset this.

---

[1] Reported by the Department of Commerce in *Survey of Current Business*, October 1947, p. 5; and January 1948, p. 6.

[2] Department of Commerce study presented to Ways and Means Committee. House of Representatives Committee on Ways and Means, *Hearings on H.R.4790* (1948), p. 143–53.

[3] Department of Commerce, *U.S. Income and Output*, 1959, Table V–1. In view of the statistical discrepancy of $3·5 billion the exact figure must be taken with reserve; the conclusion that private investment was greater than could be offset by private saving remains valid, however.

[4] *H. Rept. No. 1274*, 80th Cong., 2nd Sess.

Unless the filling of the backlogs of consumers' demand or a decline in private investment were to eliminate the excess of private investment over private saving, a reduction in the Federal surplus would exacerbate the inflation. The economic forecast on which the Administration based its policy was that there would be no significant lessening of inflationary pressure. The Secretary of Commerce told the Senate Finance Committee that nothing in the analyses prepared by the Department of Commerce indicated that inflationary pressure would not continue in the near future[1] and that in his judgement 'tax reduction should be retained for a deflationary period rather than the present time'.[2] This judgement was not influenced by the sharp fall in grain prices in February and which could have been interpreted as a sign that shortages had been made good and that excess demand was waning. Secretary Harriman held that this helped 'correct the existing imbalance' rather than indicated a dangerous situation.[3]

The Republican supporters of tax reduction in the House of Representatives did not challenge this economic forecast or attempt to demonstrate that the tax reduction could be made without adding to inflation, except in so far as they claimed that the beneficial effect on incentives would add to supply; they merely argued that if the tax reduction did add to inflationary pressure this would be more than outweighed by the improvement in the equity of the tax structure. It is clear that the effect of the proposed tax reduction on the immediate economic situation was a minor consideration in the minds of the Republican leaders in the House of Representatives. Even the prospective increases in government expenditures (mainly for foreign aid) had no effect on their approach to tax policy; Knutson said: 'instead of fitting tax reduction into foreign relief, we should fit such relief into tax reduction'.[4]

On the other hand, the Senate Finance Committee's report on H.R.4790 laid considerable emphasis on the possibility of a recession and the advantages of a tax reduction in that event. The report contrasted the Administration's firm belief that inflation would continue to be the main problem with 'a growing body of opinion among business economists' that a downturn would occur before the end of

[1] Senate Finance Committee, *Hearings on H.R.4790* (1948), p. 440.

[2] Ibid., p. 416.

[3] Ibid., p. 416.

[4] In a statement on 4 January 1948, reported in the *New York Times*. 5 January 1948.

the year.[1] One of the witnesses who had given evidence to the Finance Committee during the hearings was Dr. Roos, director of the Econometric Institute (a business research organization), who predicted that as a result of the expected decline in corporate profits, rising interest rates, and rising steel prices, investment in producers' durable goods would decline substantially from the third quarter of 1948 onwards. He predicted that this decline in investment in producers' durable goods, the decline in house building, and the fall in the export surplus would offset the expected increase in consumption. In such circumstances a surplus of the size that was in prospect if tax rates were not reduced would be very deflationary.[2] The representative of the U.S. Chamber of Commerce also declared that an addition to consumers' purchasing power was needed to maintain existing levels of output and employment.[3] Moreover, the Joint Committee on the Economic Report in its report drew attention to the possibility of a recession and the dangers of a large surplus in that event.[4] In view of the decline in grain prices these expressions of concern about the possibility of a recession in the fairly near future cannot be written off as mere rationalizations. The Senate Finance Committee's report made a serious attempt to show that tax reduction was a sound, or at any rate tenable, policy in view of uncertainties about the business outlook. Senator Millikin said in his speech introducing the bill: 'In view of the current uncertainty as to the economic prospects, it seems clear that debt reduction of such massive size (i.e. that which would occur in the absence of tax reduction) would be quite apt to be excessively deflationary. It might not merely check inflation, but might produce actual catastrophic deflation'.[5] The 'uncertainty' was not a mere figment of the imagination of the supporters of tax reduction.

THE PASSAGE OF H.R.4790

H.R.4790 was among the first items of business to be dealt with in the 1948 Session of Congress. There was not even a semblance of

[1] *S. Rept. No. 1013*, 80th Cong., 2nd Sess., p. 11–13.
[2] Senate Finance Committee, *Hearings on H.R.4790* (1948), pp. 143–5.
[3] E. Alvord to Senate Finance Committee, Senate Finance Committee, *Hearings on H.R.4790* (1948), p. 447. He was not recommending an expansionary fiscal policy proper, since he recommended that government expenditures be cut by the amount of the tax reduction.
[4] *S. Rept. No. 1358*, 80th Cong., 2nd Sess., p. 5
[5] *Congressional Record*, Vol. XCIV, p. 3126.

an attempt to relate the tax reduction to changes in government expenditure. In the Ways and Means Committee and the House of Representatives the contentions advanced for and against the bill were practically the same as in 1947: the Secretary of the Treasury found it 'unbelievable' that a tax cut which would lead to deficit financing should be pressed in the prevailing conditions,[1] and the supporters of the bill championed it as necessary to strengthen incentives and to restore some of the lost equity of the tax system.

The motion to recommit, moved by Representative Rayburn, the Minority Leader, provided for an increase in the individual exemption to $700, income splitting, and the imposition of an excess profits tax as provided in H.R.4968. It was opposed by Doughton and was rejected by 258 votes to 159. The bill itself was then passed by 297 to 120. Several members who had voted for H.R.3950 in the previous Session voted against H.R.4790 on the ground that the loss of revenue would be too great; among this group were Doughton and his North Carolina contingent, Mills, a member of the Ways and Means Committee, and Gary of Virginia.

The Senate Finance Committee approved the increase in the exemption to $600, the additional exemptions for the blind and the old, and the provisions for income splitting, but scaled down the reduction in tax rates. The reductions recommended by the Finance Committee were: 12·6 per cent of tax liability on the first $2,000 of taxable income; 7·4 per cent of liability on taxable income between $2,000 and $136,700; and 5 per cent of liability on the remainder of taxable income. The estimated loss of revenue in a full year under the Senate Finance Committee's version was $5·0 billion, compared with $6·5 billion under the House version. The Committee in their report maintained that the smaller reduction would be 'a desirable hedge against a continuation of inflationary pressure'.[2] It was true that if inflationary pressure continued the Senate version would do less damage than the House version, but a tax reduction equivalent to nearly one-eighth of total revenue could not be called 'a hedge against inflation'. An important reason why the Finance Committee scaled down the rate reduction was not mentioned in the report and was purely one of political tactics. Before the Finance Committee hearings began Senator Millikin said: 'I stated (to the Finance Com-

---

[1] The text of the Secretary's statement is printed in the *Annual Report of the Secretary of the Treasury for the year ending 30 June 1948*, pp. 300–5.
[2] *S. Rept. No. 1013*, 80th Cong., 2nd Sess., p. 11–13.

mittee) that I hoped that the ultimate bill would be conservatively based so as to be easily defensible. In my opinion the bill should have a lower reduction than the Knutson bill'.[1] There had been several hints that many Senate Democrats would support a tax reduction bill less drastic than the Knutson bill; in addition to George's expressed support for a 'very moderate' bill,[2] McClellan said that he would vote to override a Presidential veto if the loss of revenue did not exceed $5 billion.[3]

When the bill was brought to the Floor of the Senate, it was evident that its authors had succeeded in framing a bill which would attract wider support than its predecessors. Senator Lucas found his position of the previous year vindicated in that the bill embodied his substitute for H.R.1, and several Democrats announced their support for the bill because of its provisions for income-splitting. The two Republicans who had opposed the two previous Knutson bills announced that they would support H.R.4790. Morse said he did so because it would eliminate certain anomalies in the tax structure and because tax reduction was universally desired. Langer declared that he would support the bill, although he considered that the increase in the individual exemption was so small as to be an 'insult' to the lower income groups, because it would cut down the amount of money the Administration would have to spend on foreign aid.[4] O'Mahoney moved an amendment to impose an excess profits tax, which was rejected by 58 votes to 26. The few Senators who rose to oppose tax reduction all did so on the basis of the need to reduce the national debt and the prospect of increased expenditures for defence and foreign aid.

The final vote on the bill was 78 to 11; of the 78 voting in favour, 30 were Democrats. In the composition of this group there can be traced the formation of the majority needed to pass the bill. Of the 30, 11 had voted for H.R.1 or H.R.3950, namely Byrd, George, Hoey, Johnson, McCarran, McKellar, O'Conor, O'Daniel, Robertson, Stewart, and Umstead. The other important group voted against both H.R.1 and H.R.3950, but in favour of the Lucas amendment or McClellan's amendment to raise the individual exemption; there were 16 in this group, namely Chavez, Eastland, Fulbright, Hill,

[1] In a statement on 23 February 1948, quoted in the *New York Times*, 24 February 1948.
[2] See p. 85 supra.
[3] Reported in the *New York Times*, 1 February 1948.
[4] *Congressional Record*, Vol. XCIV, p. 3851.

Holland, Johnston, Lucas, McClellan, McMahon, Magnuson, May-bank, Murray, Pepper, Russell, Sparkman, and Thomas. Of the other three, Ellender and Overton had voted against all proposals for tax reduction in 1947 and Stennis did not take his seat until 1948. The second group consisted of those Senators who had opposed H.R.1 and H.R.3950 as inequitable, but had been won over by the inclusion of income splitting and the higher individual exemption for which they had pressed during the previous year. Politically it was a heterogeneous group, including Southern conservatives (such as Eastland and McClellan), Southern liberals (such as Pepper and Hill) and Northern liberals (such as Magnuson and Murray); it therefore cannot be said that the bill was passed by a Republican-Southern Democratic coalition or a Republican-conservative Democratic coalition. What happened was that nearly all Senators were in favour of tax reduction of some sort, and that H.R.4790 included something of all the widely canvassed forms of tax reduction, whereas its predecessors did not.

The House Republicans accepted the Senate's amendments with alacrity. Knutson said: 'I am reasonably well satisfied with the bill in the form in which the Senate will pass it. If we raised the amount of relief we might lose some votes in the Senate that might make it impossible to pass it over a veto. We're not taking any chances this time'.[1]

Doughton approved the Senate version as providing the same amount of tax reduction that he had recommended to the Ways and Means Committee, which ensured an even greater majority in the House.

President Truman again vetoed the tax reduction bill,[2] and the previous day sent a letter to Speaker Martin announcing that he would shortly request an additional appropriation of $3 billion for defence expenditure. The effect of this in inducing votes to sustain the veto was negligible; only three members of the House[3] and one member of the Senate[4] who had voted for the passage of the bill

[1] Quoted in the *New York Times*, 2 March 1948.
[2] The text of the veto Message is printed in the *Congressional Record*, Vol. XCIV, pp. 4164–5, and in the *Annual Report of the Secretary of the Treasury for the year ending 30 June 1948*, pp. 326–8.
[3] Representatives Harless and Dorn, Democrats, and Representative Morton, Republican. Morton so voted because the international situation presaged higher expenditures in the near future, so because he was unalterably opposed to deficit financing, tax reduction seemed unwise. *Congressional Record*, Vol. XCIV, pp. A1946–7.   [4] Senator Fulbright.

voted against the motion to override the veto. The Revenue Act of 1948 became law on 2 April 1948, the second Revenue Act to be enacted into law over the President's veto.

GOVERNMENT EXPENDITURES IN 1948

No attempt was made to align the tax reduction with reduction in expenditures or *vice-versa*. Reductions in appropriations were made in 1948, but they were not so large as those of the previous year, nor were they so controversial. The appropriations recommended for soil conservation grants and for school lunches were passed without cuts, probably due to the furore over these items in 1947.

At this time the 'Cold War' began to cast its shadow over government expenditures and fiscal policy. A decision of great importance was taken by the President. At a meeting at the White House on 13 May 1948 he read a memorandum in which he stated that he considered that $15 billion annually was the maximum defence expenditure that could be afforded in time of peace, and that the build-up of the armed forces in 1948 must not be allowed to become large enough to necessitate expenditures greater than $15 billion in ensuing years.[1] $15 billion was about the most that could be provided out of the yield of the tax rates in effect prior to the Revenue Act of 1948 without cuts in expenditure for other functions and without incurring a deficit when revenues were not depressed by a decline in economic activity. Evidently the President considered that a tax increase beyond the pre-1948 rates was unacceptable, even to finance rearmament, unless the international situation were to deteriorate severely.

In 1948 the first appropriation for the European Recovery Programme was passed. Speaker Martin and Representative Taber[2] engineered a substantial cut in the House, but in the Senate Vandenberg's influence secured the restoration of three-quarters of the cut.[3]

---

[1] W. Millis, (Ed.) *The Forrestal Diaries* (New York, 1951), pp. 435–7. James V. Forrestal was Secretary of Defense during this period.

[2] Chairman of the House Appropriations Committee.

[3] The Administration requested an appropriation of $4,265 million for the normal period of 12 months. The House reduced this to $4,000 million, to be spread over a period of fifteen months. The Senate retained the $4,000 million, but permitted its expenditure within twelve months if the President determined that this was necessary.

THE ECONOMIC EFFECTS OF THE REVENUE ACT OF 1948

The reduction in income tax under the Revenue Act of 1948 was estimated by the Treasury to be $4,737·7 million in a full year, based on a total personal income of $200 billion. Sixty-three per cent of the reduction would accrue to taxpayers with an adjusted gross income[1] of under $5,000[2]. In addition the amendments to the estate and gift tax were estimated to cost about $250 million in a full year. Total personal income in 1948 proved to be $210 billion,[3] hence the cost of the income tax reduction was about $5 billion and the total revenue reduction about $5¼ billion. The following table shows the effect of the Act on effective rates of tax, and the effects of H.R.4790 and H.R.4968 by way of comparison:

TABLE 12

Comparison of Effective Rates of Tax for a Married Couple with no Dependents

Adjusted Gross Income	Existing Law	H.R.4790	H.R.4968	Revenue Act 1948
$2,000	9·5%	5·3%	5·5%	6·6%
$5,000	16·0	11·6	14·4	12·6
$10,000	21·9	14·5	21·1	16·2
$50,000	49·6	33·2	49·4	34·4

Source: Annual Report of the Secretary of the Treasury for the year ending 30 June 1948, p. 318; and Joint Committee on Internal Revenue Taxation, Tables 8 and 8a in Congressional Record, Vol. XCIV, p. 3497.

The probable economic effect of the Revenue Act was primarily an addition to consumption demand. There might have been some effect on investment through that part of the reduction which would be received by non-corporate business or through individuals using part of their increased disposable incomes to make finance available to firms. But since available evidence does not suggest that lack of finance was an important limit on investment in mid-1948,[4] it is reasonable to regard the income tax reduction as affecting primarily

---

[1] 'Adjusted gross income' is total income minus allowable deductions for tax purposes other than the individual exemptions; it is therefore equal to taxable income plus individual exemptions.

[2] Joint Committee on Internal Revenue Taxation, data inserted in the *Congressional Record*, Vol. XCIV, p. 3495.

[3] Department of Commerce, *U.S. Income and Output*, 1959, Table II–2.

[4] See p. 89–90 supra.

consumption. The reduction in the revenue from the estate and gift tax was unlikely to have a significant effect on demand; except in so far as the estate and gift tax was paid by people who were running down their capital to maintain their consumption, the probable effect would be a small increase in consumption out of the income from the increment of capital that remained in private hands, the rest of the tax reduction resulting merely in an increase in private saving at the expense of public saving.

TABLE 13

Personal Income and its Disposition

	Personal Income	Personal Tax Payments		Disposable Income	Consumption	Saving (% of Disposable Income)
		Federal	State and Local			
1947 3rd Q.	193·8	19·7	1·9	172·3	167·2	3·0
4th	197·8	20·2	1·9	175·7	171·2	2·6
1948 1st	202·7	21·1	2·1	179·5	174·7	2·7
2nd	209·6	18·7	2·1	188·8	177·5	6·0
3rd	214·8	18·0	2·2	194·7	180·2	7·3
4th	214·4	18·2	2·2	194·0	180·8	6·8
1949 1st	209·3	16·3	2·4	190·6	179·0	6·1

Amounts in $ billion at seasonally adjusted annual rates.
Detail will not necessarily add to totals because of rounding.
Source: Department of Commerce, *U.S. Income and Output*, 1959, Table II–2.

The sharp jump in the proportion of disposable income saved that occurred in the second quarter of 1948 may have been partly due to a lag between the increase in disposable income resulting from the tax reduction and the adjustment of consumption to make use of it, but this cannot be the main reason, for the increase in saving was $6·6 billion, measured at seasonally adjusted annual rates, whereas the tax reduction was only $2·4 billion. It is highly probable that the main reason was that many consumers had made good the backlogs of demand caused by the war and in consequence were turning to a more normal rate of saving.

If it is assumed that in the absence of the tax reduction total personal income from the second quarter of 1948 to the first quarter of 1949 would have been the same as actually occurred, and if the ratio of savings to disposable incomes had been the same as actually occurred, and the average marginal rate of Federal income tax is estimated at 16 per cent,[1] then consumption in the last three quarters of 1948 and the first quarter of 1949, measured at seasonally adjusted annual rates, would have been $174·1 billion, $175·8 billion, $176·4 billion, and $173·5 billion respectively. On these assumptions the Revenue Act of 1948 added to consumption demand at an annual rate of about $4·5–$5·5 billion from the third quarter of 1948 onwards. In view of the doubt that must attend the assumptions the estimate of the addition to demand cannot be very precise; but it does suggest that the tax reduction kept consumption demand rising at something close to the previous rate until the fourth quarter, instead of levelling off at a rate somewhat below that reached in the second quarter. This probably had significant effects on other components of demand, notably inventories, whose liquidation would probably have begun sooner had the rise in sales not lasted so long.

The Consumer Price Index reached a peak in August and September 1948 and thereafter declined. The price level reached in August was about 3 per cent higher than that in April, as measured by the index. The index of wholesale prices of goods other than foods and farm products followed a course similar to that of the index of consumer prices, while the wholesale prices of farm products and foods dropped sooner and more sharply. The decline in consumption relative to disposable income that took place in mid-1948 was the main element which offset the increase in demand attributable to the tax reduction and so rendered the latter harmless in terms of inflation.

At the time nobody who analysed the situation in terms of compensatory fiscal policy had a good word for the Revenue Act. Not only were members of the Administration critical, but the *C.I.O. News* declared in an editorial that 'the present boom' called for debt reduction rather than tax reduction[2]; and in September the editors of *Fortune* called for drastic measures, including a deflationary fiscal

[1] The figure of 16 per cent is derived by comparing the increase in personal income and payments of federal personal taxes from the first quarter of 1946 to the first quarter of 1948. Since the rate of Federal income tax in the lowest bracket under the Revenue Act of 1945 was 19 per cent, an average marginal rate of 16 per cent for the whole personal sector appears reasonable since some taxpayers would be paying at a higher marginal rate, and other income receivers would have incomes too small to incur tax liability. But since quarter-to-quarter variations of personal income and tax payments do not always coincide with what one would expect from an average marginal rate of tax of 16 per cent, the figure must be taken with some reserve.

[2] *C. I. O. News*, 12 April 1948.

policy, to check inflation, and castigated the Republicans responsible for the Revenue Act for disregard of economic considerations in cutting taxes in a time of inflation.[1] At this time nobody had detected the coming turning point with any certainty and the Revenue Act still appeared as an instance of total disregard of elementary considerations of stabilization policy.

Although enacted in the teeth of rising prices, for reasons among which economic stabilization was not prominent, and enacted in 1948 rather than 1947 for reasons not of economics but of political tactics, the Revenue Act of 1948 turned out to be on balance beneficial in terms of economic stability. The economic situation changed so much and so quickly as to render it not only innocuous but useful. If there was ever a case of broadly sound economic measures being taken in very good time through good luck rather than good judgement, this was it.

A POLITICAL POSTSCRIPT:
ECONOMIC POLICY AND THE ELECTIONS OF 1948

Economic affairs in general and tax policy in particular played important parts in the election campaign of 1948. President Truman and his supporters made a major issue of the tax reduction and the reductions in expenditure for agriculture and natural resources, and the President attacked the record of the 80th Congress with ferocity. He hammered away at 'the Tabers, the Tafts, and the Martins'[2] and 'the rich man's tax bill'.[3] The Democratic platform promised tax reduction when the economic situation permitted it, of a type which would give the lower bracket taxpayers their fair share of the relief. The Republican platform advocated lower taxes and public expenditure, and included the customary denunciation of deficit financing.[4]

The campaign was fought almost entirely on domestic issues, for the bi-partisanship on foreign affairs that Senator Vandenberg inspired still held good. The results of the election were therefore an unequivocal rejection of the line of policy which the 80th Congress

[1] *Fortune*, September 1948, p. 3.

[2] Speech at Philadelphia, Pa., on 6 October 1948, of which the text is printed in the *New York Times*, 7 October 1948.

[3] Speech at St. Louis, Mo., on 30 October 1948, of which the text is printed in the *New York Times*, 31 October 1948.

[4] See the summaries of the party platforms in the *New York Times*, 15 July 1948.

had followed. Governor Dewey's defeat attracted most attention, but if Dewey fared badly with his allegedly 'me-too' policy, the Congressional Republicans fared a good deal worse, suffering a net loss of 75 seats in the House of Representatives and 9 seats in the Senate. With only the rarest exceptions the defeated Congressional Republicans trailed a long way behind Dewey.

The lesson of the 1948 elections was that a policy of reversing as much as possible of the changes made under Roosevelt would not win electoral success in and of itself, without the aid of resentment over foreign affairs and the related issue of internal communism. Since the whole approach of the 80th Congress to taxation and government expenditure had been at variance with the principle that they should be managed so as to contribute to economic stability, the outcome of the election was a significant step towards establishing as one of the facts of American public life the principle that fiscal policy should be used to contribute to the maintenance of economic stability. This conclusion was drawn by some observers at the time; the *Saturday Evening Post* commented in an editorial: 'The disagreeable truth is that the American people have given the green light to the planners and the big government boys'.[1]

[1] *Saturday Evening Post*, 4 December 1948.

CHAPTER VII

THE FIRST POST-WAR RECESSION, 1949–1950

At the end of 1948 there were signs that the general excess of demand and consequent upward pressure on prices that had been present in the American economy since the spring of 1946 might be disappearing. Several factors which tended in this direction were noted by the Council of Economic Advisers in their Annual Economic Review in January 1949. In the second half of 1948 saving had risen relative to disposable income[1] and the rate of increase of consumer credit had slowed down, indicating that much of the backlog of consumers' demand had been made good. The Council also believed that investment in many industries, especially non-durable manufacturing, had expanded enough to make good the shortages of capacity that had existed at the end of the war. They noted that there was still a need for more capacity in steel, and that there were plans for large-scale modernization in such industies as petroleum and chemicals, but their conclusion was that there would be no 'abrupt slackening' of investment,[2] a choice of words which indicates that they expected no increase in the total and perhaps a slight decline. Likewise they concluded that post-war re-stocking by businesses was practically complete, and that the ratio of inventories to sales was such that little further inventory accumulation was in prospect. Further deflationary factors noted were a decline in the number of houses started and a fall in the export surplus. The one important expansionary force noted was the prospective rise in Federal expenditures, principally defence and foreign aid expenditure authorized in 1948. The examination of the main components of demand in the private sector suggests that according to the information available when the analysis was made, the increase in total demand had come to a halt and that the outlook was one of a decline in private demand more likely than not.

None the less the Administration was reluctant to infer that the danger of inflation was over for the time being. The Council of

[1] See p. 98 supra.

[2] *Annual Economic Review*, January 1949, p. 18. The *Annual Economic Review* was published with the *Economic Report of the President*.

Economic Advisers noted that given the divergent price trends in different markets it could not be determined whether the scattered price reductions were part of a re-adjustment of the pattern of production to a changing pattern of demand, or whether they were symptoms of an emerging deficiency of aggregate demand. Twice since the end of the war, in the second quarter of 1947 and the first quarter of 1948, there had been a decline in wholesale and retail prices similar to that in the fourth quarter of 1948, only to be followed by renewed inflation.[1] The fear that inflation would emerge again, this time stimulated by the rise in defence expenditure, had a strong influence on the policy which the Administration recommended early in 1949.

Although the forces which had been responsible for the post-war inflation were clearly waning, and talk of a 'readjustment' was in the air, the halt to price increases had not lasted long enough to make it certain that inflation was no longer the immediate problem. Since the recommendation of economic policies for the year in the State of the Union Message, the Budget, and the Economic Report could not be delayed until the uncertainties about the economic outlook were resolved, the Administration was forced to choose between recommending policies to guard against a renewal of inflation and recommending no special measures for the short run economic situation until the situation clarified. If the second alternative were adopted, there might not be enough time to get the necessary measures enacted when at last it became possible to decide whether inflation or deflation was the main danger.

The course adopted was to recommend measures directed against the danger of inflation, coupled with warnings that the economic situation might change and that if it did there would be no hesitation about making necessary changes in policies. As always, there were other problems to be dealt with besides short-run economic stability. In the State of the Union Message[2] on 5 January the President recommended an ambitious programme of public investment and social welfare; the most important items were Federal subsidies for the building of houses, Federal grants-in-aid for the finance of education, an extension of the coverage and increase in the benefits of the Social Security system, the establishment of a system of

[1] *Annual Economic Review*, p. 6.
[2] The text of the Message is printed in the *Congressional Record*, Vol. XCV, pp. 74–6, and in the *New York Times*, 6 January 1949.

national health insurance, the development of river basins by means similar to those of T.V.A., expansion of publicly-owned facilities for the generation and transmission of electricity, and authority to build steel-making capacity if the industry itself proved unable to provide adequate capacity. The last would not require expenditure for a considerable time, and the health insurance and greater Social Security benefits would be paid for largely through pay-roll taxes, but all the rest would have to be financed through direct expenditure by the Treasury.

These proposals for the expansion of government expenditure on both current and capital account should be taken in conjunction with the tax increase recommended. In the State of the Union Message the President proposed that tax rates be increased to yield an additional $4 billion; most of it was to come from taxes on corporate profits, some from the estate and gift tax, and 'consideration should be given' to raising the rates of the middle and upper brackets of the personal income tax. The combination of increases in the taxes on profits and large incomes and substantial increases in government expenditure for social welfare made up a distinctly Left-of-Centre political programme, carrying on from where the New Deal had left off. This policy was very controversial, and since nearly all the items in the programme were connected with taxes or expenditures, it became intermingled with controversies over higher taxes, balancing the budget, and stabilization policy.

In the Budget Message the President said:

'In a period of high prosperity, it is not sound public policy for the Government to operate at a deficit. A budget surplus at this time is vitally important to provide a margin for contingencies, to permit reduction of the public debt, to provide an adequate base for the future financing of our present commitments; and to reduce inflationary pressures. I am therefore recommending new tax legislation to raise revenue by 4 billion dollars.'[1]

In this statement a combination of purposes can be noted, the short-run policy of accumulating a surplus to reduce inflationary pressure, and the longer run policy of tax rates high enough to support greater expenditure. In the Economic Report by far the most stress was placed on the need for a budget surplus to restrain inflation.[2] Also recommended were a variety of other measures to

---

[1] *Budget of the United States for the year ending 30 June 1950*, p. M5.
[2] *Economic Report of the President, January 1949*, p. 10.

restrain inflation. The most important were the renewal of authority to regulate the terms of consumer credit, authority for the Board of Governors of the Federal Reserve System to raise reserve requirements by up to 10 percentage points above the maximum set by the Banking Act of 1935, power to allocate scarce materials, stricter regulation of commodity exchanges, the extension of controls over exports and rents, and power to control prices and wages. The last were to be used as a last resort, if requests for voluntary restraint were disregarded.[1]

The controls recommended in 1949 were the same as those recommended in 1947 and 1948, Dr. John D. Clark, a member of the Council of Economic Advisers, told the Joint Committee on the Economic Report:

'The program now proposed by the President in his annual economic report . . . is based on the judgement that postwar inflationary forces are still strong, and probably will become more active in the near future, requiring the provision of measures now to curb spiralling prices.'[2]

By the time Clark was addressing the Committee (February 1949), signs of incipient deflation had begun to appear, but he held that because of the lack of reliable information about seasonal variation in unemployment it would not be possible to tell whether a real decline in employment had begun until April. But by April there would be developments which would 'tighten the labor market', primarily the increase in expenditures for defence and foreign aid. Once again the influence of the prospective increase in Federal expenditure on the Administration's thinking is apparent.

The increase in cash payments by the Federal government in the first half of 1949 over the second half of 1948 was $3·8 billion, expressed at seasonally adjusted annual rates, of which $1·7 billion was attributable to increased defence expenditure, $1·2 billion to foreign aid, and $0·5 billion to the increase in subsidies which resulted automatically from the fall in agricultural prices. Since cash receipts fell by $1·1 billion during this period, a cash surplus of $3·9 billion was replaced by a cash deficit of $1·1 billion.[3] The forecast

[1] Ibid., pp. 11–3.

[2] Joint Committee on the Economic Report, *Hearings on the Economic Report of the President*, 1949, pp. 425–6.

[3] Council of Economic Advisers, *Mid-Year Economic Review*, July 1949, Table A-7; and July 1950, Table A-7.

of a significant addition to demand resulting from increasing expenditure for defence and foreign aid in the first half of 1949 was thus correct; what was not foreseen was that it would be offset by declines in other components of demand.

The Budget submitted in January 1949 estimated that expenditure in fiscal 1950 would exceed that for the current fiscal year (1949) by $1,928 million, if the recommended increase in postage rates is treated as a receipt and not a reduction in expenditure. The principal increases in expenditure were for defence ($2,523 million), social welfare, including education and housing ($762 million), and natural resources ($245 million, of which $93 million was for atomic energy). This was to be partly offset by a fall in expenditures for veterans' services ($1,300 million) caused mainly by the increase in the number exhausting their rights to educational benefits under the Servicemen's Readjustment Act, and a decline in foreign aid ($510 million).[1]

Had the President's proposed increase in tax rates been enacted it would at the most have barely covered this increase in expenditure, because even if the tax increase on corporate profits had been applied to the whole of 1949 profits only about a half of the $4 billion would have been received in fiscal 1950 because of the timing of payments of the tax. Only if it is the accrual of liability to the tax rather than payment of it that influences investment and the payment of dividends by corporations would its full impact be felt in fiscal 1950.

Even so it is doubtful whether the tax changes proposed would have had a very drastic impact on effective demand. To the extent that the tax increase reduced undistributed profits after tax it would reduce private saving and increase public saving by equal amounts, which does not directly affect the level of demand unless the reduction of private saving has an effect on investment. It was the Administration's contention[2] that profits after tax were sufficiently large to permit a considerable increase in taxation without impairing the ability of corporations to finance investment needed for desirable rates of expansion. The Administration thus did not look to the tax increase to cut investment in the private sector, though the Council of Economic Advisers believed that the ratio of investment to total national income since the end of the war was too high to be sus-

---

[1] *Budget of the United States for the year ending 30 June 1950.*
[2] *Economic Report of the President, January 1949*, p. 10.

tained over the long term[1] and so would not be very concerned if the tax increase were to slow down the rate of increase of investment. To the extent that the increase in the tax on corporate profits fell on dividends it would be analogous to the increase in the rate of tax on middle and high incomes which the Administration supported.[2] It is generally believed that the marginal propensity to consume of the receivers of large incomes is lower than that of the receivers of small incomes, which seems especially reasonable when a sudden reduction of disposable income through increased tax rates is being considered. To the extent that the reduction in dividends was borne by institutional investors the effect on demand would be remote and subject to very long time lags. The increase in the estate and gifts tax also would be likely to have very little effect on consumption or investment, and again would result in a reduction of private saving and an increase in public saving by roughly equal amounts. The tax changes recommended by the Administration would in all probability have reduced private savings to a greater extent than consumption or private investment, and so would have had a much smaller deflationary effect than an increase of the same amount in other taxes.

Thus it is probable that even in the short run the deflationary effect of the proposed tax increases, if enacted, would not have been so great as might appear at first sight. In the longer run, if the Congress followed the recommendations for greater expenditures for social welfare and public investment, so using up the 'margin for contingencies' provided by the additional revenue, the result would have been inflationary. A policy of increasing government expenditure for welfare and public investment and increasing by a corresponding amount taxes which would fall heavily on private saving would be something of a return to the policies of the late 1930's which were based on the assumption of a tendency for savings to run ahead of investment demand (in an *ex ante* sense). The Council of Economic Advisers held that it was desirable that private consumption should rise from the existing proportion of 70 per cent of G.N.P. to around 75 per cent, while private investment should decline to 11–12 per cent, ratios which were thought, mainly on historical evidence, to be more sustainable over the long run than the ratios

[1] Council of Economic Advisers, *Annual Economic Review, January 1949*, pp. 61–2.

[2] At his news conference on January 13 1949 the President suggested that $6,000 might be taken as the beginning of the 'middle and upper brackets' for purposes of the proposed tax increase. *New York Times*, 14 January 1949.

which had existed since the war.[1] In view of these considerations, and the fact that the tax increases proposed would provide the minimum of deflationary 'bang for the buck' of tax increase, there can be little doubt that the selection of the taxes to be increased was determined far more by longer run policy with respect to the distribution of the national income than by any short-run need to restrain consumption.

THE TREATMENT BY THE CONGRESS OF THE ADMINISTRATION'S RECOMMENDATIONS

Despite enthusiastic prophecies of a swing to the Left in American public policy and even of a second 'hundred days' like those of 1933 as a consequence of the sweeping Democratic electoral victory, remarkably little happened.[2] The loose and informal coalition of Republicans and conservative Southern Democrats that had dominated the Congress since the elections of 1938 suffered a reduction of its power, but not enough to give effective control to the supporters of the 'Fair Deal'. Of the major measures proposed by the President in the field of social welfare and public investment, only the housing programme reached the Statute Book in 1949 in anything like the form in which the President recommended it. The Social Security revision passed the House, but was not passed by the Senate until 1950. Nothing at all came of the proposed new river valley authorities (the projected Columbia Valley Authority was the most prominent at this time), although T.V.A. received the appropriation for its first steam-operated power station. The bill to provide for Federal grants-in-aid to the states for education became bogged down in disputes between the members of the House Committee on Education and Labor, and its prospects further impaired by an acrimonious controversy over whether parochial (i.e. Roman Catholic) schools should be eligible for grants. The proposed national health insurance scheme was blocked by a formidable campaign by the American Medical Association, whose denunciations of 'socialized medicine' were to be heard throughout the land.

No action was taken by the Congress on the President's tax proposals. At first they were quite well received, Senator George

---

[1] Council of Economic Advisers, *Annual Economic Review, January 1949*, pp. 61–2.

[2] The contrast between the results of the elections of 1958 and the actions of the Congress in 1959 provide a parallel case.

(Chairman of the Finance Committee) being particularly gratified that the President had abandoned his proposal of the previous year for an excess profits tax.[1] There was, however, an evident lack of urgency in the treatment of the tax proposals; commenting on the State of the Union Message, Doughton said that the revision of the Social Security system and the extension of the Reciprocal Trade Agreements Act would have to be dealt with before the Ways and Means Committee could take up tax legislation.[2] Since both were complicated and contentious, it would be late in the session before tax legislation could be dealt with; it would inevitably be strongly opposed, and would be unlikely to become law before 1950, too late to be of any help in dealing with inflation in 1949.

Before long the signs of incipient deflation strengthened the reluctance of the leaders in Congress to proceed with the tax increase. On 9 February George told reporters that the tax increase would have deflationary effects and in view of the economic situation would be undesirable before 'late in the year at the earliest'. Doughton agreed.[3] The President did not accept this rebuff and secured the support of Speaker Rayburn in keeping the subject alive; Rayburn said after a talk with the President that the tax increase had definitely not been shelved and that the Ways and Means Committee had dealt with Social Security first at the President's request. The tax increase was needed to prevent a deficit; deficit financing would be 'a reflection on us all as a country' when national income was at such a high level.[4] Doughton commented: 'If it is necessary to avoid a deficit, we shall have to make an effort to raise some money, of course'. But when on 31 March President Truman again spoke in support of the tax increase, George said that the President would not get his tax increase,[5] and on 10 May declared that it would be 'nonsense to clap more taxes on a falling economy'.[6] Senator Douglas, in a major speech on the economic situation, agreed with this view; he held that it would be unwise to take reflationary or disinflationary action because of the uncertainty of the situation.[7]

From the remarks of Senator George and Representative Dough-

---

[1] On 17 November Senator O'Mahoney had called for the enactment of an excess profits tax, and on the following day George issued a statement in which he said that such a tax would lead to 'the destruction of business'. *New York Times*, 18 and 19 November 1948.

[2] *New York Times*, 6 January 1949.   [3] *New York Times*, 10 February 1949.
[4] Ibid., 16 February 1949.   [5] Ibid., 1 April 1949.   [6] Ibid., 11 May 1949.
[7] *Congressional Record*, Vol. XCV, p. 5961.

ton on tax reduction in 1949 it appears that the reasons for not taking prompt action to put the President's proposals into effect were not mere inertia or political distaste for higher taxation. There is no reason to doubt the genuineness of their belief that to increase taxes in a time of economic decline would accelerate the decline. On the other hand they were not led to this conclusion by a familiarity with the concepts of compensatory public finance, for George in particular was a strong supporter of proposals to eliminate the prospective deficit for fiscal 1950 by drastic cuts in expenditure. In 1949 there were few signs that many members of Congress understood that although holding down tax rates in itself adds directly to effective demand and so has a stimulating effect, when offset by a cut in expenditure the result can be at best neutral with respect to total demand even if all the additional income after tax is spent for consumption or investment. A net expansionary effect could only occur through changes in expectations which increase the marginal propensity to consume or the inducement to invest; and the existence of such effects of equal reductions in government expenditure and tax revenue is very doubtful.

THE ADMINISTRATION'S REACTION TO THE RECESSION

The Administration was slow to come to the conclusion that inflation had ceased to be the most urgent economic problem. In a memorandum to the President on 4 February the Council of Economic Advisers gave a further warning about the dangers of inflation, though Nourse appended a reservation to the effect that it did not seem to him that inflationary pressures were increasing and unabated.[1] On 17 February 1949 President Truman told his news conference that the decline in certain prices was bringing about the end to the trend of rising prices that had been hoped for for so long, and reiterated his support for increases in tax rates and stated that there were no plans to relax controls over consumer credit.[2] In a similar vein Secretary Sawyer told a conference at Chicago that he regarded the deflationary trends (presumably meaning falling prices) as 'desirable'.[3] Until at least the middle of March the Administration was of the opinion that nothing had happened to justify the abandonment of anti-inflationary policies.

In a report to the President on 1 April 1949 the Council of Eco-

---

[1] E. G. Nourse, *Economics in the Public Service* (New York, 1953), pp. 234–5.
[2] *New York Times*, 18 February 1949.   [3] Ibid., 1 March 1949.

nomic Advisers discerned a 'healthy adjustment' of price levels which was taking place in an orderly way, and that the economy was in the process of transition from the post-war boom to stable prosperity. The report recommended that 'The government by word and deed should extend every feasible encouragement to this adjustment'.[1] Despite this modification of the earlier position, the Administration had not decided that any special action was called for; on 8 April in a speech to the Executives Club at Chicago, Secretary Snyder reminded his audience that American enterprise flourishes best in an atmosphere of competition and that the nation's strength was not built by men who took a gloomy view of the future,[2] remarks which would hardly seem out of place if attributed to President Hoover eighteen or nineteen years before.

At this time signs of recession were becoming more marked. The seasonally adjusted index of industrial production fell to 184 in March and 179 in April compared with an average of 192 for the second half of 1948. Unemployment as reported by the Bureau of the Census was 3,167,000 in March and 3,016,000 in April 1949, compared with an average of 2,214,000 in the first half of 1948 and 1,914,000 in the second half. Average weekly hours worked in manufacturing industry fell to 38·3 in April 1949 compared with 40·1 in April 1948 and an average of 40·2 in the first half of 1948. Despite this there were few expressions of concern about the emerging recession. Even the C.I.O., which might have been expected to be very sensitive to rising unemployment, expressed only mild concern at this time. Representative Patman in February demanded the relaxation of consumer credit control because of rising unemployment in the durable goods industries, adding characteristically that if a depression occurred it would be 'a Federal Reserve Board depression'.[3] When the subject came up in Congress the Democrats usually accused their opponents of 'attempting to drive a sense of fear and insecurity into the American people'.[4] Representative Sabath, the Chairman of the Rules Committee,[5] admitted that there

[1] Nourse, op. cit., pp. 237–8.
[2] The text of the speech is printed in the *Annual Report of the Secretary of the Treasury for the year ending 30 June 1949*, pp. 326–9.
[3] In a letter to the Chairman of the Board of Governors of the Federal Reserve System, inserted in the *Congressional Record*, Vol. XCV, p. 1273.
[4] Representative Buckley (of Illinois); *Congressional Record*, Vol. XCV, p. 1369.
[5] At this time the only liberal on the Committee.

was 'a little unemployment', but added 'We know that from 8 to 10 per cent of our employable people are unemployed peacetimes,'[1] an extraordinary remark for a Chicago Democrat and one which would have created a considerable stir if made by a Republican in 1954 or 1958. The Joint Committee on the Economic Report in their report (issued in March 1949) dismissed the danger of serious deflation, and advocated anti-inflationary measures: 'the most rigid economy should be observed by the Government in order to balance the budget and establish a surplus'.[2] If the Administration is criticized for tardiness in abandoning its anti-inflationary posture and in coming to grips with the recession, the criticism must be qualified by noting that scarcely anyone in the country took a different view in the spring of 1949.

The change of position by the Administration was made known in the Mid-year Economic Report, published in July 1949. It noted that in the first half of 1949 there had occurred a 'moderate downward trend';[3] the principal component of demand to whose decline attention was drawn was inventory investment, though the outlook for business investment in fixed capital clearly gave the Council of Economic Advisers cause for disquiet, especially in regard to the early part of 1950.[4] The high consumption demand was cited as a source of strength, for as long as it was maintained inventory liquidation would be carried through and then production would have to rise at least to the level of sales, with cumulative effects. Also noted as sources of strength were the rise in the number of houses started and the increase in expenditures by Federal, state, and local governments. Much stress was laid on the responsibility of firms to facilitate the adjustment by reducing prices so as to increase effective consumption demand out of given (money) incomes while at least maintaining present wage rates. The Council conceded that there were uncertainties in the outlook, in that the decline had not yet been reversed and all the time the decline continued there was a possibility of the development of a deflationary spiral through the decline leading to further inventory liquidation and a postponement of investment in fixed capital. Despite this, the Council found the factors tending to sustain demand sufficiently strong to make the

[1] *Congressional Record*, Vol. XCV, p. 1368.
[2] *S. Rept. No. 88*, 81st Cong., 1st Sess., p. 7.
[3] *Mid-year Economic Report of the President, July 1949*, p. 3.
[4] *The Economic Situation at Mid-year, 1949*, a report to the President by the Council of Economic Advisers (accompanying the *Economic Report*), pp. 2–3.

emergence of a spiral unlikely; their verdict was: 'We find the prospect reassuring'.[1]

The President in the Economic Report was more forthright; after a brief survey of the economic situation, he said: 'These facts show that our economy is still operating at high levels of employment and production. The kind of government action that would be called for in a serious economic emergency would not be appropriate now'.[2]

The President recommended that the excise tax on the carriage of goods should be eliminated and the provision for the offsetting of business losses against future profits for tax purposes should be broadened to strengthen the inducement to invest under conditions of greater than usual uncertainty. The recommendation made in January for tax increases was specifically withdrawn except for the increase in the estate and gift tax, which would not depress total demand significantly. However, 'No changes in tax laws which would result in a larger net loss of revenues would be justified at this time'.[3]

Apart from these recommendations of small 'business oriented' tax reductions, the President's discussion of fiscal policy was devoted mainly to warning against attempts to balance the budget by cutting expenditures: 'if we tried to avoid a budget deficit by cutting essential expenditures, we would contribute to lower national output and lower employment, Federal receipts would fall further, and the burden upon Federal expenditures would increase. We cannot expect to achieve a budget surplus in a declining national economy'.[4]

The President stated that the situation did not call for an 'immediate and sweeping' expansion of public works,[5] but recommended certain precautionary measures, including the authorization of loans to state and local governments to cover the cost of planning public works; authorization for the Bureau of Public Roads to make advances to states for the acquisition of rights-of-way for road building; authority for the acquisition of sites by the Public Buildings Administration; and a survey of the school building needed in the nation. The other recommendation addressed specifically to the recession was the extension of the maximum maturity of RFC

---

[1] Council of Economic Advisers, *The Economic Situation at Mid-year, 1949*, p. 1.
[2] *Mid-year Economic Report of the President, July 1949*, p. 5.
[3] Ibid., p. 8. [4] Ibid., p. 8. [5] Ibid., p. 11.

loans. The President also announced that Government expenditure would be concentrated in areas of serious unemployment wherever possible.

The recommendations of the President formed a coherent policy. The situation having been analysed as primarily an inventory recession, though with some concern about investment in fixed capital, it followed that so long as consumer demand was maintained at a reasonably high level, the attempts to liquidate inventories would succeed and then production would have to rise to the level of sales, initiating a general rise unless offset by declines elsewhere in the economy. The area in which such a decline might occur was obviously fixed capital investment, hence the justification for tax reduction directed to business and the liberalization of the terms for RFC loans, with planning of public works as a longstop. Despite the drop in income, consumption did not fall much. Estimates accompanying the Economic Report showed a fall in consumption expenditure from the fourth quarter of 1948 to the second quarter of 1949 of $6 billion, measured at seasonally adjusted annual rates; from the index of consumer prices it could be estimated that about half of this was accounted for by price changes.[1] In view of the small drop the Administration was on firm ground in its belief that the inventory liquidation would take place in an orderly way and that subsequently output and employment would have to rise when liquidation could go no further because of continued high final sales. It was clear that the Administration believed that the automatic stabilizers were all that were needed to sustain consumption for the time being, but that the investment sector needed stimulation and precautionary planning.

The reliance on mild stimulants to investment, precautionary planning of public works, the automatic stabilizing effect of the budget (provided this was not interfered with by Congressional 'economizing'), and credit expansion through the Federal Reserve System, the RFC and FNMA must be regarded as a very cautious approach to the recession, especially as there was no firm evidence that the bottom of the recession had been reached, so that the danger of a deflationary spiral still existed. The mildness of the

[1] According to the latest estimates consumption expenditure at current prices *rose* by $0·3 billion between the fourth quarter of 1948 and the second quarter of 1949; measured at constant (1954) prices it rose by $5·2 billion. Department of Commerce, *U.S. Income and Output*, 1959, Tables I–3 and I–5.

anti-recession policy recommended by the Administration was noted in the following comment by the *National City Bank Monthly Letter*, which was no supporter of the Truman Administration's economic policies:

'Business was also favourably impressed by the calm tone of the President's report and its eschewal of radical proposals. It was noted with approval that the President did not follow the lead of those who are clamoring for a new round of wage increases or for a vast program of public works to increase purchasing power. Its advocacy of repealing the tax on the transportation of goods and liberalizing the provisions for the carry back of losses was regarded as recognition of the need for encouraging business.'[1]

CONGRESSIONAL ACTION ON ECONOMIC POLICY

Of the measures recommended by the President in the Economic Report that were directed specifically to dealing with the recession, the amendments to the tax system required new legislation, and so did the precautionary measures in the field of public works. The action recommended with respect to the budget was just that the regular appropriation bills should be passed without abnormal cuts. The expansion of credit could be undertaken without fresh Congressional action. No action was taken on the proposed tax changes. Doughton held that they could not be enacted without opening the whole of the tax structure to revision, so that it would be advisable to wait until the Ways and Means Committee took up a general tax revision bill in the 1950 Session. The principal struggle in the Congress, however, concerned the budget.

An economy campaign had been in the making for some time, and the prospect of a budget deficit caused by declining revenues added force to it. As always, the motives were mixed: opposition to 'spending' and demands for 'economy' were a well-tried way of waging war on the New Deal, and since so many of the measures proposed by the President at the beginning of the Session (now known collectively as the Fair Deal) would require a considerable increase in expenditure a hue and cry about 'economy' was a promising way of heading them off. Associated with this position was the opposition, still strong, to Federal deficits as such. Lastly the economy drive had the support of men such as Senator Douglas who were not outright opponents of the Fair Deal but who regarded

[1] *National City Bank Monthly Letter*, August 1949, p. 86.

the situation as auspicious for a campaign to eliminate the waste they believed existed in many government departments.

The economy drive was concentrated in the Senate, partly because the concern over the emerging deficit had not gathered strength while the main appropriation bills were before the House. Amendments were moved to most appropriation bills to require a 5 per cent cut; supporters succeeded in attaching such an amendment to the Labor-Federal Security Agency appropriation bill (H.R.3333), but the Administration and the Democratic Senate leaders secured the passage of a motion to reconsider the amendment, so that the appropriation emerged unscathed though much delayed.

After the failure of the attempt to cut the Labor-Social Security appropriation the principal vehicle of the economy drive was the McClellan resolution (S.J.Res.108); under its terms the President would be required to reduce expenditure in fiscal 1950 by an amount not less than 5 per cent and not more than 10 per cent of the total expenditure as estimated in the budget submitted in January 1949, any other reductions in expenditure brought about by other Congressional action to count towards the 5 to 10 per cent. A reduction of 5 per cent would amount to $2·1 billion, approximately the same as the reduction in receipts caused by the recession. McClellan stated explicitly that the reason underlying his resolution was that since revenues had declined, sound financial policy required a reduction in expenditure.[1] This was no 'one-man' gesture; 67 Senators signed a petition to the Majority Leader asking him to call up the McClellan resolution for a vote;[2] and 49 Senators voted for a motion to suspend the rules to permit the resolution to be attached to the National Military Establishment Appropriation Bill. It may be true that some gave their support as a gesture in the expectation that nothing would actually happen, but even so it was impressive testimony to the strength of the support in Congress for the view that it is the proper policy to cut expenditures to try to keep the budget in balance when revenues decline as a result of a recession. McClellan declared that deficit financing 'contributes a much greater threat from within to the security and survival of our liberties than does the military threat of communism from without'.[3] Ferguson

---

[1] *S. Rept. No. 498*, 81st Cong., 1st Sess., p. 1.

[2] The text of the petition and the signatures are printed in the *Congressional Record*, Vol. XCV, p. 8218.

[3] *Congressional Record*, Vol. XCV, p. 12391.

maintained that 'the shift of the economic winds' towards deflation necessitated 'trimming the government's fiscal sails'.[1] And when Pepper argued that the economy drive might make the recession worse, Capehart replied 'I cannot and will not debate the subject with anyone who does not agree that no individual, no company, no organization can long exist if it spends more money than it takes in'.[2] to which Pepper replied that he did not advocate spending more than was taken in.

The significant point is not that these extreme and obscurantist views were to be heard, but that they were to be heard so often and the contrary argument so rarely. In his statement of minority views in the report on the McClellan resolution Senator Humphrey argued that an attempt to cut expenditures would make the recession worse,[3] but he was almost alone in supporting this position in public. If there were many members of Congress in 1949 who were familiar with the concepts of compensatory public finance or even thought that the budget's properties of automatic stabilization were a contribution to the country's economic well-being, then with very rare exceptions they lay low and said nothing. The McClellan resolution encountered procedural obstacles which proved decisive. The Majority Leader refused to call it up, so that it had to go on the Calendar in the ordinary way unless it were called up by unanimous consent, which could easily be prevented; and being of a legislative character, it could not be moved as an amendment to an appropriation bill without the two-thirds majority needed to suspend the rules. The appropriations were in the end passed without abnormal cuts, as the President had recommended in the Mid-year Economic Report, but because of the strength of the support for cutting expenditures to eliminate the deficit that had been manifest in connection with the McClellan resolution, it was 'a damned close-run thing'.[4]

Late in the Session the Congress passed legislation to carry out the President's recommendation of Federal loans to state and local governments for the planning of public works. Public Law 352 authorized a programme to last for two years from October 1949, and accompanied it with appropriations and contract authorizations of $25 million for fiscal 1950. Of the specific anti-recession measures

[1] *Congressional Record*, Vol. XCV, p. 13519.
[2] *Congressional Record*, Vol. XCV, p. 6310.
[3] *S. Rept. No. 498*, 81st Cong., 1st Sess., Statement of Minority Views, p. 2.
[4] Wellington's comment on the battle of Waterloo.

recommended by the President in July 1949 this was the only one which was put into effect by Congressional action in 1949.

There was no real opposition to the Administration's anti-recession measures for not being drastic enough. Even the trade unions were generally quiescent. C.I.O. spokesmen kept drawing attention to the level of unemployment, but in the main they blamed the recession on the pricing and profit policies of business and advocated increased wages and reductions in prices and profits as the means of dealing with it.[1] Murray in the Senate and Patman in the House introduced an 'Economic Expansion bill', which would have set up a body composed of representatives of government, employers, and unions to formulate plans for economic expansion, authorized the Government to construct industrial plant as the President had recommended in January, and authorized the organization of a large 'shelf' of planned public works. The bill did not come up for a vote in either House or Senate, nor did it receive any encouragement from the Administration; Dr. Keyserling, a member of the Council of Economic Advisers, had an engagement to speak on behalf of an early version of Murray's proposal in May 1949, but cancelled it after receiving intimation that the President would regard it as an unfriendly act.[2] The Republicans made two attempts to reduce excise tax rates; on 30 June the Minority Leader, Representative Martin, introduced a discharge petition to bring to the Floor a bill he had introduced in February to reduce excise tax rates; and on the same day the Senate Finance Committee voted by 7–6 to attach provisions reducing excise tax revenue by $725 million annually to a bill dealing with the power of the Commissioner of Internal Revenue to supervise the use of industrial alcohol. Both proved abortive and were in all probability no more than gestures.

The opposition to the Administration's anti-recession policy, cautious as that policy was, came from the Right and not from the Left as in 1954. The pressure came not from those who thought the Administration was doing too little, but from those who on grounds of principle or dogma opposed the actions which the vast majority of economists had come to look on as the appropriate means of dealing with deflation. For those who wanted vigorous action there

---

[1] For instance, by the C.I.O.'s Full Employment Committee, reported in the *C.I.O. News*, 23 May 1949. Mr. P. Murray, President of the C.I.O., declared later: 'The present situation is the direct result of short-sighted and greedy business policies'. *C.I.O. News*, 18 July 1949.

[2] E. G. Nourse, *Economics in the Public Service*, p. 246.

was not much point in attacking the Administration, for to do so would have meant alliance with those whose approach to the problem of recession was one of no action at all or positive action which would make matters worse. The combination of a Democratic President and a Democratic Congress in which the anti-New Deal coalition still held sway did not, in the light of experience of 1949, look like the political situation most auspicious for effective action to deal with deflation.

THE RECOVERY FROM THE RECESSION, 1949–50

The course of the economy in the second half of 1949 and the first half of 1950 was in close accord with the analysis of the Mid-year Economic Report of 1949 and Economic Review by the Council of Economic Advisers that accompanied it. Consumption demand continued to rise, and although fixed capital investment by business declined, the decline was offset by the increase in house-building; inventory liquidation ceased and accumulation was resumed in the first quarter of 1950. The following table shows the movements of certain components of total demand:

TABLE 14

Components of Aggregate Demand, 1949–50

	1949			1950	
	II	III	IV	I	II
Consumption—Total	203·6	204·8	209·0	210·7	214·2
Durable Goods	26·0	27·1	28·5	29·0	29·8
Non-durable Goods and Services	177·6	177·7	180·5	181·7	184·3
Residential Construction (Non-farm)	10·3	11·5	12·8	14·0	15·5
Other Construction ⎫ Producers' Durable ⎬ Equipment ⎭	31·5	30·3	29·6	29·5	32·9
Inventory Investment	−6·0	−2·0	−6·0	+2·7	+5·4
Federal Government (Goods and Services)	25·8	25·9	23·8	21·1	20·0
State and Local Government	21·6	22·4	23·0	23·6	23·5
Net Exports	3·4	2·8	0·9	1·1	0·6
G.N.P.	290·3	295·6	293·0	302·7	312·0

Amounts in $ billion, measured at seasonally adjusted annual rates, at constant (1954) prices.

Detail does not necessarily add to totals because of rounding.

Source: Department of Commerce, *U.S. Income and Output*, 1959, Table I–5.

The stability of consumption expenditures in money terms and increase in real terms despite the fall in income which played such an important part in keeping the decline within bounds and in bringing the inventory liquidation to an end was the outcome of an increase in consumption relative to disposable income and a decline in disposable income which was less than the decline in personal income before tax and transfer. The latter is illustrated in the following table:

TABLE 15

Personal Income and Disposable Income, 1948–50

	Personal Income Before Tax and Transfer	Personal Tax Payments Federal	State and Local	Transfers	Social Insurance Contribution	Disposable Income
1948 4th Q.	205·9	18·2	2·2	10·7	2·3	194·0
1949 3rd Q	196·7	16·2	2·5	12·7	2·2	188·6
1949 4th Q.	197·6	16·1	2·5	12·6	2·2	189·3
1950 1st Q.	199·5	16·7	2·6	21·4	2·8	200·9
1950 2nd Q.	209·2	17·3	2·6	15·0	2·8	201·7

Note: The fourth quarter of 1948 was the peak of the quarterly personal income series and the third quarter of 1949 the trough.
Amounts expressed in $ billion, at seasonally adjusted annual rates.
Detail does not necessarily add to totals because of rounding.
Source: Department of Commerce, *U.S. Income and Output*, 1959, Table II–2.

Whereas income before tax and transfer fell by $9·2 billion, disposable income fell by only $5·4 billion. Most of the offset was the result of automatic stabilization, the exception being the reduction of about $1 billion (measured at annual rates) in Federal income tax payments that resulted from the Revenue Act of 1948.

The ratio of consumption to disposable income rose from 93·2 per cent in the last quarter of 1948 to 95·2 per cent, 95·7 per cent, and 97·2 per cent in the second, third, and fourth quarters of 1949 respectively. A considerable amount of this represented the increase in consumer credit. The amount of consumer credit outstanding at the end of December 1949 was $2·7 billion greater than at the end of June.[1] Consumer credit outstanding had been approximately

[1] Board of Governors of the Federal Reserve System, monthly statistics published in the *Federal Reserve Bulletin*.

stable in the fourth quarter of 1948, declined slightly in the first quarter of 1949, and rose very slightly in the second quarter of 1949, which lends support to the view that the increase helped finance at least part of the increase in expenditure on consumer durables.

The automatic stabilizing effect of the tax structure and the system of transfer payments thus made a considerable contribution to maintaining stability through cushioning the effect on consumption of the fall in incomes from production. Also very important was the reduction in income tax rates under the Revenue Act of 1948. Although in his Economic Report in January 1949 the President had spoken of the importance of flexibility in tax policy and of 'tax adjustments' to deal with serious deflation, it is not likely that a tax reduction could have been put into effect quickly even had the President recommended a tax reduction in January 1949 (assuming that the recession would have begun sooner had the Revenue Act of 1948 not been passed). The furore over deficit financing makes it unlikely that a tax reduction could have been secured in 1949 without great difficulty and long delays.

Government expenditures rose during the early part of the recession, as the following table shows:

TABLE 16

Federal Cash Receipts and Payments, 1948–50

	1948 2nd Half	1949 1st Half	1949 2nd Half	1940 1st Half
Federal Cash Payments				
National Defence	11·2	12·9	12·9	11·9
International Affairs and Finance	6·1	7·3	5·7	4·4
Social Security, Health and Welfare	2·2	2·6	2·9	3·1
Agriculture	2·3	2·8	3·2	2·4
Other Payments (net)	16·9	16·9	18·2	22·2 (a)
Total Cash Payments	38·7	42·5	42·9	44·0
Total Cash Receipts	42·6	41·5	41·2	41·1
Surplus or Deficit (+)	3·9	−1·0	−1·7	−2·9

Note (a) Increase due to the payment of the National Service Life Insurance dividend of $2·8 billion, which expressed at an annual rate is equal to $5·6 billion. Net of this non-recurring item cash payments would have been $38·4 billion and the surplus $2·7 billion.

Amounts expressed in $ billion at seasonally adjusted annual rates.

Source: Council of Economic Advisers, *Economic Review*, July 1949, Table A-7; July 1950, Table A-7; January 1951, Table 10, p. 162.

The following table shows Federal expenditures for public works and the purchase of mortgages:

TABLE 17

Federal Expenditures for Public Works and the Purchase of Mortgages

	1948	1949		1950
		1st Half	2nd Half	1st Half
Defence Public Works	0·2	0·2	0·2	0·3
Other Federal Public Works	0·8	1·3	1·5	1·6
Loans and Grants to State and Local Goverments for Public Works	0·8	0·3	0·5	0·6
Total Public Works Expenditure	1·8	1·8	2·2	2·5
Net Purchases of Mortgages	0·2	0·5	0·8	0·4

Amounts expressed in $ billion at seasonally adjusted annual rates.
Source: Council of Economic Advisers, *Economic Review, January 1950*, Table A-8; July 1950; Table A-8; January 1951 Table C-10.

Of the increase in government expenditures only that for the purchase of mortgages and for loans by the RFC[1] was discretionary in the sense that it would not have occurred but for deliberate decisions to take action to stimulate the economy. Part of the increase in expenditure for public works may have been discretionary in the sense that needed public works (the last backlog to be left from the war) could have been postponed again if serious inflation threatened. The other increases were automatic in that they took place under existing programmes as a result of the recession without any decision having to be taken to undertake an anti-deflationary policy; or they were autonomous in that their purpose was unrelated to short-run economic stability and that their volume would have been much the same whatever the economic situation. The increases in expenditure for social security and for agricultural subsidies were in the automatic category, and in the autonomous category were the increases in expenditure for defence and foreign aid in 1949 and the National Service Life Insurance dividend.

The boom in house building that got under way in 1949 was very

---

[1] The total of business loans extended by the R.F.C. was: 1948, $103 million; 1949, $240 million; 1950, $247 million. R. J. Saulnier, H. G. Halcrow, and N. H. Jacoby, *Federal Lending and Loan Insurance*, (Princeton, 1958), Table A-9.

important in the recovery.[1] This boom was stimulated by direct Federal expenditures through the purchase of mortgages by the Federal National Mortgage Association (FNMA or 'Fanny May'), by Federal insurance and guarantees of privately financed mortgages by the Federal Housing Administration and Veterans Administration, and by the vigorous easy money policy pursued by the Federal Reserve System.[2] The powers of the FHA to insure mortgages were greatly extended by the Housing Act of 1949; although this was a long term measure, it was probably of assistance in dealing with the recession. The total value of mortgages insured and guaranteed by FHA and VA rose from $4,354 million in 1948 to $4,634 million in 1949 and $6,103 million in 1950;[3] the increase in the volume of FNMA loans outstanding at the end of the year was $195 million in 1948, $629 million in 1949, and $519 million in 1950.[4] Total mortgage debt outstanding on residential properties housing four or fewer families at the end of 1950 was $11·9 billion more than at the end of 1948; of this increase, $6·4 billion was insured or guaranteed by the Federal government.[5]

The combination of credit relaxation, Federal insurance and guarantees, and direct Federal expenditure had a remarkable effect. The value of residential building in 1948, measured at constant (1954) prices, was $11·4 billion, which fell to a seasonally adjusted annual rate of $10·1 billion in the first quarter of 1949 and $10·3 billion in the second quarter. Thereafter it rose rapidly, and in the second quarter of 1950 it reached an annual rate of $15·5 billion in the second quarter of 1950,[6] no less than 50 per cent above the corresponding period in the previous year.

FISCAL POLICY AND POLITICS IN 1950

During the autumn of 1949 the working of the forces for recovery that were outlined in the preceding section was evident to all and there was no suggestion that further measures of stimulation would be needed. In the report of a conference on fiscal policy of University economists convened by the National Planning Association and presented to the Subcommittee on Monetary, Credit, and Fiscal

---

[1] See Table 1, p. 14 supra.
[2] For Federal Reserve policy in this period, see J. S. Fforde, *The Federal Reserve System 1945–1949*, (Oxford, 1954), Chapters XX and XXI.
[3] Saulnier, Halcrow, and Jacoby, op. sit., Tables A-10, A-17, and A-28.
[4] Ibid.   [5] *Economic Report of the President, 1959*, Table D-46.
[6] Department of Commerce, *U.S. Income and Output*, 1959, Table 1–5.

Policies of the Joint Committee on the Economic Report (the Douglas Subcommittee) on 23 September the conclusion was reached that for the time being neither an inflationary nor a deflationary change in fiscal policy was needed.[1] In November 1949 the Federal Reserve System took the first steps to reverse the easy money policy that had been in effect since June, on the ground that the rise in consumption and house building, with the end of inventory liquidation to come, indicated that the outlook for 1950 was one of mild inflation.[2] In a speech to the American Bankers' Association on 1 November Secretary Snyder declared that 'American business is having another tremendous year' and that the 'readjustment' had been achieved successfully.[3]

The controversy over taxation and the budget was revived in October 1949 when Dr. Nourse resigned from the Council of Economic Advisers, and expressed disquiet at the toleration of a deficit at such a time of high production and employment.[4] At his press conference the President replied that he too did not like deficit financing, but had no choice because of the tax reduction made by the 80th Congress, and announced that he would recommend higher tax rates when the Congress reassembled in January.[5] The announcement was greeted with disapproval by George on the Democratic side and Millikin and Martin on the Republican side; they maintained that a tax increase would imperil recovery and that the deficit should be eliminated through cuts in expenditure.[6]

The Administration's appreciation of the economic situation in 1950, as set out in the Economic Report of the President, was that recovery was definitely under way and would continue.[7] Although the Report stated that the immediate goal for 1950 was the regaining of maximum employment, defined as unemployment between two million and two-and-a-half million,[8] no further anti-deflationary measures were recommended; indeed, of the anti-deflationary measures recommended in July 1949 only the extension of the

---

[1] The text is printed in the hearings of the Douglas Subcommittee, September 23, 1949.

[2] Fforde, op. cit., Chapter XXII.

[3] The text of the speech is printed in *the Annual Report of the Secretary of the Treasury for the year ending 30 June 1950*, pp. 414–7.

[4] In a speech to the Retail Farm Equipment Association. Reported in the *New York Times*, 19 October 1949.

[5] *New York Times*, 21 October 1949.   [6] Ibid.

[7] *Economic Report of the President, January 1950*, pp. 2–3.

[8] Ibid., p. 7.

maximum maturity of RFC loans was recommended again in January 1950. Evidently the Administration considered that the forces making for economic expansion were strong enough not to need further stimulation.

The Budget recommendations in January 1950 were very similar to those of 1949. Expenditure in fiscal 1951 for social welfare, housing, and education was estimated to exceed expenditure in the current fiscal year (1950) by about $1,000 million, defence expenditure was expected to rise by $400 million, and expenditure for the development of natural resources (mainly atomic energy) was estimated to increase by $360 million. Offsetting this were expected declines in expenditure for foreign aid, agriculture, and veterans' services and benefits, amounting to about $2,560 million all told. Revenue from existing tax rates was expected to fall by just under $500 million, making an estimated deficit for the fiscal year of $5,133 million.[1] The President warned against 'drastic slashes' in government expenditure, for this was for essential services; the rise in national income in ensuing years would yield enough revenue to balance the budget.

The President's recommendations on tax policy were outlined in a Message to the Congress on 23 January 1950,[2] and set out in detail by the Secretary of the Treasury when he appeared before the Ways and Means Committee on 3 February.[3] The principal recommendations were the repeal of the excise tax on the carriage of goods; reductions in the taxes on passenger fares, long distance telephone calls, furs, luggage, toilet goods, and jewellery; the extension of the existing tax on wireless sets to television sets; an increase in the corporation profits tax to 22 per cent on profits up to $50,000 and 42 per cent on the remainder of taxable profits, so eliminating the 53 per cent 'notch' rate on profits between $25,000 and $50,000 that was imposed by existing law. Other recommendations were the extension of period for the carry-back of losses for tax purposes to five years instead of the existing two years; increases in the rates and narrowing of the exemptions and exclusions of the estate and gift tax; reduction in the depletion allowances, especially for oil; a more adequate system for the taxation of life insurance companies; and

---

[1] *Budget of the United States for the year ending 30 June 1951.*
[2] *H. Doc. No. 451*, 81st Cong., 2nd Sess.
[3] The text of the Secretary's statement is printed in the *Annual Report of the Secretary of the Treasury for the year ending 30 June 1950*, pp. 186–207.

certain provisions against tax avoidance. Anticipating the possibility that the Congress would approve the tax reductions but not the increases, the President warned in his Message that he would veto any bill which provided for a net reduction in revenue.

The Ways and Means Committee held hearings lasting for one month, in the course of which 275 witnesses were heard. Numerous demands for more sweeping reductions in excise tax rates were made, and opposition was expressed to the proposals to increase tax rates. The bill reported by the Committee, H.R. 8920, provided for reduction in the excise tax on a much wider range of items than the Administration had recommended, approximately doubling the loss of revenue under this head. The corporation profits tax was to be increased to 21 per cent on the first $25,000 of taxable profits and 41 per cent on the remainder. Deduction at source of income tax on dividends was provided for, as was the taxation of profits earned by tax-exempt organizations from business operations. No reduction was made in percentage depletion; indeed, it was extended to twenty more non-metallic minerals, including gravel stripped from hillsides. Similarly, the only change made in the estate and gift tax was the addition of two more exclusions. In contrast with the estimated increase in revenue of $1 billion under the Administration's recommendations, the bill produced by the Ways and Means Committee was estimated to cost $12 million annually.

Introducing the bill in the debate on the Floor of the House, Doughton defended it as the best that could be done without adding to the deficit in conditions of 'peak prosperity'.[1] The Republicans pressed for larger tax reductions, to be offset by cuts in government expenditure. At the opening of the Ways and Means Committee's hearings they had sought, unsuccessfully, to confine the hearings to the subject of tax reduction; the motion to recommit would have required the bill to be split, separating the tax reductions from the revenue raising provisions. The bill was passed on 29 June 1950, by which time the consequences of the outbreak of the Korean War were about to require a complete revision of American fiscal policy.

The campaign to force reductions in government expenditures was pressed with renewed vigour in 1950. The submission of a budget which estimated that there would be a substantial deficit aroused an outburst of protest; the Chairman of the House Appropriations Committee, Representative Cannon, declared that it ran counter to

[1] *Congressional Record*, Vol. XCVI, p. 9280.

most people's conception of 'sound financial book-keeping' under prosperous conditions.[1] Appropriations other than those for foreign aid were carried in 1950 in a single Omnibus Appropriation Bill instead of the usual series of bills, in the hope that the new method would make it easier to bear in mind the balance between total revenue and total expenditure. It was a change of form rather than substance, since its component parts were considered by specialist subcommittees as were the separate bills in the past, and the bill finally reported was little more than the separate bills added together. It did facilitate the 'economy' drive in that one amendment to the 'Omnibus' bill would suffice where an amendment to each separate bill would previously have been required. Two economy amendments were passed; the Taber-Thomas amendment, requiring a reduction of $600 million in funds for purposes other than defence, which was passed by 274 votes to 112;[2] and the Jensen amendment, providing that only 10 per cent of the vacancies occurring in government staffs were to be filled, which was passed by 201 to 185. The Senate Appropriations Committee rejected both the Jensen and the Taber-Thomas amendments, but on the Floor the Byrd-Bridges amendment to reduce by 10 per cent the appropriation for purposes other than defence and foreign aid was passed by 55 votes to 31. The compromise version required the Bureau of the Budget to withhold $550 million of the appropriation carried by bill in a way which would not impair the national defence. Unlike the McClellan resolution of 1949, the 'economy' measures in 1950 provided for a reduction in new obligational authority voted and not a directive to the President to reduce expenditures, a distinction of great importance. By the time the final version of the economy amendment was agreed the post-Korean rearmament had begun and reductions in civil expenditure were in order on economic grounds.

The size of the vote in favour of the Taber-Thomas amendment is impressive testimony of the strength of support for cuts in expenditure to balance the budget even in the supposedly 'liberal' 81st Congress. The Republicans were intent on making a leading issue of the budget and the deficit. In a *Statement of Republican Principles and Objectives*[3] adopted by the Republican members of Congress on

---

[1] *New York Times*, 10 January 1950.
[2] There voted in favour: Republicans, 157, Democrats 117; against: Democrats, 110, Republicans, 1 (Javits), and A. L. P. 1 (Marcantonio).
[3] Published by the Republican National Committee, Washington, D. C.

6 February 1950, it was proclaimed that the issue facing the country was 'liberty against socialism', and the first of the measures recommended to avert the threat of socialism was the end of deficit financing. On 30 March seven of the Republican members of the Ways and Means Committee advocated a reduction in the national debt limit as a means of preventing further deficit financing.[1] The Republicans made the running on this issue, since given the history of the 1930's there was no other line of attack open to them when deflation led to a deficit under a Democratic Administration; but the hold of the balanced budget doctrine was still strong enough for them to get plenty of support from Democrats, and not only from those Democrats who would be Republicans if they were not Southerners.

CONCLUSIONS ON THE HANDLING OF THE FIRST POST-WAR RECESSION

During the first half of 1950 the recovery proceeded strongly, and in May the index of industrial production rose above the previous high point in 1948. It was possible to have doubts whether the recovery would continue, because of the extent to which it was based on the housing boom and the resumption of inventory accumulation, neither of which could be looked to for additional stimulation.[2] But in the second quarter of 1950 production of producers' durable goods rose sharply, from a seasonally adjusted annual rate of $15·7 billion in the first quarter to $18·4 billion in the second and $20·6 billion in the third quarter.[3] Either the recovery of the economy and the expansion of consumers' demand had strengthened the inducement to invest, or an autonomous increase in private investment had got under way; which ever it was there would have been strong reasons for expecting further increases in output. It is thus likely that the recovery would have been sustained in the second half of 1950 even had there been no Korean war and rearmament. But subject to the slight possibility that the recovery might not have continued in the second half of 1950, it could reasonably be claimed that

[1] At the time the debt stood at $255·6 billion, and the proposal was to reduce the debt limit from the existing $275 billion to $257 billion. *Congressional Record*, Vol. XCVI, p. A2747. Nothing came of this scheme.

[2] Council of Economic Advisers, *Annual Economic Review, January 1950*, p. 71.

[3] Department of Commerce, *U.S. Income and Output*, 1959, Table I–3.

the long-awaited post-war 'adjustment' had been successfully surmounted.

Actions in the Government sector contributed to this success. The Federal Reserve System's easy money policy, the insuring and guaranteeing of mortgages by the FHA and VA, and the pumping of Federal money into the finance of house building through the purchase of mortgages by FNMA, between them made a significant contribution in stimulating the housing boom. The support given to disposable income by reduction in income tax under the Revenue Act of 1948 and by the automatic stabilizing effect of the tax and transfer system was of considerable importance, as suggested above. The increases in expenditure for defence and foreign aid at the end of 1948 and in the first half of 1949 contributed to the maintenance of aggregate demand, and the payment of the National Service Life Insurance dividend gave a further stimulus to consumption in the first half of 1950. A budget deficit emerged at a time when this was appropriate for economic stability.

But it is apparent at once that many of the actions cited above as contributing to economic stability were not purposely directed to that end. The timing of the N.S.L.I. dividend with respect to the economic situation was largely fortuitous,[1] and it was likewise fortunate that the higher expenditure for defence and foreign aid made themselves felt at a time when an addition to demand was needed. The timing of the tax reduction was not really determined by economic considerations, and had the Administration's view prevailed it is reasonably certain that there would have been no tax reduction until the recession was well under way.

The Administration did not appear to abandon the view that inflation was the immediate danger to which policy should be directed until a considerable time after the recession had begun. The President maintained his demand for tax increases, at least for the record, for a long time after it was evident that a recession was under way. Indeed, President Truman and Secretary Snyder were criticized by the editors of *Fortune* for having 'a pre-Keynesian obsession with a balanced budget'.[2] However, when it was clear

---

[1] There was a small element of administrative discretion in that the Veterans Administration had not previously been permitted by the Budget Bureau to employ the staff needed to implement this part of the law concerning servicemen's benefits. With inflation no longer pressing some of the restraints on government expenditure were relaxed and VA was allowed to add the necessary staff.

[2] *Fortune*, June 1949, p. 176.

K

beyond all reasonable doubt that the immediate problem was one of deflation President Truman adjusted his recommendations accordingly. But the policy followed was very cautious indeed. In an interview with Arthur Krock of the *New York Times*, the President said: 'a certain amount of unemployment, say from three to five millions, is supportable' and that 'it is a good thing that job seeking should go on at all times; this is healthy for the economic body'. On budgetary policy he said that he 'did not tolerate deficit financing' and that he 'hates deficit financing as much as Harry Byrd ever could'.[1] It would appear from this that President Truman, like his successor and many other Americans in public life, adhered strongly to the doctrine of the balanced budget, even if under pressure of circumstances as in July 1949 he would concede that to apply it in its entirety would be manifestly dangerous.

Throughout the period the role of longer run considerations in shaping the recommendations of the Administration about taxation and Government expenditures was as great as that of short run economic stability. The tax increase recommended in January 1949 has the appearance of being influenced by considerations of social policy and income distribution rather than the restraint of demand, and this is even more true of the tax revision proposed in 1950. Reductions in excise tax rates accompanied by an increase in the tax on corporate profits, restriction of percentage depletion, and the tightening of the estate and gift tax would have brought about a slight redistribution of income in favour of consumers at the expense of profit receivers. That its purpose was social rather than being directed to short run economic stability is suggested by the fact that although the Council of Economic Advisers considered the maintenance of a sufficiently high level of business investment in fixed capital 'an outstanding problem',[2] the major tax increase proposed might well have depressed investment somewhat and certainly would not have stimulated it.

In the Congress the contribution to the maintenance of economic stability that was made by inaction was as great as that made by affirmative action. The recommendation that taxes be increased was disregarded, and with the assistance of a certain amount of luck the

[1] The interview is printed in the *New York Times*, 15 February 1950. The quotations are from the *New York Times*, as the report of the interview is in *oratio obliqua*.

[2] Council of Economic Advisers, *Annual Economic Review*, January 1950, p. 73.

'economy' drive was held off until a change in the outlook had made it innocuous or even useful. The Housing Act of 1949, which renewed the authority of the FHA to insure mortgages and of the FNMA to purchase them was very helpful, but it was a long term measure and its arrival on the Statute Book at long last was the result of the elections of 1948 rather than the recession. No real damage was done by the 'balance-the-budget-by-cutting-expenditure' school of thought, though not for want of trying. While not all went as far as Senator Byrd, who wanted a Congressional investigation of the Council of Economic Advisers because their report in July 1949 'seemed to reflect the views of Lord Keynes rather than of American free enterprise',[1] defenders of a deficit under the conditions that prevailed in the second half of 1949 were few and far between, as were Congressional critics of the Administration who held that it was doing too little.

In the country as well as in the Congress there was little pressure on the Administration to take reflationary action sooner and more vigorously. Such pressure could not come from the regular opposition, and if Truman's Left-wing supporters were to bolt there was nowhere for them to go. The alternative in 1949–50 to the Administration's policy was not one which at least the verbal promise of more vigorous anti-deflationary measures as in 1954; it was one (at least verbally) of no action or perverse action.

The Truman Administration handled the recession with great caution, and the successful outcome was aided by good fortune in that circumstances made it possible for an expansionary effect to be exerted through the budget without the need for affirmative action specifically for this purpose. Had such action been necessary it is difficult to feel any confidence about the outcome unless the situation deteriorated badly, in view of the manifest strength of the opposition in the Congress to deficits and the demands for reduction of expenditures to eliminate the deficit. The idea that the Truman Administration took quick and drastic (or even hasty) action to deal with the recession of 1949 is without any foundation in fact.

[1] In a radio interview on 17 July 1949, reported in the *New York Times* 18 July 1949.

CHAPTER VIII

THE KOREAN WAR AND INFLATION

AT the end of June 1950 the economic situation was transformed by the outbreak of war in Korea and the intervention by the United States. In the next few weeks it became clear that a major military operation would be needed. Even more important, the outbreak of hostilities forced a reassessment of the danger of general war. It was evident that the Communist powers were prepared to go further and take greater risks than had previously been assumed. As a result the United States government decided on large-scale and rapid rearmament, a decision from which there was very little dissent.

A large increase in Federal government expenditure thus came into prospect and with it increased demands on the economy and the danger of inflationary pressure. On 5 July Secretary Snyder appeared before the Senate Finance Committee to discuss the tax revision bill,[1] explaining that he did so on the understanding that events might make it necessary to abandon the bill.[2] A week later the Finance Committee decided not to proceed with it because of the prospective increase in government expenditure. At this time nobody had any real idea of how great the increase in defence expenditure would be. The President let it be known that he had no plans for tax increases, and Senator George said that he did not expect any action on taxation before January.[3]

Inflation soon developed, but not directly from defence expenditure. Once it became apparent that the war in Korea would be no 'nine days' wonder', there was a rush by consumers to lay their hands on anything that could be stored, for fear of shortages and rationing such as had occurred in World War II. Consumers' expenditure on durable and non-durable goods in the third quarter of 1950 was at an annual rate of $138·8 billion, compared with $123·0 billion and $125·6 billion in the first and second quarters of 1950

---

[1] For details of the bill and its passage by the House, see pp. 125-6 supra.

[2] Statement printed in the *Annual Report of the Secretary of the Treasury for the year ending 30 June 1950*, pp. 227–42.

[3] Reported in the *New York Times*, 14 July 1950.

respectively,[1] an increase over the second quarter of 10·5 per cent. Defence expenditure in the third quarter of 1950 was at an annual rate of $14·1 billion, compared with $12·0 billion in the second quarter. Initially the increase in expenditure for consumers' goods was thus much greater than the increase in defence expenditure. In the last three weeks of July 1950 the value of sales by department stores was respectively 25 per cent, 46 per cent, and 42 per cent greater than in the corresponding weeks in 1949; this should be compared with the increases in June and the first week in July of 10 per cent and 9 per cent respectively over the corresponding periods in 1949.[2]

The Council of Economic Advisers described the episode as follows:

'There was a rush by consumers to buy fantastic quantities of certain goods, even though such goods were being produced under conditions which ensured the continuance of ample supplies for many months. Local stocks of sugar were exhausted; merchants were forced to limit purchases of nylon stockings; household linen flowed out of the shops and into the homes; automobile tires were eagerly seized; meat was crowded into deep freeze units.'[3]

Disposable income in the third quarter of 1950 (measured at seasonally adjusted annual rates) was $8·5 billion greater than in the second quarter, but personal consumption expenditure was $14·5 billion greater;[4] personal saving in the third quarter amounted to 2·8 per cent of disposable income, compared with 5·9 per cent in the second quarter. The increase in consumer credit outstanding in July, August and September 1950 was $200 million greater than in the preceding three months,[5] and net redemptions of Series E Savings Bonds[6] were exceptionally large during August and September.

In the six months following the outbreak of hostilities the Index of Consumer Prices rose by five per cent, while the index of prices of

[1] Department of Commerce, *U.S. Income and Output*, 1959, Table I–3.

[2] Department of Commerce, *Survey of Current Business*, August 1950, p. 2.

[3] *Economic Report of the President, January 1951*, p. 35.

[4] Department of Commerce, *U.S. Income and Output*, 1959, Table II–2.

[5] Board of Governors of the Federal Reserve System, monthly statistics published in the *Federal Reserve Bulletin*.

[6] The Series E bond is a security similar in many respects to a National Savings Certificate. The increase in redemptions that resulted from the 'buying spree' cannot be specified with precision owing to the rising trend in redemptions evident before July 1950.

wholesale prices of manufactured goods rose by 10 per cent.[1] All
this occurred before defence orders had risen enough to make a
substantial impact on demand. As the Council of Economic Advisers somewhat ruefully observed: 'The first result (of the recognition that substantial increases in defence expenditure would be
necessary) took the form of those mass movements which occasion-
ally upset economic analysis based solely on statistical data or
assuming a regular pattern of economic behaviour. Such movements, however short lived they may be, continue to influence the
economy long after the originating incident has disappeared.'[2]

The only means of preventing a 'buying spree' such as occurred
in the third quarter of 1950 is an effective system of rationing, of
which nothing existed in the United States at the time.

THE FIRST MEASURES TO CHECK INFLATION

President Truman outlined his policy for the restraint of inflation
in a Message to Congress on 19 July 1950.[3] He stressed the importance of paying for additional defence expenditure by increased
taxation, and stated that recommendations for tax increases would
be submitted 'at the appropriate time, as soon as the necessary
studies are completed'. The direct controls recommended were power
to allocate and requisition materials of strategic importance, to
regulate the use of credit for commodity speculation, and to regulate
the terms of instalment and mortgage credit. No request was made
for power to control wages and prices, although the President said
he would not hesitate to request such powers if a sharp rise in prices
made it necessary. The Congress promptly passed the Defense
Production Act, which gave to the President the powers he requested
(except for the control of credit for commodity speculation), plus
the authority to impose rationing and wage and price controls. The
last was subject to the limitation that no prices could be controlled
unless wages in the industries concerned were also controlled, and
that the controlled prices of farm products were to be not less than
the 'parity' prices if these were higher than the prices prevailing in
June 1950.

On 24 July the President submitted his first request for supple-

[1] Bureau of Labor Statistics, monthly statistics published in *Monthly Labor
Review*.

[2] *Economic Report of the President*, January 1951, p. 35.

[3] The text of the Message is printed in the *Congressional Record*, Vol. XCVI,
pp. 10626–30, and in the *New York Times*, 20 July 1950.

mental appropriations. The total requested was $17,303 million, of which $11,642 million was for the Armed Services, $4,000 million for the Mutual Assistance programme, and most of the remainder for stock-piling and research on atomic energy.

Support for increased taxation was already beginning to appear. Senator O'Mahoney, Chairman of the Joint Committee on the Economic Report, argued that adequate increases in tax rates would reduce the need for drastic controls, and began his campaign for an excess profits tax.[1] On 24 July 1950 the President revealed the Administration's recommended tax increases to the Democratic Congressional leaders in a private discussion, and on the following day the proposals were announced in a public letter from the President to Senator George. The President recommended that the rates of the individual income tax be increased to the 1945 'tentative' rates[2] and the rate of the corporation profits tax to 45 per cent.[3] The proposals were generally well received; George said that he thought that the bill to implement the recommendations could be passed within a few days, and the House and Senate Minority Leaders, Representative Martin and Senator Wherry, gave general approval on behalf of the Congressional Republicans. The approval of Martin and Wherry was coupled with a complaint about government expenditure, which, Wherry claimed, could be reduced by billions if the Administration had the will.[4] This last was one of the opening flurries of a storm which was to become prolonged and violent.

On 2 August 1950 Secretary Snyder presented the Administration's detailed proposals to the Senate Finance Committee, stressing the importance of speed in passing the increase in taxation before the additional defence expenditure strengthened inflationary pressure. He recommended that the increase in the rate of tax on corporate profits be made applicable to the whole of profits earned in 1950 and the increase in the personal income tax to the last quarter. The provisions of H.R.8920 which would raise revenue, including the taxation of the profits of business operations of tax-exempt bodies, the deduction at source of tax on dividends, the extension of the 10 per cent excise tax to television sets, and the closing of miscellaneous

---

[1] Reported in *New York Times*, 20 and 24 July 1950.

[2] I.e. the rates of tax imposed by the Revenue Act of 1945 before the reduction of liability of 5 per cent.

[3] The text of the letter is printed in the *Annual Report of the Secretary of the Treasury for the year ending 30 June 1950*, pp. 225–6.

[4] New York Times, 27 July, 1950

loopholes, should be retained. The following tables show the effect of the proposed measures:

TABLE 18

Increase in Income Tax Liability (full year)

	Effective Rate (%)			
	Single Man		Married, two children	
Adjusted Gross Income	Existing Law	Treasury Proposal	Existing Law	Treasury Proposal
$1,000	6·6	8·0	nil	nil
$2,000	11·6	14·0	nil	nil
$3,000	13·6	16·3	3·3	4·0
$5,000	16·2	18·9	8·6	10·4
$10,000	21·2	24·4	13·6	15·9
$50,000	46·4	52·8	32·2	37·8

Source: Annual Report of the Secretary of the Treasury for the year ending 30 June 1950, Table V, pp. 235–6.

TABLE 19

Increase in Revenue Resulting from the Recommended Tax Increases

	Increases, in $ million	
	Full year	Fiscal 1951
Increase in Corporation Profits Tax . .	1455·0	572·1
Increase in Personal Income Tax . . .	2932·5	1725·0
Withholding of Tax on Dividends . . .	175·0	110·0
Tax-Exempt Institutions	100·0	negligible
Life Insurance Companies	63·1	129·2
Excise on Television Sets and Deep-Freezers .	48·6	31·7
Miscellaneous loopholes	150·9	124·5
Total	4925·1	2692·5

Source: Annual Report of the Secretary of the Treasury for the year ending 30 June 1950, Table VIII, p. 242

The Treasury estimated that of the increase in the personal income tax some 55 per cent would be borne by tax payers with adjusted gross incomes of under $5,000.[1]

The Administration's recommendations were generally well received. The Senate Finance Committee accepted the Administration's recommendations about the increase in rates, and retained most of the loophole closing provisions, with the important exception of withholding of tax on dividends. The effective date for the increase in the tax on corporation profits was set at 1 July 1950 and

[1] Calculated from data in *Annual Report of the Secretary of the Treasury for the year ending 30 June 1950*, Table VI, p. 239.

not 1 January as the Administration had requested, on the ground that the latter date would require retroactive taxation. The Committee added some more relief provisions, giving more favourable treatment to stock purchase options granted by firms to their employees, validation of family partnerships for tax purposes, and certain reliefs for mining enterprises. There was little opposition worthy of name to the increases in the rates. The A.F.L. filed a protest with the Senate Finance Committee, alleging that the increases were unjust to the lower income groups,[1] but the protest rang hollow, for the increase in the personal income tax reversed those reductions which in 1947 and 1948 had been roundly denounced for favouring the wealthy.[2]

It soon became apparent that the centre of controversy about the bill would be the proposals for immediate enactment of an excess profits tax. The Administration wanted this acutely controversial issue to be held over until the first increase in tax rates was out of the way.[3] Senator George declared that the interim tax bill would pass without provisions for an excess profits tax 'or there will be no bill at all'.[4] He said shortly afterwards that he expected that the next Session of Congress would enact an excess profits tax, and hinted at the possibility of an 'excess earnings' tax,[5] which was probably a shaft aimed at the unions, who were the most vociferous supporters of an excess profits tax.

The demand for an excess profits tax gathered strength, and most of the Senate debate on H.R.8920 was taken up by this issue. George argued that the drafting of an efficient and equitable excess profits tax would require much detailed work which could not be completed quickly, so that the excess profits tax should be left till later in the Session or early next Session. He derided the excess profits tax as an anti-inflationary device, saying that it was 'the most inflationary type of tax that can be devised'.[6] Its inflationary effect, according to George, lay in the incentive it would give to wasteful expenditures by corporations. That is to say, it would result in addi-

---

[1] *New York Times,* 4 August 1950   [2] See Chapters V and VI supra.

[3] Secretary Snyder did not mention the subject in the course of his statement to the Senate Finance Committee, and informed his news conference on 8 August that an excess profits tax bill was being drafted for submission to the Congress in January. *New York Times,* 9 August 1950.

[4] *New York Times,* 9 August 1950.

[5] *New York Times,* 19 August 1950. The feasibility of an excess earnings tax was studied by the staff of the Joint Committee on Internal Revenue Taxation.

[6] *Congressional Record,* Vol. XCVI, p. 13277.

tional current expenditures (for capital expenditures are not deductible for tax purposes) and so would reduce net saving in the corporate sector. If this should occur to a significant extent it would indeed add to total demand.

Senator O'Mahoney's amendment defined excess profits as profits above 80 per cent of the average profits of the corporation for 1946–49, with excess profits so defined subject to a tax of 85 per cent gross. He argued that the revenue raised by the tax would reduce the likelihood of deficits and that the tax would deter firms from raising their prices. Most of his speech dealt with the arguments in favour of the tax on grounds of equity; he made numerous references to such ideas as 'we cannot be tender with profits and drastic with men',[1] and 'summoning business to the colors under the fiscal flag'.[2]

In view of the strength of support for an excess profits tax, George yielded somewhat and offered an amendment on behalf of himself and Millikin which would require the Finance Committee and the Ways and Means Committee to report out an excess profits tax bill retroactive to 1 July or 1 October 1950 as soon as practicable in the next Session. It did not satisfy O'Mahoney and his supporters, but was carried by 42 votes to 36, the majority consisting of the Republicans and conservative Southern Democrats.

Left-wing Democrats made vigorous attacks on the relief provisions in the bill, and moved a series of amendments to delete them. All the amendments were rejected except for that to delete the provision which would have subjected to the ordinary income tax capital gains on assets held for under three months instead of under six months as in the previously existing law. The Finance Committee's deletion of the withholding of tax on dividends was sustained, despite Senator Humphrey's criticism of the toleration of 'evasion by coupon clippers'. After a considerable amount of acrimonious debate the conservatives led by George and Millikin had their way in that the bill left the Senate without an excess profits tax and with the revenue-losing 'equity' provisions retained.

There was strong support in the House of Representatives for an excess profits tax.[3] But in order to avoid delaying the enactment of the other tax increases, to which there was no opposition in the

---

[1] *Congressional Record*, Vol. XCVI, p. 13423.

[2] Ibid., p. 13425.

[3] The 101 Members, mostly Left-wing Democrats, with a handful of Left-wing Republicans, who signed a petition advocating the immediate enactment of an excess profits tax are listed in the *Congressional Record*, Vol. XCVI, p. A6329.

House, Doughton sought to avoid the insertion of an excess profits tax amendment in order not to precipitate a struggle with the Senate (and specifically with George and Millikin) on the issue. He moved that the bill be sent to Conference, a manoeuvre which would exclude a motion to impose an excess profits tax. Seeking the necessary unanimous consent for his motion, Doughton said that he supported the principle of an excess profits tax, but that it had to be dealt with 'practically'.[1] The President, the Treasury, and the Senate were all opposed to including an excess profits tax in the present bill, so that all that Eberharter and his colleagues would achieve by insisting on the excess profits tax amendment would be to delay the urgently needed tax increases contained in the bill. The Rules Committee reported a motion to send the bill to Conference, and amendments to bind the House Conferees to insist on the inclusion of an excess profits tax were therefore ruled out of order. Eberharter thereupon moved a motion requiring an excess profits tax to be reported out during the life of the 81st Congress, which was passed by 331 votes to 2.

George denounced Eberharter's motion as 'an outright sham'[2] and moved its rejection, which was carried by 36 votes to 34.[3] The Conference version provided that if the Congress were still in session, an excess profits tax bill, retroactive to 1 July or 1 October 1950, should be reported out as soon as possible after 15 November; if the Congress was not in session at that time, then the bill should be reported as soon as possible in the 82nd Congress. This compromise proved adequate to ensure the passage of the bill. The main revenue raising provisions were left as the Senate had passed them, as was the provision, similar to that contained in the tax legislation of World War II, for accelerated depreciation allowances for investment certified by the Office of Defense Mobilization to be essential to the defence effort. The withholding of tax on dividends was not restored, but the revenue-losing 'family partnership' provisions inserted by the Senate were deleted.

The passage of the Revenue Act of 1950 coincided with the passage of the First Supplemental Appropriation Act. The speed with which so drastic an increase in tax rates was enacted reflected

[1] *Congressional Record*, Vol. XCVI, p. 14565.   [2] Ibid., p. 14821.

[3] When George's motion was put, it was carried unanimously. O'Mahoney was not on the floor at the time, and on learning what had happened, he moved that the Senate reconsider its decision. The motion to reconsider was rejected by 36 votes to 34.

credit on both the Administration and the Congress. The Administration's proposed tax increases were well chosen for raising the maximum of revenue with the minimum of controversy. Among the reasons why the Congress acted so quickly were that the spirit of united support for the intervention in Korea had not yet degenerated into the divisions and resentments that were to cause so much trouble in the next two years, and the abnormal procedural situation. The latter, together with the speed with which the proposed tax increases were sprung on the nation, gave the various interest groups little time to organize support for tax changes more favourable to them and to put on the pressure. The NAM spoke up in favour of a general excise tax[1] and there was soon some complaint from the trade unions, but nothing remotely resembling the elaborate argument and strong pressure that had been common during the Second World War and again in 1951 was apparent in the autumn of 1950.

OTHER MEASURES FOR RESTRAINING INFLATION

The Omnibus Appropriation Act of 1950 as finally approved contained a provision requiring the President to withhold $550 million of the obligational authority it contained, in a way which would not weaken the national defence. On 10 October 1950 the Bureau of the Budget accordingly issued instructions withholding $580 million, of which the largest items were: hospital construction, $75 million; rural electrification loans, $66·4 million; Bureau of Reclamation, $56·9 million; Army (civil functions), European Recovery Program, and government of occupied areas, $50 million each. This did not entail a reduction of expenditure of $580 million in fiscal 1951; most of the funds for hospital construction, the Army (civil functions) and the Bureau of Reclamation were for projects which would have taken well over a year to complete. But it reduced materially the number of new projects started, which in the next two or three years would help hold down investment expenditure in the public sector.

The authority given by the Defense Production Act for the control of installment credit was used promptly. The Federal Reserve Board re-issued Regulation W on 8 September 1950, and made the restrictions under it more drastic on 16 October. Minimum deposits were set at 33⅓ per cent for cars, 25 per cent for household appliances and wireless and T.V. sets, and 15 per cent for furniture. The maxi-

[1] *New York Times*, 1 August 1950.

mum repayment period was set at 15 months in each case. The controlled deposits and repayment periods were considerably less liberal than those which had been common before the imposition of controls, particularly in the case of household appliances and T.V. sets.[1] Instalment credit outstanding declined slightly in November 1950, and then after the usual increase in December declined steadily for six months. Consumers' expenditures on durable goods declined from an annual rate of $35·5 billion in the third quarter of 1950 to $31·2 billion in the fourth quarter, and after rising to $33·0 billion in the first quarter of 1951 remained within the range $28·0–$28·5 billion for the rest of 1951, and did not rise beyond $29·1 billion until the fourth quarter of 1952.[2] Measured at constant prices, the fall was even greater than this. It is therefore reasonable to believe that the imposition of restrictions on instalment credit had a material effect on consumer demand.

'Selective' credit control was also used to restrain house building. On 10 October the Board of Governors of the Federal Reserve System issued Regulation X, which imposed on mortgages not insured or guaranteed by FHA or VA the same conditions as to deposits and repayment periods as were imposed by FHA at the same time[3] (following the widespread American practice of 'veterans' preference' the minimum deposits required by VA were rather smaller). The scale of minimum deposits imposed on 10 October ranged from 10 per cent of the cost of a house priced at $5,000 or less to 50 per cent of that part of the cost in excess of $24,250. The decline in the value of house building after the third quarter of 1950 suggests that the restrictions had some effect. Non-farm residential building declined from an annual rate of $15·4 billion in the third quarter of 1950 to $11·8 billion in the third quarter of 1951.[4] The number of houses started in 1951 was 1,091,300, compared with 1,396,000 in 1950.

In addition to the use of 'selective' credit controls over consumer and mortgage credit, the Federal Reserve System tried to restrain the growth of bank credit by orthodox means. In August 1950 the rediscount rate was raised from $1\frac{1}{2}$ per cent to $1\frac{3}{4}$ per cent, and short

---

[1] See Department of Commerce, *Survey of Current Business*, November 1950, pp. 10–13.

[2] Department of Commerce, *U.S. Income and Output*, 1959, Table I–3. pp. 10–13.

[3] Less severe restrictions had been imposed on 18 July.

[4] Department of Commerce, *U.S. Income and Output*, 1959, Table I–3.

term interest rates allowed to rise, which caused trouble between the Treasury and the Federal System. Although the Board declared that they were prepared to use every means within their power to control inflation, they still regarded monetary policy as an adjunct to fiscal policy: 'Effective restraint on inflation must rest ultimately on the willingness of the American people to tax themselves adequately to meet the government's needs on a pay-as-you-go basis. Taxation alone, however, will not do the job. Parallel and prompt restraint in the area of monetary and credit policy is essential.'[1] The events of the second half of 1950 were a long step towards the abandonment of the policy of supporting Government bonds at par. But for the time being the commitment led the Federal Reserve System to make open market purchases and so adding to liquidity under circumstances when this conflicted with the policy of restraint.[2] Recourse was also had to 'moral suasion'. On 17 November 1950 the Chairman of the Board of Governors of the Federal Reserve System sent a circular letter to all member banks asking them not to grant loans which would add to consumer credit and mortgage credit or would be used to finance speculative accumulation of inventories.[3]

THE ENACTMENT OF THE EXCESS PROFITS TAX

Before the Congress took up the excess profits tax according to the agreement reached at the end of August, the Congressional elections took place. Although the number of seats that changed hands was not large (the Republicans made 28 gains in the House, and 6 gains and one loss in the Senate), the changes that did occur marked a definite trend to the Right. Nearly all the defeated Democratic Representatives had won their seats in 1948 and were rather Left-of-Centre; while not all of their successors were of the extreme Right, many inclined to this direction. This was also true of the Senate. The frustrations of the 'Cold War' and of the war in Korea figured prominently in the campaign, leading to the election of such candidates as John M. Butler in Maryland, Herman Welker in Idaho, and Richard M. Nixon in California, who had devoted much of their

[1] The text of the statement by the Board of Governors of the Federal Reserve System is printed in the *Federal Reserve Bulletin*, Vol. XXXVI, p. 1110.
[2] Senate Finance Committee, *Hearings on the Financial Condition of the United States*, 1957, p. 1250.
[3] The text of the letter is printed in the *Federal Reserve Bulletin*, Vol. XXXVI, p. 1582.

efforts to proving themselves less 'soft' on communism than their opponents and advocating an extreme form of 'Americanism'. The defeat of Tydings by Butler and the victories of Bennett, Dirksen, Nixon, and Welker amounted to a vote of confidence in the 'radical Right'; and the resounding victory of Taft demonstrated that there were many voters who were susceptible to a straight anti-labour appeal.

These developments were of considerable significance for economic policy. Most of the newly elected Republicans, including the Senators listed above, were strong adherents of the anti-New Deal ideology and all that that ideology implied about Federal taxation and expenditure. Moreover, it would appear that the tax increase imposed by the Revenue Act of 1950 had affected the outcome of the election.[1] For the Right-wingers there was thus a further incentive to oppose any further increase in tax rates and square this with the elementary facts of the situation by railing against 'spending'.

The impact of these developments was readily discernible when the Congress took up the excess profits tax. The tax has something of an air of radicalism about it, a distrust of certain aspects of the working of free markets, but at the time radicalism was clearly unpopular electorally. Moreover, some of the supporters of an excess profits tax had been defeated in the elections[2] and so were open to attack on this score.

The change in atmosphere was apparent when the Ways and Means Committee began its hearings on 15 November. The Administration's proposal had been outlined in a letter from the President to the Chairman of the Ways and Means Committee on 14 November, and was presented in detail to the Committee by Secretary Snyder on the following day. The scheme proposed was that excess profits should be defined as profits in excess of 75 per cent of profits in the three most profitable years for the firm in question of 1946, 1947, 1948, and 1949; or a rate of return on invested capital (the Secretary did not specify this beyond saying that it should be higher than that allowed during the Second World War). The rate of tax proposed was 75 per cent gross, that is to say, 30 per cent net of the existing corporate profits tax. The Secretary stressed equity, the need to prevent profiteering where the re-negotiation of contracts for goods

[1] See S. Lubell, *The Future of American Politics*, (Anchor Ed., New York, 1956), p. 231.

[2] Representative Young, formerly Representative-at-large from Ohio, was defeated by George H. Bender; and Representative Carroll was defeated by Senator Millikin, who was re-elected.

supplied to the Government was not applicable, rather than any anti-inflationary effect the tax might have.[1]

The Republican members of the Committee proposed that consideration of the excess profits tax be held over till the next Session, because of the damage which an 'unsound' tax would do to the economy. They were given a further grievance by the decision of the Chairman, which was approved by a straight party vote of 15–10, that the hearings should be limited to one week only, that they should be concerned solely with the excess profits tax, and that alternative schemes might not be discussed. Reed called this 'rankest steamroller tactics' and 'a stinging rebuke to the business groups of this country'.

It was undeniable that the decision was unwelcome to the business groups. The division between interest groups on the subject of an excess profits tax was clear cut. The tax was opposed by all the business groups, from the NAM, which is a by-word for far Right-wing opinions, to the relatively liberal CED. The opposition of the business community was understandable. With normal economic growth the outlook is for a gradual increase in profits, especially for progressive firms; but under an excess profits tax such increases would in a growing number of cases be liable to tax at the excess profits tax rate. The Excess Profits Tax Act did provide safeguards for growing firms, such as the application of the rate of return in the industry on capital invested, but even this was liable to penalize the most efficient firms.

In 1950 there was no means of knowing how long an excess profits tax would remain in force, once enacted. The outlook for the indefinite future was for military expenditure far greater than anything previously experienced in situations other than all-out war. After the Chinese intervention in the Korean war none could tell how long that conflict might last, and there was in addition the possibility of similar wars occurring elsewhere. In the Korean war and the 'Cold War', in contrast to World War II, there was no foreseeable prospect of victory and with it the end of war-time expenditure and war-time taxation. The justification for fearing that an excess profits tax, once enacted, would be retained for a long time was enhanced by the support for a permanent excess profits tax which existed in some Democratic and trade union circles. In 1948 President Truman had

[1] The text of the Secretary's statement is printed in the *Annual Report of the Secretary of the Treasury for the year ending 30 June 1951*, pp. 404–27.

recommended the imposition of an excess profits tax, and some Congressional Democrats had supported it.[1] The fear of a permanent excess profits tax was far from being a mere figment of the imagination of American businessmen.

In addition there were important economic considerations which arose from the fact that the mobilization would only be partial. There would remain a large civilian sector in which the maintenance of the inducement to invest, incentives, and rewards for efficiency would still be important. Likewise unusually large profits would still, *prima facie*, indicate a line of business in which an expansion of capacity would be desirable; but an excess profits tax tends to discourage investment in such lines, both by reducing the ability of firms engaged in them to finance investment from undistributed profits and by reducing the rate of return. Under conditions of total mobilization the problem is not important, for resources are allocated mainly by direct controls, but in 1950 it remained of importance.

Despite all the objections of the business world, the majority of the Committee stuck to their guns, and refused to allow consideration of the alternative schemes for a flat rate 'defence profits tax' proposed by the NAM and CED or the more drastic version[2] submitted by Professor Smithies on behalf of a group of Harvard economists. The bill (H.R.9827) reported by the Ways and Means Committee provided that the 'base' for computation of excess profits was to be 85 per cent[3] of the average for the three most profitable years of 1946 to 1949 inclusive, or else 12 per cent of the first $5 million of invested capital, 10 per cent on the next $5 million, and 8 per cent on the rest. The rate of tax on excess profits so defined was to be 75 per cent gross, provided that the effective rate of tax on the whole of a corporation's profits was not to exceed 67 per cent.

Introducing the bill in the House of Representatives on 4 December, Doughton denied that it was unreasonably harsh towards business, and said that the Committee had adopted a number of safeguards to provide 'a milder and more moderate bill'.[4] He replied to the charge that an excess profits tax would encourage wasteful expenditures with an expression of faith in the patriotism of the

[1] See Chapter VI supra.

[2] For an ordinary corporate profits tax rate of 60 per cent.

[3] A proposal that the base should be 75 per cent of profits for the years in question was rejected by the Ways and Means Committee by 12 votes to 12. *New York Times*, 29 November 1950.

[4] *Congressional Record*, Vol. XCVI, p. 16081.

nation's businessmen. The tone of the debate was angry and bitter in marked contrast to the debate on the Revenue Act. Reed made a violent attack on the bill and the means used to pass it. He said: ' "Make haste to waste" is the program of the present Democratic party. "Nothing succeeds like excess" seems to be the motto.'[1] He assailed the bill as being inspired by the C.I.O. and called on the House to recommit the bill to show that it was not dominated by the C.I.O. Most of the other Republicans in the House took their cue from Reed; for instance, Representative Woodruff declared 'It (i.e. the bill) is the result of hysteria . . . it is an excess politics bill.'[2]

The supporters of the bill based their case on equity and ethics rather than attempting to prove that the excess profits tax was economically superior to other methods of taxing corporate profits. Representative Mills, in reply to some of the charges made against the bill, defended the credit of 85 per cent of base year profits on the grounds that profits in 1946 to 1949 had been extremely high because of special factors, and so could not be considered 'normal'. As for the inflationary effect of the tax, he held that businessmen would not waste even the 25 cents out of the dollar that would come out of net profits.[3] The excess profits tax would be difficult to pass on in higher prices; in a situation approximating to orthodox perfect or imperfect competition an increase in tax on profits cannot be passed on to final purchasers at all in the short run; under oligopolistic conditions it would be possible to pass on some of the tax if the price before the tax increase was below that which would maximize joint profits. However, an excess profits tax would be more difficult to pass on than an ordinary profits tax because of its higher marginal rate (in 1950, when the rate proposed was 75 per cent, the increase in profits before tax would have to have been four times as great as the desired increase in profits after tax if the firm's base profits were such as to render it liable to the excess profits tax).

The motion to recommit the bill was rejected by 252 votes to 145, with two Democrats and eight Republicans crossing party lines. The contrast with the debates in August and September was striking; then the more enthusiastic supporters of the excess profits tax made the running, with most of its opponents lying low and saying nothing. Between then and December a marked change in the political atmosphere had occurred.

---

[1] *Congressional Record*, Vol. XCVI, p. 16083.
[2] Ibid., p. 16128.   [3] Ibid., pp. 16129–30.

The Senate Finance Committee took up the bill promptly. Millikin stated that he felt bound as a matter of good faith to do what he could to get the bill passed.[1] Secretary Snyder requested the Finance Committee to reduce the credit from 85 per cent of base year profits to 75 per cent, in order to increase the revenue yield.[2] The A.F.L. and C.I.O. reiterated the advice they had given to the Ways and Means Committee, that the rate should be sufficiently high and the credit sufficiently low to yield a revenue of between $6 and $7 billion. The most important amendments made by the Finance Committee were to cut the maximum effective rate to 60 per cent and to increase the ordinary corporation profits tax to 47 per cent with effect from 1 January 1951. Senator George explained that the reduction in the maximum effective rate was made because of the difficulty of devising adequate relief for growing firms. The lower maximum effective rate combined with the higher rate on all corporate profits would yield about the same revenue as the House version, but would distribute the burden more equitably between firms.[3] The bill passed the Senate with little controversy, in large part because Millikin supported the bill instead of opposing it bitterly as his opposite number in the House had done. O'Mahoney thanked the Finance Committee for having brought forward an excess profits tax bill; he said that although he thought the bill inadequate, he would support it as the best that could be got.[4] The bill was passed by a voice vote.

The Conference version was similar to that passed by the Senate except that the maximum effective rate was set at 62 per cent and the termination date was set at 30 June 1953. It was approved by the Senate on 22 December and by the House on 1 January. The President signed it on 3 January, and issued a statement in which he said that the Congress and its committees had acted with commendable speed, but added that the Congress might have been 'overly liberal' in its concern for corporations in special circumstances, and warned that in due course he would submit recommendations for further tax increases.[5] Passage of the Excess Profits Tax Act coincided with

[1] *New York Times*, 25 November 1950.
[2] *Annual Report of the Secretary of the Treasury for the year ending 30 June 1951*, p. 428.
[3] *Congressional Record*, Vol. XCVI, p. 16768.
[4] Ibid., pp. 16805–6.
[5] The text of the statement is printed in the *Annual Report of the Secretary of the Treasury for the year ending 30 June 1951*, p. 439.

passage of the other piece of major financial legislation dealt with after the election, the Second Supplemental Appropriation Act. It carried a total of $19,841 million, of which $16,785 million was for the Department of Defense, $1,835 million for the General Services Administration for stock-piling, and most of the remainder for the Atomic Energy Commission. A dispute about the provision of $1,500,000 for a power line in Virginia caused some delay, but the bill was signed into law on 6 January 1951.

The increases in tax rates enacted in 1950, in conjunction with the increase in revenue that resulted from rising incomes and profits, and the fall in expenditure, were adequate to offset the increase in defence expenditure until well into 1951.[1] The impact of rearmament on the economy was greater than indicated by expenditures in this period because of the effect of the placing of contracts, which preceded expenditure by a wide margin. In fiscal 1951 the value of contracts for 'hard' goods placed by the Department of Defense totalled $26,054 million, compared with expenditures of $5,173 million.[2] The surplus in the administrative budget in fiscal 1951 was $3,510 million, compared with the deficit of $5,133 million that had been estimated in January 1950. Declines in expenditure accounted for $2·3 billion of the difference: expenditure for supporting farm prices declined by $1·6 billion because of the rise in farm prices induced by the war, and expenditures for housing were $700 million below estimate because of smaller purchases and larger sales of mortgages by FNMA. Of the rise in revenue, it can be estimated that about $3 billion was the result of the increases in tax rates and the remainder the result of the rise in personal incomes and profits above the levels assumed in January 1950.[3]

In the second half of 1950 the most important sources of inflationary pressure were private consumption and inventory accumulation in the private sector, not the operations of the government. For

[1] See data in Department of Commerce, *U.S. Income and Output*, 1959, Table III-2.

[2] Department of Defense, printed in Joint Economic Committee, *Hearings on the Economic Report of the President*, 1959, pp.705-7.

[3] From the data in Table 19 supra, allowing for the fact that the corporation profits tax was increased with effect from 1 July 1950, not 1 January 1950 as the Treasury had recommended, and that the excess profits tax applied to only one-quarter of 1950 profits. Allowance must also be made for the rise in incomes and profits in fiscal 1951 above the levels assumed in their August 1950 estimates.

fiscal and monetary policy these two components of demand were as horses that had already bolted. But because of the sensitivity of the yield of the Federal tax structure to changes in the level of money incomes and of the promptness with which tax rates were raised, the fiscal operations of the government exercised a considerable restraining effect, notwithstanding the beginning of rearmament, on the inflationary pressure resulting from the increase in demand[1] elsewhere in the economy.

It was generally agreed in late 1950 that adequate taxation was the most important of the measures that could be taken to minimize the inflationary effect of rearmament. The tax increases enacted were prompt and generally adequate, though the suitability of the excess profits tax in a 'mixed economy' that is partly military and partly civilian was not very carefully investigated. Its supporters based their case on equity and ethics, the need to prevent business from making undue profits out of the war and rearmament, rather than any superiority of the excess profits tax as a means of reducing investment in the corporate sector or reducing the consumption by profit receivers. But serious problems remained at the end of 1950; there were signs that the 'buying spree' was beginning again under the impact of the Chinese intervention in the Korean war, which raised once more the spectre of prolonged and possibly extended conflict; the price increases that had already occurred would doubtless lead to claims for wage increases and might initiate a spiralling cost inflation; and the harshness of the opposition to the excess profits in the House of Representatives was an ominous portent of what was likely to happen when further tax increases were called for in 1951.

[1] That orthodox demand inflation was an important cause of the increase in the price level is suggested by the increase in corporate profits that occurred relative to national income in the second half of 1950. Corporate profits before tax, minus the inventory valuation adjustment, amounted to 15·6 per cent of national income in the third and fourth quarters of 1950, compared with 13·3 per cent and 14·2 per cent in the first and second quarters of 1950 respectively and 12·9 per cent, 14·7 per cent, 12·9 per cent, and 12·2 per cent in 1949, 1951, 1952, and 1953 respectively. Calculated from data in Department of Commerce, *U.S. Income and Output*, 1959, Table I–9.

CHAPTER IX

THE FINANCE OF REARMAMENT, 1951–1952

THE principal economic problem faced by the United States in 1951 was how to carry through a massive rearmament programme quickly and with the minimum of inflation, in circumstances short of all-out war. In the ambiguous 'betwixt-and-between' situation that existed during the Korean war, controls that interfered drastically with the economic freedom of individuals and firms were less acceptable than they had been during World War II. Drastic increases in taxation were also less acceptable than they would be under conditions of total war when the very survival of the nation might depend on the laying aside of personal and sectional interests. The political situation was especially difficult in that the unity that had followed the American intervention in Korea had worn off. The intervention of the Chinese which had driven the United Nations back to the 38th Parallel faced the United States with the choice of accepting a stalemate of unknown duration that was costly in lives and resources, or taking the appalling risks of extending the war to the Chinese mainland and possibly to Russia too. Since there appeared no way out of this unpleasant situation except retreat, it is not surprising that a mood of frustration with the war spread among large sections of the nation.[1]

The bitterness of those who opposed the conduct of the war spilled over into their attitudes to the economic policies connected with it. This was no carefully thought out, logical approach, but a mood of resentment against the conduct of the war and everything connected with it. Those who opposed further tax increases most vigorously were generally those who were most vociferous in demanding action to 'break the stalemate' and 'no appeasement', phrases which if they meant anything at all in terms of policy meant an extension of the conflict, with even greater demands on resources. The vehemence of the Republican opposition in the House of

---

[1] For this mood, which opposed the policy pursued but was unwilling to accept the alternatives of all-out war or retreat, see S. Lubell, *The Future of American Politics* (New York, 1952); and S. Lubell, *The Revolt of the Moderates* (New York, 1956).

Representatives to the Excess Profits Tax bill in November and December 1950 was the first manifestation of the effects of this resentment in arousing opposition to tax increases.[1]

THE BUDGET OF JANUARY 1951

In the Budget submitted in January 1951, the President estimated that expenditures in fiscal 1952 would be $24 billion higher than in the current year (fiscal 1951) with a deficit, at existing rates of tax, of $16,456 million. In the State of the Union Message, the Budget Message, and again in the Economic Report, the President recommended tax increases large enough to make good the deficit. But before examining the details of the proposed tax increases, it will be convenient to consider the expenditure side of the Budget, since this was very controversial and figured prominently in the debates on tax policy.

Expenditure for 'military services' was estimated to rise from $20,994 million in fiscal 1951 to $41,421 million in fiscal 1952; and expenditure for 'international security and foreign relations' was estimated to rise from $4,726 million to $7,461 million. Expenditure for all functions other than military defence, foreign aid, and interest was estimated at $15,768 million in fiscal 1951 and $16,815 million in fiscal 1952. But in order to allow completely for the increases in expenditure that were the direct result of rearmament, certain important items must be deducted from the other budget categories. Expenditures for 'defense production' and 'direct controls' (Finance, Commerce, Industry category); 'merchant marine' (Transportation and Communication); 'atomic energy' (Natural Resources) and 'civil defense' and 'defense housing' (Housing and Community Development) were so closely related to rearmament that it is proper to exclude them from the domestic civilian categories in considering the categories of expenditure which could be reduced without hindering rearmament. Expenditure under the above heads was estimated at $1,335 million in fiscal 1951 and $3,489 million in fiscal 1952. If this expenditure is treated as being for defence, then total estimated expenditure in fiscal 1951 for purposes other than defence, foreign aid, and interest was $14,433 million, and the

---

[1] This was before the disasters on the Korean battle-front in the winter of 1950–1, but the bitterness sprang from much the same causes. See the argument about the 1950 elections and the opposition to the excess profits tax in Chapter VIII, *supra*.

corresponding total in the estimates for fiscal 1952 was $13,326 million. The latter figure was based on the assumption that increases in postage rates would reduce the Post Office deficit. Since this was contingent on Congressional enactment in the 1951 session of legislation to increase postage rates, the item should be in estimating expenditures from the standpoint of January 1951. From this it emerges that the budget estimate for domestic civilian expenditure, other than interest (on the definition suggested above) for fiscal 1952 was $747 million less than the estimate for the current year (fiscal 1951).

A similar conclusion emerges from a study of the estimates of expenditure for public works.[1] When the estimates of expenditure by the Atomic Energy Commission, the Civil Defense Administration, the General Services Administration (mainly for the dispersal of government facilities), the Reconstruction Finance Corporation (whose increase in expenditure was ascribed mainly to the finance of 'underground structures'), T.V.A.,[2] and the Federal Security Agency[3] are deducted, the residual, which represented expenditure for public works other than those connected with defence, amounted to $2,079 million in fiscal 1951 and $1,747 million in fiscal 1952. An increase in expenditure for public works by the State Department of $73·2 million can also be deducted, since this was described as 'mainly foreign' and hence could not add directly to the demand for goods and services within the United States.

Total expenditure for civil purposes and expenditure for civil public works were thus estimated to be lower in fiscal 1952 than in fiscal 1951. Objection may be made to excluding foreign aid, since many American critics, both then and subsequently, tended to lump it with domestic civil expenditure as an appropriate field for cuts. But the principal purpose of foreign aid was to improve the strategic position of the United States, both through strengthening the ability of allies to defend themselves and by rendering less likely the

[1] The details are taken from the *Budget of the United States for the year ending 30 June 1952*, pp. 982-93.

[2] Most of the expansion of T.V.A.'s electricity generating capacity was used to meet the needs of the Atomic Energy Commission, whose consumption of T.V.A. power rose eleven-fold between 1950 and 1955: Tennessee Valley Authority, *A Short History of the Tennessee Valley Authority* (Knoxville, 1956).

[3] The expenditure was mainly for schools and hospitals in 'Federally impacted' areas, i.e. areas where there had been an influx of Federal employees (military and civilian) and their families as a result of rearmament.

emergence of situations which would require the use of American forces.

But although the budget estimated that expenditure for domestic civil functions would be lower in fiscal 1952 than in 1951, it was greeted by a storm of criticism. Senator Byrd said the budget represented 'the height of irresponsibility' that he had experienced during his eighteen years in the Congress in that no attempt had been made to curtail expenditures for 'non-essential' purposes and that the Administration had renewed its support for 'socialistic schemes'.[1] His Republican opposite number, Senator Bridges, was equally vehement; finding it 'shocking' that the President should recommend the provision of funds for 'unnecessary' items like Federal grants-in-aid for education and the St. Lawrence Seaway, declared: 'If the President won't be realistic, the Congress will.'[2]

There was much sharp criticism of the 'socialism' contained in the Budget. The Chairman of the Republican National Committee described it as 'a socialistic plan in the name of defense'.[3] and the Council of State Chambers of Commerce expressed similar views.[4] The increase in expenditure resulting from proposed legislation was estimated at $1,609 million. The expansion of defence production, administration of direct controls, defence housing, and the dispersal of government facilities, all part of the rearmament drive or arising directly from it, accounted for $1,268 million. The remainder, made up of grants-in-aid to states for education, aid to medical education, grants-in-aid for local health services, and the construction of the St. Lawrence Seaway and the Hells Canyon Dam, was estimated at $341 million in fiscal 1952. The amounts budgeted for the St. Lawrence Seaway and the Hells Canyon Dam were but small first instalments of the total cost that would have to be met in ensuing years if these projects were started. But even allowing for this, it cannot be argued that the amount of money in the 'Fair-Deal' proposals was large enough to make much of a direct impact on the degree of inflation in the economy. Their importance lay in their being as red rags to the Right-wing Congressional bulls, and were ill-advised in view of the need to gain Congressional support for coherent anti-inflationary budget policy. There was little chance indeed that such policies as Federal grants-in-aid to the states for education which the Congress had rejected in 1949–50 would fare better after the

---

[1] *New York Times*, 16 January 1951. [2] Ibid. [3] Ibid., 17 January 1951.
[4] Statement on 17 January, reported in the *New York Times*, 18 January 1951.

elections of 1950, and their inclusion in the Budget produced nothing in return for the commotion and ill-feeling to which they gave rise. Senators Douglas and Humphrey urged that certain 'Fair-Deal' programmes be eliminated from the Budget,[1] and if Humphrey would not support them there was small chance that anyone else in the Congress would do so.

The controversy over appropriations in 1951 was prolonged and vigorous, but as always the cuts achieved were not commensurate with the sound and fury. The Administration requested regular appropriations of $81,147 million, and the amount actually voted was $78,911 million. Not all the cuts reduced expenditures below what they would otherwise have been; for example, the appropriation for the Veterans' Administration was reduced by $483 million on the ground that claims for pensions and rehabilitation benefits might be expected to decline. Had they done so, the funds could not legally have been spent even if appropriated, and if claims did not decline the funds would have to be provided by a supplemental appropriation.[2]

The controversies over expenditures caused long delays in the passage of the appropriation bills. A particular cause was the dispute between the House and Senate over the 'Jensen rider', which provided that no agency might fill more than one-quarter of the vacancies occurring in its staff until its total staff had been reduced to four-fifths of that provided for in the Budget for fiscal 1952. The rider was attached to the Labor-Federal Security Agency, Interior, Agriculture, State-Commerce-Justice, and Independent Offices appropriation bills. The Labor-Federal Security Agency bill was the first bill containing the rider to reach the Senate; the Senate Appropriations Committee rejected the rider, but on the Floor Senator Ferguson succeeded in attaching a substitute (the 'Ferguson rider') which would reduce by 10 per cent the funds for personal services. On 11 July the Conference Committee reported a version which did not contain the Jensen rider, but Jensen and his supporters were obdurate, and on the following day the House voted by 222 to 169 to insist on the inclusion of the rider. Not until 16 August was a compromise worked out which the House would accept. Further delays were caused by the attempt of the more extreme opponents

---

[1] *New York Times*, 5 February 1951.

[2] This is what happened: additional funds for the VA in fiscal 1952 were provided by the Third Supplemental Appropriation Act of 1952.

of Secretary Acheson's policy to force his resignation by deleting provision for his salary.[1]

Although much of the sound and fury over expenditure was merely a rationalization of hostility to increased tax rates,[2] it would be erroneous to write off all demands for cuts in expenditures in this way. The Joint Committee on the Economic Report expressed themselves strongly on the point; because of the size of the national debt, they declared, deficit financing for the rearmament programme could not be contemplated without inviting 'the crack-up of the American system'.[3] The majority of the Committee concluded that 'the defense garment should be cut according to the revenue cloth'[4] and that increased military appropriations should not be voted unless adequate tax increases were in sight. Senators Benton and Douglas dissented from this, and Benton's warning against making the defence programme contingent on the 'legislative jockeying' involved in the passage of a tax bill[5] proved to be very well founded indeed. In an appendix to their report the Committee suggested economies which were estimated to save $2,035 million in a full year; they ranged from collecting uniforms from discharged soldiers instead of allowing them to be kept, to abolishing the requirement in the Taft-Hartley Act which required approval in an election conducted by the National Labour Relations Board of employees concerned before a 'union shop' agreement could be lawfully signed, in order to save the expense of holding such elections which the unions always won.[6]

The Administration did not allow the other side of the debate about public expenditure to go by default. The Council of Economic Advisers observed in their Report in January 1951:

'Because many of these services under discussion are public rather than private in nature, it may seem easier to curtail them rather than curtail non-essential private activity and spending. But in a national emergency, the question of who spends the dollar, while not unimportant, should be subordinated to the larger question of what use of resources will do most to maximize our total strength. Non-

---

[1] The terms of the amendment provided that no salary should be paid to Acheson (who was not designated by name but in an elliptical way) unless he had again been confirmed to his office by the Senate.

[2] It was frequently argued that tax legislation should not be taken up until appropriations had been dealt with.

[3] *S. Rept. No. 210*, 82nd Cong., 1st Sess., p. 1.

[4] Ibid., p. 15. [5] Ibid., p. 15, fn. 1. [6] Appendix 3, pp. 86–95.

essential government outlays should by all means be cut; but essential public outlays should have priority over non-essential private demands.'[1]

President Truman attacked the 'Budget-cutters' with his customary vigour, describing the assertion in an article that appeared in *Reader's Digest* that waste and extravagance were rampant in the Federal government as 'a pack of lies' based on 'butterfly statistics' (i.e. so meaningless that they could have been pulled out of the air with a butterfly net). He declared that expressions of fear of 'spending our way into bankruptcy' were merely a bogy flaunted year after year to frighten the electorate, and warned against 'pound foolish and penny wise' economies.[2]

In the end the great Budget-cutting drive did not produce important results, not so much because of the Administration's political strength as because Federal expenditures which did not benefit anybody other than government employees were not large enough to make possible economically significant reductions in government expenditure. If such reductions were required, either expenditures which benefit politically powerful groups had to be cut severely, or the defence expenditure had to be cut. Perhaps the last word on the argument that inflation could be dealt with by reducing 'spending' was had by Senator O'Mahoney: 'Demobilize the Army, demobilize the Navy, take the Air Force out of the air, then of course it would be possible to stop the spending which is creating our problems.'[3]

THE ADMINISTRATION'S TAX POLICY IN 1951

The primary aim of the Administration's tax policy in 1951 was to secure the prompt enactment of tax increases large enough to eliminate the deficit that was in prospect for fiscal 1952 if defence expenditures rose as expected and tax rates were not raised. The President said in his Economic Report:

'The real economic cost of this defense effort is that we must work harder, reduce consumption, and forego improvements in farm, business, and household equipment. This cost cannot be put off into the future. It must be paid by the people now, in one way or another, and it should be paid through taxation, in the manner determined

---

[1] *Economic Report of the President, January 1951*, p. 95.

[2] Speech on the occasion of the laying of the foundation stone of the new General Accounting Office building, Washington, D.C., 11 September 1951. The text of the speech is printed in the *New York Times*, 12 September 1951.

[3] *Congressional Record*, Vol. XCVII, p. 12026.

by the Congress, and not through the uncontrolled and inequitable incidence of inflation.'[1]

Taxation and inflation were regarded as alternative ways of paying for the rearmament; in the Message to Congress presenting his tax policy, the President said: 'Whatever we do about taxes, the amount of goods available for consumers to buy is only going to be what is left over after defense demands are met.'[2] There was to be no question of holding down defence expenditure as an anti-inflationary measure.

The policy recommended was rather more ambitious than the mere offsetting of increases in government expenditure by equal increases in revenue. Since in January 1951 it was estimated that there would be a deficit of $2,698 million in the 'conventional' budget for fiscal 1951, the prevention of a deficit in fiscal 1952 would require an increase in revenue nearly $3 billion greater than the increase in expenditure. The Chairman of the Council of Economic Advisers explained that the policy of 'pay-as-you-go' referred to the 'administrative' budget;[3] in the conditions prevailing in 1951 there would therefore be a substantial surplus in the 'cash' budget if the Administration's recommendation was accepted. Even allowing for some offsetting of increased taxation by reduced private saving, the tax increase envisaged should have prevented the increase in defence expenditure from having any net inflationary effect. An increase in revenue equal to the increase in expenditure would probably still lead to some inflationary effect since some of the tax increase would be offset through reduced saving. The policy of 'pay-as-you-go' recommended by the Administration, which could be and was presented as being the policy of financial rectitude by standards far antedating the theory of compensatory fiscal policy, would have results very much in accord with compensatory policy if carried out in the circumstances foreseen in early 1951.

The President recommended that tax increases to yield $10 billion in a full year be enacted forthwith, and that increases to cover the remainder of the estimated deficit be enacted as soon as the necessary studies had been made of possible additional sources of revenue. He proposed in his Tax Message that $4 billion should be obtained from higher personal income taxes, $3 billion from taxes on cor-

[1] *Economic Report of the President, January 1951*, p. 17.

[2] *H. Doc. No. 53*, 82nd Cong., 1st Sess.; also printed in the *Annual Report of the Secretary of the Treasury for the year ending 30 June 1951*, pp. 439–42.

[3] Joint Committee on the Economic Report, *Hearings on the Economic Report of the President*, 1951, p. 32.

porate profits, and $3 billion from excises.[1] But hopes for a quick tax increase as in 1950 were not fulfilled. No sooner had the President requested it than Speaker Rayburn said that it could not be done;[2] and when President Truman declared at his news conference that the Ways and Means Committee's decision to consider all possible sources of new revenue would endanger the effectiveness of the policy to control inflation, Doughton replied that extensive hearings were necessary if the Committee was to do an adequate and conscientious job of work.[3]

On 5 February Secretary Snyder presented the Treasury's detailed proposals to the Ways and Means Committee. These were that each rate of the personal income tax should be increased by 4 percentage points, the new minimum and maximum rates being 24 per cent and 95 per cent instead of the existing rates of 20 per cent and 91 per cent respectively. It was proposed that the corporation profits tax should be raised by 8 percentage points, to 33 per cent of the first $25,000 of taxable profits and 55 per cent of the remainder, to raise the rate of tax on long-term capital gains to $37\frac{1}{2}$ per cent (instead of 25 per cent) and to increase the rates of certain excise taxes. Of these the most important were spirits, beer, and wines, cigars and cigarettes; petrol, to be taxed at 3¢ instead of $1\frac{1}{2}$¢ a gallon; cars, to be taxed at 20 per cent of the manufacturer's price instead of 7 per cent; and other consumer durables, to be taxed at 25 per cent of the manufacturer's price instead of 10 per cent. The effect of these proposed tax increases is shown in the following tables:

TABLE 20

Yield of Proposed Tax Increases

		Yield in Full Year ($ million)
Personal Income Tax (incl. Capital Gains)		3,845
Corporation Profits Tax		3,280
Excise Taxes		3,252
of which Beer, Wines, Spirits	671	
Cigarettes and Cigars	547	
Petrol	606	
Cars	771	
Other Consumers' Durables	549	
Total		10,377

Source: Annual Report of the Secretary of the Treasury for the year ending 30 June 1951, pp. 479–481, Tables I–IV.

[1] *Annual Report of the Secretary of the Treasury for the year ending 30 June 1951,* pp. 440–1.

[2] *New York Times,* 4 February 1951.   [3] *New York Times,* 16 February 1951.

TABLE 21

Effective Rates of Tax under the Treasury's Proposal and under Existing Law

Effective Rate (%)

Adjusted Gross Income	Single Man		Married with Two Children	
	Present	Proposed	Present	Proposed
$1,000	8·0	9·6	Nil	Nil
$2,000	14·0	15·8	Nil	Nil
$3,000	16·3	19·5	4·0	4·8
$5,000	18·9	22·4	10·4	12·5
$10,000	24·4	28·1	15·9	19·0
$50,000	52·8	56·7	37·8	41·6

Source: Annual Report of the Secretary of the Treasury for the year ending 30 June 1951, pp. 484–5, Table VII.

TABLE 22

Allocation of the Proposed Increase in Income Tax by Income Brackets

Adjusted Gross Income	Increase in Tax Liability ($ Million)
Under $5,000	1,649·0
$5,000 and over	2,195·6
Total	3,844·6

Source: Senate Finance Committee, *Hearings on H.R.4473*, 82nd Cong., 1st Sess., p. 135.

In addition the Treasury recommended the deduction at source of income tax on dividends and interest; the elimination of certain revenue losing provisions in the Excess Profits Tax Act; the reduction of the depletion allowance for oil, gas, and sulphur to 15 per cent and for non-metallic minerals to 5 per cent; an increase in the rates and reduction of the exemptions of the estate and gift tax, as proposed in 1950; the elimination of the exemption from Federal income tax of the interest on state and local bonds issued subsequently, and the taxation of the undistributed profits of co-operatives and savings-and-loan associations.[1]

The tax increases proposed by the Treasury were thus substantial and comprehensive. No important sector of the economy escaped attention, and all the important internal taxes other than the excises on transport and communications were to be increased. The one widely canvassed tax increase that was not recommended was the

[1] Savings-and-loan associations are similar in function and nature to building societies.

general sales tax. The proposals provided the material for vigorous political controversy, both because the general increases in tax rates would if enacted make an appreciable impact on the members of most of the important groups in the nation, and because certain special groups benefited from privileges and exemptions that the Administration desired to eliminate.

When the Administration's case was presented to the Ways and Means Committee, the arguments used were mainly those outlined above,[1] the need to cover increased expenditure by increased revenue in order to prevent, or at any rate minimize, inflation. Secretary Snyder contended further that increases in tax rates would give people confidence that inflation would be controlled, and so would increase their willingness to save, which would further help to restrain inflation. Mr. Eric Johnston, Economic Stabilization Administrator, argued that since the supply of consumers' durables would have to be curtailed any way because they competed with defence production for materials, their price would rise even in the absence of a tax increase; in that case the increase would accrue in the first instance as increased profits to the manufacturers of consumers' durables; if these increased profits were used for expenditures of any kind, the result would be an addition to effective demand compared to what would happen if the increase in prices accrued to the Treasury as a result of increases in the excise tax rates.[2]

During the hearings, Chairman Doughton remarked: 'I think we all realize that we are approaching this problem of taxation from two standpoints. One to prevent inflation and the other to raise additional revenue to balance the budget.'[3]

Even within the Administration these were looked on as distinct reasons for a tax increase, instead of balancing the budget being in the prevailing circumstances one of the means of restraining inflation. In a discussion with one of the members of the Committee, Representative Mason, who drew attention to the argument that increases in taxation borne by the upper income groups would fall on savings to a greater extent than tax increases on the lower income groups and to that extent would be less effective in restraining inflation, Secretary Snyder replied: '. . . the dollar taken from the upper

---

[1] See pp. 156-7, supra.

[2] House of Representatives, Committee on Ways and Means, *Hearings on Revenue Revision*, 1951, p. 321.

[3] Ibid., p. 334.

bracket is also anti-inflationary in that it does prevent deficit financing.'[1] Mason then asked the Secretary whether the corporation profits tax was inflationary or deflationary, in general, to which he replied: 'It is revenue raising.'[2]

There is nothing to suggest that Secretary Snyder's view was influenced by the monetary effects of a deficit, the impairment of the ability of the monetary authorities to conduct a restrictive credit policy. He was opposed to an increase in the rates of interest on the national debt[3] and hence to a restrictive monetary policy. The explanation was surely that to the Secretary of the Treasury a balanced budget and 'sound finance' were one and the same thing; in the circumstances of early 1951 this indicated a substantial increase in tax rates just as the theory of compensatory fiscal policy did. 'Pay-as-you-go' thus commanded the support of all in the Administration, whether they analysed the problem in terms of the theory of compensatory fiscal policy or in terms of the traditional concept of 'sound finance'.

THE ATTITUDES OF THE MAJOR GROUPS TOWARDS TAX INCREASES IN 1951

The decision of the Ways and Means Committee to hold full hearings on the proposed tax increases meant that there would be ample opportunity for all groups to present their views, and they took advantage of the opportunity. The great economic interest groups of business (representing the upper income groups generally) and the trade unions, who on matters of taxation represent the interests of receivers of moderate-to-small earned incomes, expressed their views energetically, as did various smaller groups who felt their interests to be adversely affected by the tax increases proposed by the Treasury.

The various groups which presented their views to the Ways and Means Committee and the Finance Committee found common ground on two points; they all expressed approval of the principle of 'pay-as-you-go' and all objected to some part of the recommendations made by the Treasury. Under these recommendations every-

---

[1] Ibid., p. 83.   [2] Ibid., p. 84.

[3] He told the Ways and Means Committee that such an increase would raise the debt interest charge, which would have to be paid by higher taxation, or else would require inflationary deficit financing. House of Representatives, Committee on Ways and Means, *Hearings on Revenue Revision*, 1951, p. 41.

M

body, except for the very poor who neither smoked nor drank, would have to do part of the paying. The refrain which was common to the testimony of all groups from the NAM to the C.I.O. was that their members were doing their fair share of the paying already, and that to impose on them such large increases in their burdens would be unfair, economically dangerous, or both.

The representatives of the trade unions approved the Treasury's recommendations for higher taxes on corporate profits and for the closing of 'loopholes', but opposed the increase in the excise taxes and the form in which it was proposed to increase the income tax. Mr. Elder, on behalf of the A.F.L., claimed that the latter was inequitable in that taxpayers in the lower brackets would have their tax liabilities increased by 20 per cent whereas taxpayers in the higher brackets would have their liabilities increased by a much smaller percentage.[1] Mr. Ruttenberg of the C.I.O. proposed that the personal income tax rates should be raised by an average of four percentage points, to be achieved by an increase of two percentage points in the lowest bracket rate and steeper increases in the higher bracket. All the trade union representatives denied that the lower income groups had any 'excess purchasing power'[2] or 'loose money floating around'[3] which was contributing to inflation. Ruttenberg held that the increases in the excise taxes on consumers' durables would 'ration' these scarce goods to 'the privileged class with enough income to pay the price plus the excise tax'.[4] Representative Eberharter asked Elder whether it was likely that substantial increases in the rates of taxes borne by the lower income groups would cause a wave of demands for higher wages; Elder replied that this would be 'in accord with experience'.[5] The trade unions held that although taxes should be increased, it should be at the expense of the upper income groups and profit receivers as much as possible. Of all the possible tax changes that were mooted, it was the general sales tax to which the unions objected most strongly, however.

On the other hand, nearly all the organizations representing the interests of business and the upper income groups were in favour of a general sales tax as an alternative to some or all of the increases recommended by the Treasury. There were two variants, the 'manu-

---

[1] Ibid., p. 481. This was exactly the reverse of the argument used by the unions in 1947–8 when tax reduction was under consideration.

[2] House of Representatives, Committee on Ways and Means, *Hearings on Revenue Revision*, 1951, p. 568.

[3] Ibid., p. 604.   [4] Ibid., p. 606.   [5] Ibid., p. 496.

facturers' excise tax' and the 'retail sales tax'. The former, levied at a uniform *ad valorem* rate on all goods manufactured and sold in the United States with the exception (under most schemes) of food and medicines, would be collected from the manufacturer and based on his price. The retail sales tax would be levied on retailers on the basis of their sales, with the same exclusions as in the manufacturers' excise tax, though under a retail sales tax certain services could also be taxed. The manufacturers' excise tax was undoubtedly superior from the standpoint of administrative efficiency and convenience. It was estimated that there were about 300,000 manufacturers who would fall within its field, whereas there were about 3,000,000 retailers, each of whom would have to be checked from time to time.[1] Moreover, many states and some cities and counties levied a retail sales tax, so that it could be asserted that a Federal sales tax would be trespassing on state and local 'territory', as well as being inconvenient for retailers, who would be obliged to keep two sets of sales tax accounts. On the other hand it was argued that the manufacturers' excise tax would be 'pyramided', that is to say, the manufacturer's price plus the tax would be taken as the base to which wholesalers and retailers would apply their usual margins; if this were so, the increase in the price paid by the consumer would be greater than the tax, the difference accruing to the wholesaler and retailer. The supporters of the manufacturers' excise tax claimed that competition among distributors would prevent 'pyramiding'; this was probably true in the long run, but would be less likely in a situation of excess demand such as existed early in 1951.

The general sales tax was supported as an alternative to other possible tax increases on two main grounds; firstly, opposition to increased taxes on profits and large incomes, both for the obvious reason and because of the harmful economic effects believed to flow from such tax increases; and secondly, for industries whose products were the subject of increases in excise taxes recommended by the Treasury, a general sales tax at the rates commonly canvassed would have a smaller impact than the Treasury's proposed increases. This last is probably the reason why the associations of motor dealers and electrical goods manufacturers were to be found among the supporters of the general sales tax. The other supporters were

---

[1] National Association of Manufacturers to Ways and Means Committee. Effective enforcement of a retail sales tax would require 'a swarm of Treasury agents who would cover the land like locusts'. Ibid., p. 723.

the NAM, the Chambers of Commerce, and other groups representing the interests of the upper income groups and profit receivers.

The general sales tax was opposed on the ground that it imposed
a disproportionately heavy burden on those least able to bear it,
and because of cost-inflationary effects through raising prices paid
by farmers and hence raising the 'parity' prices of agricultural products, through increasing automatically those wages linked to the
cost of living index, and through stimulating wage demands by
others. The equity arguments were the most frequently heard, and
had strong support both in the Administration and in the Congress.
Chairman Doughton remarked:

'I do not think it (a general sales tax) bears any relation whatso-
ever, or very little relation, to the ability to pay. . . . In my opinion
the sentiment is overwhelmingly against it. . . . We went through
World War II without this Committee reporting out a general sales
tax. Now certainly this emergency is not as great as it was then.'[1]

In addition to opposition to the Treasury's proposed tax increases
because of the distribution of the burden between low incomes and
profits, there was much complaint from particular industries about
the proposed increases in the excise tax rates. Most attempted to
show that their product was in some way or other essential to the
defence effort. The Assistant Sales Manager of the American Re-
frigerator Co., expressing opposition to the extension of the tax to
deep-freeze units, submitted a paper entitled 'Essentiality of a Food
Freezer in a War-time Economy';[2] and the Chairman of the Taxation
Committee of the Automobile Manufacturers Association opposed
the increase in the tax on cars on the ground that the highest possible
output of cars was desirable because cars were essential to a defence
economy.[3] The trade unions concerned in these industries opposed
the tax increases on the grounds that the reduction in sales would
lead to unemployment. The General Counsel to the U.S. Brewers
Federation claimed that beer is 'an essential food'[4] and so should
not be subject to increased taxation, and the President of the union
representing brewery and distillery employees[5] asserted in a letter
to the Senate Finance Committee that 'dry' supporters were behind

---

[1] House of Representatives, Committee on Ways and Means, *Hearings on
Revenue Revision*, 1951, pp. 1837–8.
[2] Ibid., p. 2299.   [3] Ibid., p. 2206.
[4] House of Representatives, Committee on Ways and Means, op. cit., p. 2102.
[5] United Brewery, Flour, Cereal, Soft Drink and Distillery Workers of America,
C.I.O.

the proposed increases in excises on alcoholic drinks.[1] The National Tax Equality Association continued its old feud with the tax-exempt or partially tax-exempt co-operatives and mutual savings banks, and officials of state and local governments appeared in strength to oppose the withdrawal of the tax exemption from new issues of state and local bonds, both on the ground that it would be unconstitutional and because of the additional costs to state and local governments.

At the end of the hearings, Chairman Doughton complained:

'Witnesses who appeared before our Committee at the public hearings, while all for preparedness, would preface their statements by saying that while those who they represented or spoke for wanted to do their full part in producing the revenue necessary to finance emergency expenditures, they usually, with few exceptions, claimed they were paying as much or more in taxes than they should and that any additional revenue should be raised from some other source. We were not given much help as far as the other sources were concerned, except a few I believe did recommend a general sales tax.'[2]

It was not so much that there was no advice about what taxes might be raised; it was that none of the major groups would give their support to tax increases which did not fall primarily on somebody else. Both the C.I.O.'s suggestions of drastic increases in the rates of tax on large incomes and profits and the business groups' suggestions of a general sales tax were relevant in that the desired amounts of revenue could be raised from them; but neither suggestion was one which could secure general acceptance. What the hearings did reveal was that there was no possibility of a tax programme which could be generally agreed on yet would be sufficiently anti-inflationary (or revenue raising).

THE EMERGENCE OF THE REVENUE ACT

The Ways and Means Committee voted on 9 May 1951 by 13 to 12 in favour of an increase of three percentage points in each of the bracket rates of the personal income tax, rejecting a Republican proposal for a 10 per cent increase in tax liability by a straight party vote of 15 to 10.[3] On the following day the Committee voted, again by a straight party vote, in favour of an increase of five percentage points in the corporation profits tax. In an important reversal of position the Democratic members of the Committee decided at a

[1] Senate Finance Committee, *Hearings on H.R.4473*, 1951, p. 1841.
[2] House of Representatives, Committee on Ways and Means, op. cit., p. 2809.
[3] *New York Times*, 10 May 1951.

meeting on 22 May to adopt a plan put forward by Representative Eberharter for an increase of 12½ per cent in tax liability instead of the increase of three percentage points in each bracket rate, the revenue yield being about the same in each case.[1] This drew a strong protest from the Republicans, and aroused considerable criticism from conservative commentators because of the heavier burden it would impose on the upper income groups and therefore the greater likelihood that a significant part of the increased tax would be absorbed by a reduction in personal savings.[2] Shortly afterwards the Committee voted to increase the excess profits tax rate to 82 per cent gross, i.e. to retain the rate of 30 per cent net. There followed a considerable amount of manœuvring on such issues as the excise taxes on consumers' durables and the exemption of savings bank interest from deduction of tax at source, but on 15 June the Committee formally approved the draft tax bill by a vote of 19 to 6. The majority was composed of the Democratic members plus Representatives Woodruff, Kean, Holmes, and Byrnes; the other six Republicans were irreconcilably opposed.[3]

The provisions of the bill reported by the Ways and Means Committee, H.R.4473, differed in many important respects from the Treasury's recommendations. The bill provided for an increase of 12½ per cent in liability to personal income tax, with a maximum rate of 94·5 per cent on income over $80,000, with a maximum effective rate of 90 per cent. The effective rates under the House bill are compared with those under existing law (Revenue Act 1950) in the following table:

TABLE 23

Effective Rates under Existing Law and H.R.4473

Effective Rate (%)

Adjusted Gross Income	Single Man		Married, Two Children	
	Existing Law	*H.R.4473*	*Existing Law*	*H.R.4473*
$1,000	8·0	9·0	Nil	Nil
$2,000	14·0	15·0	Nil	Nil
$3,000	16·3	18·3	4·0	4·5
$5,000	18·9	21·2	10·4	11·7
$10,000	24·4	27·4	15·9	17·9
$50,000	52·8	59·4	37·8	42·5

Source: Annual Report of the Secretary of the Treasury for the year ending 30 June 1951, pp. 484–5, Table VIII.

[1] *New York Times*, 22 May 1951.
[2] See, for instance, E. H. Collins in *New York Times*, 28 May 1951.
[3] *New York Times*, 16 June 1951.

On incomes above $20,000 not eligible for 'split income' treatment the rates in H.R.4473 would have resulted in a greater tax liability than the increase proposed by the Treasury. The Treasury estimated that of the increase in tax liability (at prevailing levels of personal income) under the House bill of $2,902 million, $1,032 million, or 36 per cent, would be borne by taxpayers with adjusted gross incomes of under $5,000[1] compared with 43 per cent under the Treasury's proposal. Deduction at source of tax on dividends and interest was provided for, as was a tax reduction amounting to half of full 'income-splitting' for 'heads of households' who were not eligible for income splitting under the Revenue Act of 1948. The Treasury estimated the cost of this concession at $45 million in a full year.[2] The increases in the individual income tax were to come into effect on 1 September.

The corporation profits tax was to be increased to 30 per cent of the first $25,000 of profits and 52 per cent of the remainder. The rate of the excess profits tax was retained at 30 per cent net, but the base for the computation of excess profits was reduced to 75 per cent of profits in the base years. The increases were to apply to the whole of 1951 profits.

The bill provided for increases in the excise taxes on alcoholic liquor, cigarettes, petrol, and cars, though the increases were much smaller than the Treasury had requested. In addition it provided for the imposition of a new tax on diesel oil, and an increase in the tax on some photographic goods and sporting goods, which the Treasury had not recommended, and repealed the tax on $3\frac{1}{3}$ per cent on electricity sold by private firms, and the tax on baby powders and lotions and toilet preparations used by hairdressers and beauty parlours. Deep-freeze units and certain other consumers' durables hitherto untaxed were subjected to tax, but the excise on household appliances already subject to tax was not raised.

The bill provided for an increase in the rate of tax on long term capital gains of one-and-one-eighth percentage points, an increase of the same proportion as that in the income tax rates. The yield of this increase was more than offset by the cost of the provision under which the capital gain from the sale of a residence would be exempt

[1] Calculated from data in Senate, Committee on Finance, *Hearings on H.R.4473*, 1951, p. 135.
[2] *Annual Report of the Secretary of the Treasury for the year ending 30 June 1951*, p. 477, Table I.

if the seller bought a new *bona-fide* residence within one year and the higher cost of the latter offset the gain. This remedied a long-standing hardship in a period when property values were rising. There was also a new tax on wagering, of $50 per person employed in a wagering business and 10 per cent of the gross stakes received. There were a series of revenue-losing provisions; the Committee not only disregarded the Treasury's proposal to restrict the percentage depletion allowances, but extended them to a wide range of minerals hitherto ineligible, on the ground that the existing state of affairs discriminated against the producers of minerals that were not eligible for the allowance. Moreover, the bill contained a provision which would validate 'family partnerships' for tax purposes, along the lines of the provision inserted by the Senate but deleted in Conference in 1950.

The yield of the increases in tax rates provided in H.R.4473 was estimated by the Treasury at $6,830 million, of which $2,902 was from the increases in the rates of the individual income tax, $2,699 million from corporation profits tax and the excess profits tax, $806 million from the increases in excise tax rates, $300 million from the tax on wagering, and the remainder from miscellaneous changes such as the provision for deduction at source of tax on dividends and interest.[1] The short-fall below the Administration's recommendations was greatest in the yield of the excise taxes, which was only one-third as great as that requested. The increase in the tax on spirits was one-half of the Treasury's request, on beer one-third, and even less on cigarettes. The tax on petrol was to be increased by $\frac{1}{2}$¢ instead of $1\frac{1}{2}$¢, and the tax on cars was raised to 10 per cent instead of 20 per cent. The increase in the revenue from the personal income tax was nearly two-thirds as great as requested, and that from taxes on corporate profits five-sixths as great. When this is set beside the distribution of the increase in the personal income tax among income groups, it is clear why the writers of the *C.I.O. News* headed their article on the tax bill: 'House Framers of Tax Bill Heed Voice of the People'.[2]

When Doughton brought the bill to the Floor of the House on 20 June 1951 he spent most of his time defending the equity of its provisions. He agreed that the increase in revenue was considerably less than the Administration had requested, but 'it is, in the judgement of our Committee, as large an amount as can be safely collected

[1] *Annual Report of the Secretary of the Treasury for the year ending 30 June 1951*, p. 477, Table I.
[2] *C.I.O. News*, 28 May 1951, p. 12.

from the economy under present conditions'.[1] In the course of the debate there was a certain amount of complaint from the Democratic side of the aisle about the increases in excise taxes,[2] mild as they were, and a suggestion that the increase in the income tax should apply only to incomes above $10,000, since the man earning $2,000 or $3,000 does not really live but 'merely exists'.[3] But on the whole the Ways and Means Committee succeeded in drafting a programme of tax increases which the House Democrats would support without too much reluctance.

It aroused strong opposition on the Republican side, however. Two Republicans spoke in favour of the bill; Representative Byrnes of Wisconsin said that he supported the bill because after all the discussion there had been about what constituted sound fiscal policy, it seemed to him that there were 'two basic principles of conduct that are still sound and still honourable. The first is that one should not spend more than he can afford, and the second is that one should pay his bills'.[4] Representative Kean strongly criticized the apportionment of the burden of the tax increases under the bill, declaring it to be 'cold murder' on the upper income groups, but, since 'the Government is going to spend the money anyway'[5] as a result of the appropriations already voted, considered that under the circumstances it would be better to have a bad bill rather than no bill at all.

But apart from this the position taken by the Republicans was one of extravagant railing against 'spending', opposition to any tax increases whatever, and a denial that tax increases could make any contribution to the restraint of inflation. Both Reed and one of the wilder spirits among the Right-wing Republicans, Representative Sheehan, declared that the use of increased taxation and not cuts in government expenditure to control inflation was the work of those who 'seek to destroy the American system' (Reed)[6] or 'a socialist dream to bring on socialism without revolution' (Sheehan).[7] But most striking of all, because of his position in Congressional life, was the stand taken by the Minority Leader, Representative Joseph W. Martin:

'The Administration's contention that this tax bill is needed to

---

[1] *Congressional Record*, Vol. XCVII, p. 6894.

[2] For instance, by Representative Dingell. *Congressional Record*, Vol. XCVII, pp. 6906–7.

[3] This remark was made by Representative Sabath. Ibid., p. 6832.

[4] Ibid., p. 6963.   [5] Ibid., p. 6909.

[6] *Congressional Record*, Vol. XCVII, p. 6893.   [7] Ibid., p. 6929.

control inflation is economic voodoo talk. No set of controls and no pyramid of taxes ever devised by man will stop inflation in America when the root of the evil is government spending.

'And the only way in which we are going to stop this government spending is to stop excessive taxation and stop the borrowing. The American taxpayer is going to have to do to his government what the father does to his wasteful son—cut off the spending money.'[1]

Except for Kean and Byrnes, as mentioned above, all the Republicans who spoke expressed sentiments similar to those of Martin. Partisan bitterness, hostility to higher tax rates, and an inarticulate but none-the-less intense dislike of the changes in the role of the Federal government which were responsible for expenditures for civil purposes being higher than they were a quarter century previously thus blinded most of the House Republicans to the most elementary considerations of economics, not merely of compensatory theory but of the older principles of 'sound finance' as well. Martin and his colleagues were in the position of willing the end, rearmament (many of them advocated an even more militant policy towards Russia and China), but refusing to will the means, higher taxation to divert the resources from civil to defence uses.

The motion to recommit the bill was rejected by 220 votes to 171. One Democrat (Garmatz) voted in favour of the motion to recommit and one more (Wheeler) was paired in favour. The Virginia delegation voted unanimously for the increase, presumably because a deficit would be even more distasteful than the tax increases. Thirteen Republicans voted against the motion to recommit, namely Byrnes, Bakewell, Case, Holmes, Hope, Javits, Johnson, Morton, Norblad, Saylor, Hugh Scott, Stockman, and Tollefson.

Secretary Snyder appeared before the Senate Finance Committee on 28 June.[2] By this time the prospective increase in expenditures in fiscal 1952 and hence the deficit were not so great as had been expected in January. The estimate of total expenditure was revised from $71·6 billion to $68·4 billion. The estimate of defence expenditures was revised downwards by $3·1 billion to $44·0 billion because the delivery of goods contracted for was proving slower than had been assumed when the estimates were drawn up in January; the estimate of expenditure for defence production was revised down-

---

[1] Ibid., p. 6983.

[2] The text is printed in the *Annual Report of the Secretary of the Treasury for the year ending 30 June 1951*, pp. 464–76.

wards by $0·7 billion since the January estimate had been very tentative, made before a fully detailed programme had been drawn up; on the other hand, sales of mortgages from the FNMA portfolio had proved smaller than expected because of the rise in interest rates; net purchases of $0·2 billion were now expected in fiscal 1952 instead of net sales of $0·5 billion. The Secretary urged the Senate to enact the increases in taxation recommended by the Treasury, and in this he was supported by Mr. Johnston, the Economic Stabilization Administrator, who warned that the direct controls would not be effective for 'protracted periods' unless 'stern steps' were taken to reduce demand.[1] Johnston was uneasy about the effect of the changes in the personal income tax provided by the House bill, for he held that they would seriously impair incentives.[2] In this he had the support of the Director of Defense Mobilization, Mr. Charles E. Wilson,[3] who had said that the House bill 'had an unfortunate element of "soak the rich" in it'.[4]

In the course of the hearings before the Finance Committee the various groups tried to get the Senate to take care of the points on which the House had failed them. NAM and the other business groups again championed a general sales tax, though with little success if the remarks of members of the Committee during the hearings are any guide. Taft, whose support was necessary if there was to be any prospect of the enactment of a general sales tax, asked a number of hostile questions, such as the following about a claim that had just been made that a sales tax would have a less injurious effect on incentives than would a higher income tax: 'What difference does it make to a man whether he gets less income . . . or whether he gets more income and has to pay more for the stuff he buys. What difference does it make? I cannot see the difference in incentive.'[5] No satisfactory answer was given to the question.

The business groups criticized severely the provisions of the House bill for increases in the personal income tax; the NAM held that they made worse a progression that was already too steep,

[1] Senate, Committee on Finance, *Hearings on H.R.4473*, 1951, p. 220.
[2] Ibid., p. 228.
[3] Prior to appointment as Director of Defense Mobilization, Mr. Wilson was president of General Electric; he should not be confused with Charles E. Wilson of General Motors, Secretary of Defense under President Eisenhower.
[4] In a television interview, 'Meet the Press' on 17 June 1951. Reported in *New York Times*, 18 June 1951.
[5] Senate, Committee on Finance, op. cit., p. 343.

and savoured of Marxism.[1] The representatives of organized labour also criticized the provisions relating to the personal income tax as unfair to those in the very low income group,[2] but made their strongest attacks on the increases in the excise tax rates. They opposed with all their strength the proposals for a general sales tax, knowing well that its supporters looked to it not just as an emergency revenue raising device but as a permanent modification in the tax structure.[3] Their attitude in opposing the general sales tax was very similar to that of the business groups in opposing the excess profits tax in 1950. The unions' representatives proposed, as usual, to make up the loss of revenue entailed by their recommendations by higher taxation of profits and large incomes, both by increases in the rates and by withdrawal of exemptions and exclusions.

Exception was taken to other features of the House bill. Investors' organizations objected to the provision for the taxation at source of interest and dividends; for example, W. Jackman, giving evidence on behalf of the Investors League, Inc., described the provision as 'insulting' in that it implied that 'upright, loyal Americans' were 'crooks',[4] while the representative of a similar organization regarded it as a 'police state' method of tax collection,[5] a remarkable description indeed for an administrative technique introduced into British tax procedure by Addington. The pros and cons of the tax treatment of cooperatives and mutual insurance companies were argued again, this time with the cooperatives very much on the defensive because of the announced intention of a member of the Committee, Senator Williams, to try to persuade his colleagues to make provision in the bill for the withdrawal of their exemptions.

There was a general impression, which proved to be well founded, that the Senate Finance Committee would reduce the size of the tax increases. The Committee considered a proposal to increase the income tax by three per cent of the first $2,000 of 'residual' income (i.e. income net of all exemptions, including personal exemptions, and net of tax at existing rates) and four per cent of the remainder, but dropped it when they found that under it some middle income-

---

[1] Senate, Committee on Finance, *Hearings on H.R.4473*, 1951, p. 354.

[2] Mr. Elder, the A.F.L.'s representative, proposed that there should be no increase in the tax on the first $1,000 of taxable income. Ibid., pp. 751–2.

[3] The NAM representative gave as one of his reasons why the manufacturers' excise tax should be preferred to the retail sales tax the former's greater prospect of permanency. Ibid., p. 362.

[4] Ibid., p. 624   [5] Ibid., p. 664.

group taxpayers would be more heavily taxed than under the House bill.[1] In their report on the bill,[2] which was presented on 18 September 1951, the Finance Committee recommended that the personal income tax be increased by 11 per cent of tax liability under existing law or 8 per cent of income after tax, whichever was the smaller. The yield of this increase was estimated at $2,367 million in a full year. The Committee proposed that the corporation profits tax be increased to 27 per cent on the first $25,000 of taxable profits and 52 per cent on the remainder, a way of allocating the increase of five percentage points which would be more advantageous to smaller firms and collect slightly less revenue than the House provision. The rate of the excess profits tax was to be retained at 30 per cent net, but the provision in the House bill to cut the base to 75 per cent of profits in the base years was rejected, and the ratio of excess profits tax liability to total profits restricted to 5 per cent in the first and second years after the passage of the Act, 8 per cent in the third year, 11 per cent in the fourth, 14 per cent in the fifth, and 17 per cent in the sixth and subsequent years. The increases in taxes on corporate profits were estimated to yield $2,060 million in a full year. The only important change recommended by the Finance Committee from the provisions of the House bill relating to excise taxation was the rejection of the proposed tax on diesel fuel. The increase in the capital gains tax and the provision for the deduction at source of tax on interest and dividends were rejected. The depletion allowance was extended to a few miscellaneous minerals that were not so treated under the House bill; and retained earnings of cooperatives not allocated to members were to be taxed at the rate applicable to corporate profits.

Before the bill was reported by the Finance Committee, but after it had become common knowledge that the revenue yield of the Committee's version would be considerably less than that of the House bill, a group of Senate Democrats, among whom Humphrey and Douglas were the most prominent, let it be known that they would bring forward amendments to stiffen the bill when it reached the Floor of the Senate. In this they were supported by the Administration. In a letter to the Vice-President, who read it at the beginning of the debate on 20 September, the President exhorted the Senate to increase the rates of the personal income tax and the corporation

---

[1] *New York Times*, 27 August 1951.
[2] *S. Rept. No. 781*, 82nd Cong., 1st Sess.

profits tax above the levels recommended by the Finance Committee, and condemned the provisions which lightened the load borne by certain favoured classes of taxpayers.[1]

In his speech introducing the bill, George asserted that the personal income tax had reached the point of diminishing returns, and that further increases in taxation on business would encourage extravagance. Any further increase in the excess profits tax would cripple the growing firms and thereby tend to promote the development of monopoly. Any increase in taxation above that provided in the Finance Committee's recommendations would have to come from 'entirely new' forms of taxation (by which he presumably meant a general sales tax).[2]

George was supported by the conservative and 'middle-of-the-road' Democrats, and by the Republican leaders, notably Millikin. He and George defended the bill together, against the attacks both of the Democratic Left and of the Republican far Right. The latter took the same position as their colleagues in the House, that of hostility to any tax increases at all, coupled with vitriolic denunciations of Federal expenditures, 'bureaucrats' and the 'secret government', and demanding a return to 'the pure American political doctrine'.[3] The number of Republicans who felt sufficiently strongly in this way to oppose their colleagues of the Finance Committee was fairly small, and in consequence the interest in the Senate's debates centred on the efforts of Humphrey, Douglas, and their colleagues to 'stiffen' the bill.

The Democratic critics of the bill concentrated on the fact that most of the reductions made by the Finance Committee would accrue to the wealthy, and on the thesis that it was impossible to increase tax rates any further without dire consequences. As Humphrey pointed out, there was something wrong with the case against higher taxation of corporations when on one hand it was held that the rates already in effect were a tremendous burden on business, and then in the next breath it was said that corporations passed on any increases in taxes on profits in the form of higher prices.[4]

The first vote taken was on a relief provision modifying the excess

---

[1] The text of the letter is printed in the *Annual Report of the Secretary of the Treasury for the year ending 30 June 1951*, p. 490.

[2] *Congressional Record*, Vol. XCVII, p. 11597.

[3] This was the opinion of Senator Jenner. *Congressional Record*, Vol. XCVII, pp. 11942–51.

[4] Ibid., p. 11715.

profits tax, to which O'Mahoney objected. After George had declared that to pass O'Mahoney's amendment would amount to a vote of no confidence in the Finance Committee, it was rejected by 65 votes to 22. Of the 22 voting in favour of the amendment, all but two (Morse and Langer) were Democrats. These voting strengths were repeated, give or take half-a-dozen votes, in all divisions on amendments to strengthen the bill. Humphrey, Douglas, and Lehman moved amendment after amendment, but the only one to receive more than 30 votes was that to make 1 January 1951 the effective date of the increase in the corporation profits tax instead of 1 April, but even this was defeated by 54 votes to 33.

All the extensions of the depletion allowances were approved, despite Humphrey's sarcasm about the usefulness of oystershell (which had been made eligible for percentage depletion)[1] to the defence effort: 'if oystershells and clamshells can be included in the bill, then anything can be included. Why not include duck feathers. Or canary birdseed, or dried up beetles, or anything'.[2] In the debate on the depletion allowances for coal and oil there was much evidence of shameless log-rolling; against the massed forces of those whose states contained industries that benefited from the extended depletion allowances, Humphrey's group could achieve nothing.

Senator Moody's amendment to exempt vacuum cleaners from excise tax was passed after George declared himself indifferent to whether it passed or not. Jenner succeeded in attaching to the bill a rider to prevent the Federal Security Administrator from withholding grants-in-aid for public assistance because a state allowed members of the general public to inspect the list of recipients of such aid.[3] The bill finally passed by 57 votes to 19. Some of the Left-of-Centre Democrats agreed with Moody that although the increase in revenue provided under the Senate version of the bill was inadequate, it was better than nothing, and therefore voted for the bill; Douglas, Humphrey, Lehman, and Morse in a last gesture of protest voted

[1] Oystershell is a *bona fide* mineral; as was pointed out in the debate, it is a commercial source of calcium carbonate and comes from deposits half a million years old, not from the refuse bins of restaurants.

[2] *Congressional Record*, Vol. XCVII, p. 12318.

[3] The legislature of Indiana in its 1951 session had passed an Act authorizing members of the public to inspect lists of the recipients of state assistance, ostensibly as a means of preventing frauds. This violated the regulations concerning Federal grants-in-aid, and the Federal Security Administrator suspended payment of grants to Indiana. Attempts to upset this in the Courts failed.

against it along with those of the far Right who opposed any increase at all.

The Conference version of the bill provided for an increase in the personal income tax of 11¾ per cent of liability (splitting the difference between the 11 per cent of the Senate version and the 12½ per cent of the House version) or 9 per cent of income after tax. The base for computation of excess profits was set at 83 per cent of profits in the base year, with a maximum effective rate of 18 per cent of total profits. The corporation profits tax was to be raised to 30 per cent on the first $25,000 of taxable profits, and 52 per cent on the remainder, as in the House version, and the capital gains tax left at its existing rate. The collection of tax at source on dividends and interest, deleted by the Senate, was not restored.[1]

The House conferees defended the Conference version as the best that could be got, and Doughton said that he did not believe that any further increases in tax rates could be passed in conditions short of all-out war. Reed returned to his attack, denouncing the view that tax increases could do anything to prevent inflation as 'one of the most dangerous fallacies of the Truman spenders'.[2] There then occurred what the *New York Times* called 'the greatest surprise of the session', the House's rejection of the Conference Report by a vote of 204 to 157. Sixty-two Representatives, all of them Democrats, who had voted or were paired against the motion to recommit voted or were paired against the Conference Report. Nearly all of them were from Northern industrial states, which makes it likely that they were influenced by the C.I.O.'s campaign to defeat the bill in its existing form; its legislative representatives sent letters to most Members, and the *C.I.O. News* claimed that the rejection of the Conference report had been achieved 'largely through C.I.O. efforts'.[3] The House Republican leaders were delighted, of course; Reed declared that the vote gave the Administration notice that 'the people will not submit to higher taxes without some show of economy in government'.[4]

The bill was returned to Conference, and reported again the next day with a few small alterations; the increase in tax in the lowest

[1] The text of the Conference Report is printed in the *Congressional Record*, Vol. XCVII, pp. 13238–70.
[2] Ibid., p. 13271.
[3] *C.I.O. News*, 22 October 1951, p. 2.
[4] Reported in *New York Times*, 17 October 1951.

bracket was set at 11 per cent of liability instead of 11¾ per cent, the capital gains tax raised to 26 per cent, and two small changes made in the coverage of the excise tax. The House conferees were forced to yield over the tax on the profits of co-operatives by George's threat that if the House would not agree he would see to it that there would be no tax bill at all.[1]

The Administration did what it could to get the bill accepted. When Representative Yorty called at the White House the President asked him to support the bill as the best that could be got;[2] when asked at his news conference whether he was confident that the Congress would pass the bill, the President replied that he was never confident about anything the Congress would do, but he hoped that they would.[3]

The second Conference version was approved on 19 October by 185 votes to 160. Twenty-four of those Democrats who voted against the first Conference report voted in favour of the second. All were from the liberal wing of the Democratic party, including men such as Bolling, McCarthy, and Eberharter who had a firm grasp of the economics of tax increases and deficits. The only explanation of the defeat of the first Conference report is that many Representatives who regarded the bill as inequitable, though they would prefer it to no bill at all, wanted to register a protest against its inequity, but failed to realize that there were enough of them to defeat the bill if they voted, as they had to, along with the orthodox Republicans.[4] Since they preferred a bill which to them seemed inequitable rather than no tax increase at all, they voted in favour of the second report. None the less, support for the view that an inequitable tax increase was worse than no tax increase at all was strong, and it came perilously close to there being no increase at all.

President Truman signed the bill at once. He issued a statement criticizing it on the ground that the tax increases it carried were so inadequate as to be 'a serious departure from the standards of sound government finance'. If the revenue were not so urgently needed he would not have approved a bill containing the relief provisions and the Jenner amendment. In conclusion he warned that he would urge

[1] Ibid., 18 October 1951.   [2] Ibid., 19 October 1951.
[3] News conference held on 18 October. Reported in the *New York Times*, 19 October 1951.
[4] The Indiana Republicans were an exception; all except Representative Wilson voted in favour of both the first and second Conference reports, obviously to secure the enactment of the Jenner rider.

the Congress to give 'major attention' to improving the tax laws in the next session.[1]

The Treasury's estimate of the revenue yield of the Act as it finally reached the Statute Book[2] is shown in the following table:

TABLE 24

Changes in Revenue Yield under the Revenue Act of 1951

	Change in Revenue ($ Million)	
	Full Year	*Fiscal 1952*
Individual Income Tax	2,455·6	1,340·9
Corporation Profits Tax	2,286·6	940·9
Excise Taxes (excluding wagering)	760·6	537·3
Wagering	300·0	50·0
Life Insurance Companies	73·0	51·0
Depletion Allowances	− 63·9	− 40·9
Excess Profits Tax	−102·0	−102·0
Miscellaneous	−271·9	−321·2
Total	5,438·0	2,455·1

Source: Annual Report of the Secretary of the Treasury for the year ending 30 June 1951, p. 501, Table I.

The increase in the effective rates of the personal income tax are shown in the following table:

TABLE 25

Effective Rates under the Revenue Act of 1951 and under Existing Law

	Effective Rate (%)			
	Single Man		Married, Two Children	
Adjusted		*Revenue Act*		*Revenue Act*
Gross Income	*Existing Law*	*1951*	*Existing Law*	*1951*
$1,000	8·0	13·3	Nil	Nil
$2,000	14·0	15·5	Nil	Nil
$3,000	16·3	18·1	4·0	4·4
$5,000	18·9	21·0	10·4	11·5
$10,000	24·4	27·2	15·9	17·7
$50,000	52·8	56·9	37·8	42·2

Source: Annual Report of the Secretary of the Treasury for the year ending 30 June 1951, p. 502, Table III.

The Revenue Act of 1951 was a piece of legislation which pleased nobody. To the Administration the increases in rates appeared in-

---

[1] The text of the President's statement is printed in the *Annual Report of the Secretary of the Treasury for the year ending 30 June 1951*, p. 491.

[2] For a summary of the provisions of the Act, see ibid., pp. 492–507.

adequate and the numerous provisions for special relief were unwelcome in that they further complicated the tax code and mitigated still further the progressivity of the tax on incomes which are not simple salaries. The Left-wing Members of Congress considered it inequitable because of the special relief provisions and because more of the increased burden was not placed on the upper income groups and profit receivers. To the business community and conservatives in general it was unwelcome for exactly the opposite reason, that most of the additional revenue was raised from taxes on personal incomes and corporate profits and not from a general sales tax. The *New York Times* found in the Administration's unwillingness to support a general sales tax 'a conspicuous example of the nation's lack of leadership'.[1]

It is clear that the primary reason why the tax increase fell so far short of that originally requested by the Administration was one of political stalemate. Opposition to a general sales tax, on grounds of equity, was sufficiently strong in the Administration, the Congress, and in the country to prevent its having a real chance of being enacted. On the other hand, those who opposed a general sales tax did not have the strength to force through large increases in direct taxation in the teeth of the opposition of business and the upper income groups, just as had happened during the Second World War.

Resistance to further tax increases was very strong in all sections of the community, which is not surprising in view of the speed and magnitude of the increases that had already been enacted. By late 1951 it had become the generally accepted view in Congress that no further tax increases were possible unless general war should break out. While generally held views about the increasing ill effects of rising tax rates had something to do with the hostility to further tax increases, those most strongly opposed did not make serious efforts to demonstrate that attempts to use tax increases to impose a further check on inflation would be futile because it would reduce supply (though the effect on incentives and inducements to invest) more than it would reduce demand (because of induced dis-saving). No evidence was adduced which pointed towards the conclusion that the United States had reached the limit of taxable capacity in any economic sense. The limit to tax increases reached in 1951 was political, not economic.

[1] Editorial on 13 October 1951.

TAX AND EXPENDITURE POLICY IN 1952

The fiscal developments of 1952 were an epilogue to those of 1951. Following the President's statement that he would recommend revision of the tax laws,[1] there were rumours that he would propose tax increases to the next session of Congress as a result of the prospective increase in defence expenditure in fiscal 1953.[2] In his Budget Message submitted in January 1952 the President recommended that revenue be increased sufficiently to make up the difference between the yield of the Revenue Act of 1951 and the increase originally recommended in January 1951 (that is to say five to five-and-a-half billion dollars). Discussing how it should be raised, the President said: 'Glaring inequities in our tax laws should be eliminated before those of modest means are asked to pay more'.[3] Even this increase was inadequate to offset the increase in expenditure expected in fiscal 1953, which was estimated at $85,444 billion, as against revenue estimated, rather optimistically, at $70,998 million. The increase in expenditure over the estimate for fiscal 1952 was $15 billion, of which $12 billion was for 'military services' and the other $3 billion for 'international security and foreign relations'. In the face of such large increases in expenditure the policy of strict 'pay-as-you-go' had to be abandoned.

The reaction in Congress to the proposal for further tax increases was one of almost unanimous opposition. The Democratic leaders in both House and Senate declared that there was no likelihood of there being enough members who would support an increase.[4] Senators Douglas and Humphrey supported measures to close the 'loopholes',[5] but it was soon clear that no action would be forthcoming. The Administration did not present a detailed programme of tax increases to yield the five billion dollars, and no special Tax Message was sent up as in 1951. It is evident that the Administration regarded the cause as hopeless. As the Presidential election campaign gathered momentum in the spring of 1952 consideration of the

[1] See pp. 177-8, supra.
[2] Especially after a discussion between the President and the Director of the Bureau of the Budget on 17 November 1951.
[3] *Budget of the United States for the year ending 30 June 1953.*
[4] *New York Times*, 9 January 1952.
[5] Humphrey prepared a pamphlet entitled *Tax Loopholes*, published by the Public Affairs Institute on 24 February 1952.

part tax policy should play in the control of inflation became submerged under pre-election tax cut talk.

The Administration strongly opposed cutting the rearmament programme because of the inability to secure further tax increases. In the course of the hearings on the Economic Report, Dr. Blough, a member of the Council of Economic Advisers, advanced the idea of accepting a deficit in the peak year of rearmament, covering the whole cost of rearmament through taxation taking one year with another.[1] Keyserling took the more extreme position of warning that there are worse things than inflation, that if Russia overran Western Europe as a result of an inadequate American defence establishment it would take more than a balanced budget to protect the United States.[2] Charles E. Wilson, Director of Defense Mobilization, also expressed strong opposition to slowing down rearmament if additional taxes were not voted.[3]

The treatment of appropriations by the Congress in 1952 was similar to that in 1951; nearly all appropriations were cut to amounts well below what the Administration requested. The Jensen rider of the previous year (the Conference Committee version) was attached to the Agriculture, Independent Offices, Interior, Labor-Federal Security Agency, and State-Commerce-Justice appropriation bills, and a rider was attached to the Independent Offices bill forbidding civil service officers from carrying over paid leave from one year to the next. The programme of Federally subsidized housing authorized by the Housing Act of 1949 was cut severely, only 35,000 houses being authorized for fiscal 1953 as against the 75,000 the Administration requested; even this was achieved only after a long struggle, for the majority in the House were obdurate in their demand that the programme should be limited to 5,000 houses only, The largest cut was in the military appropriation, of nearly $5 billion; foreign aid (military and civil) was cut by $1·7 billion. The Administration requested $600 million in the First Supplemental for civil defence, mostly for the construction of public shelters; the Congress appropriated $37·5 million, none of it for shelters, as the enabling legislation to authorize the shelters was not passed.

Expenditures did not rise so much in fiscal 1953 as had been expected, partly because of Congressional cuts, but also because the

---

[1] Joint Committee on the Economic Report, *Hearings on the Economic Report of the President*, 1952, p. 53–4.
[2] Ibid., p. 36.   [3] Ibid., p. 170.

deliveries of military goods fell behind the necessarily tentative early estimates.[1] The estimates published in January 1953[2] put expenditures for 'military services' at $6·8 billion less than the estimate of the previous January and expenditures for 'international security and foreign relations' at $4·8 billion less. As a result the January 1953 estimate of the deficit in fiscal 1953 was only $5·9 billion (the out-turn was a deficit of $9·4 billion).

THE ECONOMIC EFFECTS OF THE REVENUE ACT OF 1951 AND OTHER MEASURES TO RESTRAIN INFLATION

Although if judged by the criteria of economic stabilization in the circumstances foreseen in early 1951 the tax increases enacted were too little and very late, none the less by the time President Truman signed the Act the worst of the post-Korean inflation was already over. The index of wholesale prices began in May a decline which continued into the spring of 1952. The index for March 1951 was 116·5, for March 1952 112·3.[3] The index of wholesale prices other than those of farm products and food declined by the same amount. In the spring and summer of 1951 the rise in the consumer price index slowed almost to a halt; and a rise in the fourth quarter of 1951 was followed by a slight decline in the first quarter of 1952.[4] From the spring of 1951 onwards the price indices were thus extraordinarily stable for a period in which rearmament was proceeding apace,[5] although the increases in taxation actually enacted fell far short of what the Administration requested. In considering why this was so, attention must be given to other measures taken to restrain demand.

Among these was the more vigorous use of orthodox monetary policy. The dispute between the Federal Reserve System and the Treasury over the nature of the System's obligation to ensure the success of the Treasury's debt operations and what obligation the Treasury had to determine the conditions of its issues so as not to

[1] The steel strike was an important factor in slowing down deliveries of military goods.

[2] *Budget of the United States for the year ending 30 June 1954.*

[3] Department of Labor, published in *Survey of Current Business*, March 1952, p. 22, and in monthly statistics thereafter.

[4] Department of Labor; published in *Survey of Current Business*, April 1953, p. 23.

[5] The implicit deflator in the series for G.N.P. at constant prices rose by 1·8 per cent between the second quarter of 1951 and the second quarter of 1952. Department of Commerce, *U.S. Income and Output*, 1959, Table VII–3.

conflict with the System's policies came to a head early in 1951, and ended with the famous 'accord' of 4 March 1951 whereby the Federal Reserve System was freed from the commitment to support the prices of U.S. Government bonds at par. At first this permitted only a slight tightening of credit policy, for one of the elements of the accord was an understanding that unless something cataclysmic happened the rediscount rate would not be raised in the remainder of 1951.[1] Since the rediscount rate cannot get too far out of line with market rates without member banks increasing their borrowing from the Reserve Banks to carry additional earning assets, the System was closely limited as to the restrictive policy it could pursue in 1951. Some restriction was undertaken; the rate of interest on long term U.S. Government bonds rose from 2·47 per cent in March 1951 to 2·70 per cent in December, and the average rate on bank loans rose from 3·02 per cent to 3·27 per cent in the same period. In the first half of 1952 rates of interest on bank loans continued to rise, but other rates of interest remained steady.[2]

The Council of Economic Advisers looked on these developments in monetary policy with a somewhat jaundiced eye; they said in the Economic Report of January 1952: 'The increase in interest rates is an increase in the cost of capital, and this involves an increase in the cost of production which may tend to press prices upwards'.[3] Dr. John D. Clark added a separate note[4] in which he said that the increase in interest rates had had 'utterly perverse' consequences. On the other side, however, the 'accord' and the increase in interest rates, including the issue by the Treasury of non-marketable bonds at $2\frac{3}{4}$ per cent, were hailed as extremely important. The editors of *Fortune* wrote: 'Many of the mildly deflationary trends evident in the U.S. economy during the second quarter were traceable to this momentous tinkering with the structure of the Federal debt'.[5] The drop in building was cited as the most important deflationary effect.

The decline in house building that took place in 1951 was considerable,[6] but the extent to which this was due to monetary policy

---

[1] See the testimony of the Chairman of the Board of Governors of the Federal Reserve System to the Senate Finance Committee. Senate, Committee on Finance, *Hearings on the Financial Condition of the United States*, 1957, p. 1321.

[2] Board of Governors of the Federal Reserve System, monthly statistics. The rates of interest on bank loans are averages of rates reported from 19 cities.

[3] *Economic Report of the President, January 1952*, p. 140.

[4] Ibid., pp. 142–4.   [5] *Fortune*, editorial, July 1951.   [6] See p. 141, supra.

is open to question. The imposition of direct restrictions on credit for house building in August to October 1950[1] was followed by a decline in building, before any effective restriction of credit by conventional means had occurred. In view of the extent to which changes in the amount of house building have corresponded to changes in credit policy in the United States since 1949 it is reasonable to suggest that monetary policy played some part in the restraint of house building, but it cannot be determined exactly how much.

In this period the Administration had resort to price and wage controls, with an apparent reluctance that was in marked contrast to the readiness with which authority to impose such controls was requested from the 80th Congress. General price and wage controls were not brought into effect until 25 January 1951. The controlled prices were to be those prevailing in the base period of 19 December to 25 January. The increases granted in subsequent wage settlements were not to bring wages more than 10 per cent above the level prevailing in January 1950. Neither business nor the unions were happy with the controls. As in 1945–46 many businessmen seemed to fear that the controls might be used to squeeze profits by holding down prices while wages were allowed to rise. As far back as July 1950 union leaders had been demanding immediate and thorough-going price control but criticizing 'unfounded talk' about wage control.[2] In December 1950 the United Labor Policy Committee (composed of leaders of the A.F.L. and C.I.O.) agreed to 'wage stabilization' provided it did not become 'wage freezing', and permitted cost-of-living adjustments and the removal of inequities and substandard rates.[3]

The increase of 10 per cent over January 1950 was not generous. In January 1951 the consumer price index was 8 per cent above the level of the previous January, so that unless the increase in prices came to a halt very quickly, which was not expected by the officials concerned,[4] wage earners would have to accept an appreciable cut

[1] See p. 141, supra.

[2] For instance, a statement by Mr. Emil Rieve, Chairman of the C.I.O. Full Employment Committee, in which the quoted phrase appeared. Reported in the *New York Times*, 1 August 1950.

[3] Reported by *C.I.O. News*, 5 December 1950, p. 3.

[4] The Director of Price Stabilization told the Joint Committee on the Economic Report in January 1951 that he expected that it would be 'several months' before price stability could be achieved. Joint Committee on the Economic Report, *Hearings on the Economic Report of the President*, January 1951, p. 140.

in their real income. The average working week had lengthened in the second half of 1950, but this trend did not continue in 1951, so no offset to a decline in real wage rates could be expected from this source.

Within a short time the severity of both price and wage controls was moderated by legislation and administrative decision. Whereas the regulations of the Office of Price Stabilization provided that price increases to cover increased costs would be allowed only to the extent necessary to bring profits before tax up to 85 per cent of average profits in 1946–49 (the standard then in effect for computing 'excess profits' for tax purposes), the Capehart and Herlong amendments to the Defense Production Act of 1951 required the Office of Price Stabilization to allow price increases to offset all increases in costs since 26 June 1950 and to allow profit margins in effect at that time to be retained. Similar relaxation of the original severity of wage control was achieved by administrative decision. The problem soon arose of increases under cost-of-living 'escalator' clauses which would exceed the limit of 10 per cent above January 1950; the solution adopted was to permit such wage increases, but to prohibit the inclusion of 'escalator' clauses in agreements negotiated subsequently. This treatment discriminated against those not covered by 'escalator' agreements, who were prevented from obtaining a 'cost-of-living' increase by means of a conventional wage claim. The Wage Stabilization Board adopted the only feasible solution, to permit ordinary wage increases provided they did no more than offset increases in the cost of living that had already occurred.

Clearly, controls legislated and administered in this way could not be expected to do more than slow down the upward adjustment of prices and wages to any large excess of effective demand. It is probable, however, that some delaying effect was exerted on wage increases, and the imposition of price controls were useful in diminishing consumers' expectations of further price increases, a point which will be discussed in more detail below.

The next step is to examine the extent to which the tax increases, monetary restraint, selective credit controls, and other controls restrained demand. But first, account should be taken of the increase in real output that occurred in the year following the outbreak of the war in Korea. G.N.P. measured at constant (1954) prices rose from a seasonally adjusted annual rate of $312·0 billion in the second quarter of 1950 to $340·0 billion in the second quarter of 1951, an increase of 9 per cent. A further, though smaller, increase took place in the remainder of 1951 and 1952.[1] Part of this was obtained by bringing into use the 'slack' in the economy left over from the recession; unemployment in June 1950 as reported by the Bureau of the Census was 3,384,000, which fell to 1,980,000 in June 1951.[2] Employment in non-agricultural establishments rose by approximately the same amount, but the number in the armed forces rose by 1,700,000 in the same period, so that the increase in demand must have attracted into employment a substantial number who were previously not in the labour force (or at any rate not detected by the statistical measures of it). The average number of hours worked per week in manufacturing also rose.

In 1950 this increase in production was absorbed by increased consumption and inventory accumulation, the effects of the 'buying spree' and the stock-rebuilding that followed it, and the attempts to build up stocks in anticipation of controls. The impact of these increases in demand was sufficient to generate serious inflationary pressure even though the burden of rearmament that had so far affected the economy was a fraction of what was in prospect for the future. The factors which made that increase in defence expenditure possible without further serious inflation were the further increases in production, the effect of the demand-reducing measures taken by the authorities, and autonomous developments reducing effective demand.

The tax increases were indeed very important. The ratio of Federal personal tax payments to personal income in the first quarter of 1952, when the increases under the Revenue Act of 1951 were in full operation, was 11·6 per cent, compared with 7·8 per cent in the second quarter of 1950.[3] At the level of personal income and the ratio of consumption to disposable income prevailing in the first quarter of 1952 this was equivalent to a reduction of $10 billion in disposable income and $9·2 billion in consumption demand. Even more striking was the effect of the tax increase on corporate profits.

[1] The increase in real G.N.P. from the second quarter of 1951 to the fourth quarter of 1952 was 6·8 per cent. Department of Commerce, *U.S. Income and Output*, 1959, Table I–5.

[2] Department of Labor; printed in the *Economic Report of the President*, 1953, Table B–12.

[3] Calculated from data in Department of Commerce, *U.S. Income and Output*, 1959, Table II–2. There would probably have been some rise in the ratio even without the increase in rates on account of the progressivity of the personal income tax.

Profits after tax after the outbreak of the Korean war exceeded the amount for the second quarter of 1950 only in the third and fourth quarters of 1950 and the first quarter of 1951, when taxable profits were inflated by the rise in the value of inventories. If the inventory valuation adjustment is deducted, net corporate profits after tax rose hardly at all in 1951 and 1952, and were only marginally greater than in the second quarter of 1950.[1] Gross profits after tax minus the inventory valuation adjustment rose,[2] but the increases must be adjudged small in a situation where total income was rising so quickly. It is reasonable to suggest that this near-stability of corporate profits after tax was an important cause of the stability of non-residential construction and the output of producers' durable equipment after mid-1950. Measured at constant prices, these components of demand totalled $32·9 billion (at seasonally adjusted annual rates) in the second quarter of 1950 and $34·8 billion in the third quarter; in no quarter of 1951 or 1952 was the latter figure exceeded by more than $1 billion, and the average of the quarters for the two years was $35·1 billion.[3] In a situation where demand was high and rising one would expect the inducement to invest to be strong; the prevention of any substantial increase in commercial fixed capital investment in real terms, when investment was not subject to stringent direct controls, was an important contribution to the maintenance of economic stability and which may be attributed in substantial measure to the severity of the taxation of corporate profits.

Falls in total demand in 1951 compared with the second half of 1950 were not caused solely by the increases in taxation. While the tax increases reduced personal disposable income relative to personal income before tax, consumption also fell markedly relative to disposable income. The ratio of consumption to disposable income was 92·5 per cent and 94·5 per cent in the first and second quarters of 1950, rising to 97·0 per cent in the third quarter when the 'buying spree' was at its peak, But after some revival of the buying spree early in 1951, consumption in the last two quarters of 1951 and the first two quarters of 1952 was very low in relation to disposable income, the ratios being 90·7 per cent, 91·2 per cent, 92·5 per cent

---

[1] *U.S. Income and Output*, 1959, Table I–9.

[2] Estimates of *gross* corporate profits quarterly are not available. Gross corporate profits after tax minus the inventory valuation adjustment were: 1949, $17·6 billion; 1950, $16·5 billion; 1951 $18·6 billion; and 1952, $19·7 billion. *U.S. Income and Output*, 1959, Tables VI–7, VI–11, and VI–18.

[3] *U.S. Income and Output*, 1959, Table I–5.

and 92·6 per cent respectively.[1] It is reasonable to attribute at least part of the decline in expenditures on consumers' durable goods to the effect of Regulation W, for expenditure on them declined considerably more sharply relative to disposable income than did expenditures for non-durable goods. Another probably important factor was what J. P. Lewis has called the 'morning after' effect,[2] the reaction to the very heavy buying in the previous period. The buying had left consumers with abnormally large stocks of goods; and the imposition of price control, at long last, gave ground for expectations that there would be no rapid rise in prices in the near future, so removing the incentive of consumers to add to their stocks still more.

A similar 'morning after' effect reduced the rate of increase of business inventories. The rate of inventory accumulation in the fourth quarter of 1950 and the first two quarters of 1951 ($15·5 billion, $10·0 billion, and $14·5 billion, measured at seasonally adjusted annual rates at constant (1954) prices)[3] was so great that it could not continue for long. In the third quarter of 1951 a marked decline in the rate of inventory accumulation began, which continued to mid-1952.

The increase in production, combined with a decline in the rate of inventory accumulation, near stability of commercial investment in fixed capital, and the reduction in consumption relative both to personal income before tax and to disposable income, 'made room' for the increase in defence expenditure, without serious inflationary pressure. Federal purchases of goods and services for 'national defense'[4] rose from an annual rate of $12·0 billion in the second quarter of 1950 to $24·3 billion in the first quarter of 1951 and $46·2 billion in the second quarter of 1952.[5] The whole of the increase after the first quarter of 1951 was in real terms.[6]

---

[1] Calculated from data in Department of Commerce, *U.S. Income and Output*, 1959, Table II–2.

[2] See his article 'The Lull that Came to Stay', *Journal of Political Economy*, Vol. LXIII (1955), pp. 1–19.

[3] *U.S. Income and Output*, Table I–5.

[4] For the definition of this concept and the difference in coverage from classifications previously used, see *Survey of Current Business*, December 1958, p. 12, footnote 1.

[5] *U.S. Income and Output*, Table I–3.

[6] *U.S. Income and Output*, Table VII–3. A deflator for Federal purchases of goods and services for national defence is not available, but the deflator for all Federal purchases is a reasonable approximation because of the high ratio (in 1951–2) of Federal purchases for defence to other Federal purchases, and the absence of evidence of divergent price trends.

It is necessary to consider to what extent the declines in demand in the private sector, which reduced the need for increased taxation below what seemed appropriate in January 1951, were foreseen or noticed while the tax legislation was under consideration. The Administration clearly believed that the slackening in inflationary pressure, evident by the late spring and early summer of 1951, did not call for any revision of its tax policy. Secretary Snyder told the Senate Finance Committee on 28 June 1951: 'We must not conclude from developments of recent months that the inflationary danger has passed',[1] and President Truman's strictures on the inadequacy of the tax bill have already been noted.[2]

In the Congress there was nowhere any suggestion of opposition to the Administration's recommendations on the ground that the prospective excess of demand was not great enough to call for tax increases as large as those proposed. As was outlined above, the reasons why the tax increases passed by the Congress fell far short of what the Administration had requested were mainly political. The Joint Committee on the Economic Report issued a report[3] entitled *Inflation Still a Danger*; this was a report by the Committee's staff, but in an introduction signed by the whole Committee it was said that 'fundamental inflationary pressure' would continued to mount in ensuing months as defence expenditure increased, calling for renewed efforts to reduce Federal civil expenditures and for tax increases 'sufficient to balance a carefully planned administrative budget' during the current fiscal year (i.e. fiscal 1952). Members of Congress who looked at the problem in terms of the economics of stabilization did not conclude that the situation had changed or was likely to do so in a way that would make a less drastic fiscal policy consistent with stability. The conclusion cannot be avoided, therefore, that the shortfall of the tax increases below the increase recommended by the Administration was a political failure if judged by the interpretation of the economic outlook generally accepted throughout 1951, and that the American economy was spared the inflation which had been predicted to occur in the event of such a failure only by developments which were not foreseen or whose significance was not fully appreciated at the time.

[1] Senate, Committee on Finance, *Hearings on H.R.4473*, 1951, p. 63.
[2] See p. 177, supra.
[3] *S. Rept. No. 644*, 82nd Cong., 1st Sess. The quotations are from the introduction on p. 1 of the report.

CONCLUSIONS ON FISCAL POLICY IN 1951-52

It has been the contention of this chapter that the primary reliance on fiscal policy as the means of preventing inflation, with the direct controls not widespread or stringent enough to be more than subsidiaries (albeit very useful subsidiaries), indicated in the circumstances of early 1951 a policy of drastic tax increases such as the Administration proposed; that this policy was only partially put into practice because of Congressional sentiment about what was the maximum tax burden in circumstances short of general war and the working of 'interest-group' politics in producing a stalemate in which each group was able to block a drastic increase in those taxes most unacceptable to it; and that the American economy was rescued from the consequences of this apparent political failure by demand-reducing developments in the private sector that were not apparent in early 1951 and whose significance was not fully appreciated for many months.

If the timing and magnitude of the tax increases are contrasted with those in World War II[1] the Truman Administration and the 81st and 82nd Congresses (especially the former) and their tax specialists emerge with credit, enough to justify Professor Smithies in seeing in February 1951 'a high degree of economic enlightenment in Washington, a much higher degree than there has been in previous crises'.[2] None the less, the high degree of stability that existed after mid-1951 owed quite a lot to the 'concatenation of special circumstances',[3] notably the decline in consumption relative to disposable income and the decline in inventory accumulation. Or, another way of putting it, the United States owed the combination of nearly steady prices (after mid-1951) and rapidly increasing defence expenditure in part to good luck as well as to good judgement.

The contrast between the virtual unanimity with which the tax increases under the Revenue Act of 1950 were passed and the bitter and long drawn-out struggle over the Revenue Act of 1951 is striking. Among the reasons that may be suggested are the speed with which

[1] Federal receipts as shown in the national income accounts were 21·2 per cent of G.N.P. at factor cost (G.N.P. minus indirect business taxes plus subsidies) in 1952 compared with 20·7 per cent in 1944. *U.S. Income and Output*, 1959, Tables I–17 and III–1; *National Income*, 1954, Table 8.

[2] Joint Committee on the Economic Report, *Hearings on the Economic Report of the President*, February 1951, p. 309.

[3] Lewis, op. cit., p. 19.

the first tax increases were sprung upon the country, and the mood of united support for the intervention in Korea and the rearmament. After the elections of 1950 and the Chinese intervention in Korea this mood of unity dissolved into acrimonious conflict, bringing on the worst 'era of bad feelings' in recent times. This added strength to those who for nearly twenty years had maintained unrelenting opposition to the expansion of the role of the Federal government in economic affairs[1] and the levels of taxation and expenditure which resulted. The resurgence of a Right opposed to high taxation and opposed on ideological grounds to all techniques of economic control except possibly monetary policy, and believing firmly that large parts of government expenditure could properly be eliminated,[2] was an important obstacle to the effective use of fiscal policy to restrain inflation, which in practice meant tax increases. This group, which included many of the Republican leaders in the House, did not fail to block all tax increases in 1951 from want of trying, and came perilously near to success.

Such was the opposition to the Revenue Act of 1951 that it was accepted by all in Congress that further increases in taxation were not 'on'. The Joint Committee on the Economic Report in its 1952 report[3] regarded this as a fact of the situation and confined its discussion of the use of the Federal budget for the restraint of inflation to considering possible reductions in expenditure. Given the small prospect of economicaly significant reductions in expenditure unless the rearmament programme were substantially cut, the political barrier to further tax increases would have rendered fiscal policy powerless to exercise any further restraint if developments in the private sector had led to a rise in demand greater than the increasing output could meet. Since this situation did not arise, one can only speculate about what would have happened if it had. Since the attitude of the Administration[4] was that the rearmament programme was essential to the nation's survival and that if the nation was unwilling to pay for it through taxation it would have to pay for it the other way, reliance would have to have been placed on direct controls, the economy getting along with inflation that was in part suppressed.

In appraising the conduct of general economic policy in the United

[1] See Chapter II, supra.
[2] The *Congressional Record* for 1951–52 is full of such assertions.
[3] *S. Rept. No. 1295*, 82nd Cong. 2nd Sess.   [4] See p. 157, supra.

States during the period, it is of interest to compare it with that of Great Britain, where the problem was similar in that it was decided that the national interest required an extensive rearmament. There were important differences in the economic situations in the two countries, however, notably the existence in the United States of a certain amount of 'slack' left over from the recession of 1949 which had no counterpart in Britain; the absence of difficulties with the balance of payments to plague American policy makers; and the existence in Britain of direct controls effective enough to prevent the emergence of a 'buying spree' of the magnitude experienced in the United States. The comparison also throws interesting light on differences between American and British attitudes to taxation.

The magnitude of the rearmament in the United States was much greater than in the United Kingdom. Defence expenditure rose from 5·8 per cent of G.N.P. at factor cost in 1949 to 14·5 per cent in 1952, compared with 6·9 per cent and 10·4 per cent in those years in the United Kingdom.[1] The policy the United States government tried to follow was to match all of the increase by taxation. This it was unable to do, but the existence of the 'slack' when rearmament began provided a margin which offset much of the shortgall in taxation. The British government did not try to do this, for reasons expounded in the Chancellor's budget speech in 1951. Other developments, notably a decline in the export surplus and a decline in home investment were relied upon to free some of the resources needed for rearmament. Had it been thought necessary to offset the whole of the increase in defence expenditure by taxation, there can be little doubt that it would have led to a revision of the estimate of the additional burden that could safely be borne.

There could be few greater contrasts than between the reception accorded to Gaitskell's Budget and that accorded to the Truman Administration's fiscal proposals. The former was generally regarded as fair and reasonable even by the Opposition, despite their qualms about the increase in the Profits Tax on distributed profits. Whereas when the U.S. Treasury proposed that the tax on cars, gas and electric appliances, and wireless and T.V. sets should be raised to 20 per cent and 25 per cent, strong opposition was aroused and only a small increase in the tax on cars actually enacted,[2] the Chan-

[1] Calculated from data in *U.S. Income and Output*, 1959, Tables I–1 and I–17; and *National Income and Expenditure*, 1959, Tables 1 and 35.

[2] See p. 168, supra.

cellor raised the tax on these items to 66⅔ per cent and hardly a dog barked. The Secretary of the Treasury recommended on 5 February 1951 that the tax on petrol be increased by 1½¢ a gallon, and on 1 November it was raised by ½¢ a gallon; but the Chancellor could announce on the afternoon of 10 April that the tax would be increased by 4½d. a gallon with effect from 6 o'clock that evening.

In view of the generally expressed belief in the United States that no further increases in taxation were possible in conditions short of total war (and the fact that the 1951 rates in the United Kingdom were the post-war 'peak'), a comparison of the tax burdens is of interest. The measure taken, total receipts of all units of government as a percentage of G.N.P. at factor cost, is only a rough measure, since the services rendered by the public sector are relevant in a comparison of the burden; the most important example is the Health Service; to the extent that the difference in tax ratios was offset (taking the nation as a whole) by the payments Americans have to make privately for medical care, the 'burden' in the United States was not really less than in the United Kingdom.[1] The table overleaf compares Gross National Product at factor cost and government revenues (including in both cases local governments and social insurance funds). For comparability, 'additions to tax reserves' by companies in the United Kingdom are added to revenue, since in the United States national income accounts corporate profits taxes are entered under government revenue as liability accrues and not when they are paid. Grants from abroad on current and capital account have been deducted from the revenues of the government of the United Kingdom.

By 1952, when the full increases were in effect, the burden of direct taxation (counting Social Security and National Insurance contributions as direct taxation) was only marginally smaller in the United States than in the United Kingdom. The great difference lay

[1] Consumers' purchases of medical services and related goods in the U.S. in 1950–52 averaged 3·2 per cent of G.N.P. at factor cost; *U.S. Income and Output*, 1959, Table II–4. These purchases are valued at market prices and so contain a certain amount (probably very small) of indirect tax. Also, there was still some private expenditure for medical care and 'medical goods' in the United Kingdom, though the National Income Blue Book does not estimate how much. Expenditure on 'chemists' goods', a classification similar to the U.S. 'drug preparations and sundries', averaged 0·9 per cent of G.N.P. in the United Kingdom in 1950–52. The amount of expense for medical care which in the U.S. was paid for privately but which was paid for through taxation in the United Kingdom was thus about 2·3 per cent of G.N.P.

O

TABLE 26

Ratios of Taxes to Gross National Product in the United States and the United Kingdom, 1949–52

	United States				United Kingdom			
	All	Indirect	Corporate	Other	All	Indirect	Corporate	Other
	(%)	(%)	(%)	(%)	(%)	(%)	(%)	(%)
1949	23·8	9·2	4·4	10·2	39·7	17·8	6·7	15·2
1951	28·2	8·5	7·4	12·3	43·2	17·7	10·0	15·5
1952	28·4	8·8	6·1	13·5	38·5	16·3	7·0	15·2

Notes: 'Corporate' taxes in United Kingdom include tax payments and additions to tax reserves by companies and public corporations.

'Indirect' taxes are those classified as 'indirect business tax liability' in the U.S. national income accounts and those classified as 'taxes on expenditure' in the British national income accounts, including in both cases local rates and property taxes.

Source: U.S. Income and Output, 1959, Tables I–17, III–2, and III–3; and *National Income and Expenditure 1959,* Tables 1, 25, 31, 35, 38, 39, and 40.

in indirect taxation, as was (and in 1960 still is) readily apparent on comparison of British and American rates of tax on tobacco, alcoholic liquor, petrol, and consumers' durables. If the political resistance to high taxation was greater in the United States than in the United Kingdom, it was principally so in relation to indirect taxation, which is generally thought of as being the least progressive and therefore the most objectionable to the Left.

Despite all that has been said above about the political obstacles to tax increases in 1951 and the delays they caused, there is justification for describing the tax increases of 1950–51 as 'the most timely and most nearly adequate anti-inflationary tax program that it (the Federal government) has ever brought to bear on a serious inflationary problem'.[1] But had further fiscal restraint been needed the signs are that it would have been impossible to obtain barring a sudden change of heart by the major interest groups and numerous Members of Congress. Moreover, it was a special case in the sense that the increase in taxation could be presented as being necessary to 'pay for' the Korean war and rearmament, an argument that would make sense to many more people than those who looked at the problem in terms of compensatory fiscal policy. Both the older and the newer conceptions of 'sound financial policy' pointed to the same measures.

[1] Lewis, op. cit., pp. 6–7.

CHAPTER X

THE REPUBLICAN VICTORY AND ORTHODOX DEFLATIONARY POLICY, 1952–1953

THE forces which had so reduced the inflationary pressure in 1951 were still present in 1952. Output rose, especially in the second half of the year, and although a deficit emerged in fiscal 1952 there were no signs of an immediate return of open inflation. When the Defense Production Act was renewed in 1952 the direct controls were weakened still further; the power to control instalment credit was not renewed, and the power to control mortgage credit was renewed subject to the condition that the power was to lapse if housing starts as reported by the Department of Labor were to fall below a seasonally adjusted annual rate of 1,200,000 in three successive months. The combination of business and other conservatives who were opposed to controls on principle and the trade unions whose members were employed in the industries affected by the controls was able, because of the absence of any immediate problem of inflation, to secure the removal of many of the controls.

In the second half of 1952 and the first half of 1953 the price level remained almost steady. The implicit deflator for G.N.P. rose from 97·7 in the second quarter of 1952 to 98·8 in the second quarter of 1953; the rise in the implicit deflator for consumption expenditure in the same period was almost identical.[1] There was little sign of the existence of unused resources in the economy; unemployment as measured by the Bureau of the Census averaged 2·4 per cent of the civilian labour force in the second half of 1952 and 2·6 per cent in the first half of 1953. In these circumstances it was reasonable to look on the increase in the rate of inventory accumulation[2] and the continued rise in defence expenditure[3] as potential sources of inflation

---

[1] *U.S. Income and Output*, 1959, Table VII–3.

[2] Investment in inventories, measured at current prices at seasonally adjusted annual rates, was + $5·1 billion − $2·2 billion + $4·3 billion and + $5·3 billion in the first, second, third, and fourth quarters of 1952 respectively. *U.S. Income and Output*, 1959, Table I–3.

[3] Purchases of goods and services for national defence rose from a seasonally adjusted annual rate of $46·2 billion in the second quarter of 1952 to $50·5 billion in the second quarter of 1953. *U.S. Income and Output*, 1959, Table I–3.

and regard inflation as the main immediate danger to be guarded against despite the stability of the price level. The Federal Reserve System took this view; in the autumn of 1952 it restricted its purchases of securities to less than the amount needed to meet the seasonal increase in the demand for credit.[1]

ECONOMIC STABILITY AS AN ELECTION ISSUE IN 1952

While most observers do not credit economic issues with having an influence on the result of the election comparable with the famous 'three C's' (i.e. Communism, Corruption, and Korea),[2] the Presidential candidates and their supporters made frequent reference to economic issues, and in view of the result of the election the positions taken by General Eisenhower are of particular interest and importance.

An emphasis on inflation is to be found in the speeches of both Eisenhower and Stevenson; it was common ground that the immediate economic problem to be dealt with when the next President took office would be inflation and not incipient recession. Governor Stevenson said on 23 September in a speech at Baltimore that 'we have inflation today' because of defence expenditure being loaded upon an already fully employed economy. He proposed a budget policy of 'pay-as-you-go' for defence, with no tax cut until the budget could be balanced. He proposed 'a program of restraints' to check the growth of credit, and a tightening of price and wage controls, the controls which, he said, were preventing the inflation from getting out of hand at the moment of speaking.[3] This speech placed the emphasis on inflation as strongly as any of Eisenhower's speeches did; the stress laid on inflation in so many Republican speeches cannot be dismissed as mere partisan imagination or the result of believing that budget deficits must of necessity cause inflation under all circumstances.

Eisenhower attributed the inflation to the policies of the Democratic Administration, notably large government expenditures and budget deficits. In a speech at Wilmington, Del., on 17 October he

---

[1] See the account of Federal Reserve policies submitted by the Chairman of the Board of Governors of the Federal Reserve System in *United States Monetary Policy: Recent Thinking and Experience*, hearings before the Economic Stabilization Subcommittee of the Joint Committee on the Economic Report, December 1954, p. 14.

[2] See L. Harris, *Is There a Republican Majority?* (New York, 1954), Chapter 3.

[3] The text of the speech is printed in the *New York Times*, 24 September 1952.

declared that if elected he would put an end to 'wild spending' and 'recurrent deficits' that cause inflation.[1] These sentiments, expressed in similar language, are to be found in all the speeches in which Eisenhower touched on home economic policy. In a speech at Columbia, S.C., he said: 'Isn't it time we had an administration that will keep spending down . . . that believes that an unbalanced budget is dangerous to every one of us'.[2]

The principal Democratic talking point was the high level of income and employment, contrasted with the 'Hoover depression', with such slogans as 'you've never had it so good' and 'don't let them take it away'. It was an appeal to results; whatever the rights and wrongs of deficits and government spending, real incomes and employment were indubitably better than they were in the last years in which a Republican Administration had held office. From this it was inferred, sometimes in so many words, that the election of a Republican President would result in a reversion to the conditions of 1930–3. Senator Sparkman,[3] deriding the Republican slogan about it being 'time for a change', declared that among the changes a Republican Administration would bring would be a depression.[4] Governor Stevenson did not present the argument in such extreme terms as this.

The principal Republican reply was that the prosperity under Democratic Administrations had been what Governor Dewey called 'bloodstained prosperity'.[5] Putting the argument in more restrained terms, Eisenhower argued that not the New Deal but the Second World War had brought full recovery from the Great Depression, and when the war was over the accumulated backlogs kept the economy going at high levels; just when this stimulus was weakening, the Korean war and rearmament supervened and provided the necessary impetus to maintain prosperity.[6]

General Eisenhower and his advisers evidently believed that election-time economic history was not enough to allay doubts about whether a Republican Administration could maintain prosperity

[1] Text in *New York Times*, 18 October 1952.
[2] 30 September 1952. Text in *New York Times*, 1 October 1952.
[3] Democratic candidate for Vice-President.
[4] Speech at Beckley, Va., on 7 October. Reported in *New York Times*, 8 October 1952.
[5] Broadcast on 21 October, reported in the *New York Times*, 22 October 1952.
[6] Speech at Peoria, Ill, 2 October. Text in *New York Times*, 3 October 1952.

and high (or full) employment; this was probably the one issue that might just pull the Democrats through. Eisenhower gave stronger and stronger pledges in the closing stages of the campaign that he would not attack the schemes of social welfare enacted under the Administrations of Roosevelt and Truman, and that he would do everything possible to prevent depression. He said in a speech at Worcester, Mass., on 20 October: 'Anyone who says it is my purpose to cut down social security, unemployment insurance, leave the ill and aged destitute, is lying'.[1] He gave the following pledge on full employment in a speech at Harlem on 25 October: 'If the finest brains, the finest hearts, that we can mobilize in Washington, can foresee the signs of any recession and depression that would put honest hard working men and women out of work, the full power of private industry, of municipal government, of state government, of the Federal government will be mobilized to see that it does not happen. I cannot pledge you more than that'.[2]

The impression given by Eisenhower's campaign speeches about economic policy was that he believed that Federal expenditures were too high and that budget deficits were 'bad things' because they were inflationary. He undertook to reduce Federal expenditures to an annual rate of $60 billion within four years if the 'Cold War' did not worsen.[3] He also declared that he would have the Treasury work as the partner of the Federal Reserve System and not as its rival; since he spoke of the need to overthrow the Truman Administration's 'idol' of cheap money,[4] it is clear that he meant that the Treasury was to cooperate when the Federal Reserve System considered a restrictive monetary policy to be necessary.

Eisenhower's views about fiscal policy thus appeared in tune with the traditional orthodoxy and the views expressed by most Republicans during their years of Opposition. This was only to be expected, for this was a subject that was quite new to him. There is no reason to question the sincerity of his promise to do everything possible to prevent a depression, but he gave no details as to what he considered appropriate policies, and in particular gave no sign of realizing that the commitment might require actions which ran counter to his expressed views about government expenditure

---

[1] Text in *New York Times*, 21 October 1952.
[2] Text in *New York Times*, 26 October 1952.
[3] Speech at Peoria, Ill., 2 October. Text in *New York Times*, 3 October 1952.
[4] Speech at Troy, N.Y., 22 October. Text in *New York Times*, 23 October 1952.

and deficits. Almost certainly this was because he was as yet unfamiliar with the problem.

THE REPUBLICAN VICTORY AND THE FORMATION OF THE EISENHOWER ADMINISTRATION

The Republican victory in 1952 was a victory for Eisenhower rather than for his party. The Republican majorities in the incoming 83rd Congress were narrow; 221 to 214 in the House of Representatives and 48 to 47 in the Senate.[1] Although the results of the elections, especially those for the Senate, cannot be said to have amounted to a vote of confidence in the extreme Right,[2] the Republican victory majority in the Congress did place in positions of leadership men whose opinions were far out towards the Right, in many instances the same men who had held those positions during the 80th Congress.

In appointing his Cabinet and other leading members of his Administration, Eisenhower drew heavily on the business world. As Secretary of the Treasury he appointed George M. Humphrey, a leading Cleveland steel executive and a man of strong personality and decidedly 'orthodox' views on finance and economic policy, in whose judgement he came to place great trust. Joseph M. Dodge, who became Director of the Bureau of the Budget, was another convinced believer in 'economy' and balanced budgets. The new Secretary of Commerce, Sinclair Weeks, held similar views. The generally 'orthodox', business oriented views about economic policy that Eisenhower expressed in his campaign were thus reflected in his appointments to the Departments directly concerned with economic policy.

THE SURVIVAL OF THE COUNCIL OF ECONOMIC ADVISERS

The way in which President Eisenhower dealt with the Council of Economic Advisers would be an early indication of the extent to which he was prepared to make use of up-to-date economic analysis

---

[1] The other Senator was Wayne Morse, who although re-elected in 1950 as a Republican disassociated himself from the party out of disapproval of Eisenhower's agreement with Taft, and styled himself an independent until 1955 when he became a Democrat.

[2] Three extreme Right-wing Senators, Kem of Missouri, Cain of Washington, and Ecton of Montana, for each of whom Senator McCarthy campaigned, were all defeated although Eisenhower carried their states.

in fulfilling his campaign promise to take all possible action to prevent a depression. When he took office, the very survival of the Council was in question. The 82nd Congress had appropriated funds sufficient for only the first nine months of fiscal 1953 instead of for the customary full year, with the result that early in 1953 the Council was forced to wind up its operations. The reason was that the Council had fallen into disfavour with substantial sections of Congressional opinion, especially on the Right. This was partly because the Council's Chairman, Dr. Keyserling, had considered it his duty to support in public the Administration's economic policies and in consequence had made numerous speeches on controversial political issues, leading many Congressmen who disagreed with the Administration's and Dr. Keyserling's views on these issues to regard the Council of Economic Advisers as merely a propaganda agency for Fair Deal policies.

Unfortunately, this was not the only cause of the trouble. A more fundamental cause was the rift which still existed between the thinking of economists about economic stability and the policies needed to achieve it and the thinking of powerful groups both in Congress and the country. The belief that 'Keynesian' economics was not neutral analysis but political party doctrine and undesirable doctrine at that[1] had far from disappeared. Since the 'New Economics' was associated in the minds of many Americans with the New Deal, it is not surprising that it should have come under fire from the 'radical Right' from 1950 onwards. It was not at all uncommon to find deficit financing and large government expenditures denounced in the name of 'Americanism'.[2] In the course of some advice on the subject of 'how to tell a communist' Senator Mundt wrote: 'Communists and those supporting their nefarious program are always among those supporting fiscal extravagance and deficit spending'.[3] William F. Buckley Jr. in his book *God And Man At Yale*[4] (which was a best seller for a time) complained that that university was atheistic with respect to religion and Keynesian in economics, both of which he regarded as equally objectionable. This was not the only attack on economics as taught in the universities. This onslaught on

---

[1] See Chapter II, supra.

[2] The *Congressional Record* for these years is full of examples; to take one, see the speech by Senator Martin to a Republican Committee dinner in Mifflin County, Pa., whose text is printed in the *Congressional Record*, Vol. XCVIII, pp. A399–401.

[3] *Congressional Record*, Vol. XCVIII, pp. 383–5.　　　　[4] (Chicago, 1951).

economics is explicable only in terms of 'the politics of revenge'[1] against the New Deal.

It would be out of place here to go into any detail about the causes of the upsurge of the 'radical Right' and the sources of its strength,[2] but the damage it was capable of doing to the effectiveness of sound economic analysis in the formulation of American economic policy needs to be stressed. It was essentially an alliance between the 'unreconstructed' opponents of the New Deal seeking revenge[3] and those who objected to the foreign policy of resisting communist aggression by limited local action in cooperation with other countries. In view of the evidence from the public opinion polls that support for Senator McCarthy (the most readily available measure of support for the radical Right) was proportionately greatest in the lower income groups[4] it is tolerably safe to say that numerically most of the support for the radical Right came from those with 'Cold War' grievances rather than from those who really wanted to restore the economic *status quo ante* 1933. It is therefore likely that this Right-wing coalition was viable only in times of prosperity and inflation; a depression would lead those in the lower income groups who were vulnerable to unemployment to demand that the government 'do something' about it, and the 'something' would have to be so like the New Deal fiscal policy as to offend those who supported the extreme Right because of economic grievances. But in 1953 there was nothing to strain this Right-wing alliance, which gave the appearance of the existence in the United States of a formidable body of support for men whose expressed views on economic policy suggested that for ideological reasons they were disposed to ignore practically all that had been learnt since 1933 about the contribution the government can make to the maintenance of economic stability.

These were the forces that had created distrust of the Council of Economic Advisers. The House Appropriations Committee provided in the supplemental appropriation bill for a single economic adviser only, instead of the full Council. The Council was thus discontinued,

[1] The phrase is from S. Lubell, *The Revolt of the Moderates* (New York, 1956), Chapter III.

[2] These topics are ably dealt with by the writers of the seven essays collected in D. Bell (Ed.), *The New American Right* (New York, 1955).

[3] Bell, *op. cit.*; and also the following opinion by Charles R. V. Murphy in *Fortune*: 'many businessmen look to McCarthy to keep the albatross hung about the neck of the New and Fair Deals'. *Fortune*, April 1954, p. 180.

[4] Bell, *op cit* ., Chapter VII.

with the result that the employment of its staff came to an end.[1] The prime mover in this was Representative Taber, a veteran opponent of the New Deal and the Fair Deal who had a low opinion of economists. The Senate restored the funds for the full Council, thanks largely to the efforts of Senator Taft (who had been Chairman of the Joint Committee on the Economic Report during the 80th Congress). But the Conference Committee adopted the House version. The same fate as befell the National Resources Planning Board in 1943[2] appeared to have befallen the Council of Economic Advisers ten years later. In many respects this marked the nadir of the influence of economic analysis on the general economic policies of the United States government and the respect felt for economic analysis by those engaged in making those policies. The doctrines of what one noted academic supporter of 'modern capitalism'[3] has called 'suicidal conservatism' appeared to rule the American political roost.[4]

In a situation that was full of uncertainty about the future of 'economics in the public service' the actions of President Eisenhower were very significant. He appointed Dr. Arthur F. Burns, Director of Research of the National Bureau of Economic Research and a specialist in the study of business cycles. After the full Council had expired for lack of funds, Dr. Burns became the single economic adviser provided for in the supplemental appropriation. The President decided that the full Council as provided for by the Employment Act should continue, and requested an appropriation of $300,000 for fiscal 1954. At the same time he submitted to the Congress a reorganization plan, which was approved, which centralized authority in the hands of the Chairman. The House voted an appropriation of $200,000 in the regular Independent Offices appropriation bill, which was increased by the Senate to $275,000, whose version was retained by the Conference Committee. In addition the President set up the Advisory Board on Economic Growth and Stability under

[1] The staff were covered by Civil Service rules, which preclude dismissal except for cause, unless the employing agency is discontinued.

[2] See p. 35, supra.

[3] T. Wilson, *Modern Capitalism and Economic Progress* (London, 1950), p. 248.

[4] As evidence of this, note the vote of the House of Representatives to authorize Representative Reece to investigate the tax-exempt foundations after he had declared that they were engaged in a 'diabolical conspiracy' whose aim was 'the furtherance of socialism in the United States'. (*Congressional Record*, Vol. XCIX, p. 10015.)

the chairmanship of the Chairman of the Council of Economic Advisers; composed of representatives (usually Under-Secretaries) of the Treasury, Agriculture, Commerce, and Labor Departments, the Bureau of the Budget, and the Board of Governors of the Federal Reserve System, its principal function was to strengthen the channels of communication between the Council of Economic Advisers and the other departments and to bring its views to their attention.

The appointment of Dr. Burns was well received. It was welcomed in Congress, and the comments of the business journals were laudatory.[1] Burns was a highly qualified 'economist's economist' who had not been embroiled in political controversy; and the appointment was an important step by the President in fulfilling the promise to take all possible measures to prevent a depression; the selection of a specialist in the study of business cycles appears especially significant in this context. Congressional distrust of the Council waned, and even Representative Taber ceased to be the resolute opponent of the Council that he previously was.

THE END OF CONTROLS AND THE DEFLATIONARY MONETARY AND FISCAL POLICY

Among the earliest actions of the Administration was the ending of the remaining direct controls. President Eisenhower announced his intention of doing this in his State of the Union Message on 2 February 1953, and in an Executive Order on 6 February he abolished all wage controls and many price controls; the remaining price controls were abolished on 18 March. Secretary Humphrey was in large measure responsible for the abolition of controls. He believed that this could be done without any increase in prices, the more so because of the restrictive credit policy;[2] subsequent events vindicated his judgement.

The fiscal measures recommended by the Administration were in accordance with the positions taken during the campaign in the previous autumn, that government expenditures should be cut, the budget deficit reduced, and tax reduction held over till a balanced budget was within reach. It soon became apparent that the President would have strong support in the Congress for reducing appropria-

[1] See *Fortune*, April 1953, and *Guaranty Survey*, July 1953.
[2] 'The Eisenhower Shift', by Charles R. V. Murphy in *Fortune*, February 1956, p. 113

tions below the amounts requested in President Truman's Budget Message, but that he would have difficulty over tax reduction. As the law (the Revenue Act of 1951 and the Excess Profits Tax Act of 1950) then stood the excess profits tax would expire on 30 June 1953; the increase in the personal income tax on 31 December 1953; and the increase in excise taxes on 31 March 1954. Representative Reed, now Chairman of the Ways and Means Committee, had introduced a bill, H.R.1, to make the reduction in income tax effective on 30 June 1953 to coincide with the end of the excess profits tax. The Ways and Means Committee reported the bill on 16 February, but the Republican leaders in the House had the bill held in the Rules Committee to give the Administration time to prepare its tax policy.

The Administration's recommendations were submitted to the Congress in a special Message on 20 May 1953.[1] The principal recommendation was that the excess profits tax should be continued at its existing rate for a further six months. The President expressed the hope that it would be possible to allow the tax reductions scheduled for 1 January 1954 to go into effect, and stated that in the following Session he would submit recommendations for a 'modified' system of excise taxation. A number of sharp reductions in appropriations were proposed. Whereas in his Budget Message President Truman had recommended appropriation of $40,720 million for the Department of Defense, President Eisenhower reduced this to $35,772 million; the requested appropriation for Mutual Security was similarly cut from $7,614 million to $5,139 million; the requested appropriation for the Atomic Energy Commission was cut from $1,593 million to $1,096 million, that for the Army (Civil Functions) from $683 million to $499 million, that for the Department of the Interior from $607 million to $491 million, and that for the Department of Commerce from $1,131 million to $962 million.[2]

The Congress approved these cuts and added some of its own, none of them large except for the cuts in the Mutual Security and Army appropriations. The cuts in the military appropriations were the financial consequence of an important decision in defence policy, to slow down the rate of rearmament and to rely more on retaliatory power than on strength in conventional weapons. The retaliation

---

[1] Its text is printed in the *Annual Report of the Secretary of the Treasury for the year ending 30 June 1953*, pp. 204–7, and in the *Congressional Record*, Vol. XCIX, pp. 5277–9.
[2] *Congressional Quarterly Almanack*, (Washington, 1953).

was to be accomplished with an Air Force that was smaller than that provided for in the Truman Administration's plans, and the cut in the Air Force appropriation ($4·8 billion) was the sharpest of all. This cut in the Air Force appropriation was the most severely criticized of all the Administration's recommendations on appropriations.

The extension of the excess profits tax was achieved only after a considerable struggle. Secretary Humphrey told the Ways and Means Committee on 1 June 1953 that although the excess profits tax was inequitable, it should be continued for a further six months because the loss of $800 million of revenue entailed by its expiration could not be afforded. In the course of the hearings nearly all the business representatives held that the tax should be allowed to expire. The Committee for Economic Development supported its continuation for six months and the C.I.O. wanted it to be continued indefinitely.

Chairman Reed was resolutely opposed to the bill, and let it be known that he would not allow it to be reported out of his Committee.[1] However, the Republican leaders in the House were prepared to invoke a seldom used power of the Rules Committee to bring the bill to the Floor.[2] At this Reed yielded and summoned the meeting which voted to report the bill. The vote was 16 to 9, 9 Republicans and 7 Democrats voting in favour.[3]

Representative Kean, who introduced the bill, stressed the argument that to reduce tax rates before the decline in government expenditure had begun would be inflationary under the conditions then prevailing; although the excess profits tax had its defects, so did other taxes, and there was no good reason why those liable to the excess profits should have priority in the redress of their grievances.[4] He was supported by Representative Cooper, the senior Democrat on the Ways and Means Committee, who said that 'sound fiscal policy' required the extension of the tax.[5] Most of the criticism of the bill came from the Republican side; Reed denounced it as a 'breach of faith'.[6] The motion to recommit was rejected by 275 votes to 127 and the bill passed by 325 votes to 77.

[1] The rules of the Ways and Means Committee provide that it shall meet at the call of the Chairman, so that Reed could prevent the bill being reported out by declining to call a meeting of the Committee for the purpose.
[2] *New York Times*, 25 June 1953.   [3] *New York Times*, 9 July 1953.
[4] *Congressional Record*, Vol. XCIX, pp. 8488–9.   [5] Ibid., p. 8489.
[6] Ibid, pp. 8491–3.

Debate in the Senate was brief and centred on the amendment moved by Senator Williams to increase the minimum exemption from $25,000 to $100,000 to help small businesses. The amendment was rejected by 52 votes to 34 and the bill passed by a voice vote. Senator Long held that since economists were expressing concern about a coming recession, it would be preferable to let the tax expire and so give an incentive to the investment of venture capital.[1] Introducing the bill, Millikin spoke of its importance in helping to balance the budget.[2]

The fiscal policy pursued in 1953 was thus fairly strongly deflationary. The Administration insisted on the maintenance of existing tax rates despite a considerable drop in expenditure that was to be brought about both through Congressional cuts in appropriations (in most instances at the Administration's behest) and through direct economy within the Administration. One of the first actions of the new Director of the Bureau of the Budget was to place the various departments under stringent restrictions on expenditure and replacement of staff. On 11 August 1953 the President in a letter to all agency heads instructed them to make renewed efforts to hold down their agencies' expenditure and to reduce their requests for appropriations for the next fiscal year.[3] He also used a 'pocket veto' to prevent the passage of the bill to abolish the tax on admissions to cinemas, declaring in a 'memorandum of disapproval'[4] that the loss of revenue could not be afforded. From the remarks of the President and the Secretary of the Treasury on numerous occasions it is clear that the Administration was not so much pursuing a deliberately deflationary fiscal policy as trying to 'get the budget under control' in a more old-fashioned sense. The widening deficit and the rising trend of Federal expenditures were regarded as undesirable in themselves, so that it was necessary to reverse them, whether or not the situation in the economy was inflationary enough to call for such measures. The ideas expressed in the campaign speeches still held sway. There was very little Congressional criticism of the deflationary fiscal policy as such; there was plenty of criticism of the cut in defence expenditure, but almost none of the general policy of maintaining existing tax rates while cutting expenditures.

[1] *Congressional Record*, Vol. XCIX, p. 8876.
[2] Ibid., p. 8848.   [3] *New York Times*, 12 August 1953.
[4] Text printed in *New York Times*, 8 August 1953.

In contrast, the restrictive policy pursued by the Federal Reserve System in the first four months of 1953 was very controversial. The System reinforced the restrictive policy that had begun in the autumn of 1952 by raising the rediscount rate in January 1953 and making substantial sales of securities.[1] The Administration approved this policy, and the Treasury reinforced it by announcing in April the issue of $1 billion of 30 year bonds at $3\frac{1}{4}$ per cent, the highest rate of interest offered on any issue of U.S. Government securities since 1933.

These policies indicated clearly that the Federal Reserve System believed that inflationary pressures threatened. In the hearings on monetary policy held by the Economic Stabilization Subcommittee of the Joint Committee on the Economic Report both Secretary Humphrey and Chairman Martin were closely questioned as to what factors in the situation seemed to them to indicate a danger of inflation at a time when the general price level was fairly stable. Martin said that early in 1953 there was forming what he called 'a bubble on top of a boom'.[2] He was particularly concerned about the increase in inventories, a point which Humphrey also stressed. Humphrey argued that the removal of price control might have led to a speculative accumulation of inventories, which at the time might well have led to an increase in prices.[3]

There are two ways in which a restrictive policy can check the accumulation of inventories: by checking the growth of total income and sales, which after a time will check the growth of inventories, depending on the original ratio of inventories to sales and the ratio that the sellers of goods desire; and the more direct means of raising the cost of carrying inventories. It is evident from the testimony that it was the second of these means that was the purpose of the restrictive monetary policy in 1953.[4] It was claimed that but for the restrictive policy the accumulation would have been greater and the subsequent liquidation correspondingly more severe. This is a separate argument, the need to avoid undue fluctuations in inven-

[1] See account of Federal Reserve actions submitted by the Board of Governors to the Economic Stabilization Subcommittee of the Joint Committee on the Economic Report: *United States Monetary Policy: Recent Thinking and Experience*, Hearings before the Economic Stabilization Subcommittee of the Joint Committee on the Economic Report, December 1954, p. 14.

[2] *United States Monetary Policy: Recent Thinking and Experience*, hearings before the Economic Stabilization Subcommittee of the Joint Committee on the Economic Report, December 1954, p. 246.

[3] Ibid., p. 209   [4] Ibid., pp. 209, 213.

tories, and to be distinguished from the contention that the accumulation of inventories if unchecked would have caused an excess of effective demand.

The effect of the restrictive measures on the credit market was greater than had been expected. The new $3\frac{1}{4}$ per cent bonds fell below par and something of a 'scramble for liquidity' took place, and the situation was subsequently described officially as one of 'undue tension'.[1] The editor of a well-known business journal was moved to write: 'It's good to know the brakes work but we don't want to go through the windshield'.[2] The restrictive policy was reversed early in May; large purchases of securities were made, the purpose being described by the Federal Reserve System as 'relief of money market tensions'.[3] It soon became evident that the restrictive policy had been reversed altogether, for in July reserve requirements were reduced.

The effect of the restrictive credit policy on the economy outside the credit markets is hard to estimate. Inventories continued to rise for about four months after the policy had been reversed, so that unless there were some very complex delayed-action effects it can hardly be said that the policy was responsible for the swing from inventory accumulation to liquidation that was an important feature of the recession that began later in the year. It may well be that the monetary policy slowed down the rate of inventory accumulation in the early part of the year, with the result that the subsequent liquidation was less severe than it would otherwise have been.

The restrictive credit policy was the subject of vigorous controversy both at the time and subsequently. It was attacked on the ground that it would lead to reduced employment and economic activity[4] and that the higher rates of interest on the national debt were an unnecessary burden on the taxpayer for the benefit of banks and the financial community generally. There was even a demand that the Federal Reserve System should once more be required to support the Government bond market.[5]

[1] Ibid., p. 8.   [2] *Business Week*, editorial, 9 May 1953.
[3] *United States Monetary Policy*, p. 14.
[4] See the statement by Senator Douglas on August 3 1953 *Congressional Record*, Vol. XCIX, p. 11027–9, and the statement of minority views on the Democratic members in the 1954 report of the Joint Committee on the Economic Report.
[5] A resolution to this effect (H. Con. Res. 98) was introduced by Representative Patman with the support of Rayburn and McCormack. Text and explanatory statement in *Congressional Record*, Vol. XCIX, p. 4747–8.

CONCLUSION

In his references to economic policy in the course of the campaign Eisenhower gave the impression that he shared the devotion to the principle of small, balanced Federal budgets that had been professed in the Republican platforms and by party spokesmen in the Congress and elsewhere during the Administrations of Roosevelt and Truman. In the first six months or so of the Eisenhower Administration a start was made towards putting those principles into practice. The 'new look' in defence policy attempted to fulfil the Republican promises that more effective defence could be achieved with smaller expenditures. The drastic cuts in appropriations for Federal electric power development, in which the Congress went further than even President Eisenhower requested, reflected the 'free enterprise' ideology that the Republicans had so long supported with respect to natural resources. The fact that the Administration insisted on the retention of the excess profits tax after the Federal Reserve System had reversed its restrictive policy suggests that either the Administration disagreed with the Federal Reserve System's judgement that the inflationary pressures that had threatened earlier in the year had begun to recede, or else that the Administration's budgetary policy was strongly influenced by considerations other than compensatory policy. There is little doubt that the latter was the correct explanation.

Reliance on monetary policy as a means of stabilizing the economy was greatly increased. In the first half of 1953 the Federal Reserve System's policy was directed to checking inflation and then swinging over to avoid exerting deflationary pressure, whereas the budgetary policy was determined primarily by other criteria. The Administration supported the restrictive monetary policy and used its operations with the National Debt to reinforce it. In undertaking a deflationary policy at a time when the general price level was practically stable, the Federal Reserve System and the Administration were running a risk of deflation in order to guard against an inflation that was potential and not actual. In reply to a question from Senator Douglas, Secretary Humphrey said that the restrictive monetary policy was occasioned not by price increases that had already occurred but by price increases that were expected in the future.[1] The use of monetary

[1] *United States Monetary Policy: Recent Thinking and Experience*, hearings before the Economic Stabilization Subcommittee of the Joint Committee on the Economic Report, December, 1954, p. 212.

policy as the means of promoting short run economic stability while directing budgetary policy to other ends did no great harm in the first half of 1953 when the deflationary effects of the budgetary policy, though only incidental to its main purpose, were not sufficient to do more than offset the rise in private demand. The full consequences of the decisions made in the first half of 1953 were not felt until later when the cuts in defence expenditure took effect. The conduct of fiscal policy in the first half of 1953 left open the question of what use the Eisenhower Administration would make of fiscal policy if called upon by events to fulfil the promise to do everything possible to prevent depression.

CHAPTER XI

THE REPUBLICAN ADMINISTRATION AND THE RECESSION, 1953-1955

DURING the summer of 1953 the increase in production came to a halt, and by the end of September a decline had definitely set in. The danger of such a recession had been foreseen several months before. The rearmament programme had been scheduled to reach its peak late in 1953 and then decline steadily until defence expenditure reached an annual rate of about $40 billion. It was generally realized that such a decline in defence expenditure would cause serious problems of readjustment. The question was discussed in some detail by the Council of Economic Advisers in their *Annual Economic Review* in January 1953; their conclusion, based on a survey of trends in productivity, growth of the labour force, investment, the foreign balance, and the propensity to save, as well as the decline in defence expenditure, was that there would be a tendency towards a deficiency of demand over the next three years or so.[1] The rapid accumulation of inventories, at what looked like an unsustainable rate, also gave cause for concern.[2]

The following tables give an indication of the nature and magnitude of the recession:

TABLE 27

Selected Indicators of the Recession, 1953–4

	G.N.P. ($ billion at 1945 prices)	Industrial Production	Production of Durable Goods	Unemployment (% of Civilian labour force)
1953 Peak	373·2	142	162	2·6
	(*2nd Quarter*)	(*July*)	(*July*)	(*August*)
1954 Trough	359·5	128	136	6·2
	(*2nd Quarter*)	(*Feb.–Apr.*)	(*Mar.–Apr.*)	(*September*)

Sources: G.N.P. at constant prices: *U.S. Income and Output,* 1959, Table I–5. Industrial Production and Production of Durable Goods: Federal Reserve revised seasonally adjusted indices, published in *Federal Reserve Bulletin,* December, 1959, pp. 1469–71.
Unemployment percentages (seasonally adjusted): *Survey of Current Business,* April 1960, p. 22.

[1] The *Annual Economic Review* accompanied the *Economic Report of the President.* The analysis referred to is in Chapters III and IV.
[2] *Fortune,* February 1953, p. 30–2; *C.I.O. News,* 6 July 1953.

TABLE 28

Changes of Components of G.N.P.

	Change from 2nd Quarter 1953 to:			
	1953 4th Qtr.	1954 2nd Qtr	1954 4th Qtr.	1955 2nd Qtr.
Personal Consumption	−2·1	0·2	7·0	17·5
Non-Farm Housing	−0·3	1·0	3·1	4·7
Other Private Domestic Investment in Fixed Capital	0·5	−1·0	−1·5	1·2
Change in Inventories	−7·8	−6·1	−2·4	3·3
Net Exports	0·6	2·0	3·5	1·5
Government Purchases of Goods and Services:				
Federal	−1·3	−12·3	−16·1	−16·1
State and Local	1·1	2·4	3·2	4·6
Total G.N.P.	−9·3	−13·7	−3·1	16·6

Changes expressed in $ billion at seasonally adjusted annual rates at constant (1954) prices. Detail does not necessarily add to totals because of rounding.
Source: Department of Commerce, *U.S. Income and Output*, 1959, Table I–5.

In the initial stages of the recession the swing from inventory accumulation to liquidation was the strongest deflationary force in the economy. The Council of Economic Advisers considered that the main cause of the swing was what they called an 'imbalance' between income and demand for goods in 1953,[1] which led to an undesired increase in inventories, followed in due course by liquidation as producers and sellers of goods sought to bring their inventories more into line with their sales. Another cause was the cut in orders for military goods, which reduced the inventory requirements of firms doing defence work. A third possibility was that the reduction in inventories was the direct result of the restrictive monetary policy pursued in the early months of 1953. The last explanation does not seem the most likely because of the length of the lag between the reversal of the restrictive monetary policy and the onset of inventory liquidation.[2]

The 'imbalance' was caused by the fact that in 1953 consumers' expenditure for goods did not rise in proportion to the increase in disposable income. From the fourth quarter of 1952 to the third quarter of 1953 disposable income rose by $8·2 billion, measured at seasonally adjusted annual rates.[3] During this period consumers'

[1] *Economic Report of the President, 1954*, pp. 20–1.
[2] See p. 208 supra.   [3] *U.S. Income and Output*, 1959, Table II-2.

expenditure for goods rose by only $2·1 billion.[1] Measured at constant (1954) prices the increase was $3·5 billion.[2] The reason why consumers' purchases of goods rose abnormally slowly is hard to determine. During the first seven months of 1953 total consumer credit outstanding rose by an average of $400 million a month; the rate of increase fell to $200 million a month in August, a rate that continued until December.[3] Since the rate of increase in purchase of goods was greater in the first and second quarters of 1954 when total consumer credit outstanding was declining than it was in 1953, it is unlikely that the low rate of increase of purchases of goods was due to the effects of restrictive monetary policy on the cost and availability of consumer credit.

In the course of a discussion during the hearings of the Joint Committee on the Economic Report, the Chairman of the Council of Economic Advisers held that the swing from inventory accumulation to liquidation was mainly due to the 'imbalance', though he agreed that the reduction in defence orders had also reduced inventory requirements.[4] This analysis appears correct, for inventory liquidation occurred in the non-durable goods sector[5] as well as the durable goods sector which bore the brunt of the cut in defence orders. Reduced defence expenditure could have caused a reduction in sales of non-durable goods, and hence in inventory requirements, through multiplier effects, but the decline in sales of non-durable goods that would be an essential part of such a process did not occur.

After the beginning of 1954 the reduction in defence expenditure became the main deflationary force in the economy. Purchases of goods and services for national defence declined from an annual rate of $50·5 billion in the second quarter of 1953 to $47·6 billion in the fourth quarter, $41·5 billion in the second quarter of 1954, and $38·4 billion in the fourth quarter.[6] The whole of the decrease represented a decrease in real terms.[7]

---

[1] Ibid., Table I–3.   [2] Ibid., Table I–5.

[3] Board of Governors of the Federal Reserve System, monthly statistics published in the *Federal Reserve Bulletin*.

[4] Joint Committee on the Economic Report, *Hearings on the Economic Report of the President*, 1955, pp. 46–8.

[5] Department of Commerce, *Business Statistics*, 1955, p. 18.

[6] *U.S. Income and Output*, 1959, Table I–3.

[7] In the absence of a separate deflator for Federal purchases of goods and services for defence, that for all Federal purchases of goods and services is used. *U.S. Income and Output*, 1959, Table VII–3.

THE BEGINNING OF THE RECESSION AND THE TAX
REDUCTION OF 1 JANUARY 1954

On 22 September 1953 the Secretary of the Treasury announced that the Administration would not request legislation to postpone the tax reductions scheduled for 1 January 1954. The reductions were substantial; the cost of the expiration of the excess profits tax was estimated at $2 billion in a full year, and the cost of the reduction in income tax at $3 billion.[1] The reduction would restore the rates of income tax in effect under the Revenue Act of 1950. In his speech announcing the reductions[2] Secretary Humphrey said:

'. . . it is the definite intention of this administration, through tax reduction to return to the people to spend for themselves all the real savings in Government spending that can be reasonably anticipated.'

The Secretary continued:

'I can assure you that this Government is dedicated to the maintenance of a high level of employment and production and it will pursue policies to foster that end.'

Although the speech included a remark that it is not a calamity if the day of the order-taker is passing and salesmen are again needed, there is a marked difference in the tone of the speech from those made by Secretary Humphrey and other members of the Administration earlier in 1953; the last passage quoted is particularly significant. Clearly, the Secretary of the Treasury was trying to foster confidence in the ability of the economy, and of the new Administration, to cope with the threatened recession.

The reference to 'returning to the people the savings in Government expenditure' is worthy of note, for this was a theme to which Secretary Humphrey was to return frequently during the debates on tax reduction in the following year. Humphrey was no supporter of the principle of a compensatory fiscal policy,[3] but he did not maintain that a budget surplus must already have been achieved before tax reduction was permissible; the tax reduction should coincide as

---

[1] *Annual Report of the Secretary of the Treasury for the year ending 30 June 1954*, p. 44.

[2] To the American Bankers' Association. Text printed in the *Annual Report of the Secretary of the Treasury for the year ending 30 June 1953*. The extracts quoted are at p. 249.

[3] He was reported as saying at his news conference on 16 January 1957 that he would probably resign if the Administration were to decide on a deficit-financed tax cut during a recession. *New York Times*, 17 January 1957.

nearly as possible with the reduction in expenditure so that increased private spending can offset the reduction in demand caused by the cut in Government spending.

It is a moot point whether the tax reduction which became effective on 1 January 1954 was in any real sense discretionary. The Secretary of the Treasury in the speech quoted above treated it as an act of deliberate policy, while the Economic Report of the President in January 1954[1] and Dr. Burns in his Millar Lectures in 1957[2] treated it as a piece of counter-cyclical policy put into effect in very good time. But it is equally possible to contend that the tax reductions would have gone into effect just the same had the threat been one of inflation rather than deflation, because of the political impossibility of getting the Congress to pass the legislation needed to continue the existing rates. The extension of the excess profits tax in 1953 had been achieved with great difficulty;[3] the President in his 1953 Tax Message had held out the expectation of tax reduction in 1954; and given the views among Congressional Republicans about high taxation it is very unlikely that the seldom-used powers of the Rules Committee would be invoked to thwart Representative Reed again, for the authority of Committee Chairmen is jealously guarded by Congressional practice. It is thus likely that even had it wanted to, the Administration would not have been able to prevent the tax reductions from going into effect unless severe inflation existed.

One of the reasons for the insertion of the time limit to the tax increases was the belief that defence expenditure would reach a peak in 1953 and thereafter decline. Of course, any forecast made in 1951 concerning the economic and budgetary outlook at the beginning of 1954 had to contain a high proportion of guesswork, but it was not entirely by chance that automatic tax reduction coincided with the reduction in defence expenditure. It can scarcely be denied, however, that there was a considerable element of good fortune in that existing law brought about a substantial tax cut quite early in the recession, at a time when a truly 'discretionary' tax reduction could not be achieved without summoning a Special Session of the Congress.

At about the end of August the Chairman of the Council of Economic Advisers came to believe that a recession was in the offing[4]

---

[1] *Economic Report of the President, 1954*, p. 52.
[2] Published as A. F. Burns, *Prosperity Without Inflation* (New York, 1957).
[3] See p. 205 supra.
[4] A. F. Burns, *Prosperity Without Inflation*, (New York, 1947) p. 30.

and on 25 September 1953 he reported to the Cabinet that there were many signs that a recession was beginning.[1] He said that the immediate measures which the Council of Economic Advisers had in mind were liberal monetary policy, tax reductions, and Federal lending programmes rather than large increases in Federal construction expenditure, and stressed the importance of planning well in advance. A considerable amount of work was done in the second half of 1953 to hasten the planning of Federal public works and to prepare detailed information about what Federal expenditures could be increased quickly should the need to do so arise. Planning had started before the onset of the recession was definitely noted; on 9 July the Budget Bureau had issued the following directive: 'Increased emphasis will be given to the development of plans for authorized high priority projects to a stage where these projects would qualify for construction at a time when construction starts would be consistent with a less restrictive budget policy.'[2] The language could scarcely be more guarded, but it does indicate that the Budget Bureau was thinking ahead to the time when it might be necessary to add to demand, even though 'economy' was still the public watchword. The work done in accordance with this directive led to the inclusion in the Budget for fiscal 1955 of twenty new projects and the resumption of work on six more. They were all flood control, navigation, or irrigation projects, the last group under the control of the Bureau of Reclamation and the others under the Corps of Engineers.[3] The total cost of the projects was estimated at $184 million, of which $25 million would be spent in fiscal 1955.[4] This in itself was a very small amount, but far more important was the planning done which would shorten the time lag before contracts were let and men employed if it were necessary to expand works construction very quickly. At the request of the Council of Economic Advisers the Bureau of the Budget also made a study of what expenditures could be increased by administrative decision and how quickly.

The President in his Message transmitting the Economic Report

[1] R. J. Donovan, *Eisenhower: The Inside Story*, (New York, 1956), p. 165. Donovan was given access to Cabinet minutes for his book.

[2] Cited in *Economic Report of the President*, 1954, p. 54.

[3] The Corps of Engineers, although technically part of the U.S. Army, has numerous civil responsibilities, including the construction and operation of canals and locks.

[4] Assistant Director of the Budget to the Joint Committee on the Economic Report; Joint Committee on the Economic Report, *Hearings on the Economic Report of the President*, 1954, p. 28–9.

stressed the Administration's determination to deal effectively with the recession:

'The arsenal of weapons at the disposal of the government is formidable. It includes credit controls administered by the Federal Reserve System; the debt management policies of the Treasury; the authority of the President to vary the terms of mortgages carrying Federal insurance; flexibility in the administration of the budget; agricultural supports; modification of the tax structure; and public works. We shall not hesitate to use any or all of these weapons as the situation may require.'[1]

This was a vigorous enough statement of intentions, and one could hardly expect more from any Administration.

The Budget for fiscal 1955, submitted in January 1954, did not contain any provision for the use of Federal expenditure to deal with the recession; the emphasis was still on the reduction of expenditures, and the Budget Message pointed with obvious satisfaction to the fact that the budget deficit estimated for fiscal 1954 was only $3·3 billion compared with the $9·9 billion estimated in the budget submitted by President Truman in January 1953. The estimate for fiscal 1955 was for a reduction of about $5 billion in both revenue and expenditure, with a deficit of $2·9 billion. On the face of things it appeared that the budget would reduce demand slightly through a 'balanced budget multiplier' effect unless the removal of the excess profits tax proved a strong stimulant to investment.

The reduction in defence expenditure was responsible for almost the whole of the projected decline in Federal expenditure.[2] There were three main causes of the decline: the decline from a peak reached in 1953 as envisaged in the plans prepared during the Truman Administration, the end of hostilities in Korea,[3] and the changes in defence policy made in 1953 by the Eisenhower Administration that were popularly summarized as getting 'more bang for the buck'.

---

[1] *Economic Report of the President*, 1954, p. iv.

[2] The other category of expenditure which declined substantially in fiscal 1954 was 'housing and community development'. This decline was caused by the substitution of private financing for Treasury financing of certain local housing projects. The Treasury's loans were repaid from the proceeds, which reduced net expenditure as shown in the budget accounts, but was merely a financial transaction and deflationary only insofar as it absorbed investible funds in the private sector which would otherwise have been used to finance investment that could not be carried out for lack of finance from other sources.

[3] The armistice was signed on 27 July 1953.

The rate of decline of defence expenditure was under-estimated. Expenditure for goods and services for 'major national security' (a category in use in the national income accounts in 1954–7 which corresponded to the category of the same name in the Budgets in that period) in the fourth quarter of 1953 was at an annual rate of $49·4 billion.[1] The Budget in January 1954 estimated total expenditure for 'major national security' in fiscal 1954 at $48·7 billion and in fiscal 1955 at $44·1 billion. The drop in defence expenditure expected to occur between the beginning of 1954 and the beginning of 1955 was thus about $6 billion. The actual expenditures for 'major national security' in fiscal 1954 was $46·5 billion, $2·2 billion less than the estimate published in January 1954, and the estimate for 'major national security' expenditure in fiscal 1955 that was published in the Budget in January 1955 was only $40·6 billion compared with the previous January's estimate of $44·1 billion. Purchases of goods and services for 'major national security' in the fourth quarter of 1954 were at a seasonally adjusted annual rate of $40·2 billion.[2] Defence expenditure thus declined in 1954 by about $3½ billion more than had been estimated at the beginning of the year. This was not caused by any decision to make further cuts in defence expenditure to balance the budget or for any other purpose. The reorganization and reduction in the strength of the U.S. armed forces that followed from the decisions taken in 1953 were carried through more quickly than had been expected; 'It wasn't planned that way, it just happened'. This led to the inclusion in the Economic Report of the President (1954) of an erroneous forecast of government expenditure for the forthcoming year which was noticed and criticized.[3]

The tax reductions supported by the Administration approximately offset the expected reduction in defence expenditure of $6 billion. The expiration of the excess profits tax and the reduction in income tax that became effective on 1 January 1954 were estimated to cost between them $5 billion in a full year, and the loss of revenue through the provisions of the proposed new Internal Revenue Code was estimated at $1·4 billion.[4] Against this must be set the increase in the Social Security tax, which was automatic under existing law, on 1 January 1954 which yielded $1 billion in a full year, making a

[1] *Economic Report of the President, 1957*, Table E–1.   [2] Ibid.

[3] B. W. Sprinkel, 'The 1955 Economic Report of the President,' *Journal of the American Statistical Association*, Vol. L, p. 247.

[4] *Annual Report of the Secretary of the Treasury for the year ending 30 June 1954*, p. 44.

net reduction of $5·4 billion. Secretary Humphrey's principle of tax reduction proceeding in line with reductions in government expenditure was thus being adhered to. The amount of the tax reduction, which barely offset the reduction in expenditure, showed considerable caution, and given that some of the reduction in the income tax would add to savings rather than to consumption it is probable that the result would have been a reduction, probably slight, in total demand; the size of the reduction cannot be specified with precision because of the uncertainty about the effect of the elimination of the excess profits tax. It would be going too far, however, to describe the budget as 'a plan for more deflation'.[1]

This leaves open the question of whether the Administration's tax policy would have been different had the course of defence expenditures been foreseen more accurately. It is not at all unlikely, for even the Secretary of the Treasury, whose opposition to deficits was the strongest of any member of the Administration, might have followed his own principle and 'returned to the people' the $9–9½ billion of savings in expenditure instead of the $6 billion that there was expected to be at the time.

THE ADMINISTRATION, CONGRESS, AND TAX REDUCTION

Two important pieces of tax legislation were due for consideration during the 1954 session of Congress. The increases in the rates of excise tax and the corporation profits tax that had been imposed by the Revenue Act of 1951 were due by the terms of that Act to expire on 31 March 1954. Legislation had to be passed promptly unless it were decided that excise tax reduction was appropriate.[2] Also scheduled for consideration was the proposed revision of the Internal Revenue Code; this had been the subject of discussion between Treasury and Congressional experts since the spring of 1952[3] and was mainly a consolidating measure, but it contained some very controversial reforms, and would provide the means to keep open the question of tax reduction for most of the Session.

The Administration's position, expounded in the State of the

---

[1] Senator Morse, in *Congressional Record*, Vol. C, p. 862.

[2] The reduction in the corporation profits tax would not affect tax *payments* until the first instalment of tax on 1954 profits became due (March 1955), so that no inconvenience would be caused if legislation to continue the tax at existing rates was passed later in 1954. The reduction in the excise tax would go into effect at once unless prevented by fresh legislation.

[3] *Congressional Record*, Vol. C, p. 8993.

Union Message and the Budget Message,[1] was that the existing excise and corporation tax rates should be continued, and that no revenue-losing provisions should be included in the bill to enact the new Internal Revenue Code except the reforms proposed in the Budget Message; in particular, general reductions in the tax rates were opposed.

On the other hand, there was strong support both in the Congress and in the country for the contention that more drastic tax reduction was needed to deal with the recession, and that the revision and reforms proposed were inequitable. Taking this view were most of the Congressional Democrats (the Virginia delegation excepted, of course), leading Democrats outside the Congress, the trade unions, and other groups with a 'Fair-Dealish' outlook. Support for tax reductions as a means of dealing with the recession extended beyond the Democrats and their supporters, however; the Joint Committee on the Economic Report in a unanimous report stated that they expected the President to recommend reductions in excise and income taxes if the recession worsened.[2]

It soon became apparent that the Administration would have great difficulty in securing the extension of the existing rates of excise tax. Chairman Reed expressed his opposition almost at once, on the ground that tax reduction was needed to increase consumers' purchasing power and to encourage industry,[3] and it was soon evident that he had support from other Republican members of his Committee. On 27 January 1954 Speaker Martin endorsed a plan devised by Representative Simpson (a senior Republican member of the Ways and Means Committee) to reduce to 10 per cent all excise tax rates higher than this except for those on liquor and tobacco. The rates of tax on liquor and tobacco imposed by the Revenue Act of 1951, and the other increases which did not raise the rates above 10 per cent (of which the tax on cars was the most important) were to be continued. This plan was embodied in the bill H.R.8224 which was approved by the Ways and Means Committee on 4 March 1954.

In the Report by the Ways and Means Committee on H.R.8224[4] the majority laid much stress on the argument that the tax reduction would stimulate production and employment. Although this claim is

[1] The recommendations on tax policy are outlined in the *Budget of the United States for the year ending 30 June 1955*, pp. M16–23.

[2] *H. Rept. No. 1256*, 83rd Cong., 2nd Sess., p. 6.

[3] Reported by the *New York Times*, 8 January and 25 January 1954.

[4] *H. Rept. No. 1307*, 83rd Cong., 1st Sess.

always made for any and every proposed tax reduction, the arguments used to support the claim do indicate that Martin, Reed, Simpson, and their colleagues did oppose the Administration on this issue at least in part because they believed that further measures ought to be taken to check the decline in business activity. The estimated cost of the tax reductions in a full year was $912 million.[1] The most important items in terms of loss of revenue were: telephones, telegrams, and cables, $360 million; admission to public entertainments, $175 million; and jewellery, $100 million.

The Administration continued to oppose the tax reduction. In a television interview on 28 February Secretary Humphrey would approve only 'selective' reduction in excise taxes.[2] The Treasury's view was that cinemas and the fur trade were the cases most deserving of the 'selective' relief.[3] When the bill was brought before the House on 9 March 1954 the majority argued for it in terms of the general desirability of tax reduction and of the contribution tax reduction would make to overcoming the recession. In the latter context Representative Kean pointed out: 'Enactment of this bill (H.R. 8224) will add nearly a billion dollars a year to the spending ability of our people. . . . This added purchasing power of our people should aid in reversing the business trend'.[4] There was only desultory opposition to the bill from Congressional Democrats, and the motion to recommit provided merely for the exemption from tax of admission to entertainments costing 50¢ or under. It was rejected by a straight party vote of 213–200 and the bill passed by 411 to 3.

The Senate Finance Committee in their report on H.R.8224 endorsed the reasons given in the Ways and Means Committee's report for reduction of excise taxes, though laying more stress on the argument that 'whenever the budgetary situation permits' the opportunity should be taken to reduce excise taxes.[5] The Committee made a few small changes, resulting in a net loss of revenue of $46 million compared with the House bill.

When the Senate debated the bill on 24 and 25 March the use of

[1] *Congressional Record*, Vol. C, p. 3015.
[2] Reported in the *New York Times*, 1 March 1954.
[3] Representative Hale Boggs (a member of the Ways and Means Committee) stated that this view was conveyed to the Committee by Dr. D. T. Smith, Special Assistant to the Secretary of the Treasury; *Congressional Record* Vol. C, p. 3029.
[4] *Congressional Record*, Vol. C, p. 3021.
[5] *S. Rept. No. 1085*, 83rd Cong., 2nd Sess., p. 1–3.

fiscal policy to counteract the recession figured prominently. The leading supporter of more drastic tax reduction to add to demand was Senator Douglas, who moved amendments to repeal the tax on household appliances, to reduce the rate on radio and television sets from 10 per cent to 5 per cent, and that on cars from 10 per cent to 7 per cent. These were opposed by several Senators on the familiar ground of the dangers of tax reduction 'out of borrowed money'.[1] Not for the last time Douglas had the embarrassment of having quoted at him the view expressed in his book[2] that to incur an anti-deflationary deficit when unemployment was below 8 per cent would run too serious a risk of inflation. His amendments to reduce the tax on cars and wireless and T.V. sets were easily defeated, but Millikin (Chairman of the Finance Committee) yielded and accepted Senator Capehart's amendment to reduce the tax on household appliances to 5 per cent. Capehart, a conservative Republican from Indiana, put forward this proposal purely because the household appliance industry (of which a considerable part was located in Indiana) was suffering from the recession. This amendment was carried by 64 votes to 23, with many of the Right-wing Republicans voting in favour.

The supporters of a balanced budget attempted to block the tax reduction. Senators Byrd and Williams moved an amendment to delete all the tax reductions except that in the tax on admission to entertainments. Williams argued for the amendment in the following terms: 'I do not think any member of the Senate will question the sound premise that the budget should be balanced before tax cuts are made. . . . We have already reduced taxes by $5 billion this year. There still remains a big question of whether or not that went too far'.[3] The amendment was supported by several Senators (of whom Symington was the most prominent) who believed that the national interest required larger defence expenditure than the Administration planned and that tax rates should be kept up to pay for this increased expenditure.[4] The amendment was defeated by 54 votes to 34; the

---

[1] E.g. Senator Bush, who quoted Mr. Micawber approvingly; *Congressional Record*, Vol. C, p, 3835.

[2] P. H. Douglas, *Economy in the National Government*, (Chicago, 1952). Senator Douglas did not define the measure of unemployment in his book; but in the absence of such a definition it was not unreasonable to assume that it referred to unemployment as measured by the Bureau of the Census and the Bureau of Labor Statistics.

[3] *Congressional Record*, Vol. C, p. 3859.   [4] Ibid., p. 3862.

division cut across party lines, 16 Democrats and 18 Republicans being in favour, and 25 Republicans and 29 Democrats against. Those voting against the amendment and thus in favour of the tax reduction included such unlikely allies as Jenner and Malone and Humphrey and Douglas.

The Conference version of the bill was identical with the Senate version except that cinemas were not quite so generously treated. The estimated cost in a full year was $999 million.[1] By this time the Administration had relented in its opposition. When the President made his broadcast about tax reduction on 15 March 1954 he did not mention the reduction in excise taxes; since the purpose of the broadcast was to oppose a reduction in the personal income tax, there was no reason why he should not have appealed to the Senate to reject the excise tax reduction had he felt this to be necessary. When Senator Knowland and Representative Martin discussed the Congressional situation, including H.R.8224, with the President on 22 March he did not raise the question of a smaller tax reduction.[2] On 29 March it was reported that 'The President's economic counsellors' advised him that the reduction in excise tax rates would stimulate consumption demand and thus promote recovery.[2] Presumably this meant the Council of Economic Advisers; on this point the *New York Times* was, as usual, well-informed. The President signed the bill on 31 March 1954, and said on that day at his press conference that he signed the bill 'wholeheartedly', expressing the hope that it would so stimulate business that the loss of revenue would not be as great as originally estimated. The tax reduction thus accomplished was without doubt useful in dealing with the recession, but the initiative came from Congress, not from the Administration.

INCOME TAX REDUCTION AND OTHER MEASURES TO COUNTERACT THE RECESSION

The measures on which the Administration relied to bring about recovery, other than the automatic tax reductions and the excise tax reduction, were the easy money policy, the stimulation that would be given to investment by the more liberal provisions for depreciation in the proposed new Internal Revenue Code,[3] and certain minor measures.

These measures included the stockpiling of lead and zinc; the

---

[1] *Congressional Record*, Vol. C, p. 4061.
[2] *New York Times*, 29 March 1954.   [3] See p. 230 infra.

setting up of a new programme of subsidized shipbuilding; speeding up the handling of applications for FHA and VA mortgage insurance and guarantees; the speeding-up of tax refunds, and of the payments by the Department of Agriculture for the construction of grain elevators; and the placing of Government contracts in areas where unemployment was high.[1] In addition an attempt was made to reschedule some defence expenditure so that more would be spent in the first half of fiscal 1955. But in this respect too defence expenditure proved to be something of a rogue elephant from the point of view of economic stabilization; the re-scheduling did not have any effect until the second half of fiscal 1955 when the extra stimulation was not really needed.[2]

Both the Administration and outside observers attached great importance to monetary policy during the recession. Indeed, Neil H. Jacoby, a member of the Council of Economic Advisers during the period, has maintained that credit policy was 'even more significant' than the tax reduction in promoting recovery from the recession.[3] Relations between the Federal Reserve System and the Treasury and the other Executive departments were cordial and co-operation close during this period. The Treasury's issues of securities were all medium- or short-term; there was an issue of $2·2 billion on 9 November 1953 at $2\frac{3}{4}$ per cent for 7 years 10 months; another $2·2 billion on 17 May 1954 at $1\frac{7}{8}$ per cent for 4 years 9 months; and $4 billion on 4 October 1954 for 2 years $7\frac{1}{2}$ months at $1\frac{5}{8}$ per cent. There were no attempts to repeat the $3\frac{1}{4}$ per cent loan of April 1953. The Secretary of the Treasury stated that shorter-term finance had been used so as not to compete with State and local governments, business, and home-owners for long-term investible funds. Between the end of May 1953 and the end of October 1954 the banks' holdings of U.S. Government securities increased by $11·9 billion.[4] The Treasury's financing was in effect being done out of 'new money'.

Well before the recession had begun the policy of the Federal Reserve System became steadily more liberal. Once the recession was under way the policy became one of 'active ease'. The quantity of credit increased substantially, and interest rates declined, as is shown in the following table:

[1] A. F. Burns, *Prosperity Without Inflation*, (New York, 1957), pp. 32–3.
[2] Burns, op. cit., p. 34.
[3] N. H. Jacoby, *Can Prosperity Be Sustained*, (New York, 1956), p. 39.
[4] *Federal Reserve Bulletin*, Vol. XXXIX, p. 1067; and Vol. XLI, p. 517.

TABLE 29

Selected Interest Rates, June 1953 and 1954

	June 1953	June 1954
Treasury Bills	2·11%	0·64%
Prime Commercial Paper	2·75	1·56
Bank Loans (a)	3·73	3·60
U.S. Government Bonds (long term) (b)	3·29	2·70
Commercial Bonds (Moody's Aaa)	3·40	2·90

(a) Average for the three months ending in June of the rates on short-term bank loans in 19 cities.
(b) Due 1978–83, bearing 3¼ per cent interest
Source: Board of Governors of the Federal Reserve System, monthly statistics published in the *Federal Reserve Bulletin.*

The supply of credit was certainly adequate during the recession of 1954. Indeed, it subsequently became the general opinion in the Federal Reserve System that the policy of 'active ease' had been too active.[1] Business investment in fixed capital declined steadily, if slowly, throughout 1954, and not until September 1954 did new orders for machinery begin a definite rise; it is therefore doubtful whether the easy money policy played much of a part in checking the decline in investment in fixed capital by business, although it is possible, but not open to proof, that but for the relaxation of credit policy the decline in fixed capital investment by business would have been even greater. Likewise, consumer credit outstanding declined during the first half of 1954, the period when the greatest monetary 'ease' prevailed, and did not begin to rise strongly until the policy of 'active ease' was being reversed. The swing from inventory liquidation to accumulation came at the same time, indicating that the influence of monetary policy on these components of demand had been outweighed by other forces.

There is stronger evidence of the effect of the credit policy on housing, however. Non-farm house building, measured at seasonally adjusted annual rates at constant (1954) prices varied between $13·5 billion and $13·8 billion in the four quarters of 1953 and in the first quarter of 1954, but in the second quarter a steep increase began; in the fourth quarter of 1954 non-farm house building reached an annual rate of $16·9 billion (at constant 1954 prices), and in the second quarter of 1955 reached a peak of $18·5 billion.[2] The value

[1] Chairman of the Board of Governors of the Federal Reserve System to the Senate Finance Committee. Senate, Committee on Finance, *Hearings on the Financial Condition of the United States*, 1957, p. 1305.

[2] *U.S. Income and Output*, 1959, Table I–5.

Q

of house building contracts awarded began a definite rise in February 1954, and in the third and fourth quarters of the year was 33 per cent and 50 per cent greater than in the third and fourth quarters of 1953 respectively.[1] The fact that in 1955 house building declined fairly soon after the Federal Reserve System had begun a more restrictive monetary policy[2] suggests that the increase was caused at least in part by the easy money policy; both in 1949–50 and in 1958–59 the relaxation of credit as an anti-deflationary measure was followed by an increase in house building.

The monetary policy was not the only factor tending to stimulate house building. The VA and FHA were very active in using their authority to guarantee and insure mortgages for the finance of house building. The Housing Act of 1954 authorized the FHA to insure mortgages with smaller deposits and longer repayment periods than hitherto.[3] The number of housing starts in 1954 that were financed by mortgages insured or guaranteed by the FHA and VA was 583,300 (48·5 per cent of all privately-financed houses started) compared with 408,600 (38·3 per cent of all privately-financed houses started) in 1953.[4] Since the Housing Act and the Servicemen's Readjustment Act set maximum limits to the rate of interest on mortgages insured and guaranteed, the reduction in interest rates added much to their effectiveness. It is not possible to apportion responsibility for the housing boom exactly between 'pure' monetary policy and the Federal mortgage underwriting agencies. But in the absence of any evidence of a fall in building costs relative to personal income or of a sudden change in the demographic factors influencing the demand for houses, it is reasonably clear that the housing boom of 1954–5 was the result of the measures taken to stimulate the economy.

Whether or not these measures were adequate to bring about

[1] Calculated from F. W. Dodge Corp. series based on reports from thirty-seven states east of the Rocky Mountains. Printed in Dept. of Commerce, *Survey of Current Business*, monthly statistics.

[2] See p. 250 infra.

[3] The maximum insurable amount of the mortgage was set by the Housing Act of 1954 at 95 per cent of the first $9,000 of the cost of the house and 75 per cent of the remainder. Under the previously existing law (Housing Act 1949) the amounts were 95 per cent of the first $7,000 and 70 per cent of the remainder in the case of a new house where the mortgage was approved before construction, and in other cases 80 per cent of the cost. The maximum repayment period was extended from 25 years to 30 years.

[4] *Economic Report of the President, 1957*, Table E–31.

recovery was vigorously debated in the first six months of 1954. The Administration's view was that the tax reductions that had gone into effect on 1 January, and the reduction in excise tax rates, the easy money policy, and the more minor stimulating actions outlined above were adequate in the light of available information, and that more drastic measures would not be needed unless the situation deteriorated.

On the other hand, most Democrats, the trade unions, and other 'Left-of-centre' organizations held that further measures were needed, either tax reduction, additional public works expenditure or sometimes both. The proposed tax reduction received the wider support. The type of reduction most widely advocated was an increase in the individual exemption from income tax from the existing level of $600 to $700, $800 or in extreme cases even $1,000. The rationale of these proposals was that the recession was caused by a deficiency of effective demand, especially of consumer demand. The increase in consumer demand would result in a fuller use of productive capacity and so would increase the inducement to invest in new capacity. An increase in consumers' expenditure would permit the inventory liquidation to be carried out more quickly and thus hasten the resumption of inventory accumulation with the consequent stimulus to recovery.

The alternative to this approach was that supported by the Administration, that of direct stimulation of investment by tax concessions directed specifically to that end. The Administration held further that a large tax reduction would entail too great a risk of inflation. Secretary Humphrey told the Senate Finance Committee that an increase in the deficit would be 'the worst thing we could do'[1] because of its inflationary consequences. When asked by Senator Long: 'At this moment, you are not worried about further inflation, are you?' the Secretary replied: 'I would be very worried about it if you put another $3 or $4 billion worth of deficit on our present deficit'.[2]

Before tracing the course of the debate and its outcome, it is worth examining the background to the demand for 'an emergency transfusion of purchasing power'.[3] Between the third quarter of 1953 and

[1] Senate, Committee on Finance, *Hearings on H.R.8300*, 1954, p. 145.
[2] Ibid., p. 146.
[3] The phrase is from the Report of the Executive Committee of the A.F.L. to the A.F.L. Annual Convention, 1954; reported in the *Monthly Labor Review*, Vol. LXXVII, pp. 1250–1.

the second quarter of 1954 personal income before tax and transfer and before payment of contributions for social insurance declined from an annual rate of $279·6 billion to $276·0 billion. Between those quarters transfer payments rose by an annual rate of $1·9 billion, against which must be set an increase in personal social insurance contributions of $0·5 billion; Federal personal tax payments fell by $3·4 billion, while state and local tax payments rose by $0·3 billion.[1] The fall in Federal personal tax payments and the rise in transfer payments were more than enough to offset the fall in personal income before tax and transfer, disposable income rising by $1·0 billion.[2] Although the level of personal income before tax and transfer in the second quarter of 1954 was the lowest reached in the recession, disposable income was higher than the pre-recession peak, as was consumption. Although small changes from quarter to quarter as shown in the national income accounts must be treated with caution because of the 'statistical discrepancy',[3] there is every reason to regard as correct the view held at the time in official circles that disposable income and consumption expenditure for goods as well as services was being well maintained despite the recession. As long as this was so the attempt to reduce inventories would succeed and before long inventory liquidation would have to come to a halt, with a consequent increase in total demand and production. The danger was that the fall incomes caused by the reductions in output made in order to reduce inventories might lead to such a drop in consumers' demand that the attempt to liquidate inventories would fail, leading to another round of cuts in output. The cut in incomes resulting from the fall in defence expenditure could intensify such a spiral.

But in the early months of 1954 there was no sign of such a development. Retail sales of non-durable goods rose steadily, the total in each month except March being above that for the corresponding month in 1953, and in April equalled the previous high point (July 1953).[4] Sales of consumers' durable goods were below the 1953 levels throughout 1954, but in February and succeeding months were well above the low point of December 1953 and January 1954. The movements of disposable income and retail sales indicated that the fall in

[1] *U. S. Income and Output*, 1959, Table II–2.
[2] Detail does not add to total because of rounding.
[3] *U.S. Income and Output*, 1959, Table I–18.
[4] Department of Commerce, *Business Statistics* (1957 edition), p. 16.

production and in incomes derived from it was not causing a deflationary spiral, so that it was likely that the combination of reduced output and stable sales would run down inventories fairly quickly. It was reasonable to reach this conclusion in March or April 1954.

The above conclusion indicated that the consumption sector of the economy would be able to get by with the tax reduction already enacted, with the reduction in excise tax rates just to be on the safe side. The Administration's approach was cautious; in March and April 1954 definite evidence that the trough of the recession had been reached was not yet available and there were no grounds for believing that recovery had begun; the risk of a deflationary spiral still existed. The Administration decided to take the risk, which indeed did not appear a large one, in order to avoid risking the inflation that might develop once recovery was well under way if the tax reduction could not be reversed quickly.[1] While it was quite legitimate to argue that the risk of inflation should have been accepted and tax rates reduced, it cannot be justifiably asserted that the issue was whether any attention at all should be paid to consumption;[2] talk about 'a massive transfusion of purchasing power' implied that the consumption sector of the economy was in a much worse state of ill-health than it really was.

The main tax bill of 1954, that to enact a new Internal Revenue Code,[3] was a measure of revision and reform. Indeed, the slow, deliberate progress that it had made since its inception in 1952 suggests that its coinciding with a recession was fortuitous, though had there been inflation serious enough to make any tax reduction undesirable it could presumably have been held over for a year or so. The majority of the Ways and Means Committee stated in their report on the bill:

'This bill is a long overdue reform measure which is vitally necess-

---

[1] It is most unlikely that had the exemption from income tax been raised it would have been lowered again should recovery turn into inflation. When tax rates were raised in 1950 to rates higher than those in effect before the Revenue Act of 1948, the individual exemption was not cut although it had been increased from $500 to $600 in 1948.

[2] This assertion was freely made; for example, S. H. Ruttenberg, representing the C.I.O., expressed to the Joint Committee on the Economic Report the view that the Administration had insisted on stimulating investment only, thus putting the cart before the horse. Joint Committee on the Economic Report, *Hearings on the Economic Report of the President*, 1955, p. 159.

[3] The last complete revision and consolidation of the Internal Revenue Code had been in 1875.

ary regardless of momentary economic conditions and should not be confused with other measures which may be, or might become, appropriate in the light of a particular short run situation. . . .'[1]

There was no reason why a tax reduction should not have been added to the reforms if the economic situation rendered this desirable. The most contentious provisions were the dividend credit and the more liberal depreciation allowances. The latter provided that the taxpayer might use the 'sum of years digits' method[2] of computing depreciation, or declining balance at double rate (i.e. if the asset had a life for tax purposes of 10 years the annual allowance would be 20 per cent of the value not yet written off). The new formulae for computing depreciation allowances were to apply only to depreciable assets acquired after the Act had come into force, and thus were evidently intended as a device for encouraging investment rather than as an improvement in the equity of the tax system. The Administration proposed that the first $50 of personal income from dividends should be exempt from tax in 1954 and the first $100 in subsequent years, and that the taxpayer should be allowed to deduct from his tax liability 5 per cent of his income from dividends in the first year after the Act had come into force, 10 per cent in the second year, and 15 per cent in the third and subsequent years.[3] The bill reported by the Ways and Means Committee (H.R.8300) followed the Administration's recommendations except that the credit of dividends against tax liability was limited to 10 per cent. The dividend credit had no relevance to the immediate economic situation; it was supported on grounds of equity, as a means of providing relief from the 'double taxation' of dividends.[4]

The minority report of the Ways and Means Committee denounced the dividend credit as an indefensible discrimination in favour of unearned income and as embodying the 'trickle down' approach to tax reduction.[5] The changes in the depreciation allow-

---

[1] *H. Rept. No. 1337*, 83rd Cong., 2nd Sess., p. 1.

[2] This system is best explained by an example. The years of depreciable 'life' remaining to an asset in each year of that life are added together. In the case of an asset with a life of 5 years $5+4+3+2+1=15$. In the first year $\frac{5}{15}$ of the cost is taken as the depreciation allowance, in the second year $\frac{4}{15}$ in the third $\frac{3}{15}$, in the fourth $\frac{2}{15}$, and in the last $\frac{1}{15}$.

[3] *Budget of the United States for the year ending 30 June 1955*, p. M18.

[4] *H. Rept. No. 1337*, 83rd Cong., 2nd Sess., p. 4. Prior to 1954 dividends were not regarded under American tax law as having borne tax before being distributed. For a full discussion of the subject, see D. M. Holland, *The Income Tax Burden on Shareholders*, (Princeton, 1958). [5] Ibid., p. B–7.

ances were criticized on the ground that the fuller use of capacity that would result from an increase in consumption demand would be a more reliable inducement to investment, for since much existing capacity was not being fully used tax relief directed specifically to investment would not have much effect.[1]

The proposal for an increase in the individual exemption from income tax had almost[2] unanimous support from the Democrats, including Representative Rayburn, House Minority Leader, and Senator George, the senior Democratic member of the Finance Committee, which made it 'official' Democratic policy if anything could. There were also signs of Republican support.[3]

The Administration was sufficiently concerned for the President to make a special broadcast on the subject on 15 March, two days before the bill was due to be debated in the House of Representatives. After stressing the need to encourage investors to buy 'lathes, looms, and great generators' the President expressed hostility to the proposed increase in the individual exemption on the ground that it would exempt a large number of taxpayers from tax liability altogether:

'When the time comes to cut income taxes still more, let's cut them. But I do not believe that the way to do it is to excuse millions of taxpayers from paying any income tax at all . . . every real American is proud to carry his share of any burden. . . . I simply do not believe for one second that anyone privileged to live in this country wants someone else to pay his fair and just share of the cost of his Government'.[4]

The debate on the bill in the House on 17 and 18 March 1954 took the form outlined above, with sundry Democratic assertions that since their opponents had decided to something as reckless as to reduce taxation in face of a deficit, it might as well be a more equitable tax reduction.[5] The motion to recommit provided that the dividend credit and the depreciation provisions should be deleted and an increase in the individual exemption to $700 inserted. It was rejected by 210 to 204, eight Republicans voting in favour and seven

---

[1] Ibid., p. B–4.

[2] Senator Byrd and his supporters from Virginia were opposed.

[3] For instance, Representative Edith Rogers, who was supporting an increase in the exemption to $1,000. See *Congressional Record*, Vol. C, pp. 2966–9.

[4] The text of the broadcast is printed in the *Annual Report of the Secretary of the Treasury for the year ending 30 June 1954*, pp. 221–4.

[5] For instance, Rep. Camp; *Congressional Record*, Vol. C, p. 3444–5.

Democrats against. Not all of those voting in favour of the motion were voting in favour of a reduction of the income tax; if the motion to recommit had been carried it would probably have been the end of the bill for the Session unless the economic situation were to deteriorate. Among those whose votes appeared to be influenced by this consideration were the Democrats from Virginia[1] and Representative Cannon.[2] There are signs that the President's efforts were effective in whipping-in some of the Republican stragglers; one of these, Representative Ayres, said that he had thus changed his mind.[3]

When the Senate Finance Committee opened hearings on the bill on 7 April 1954 Secretary Humphrey held firmly to the position that the measures already taken, plus the stimulation that the depreciation provisions of the bill would give, were adequate to deal with the recession, and that a further tax reduction would be inflationary. The representatives of NAM and the U.S. Chamber of Commerce supported the Administration's position, but the Chamber's representative recommended that personal income tax should be reduced by 5 per cent of liability and that expenditures should be cut sufficiently to make the tax reduction possible without further unbalancing the budget.[4] The trade unions gave vigorous support to the increase in the individual exemption from income tax. Mr. Reuther said that there was 'nothing wrong in the American economy that an increase in the purchasing power in the hands of the American people will not cure'.[5] There was also the usual pleading for special relief and grinding of axes; the General Counsel to the National Institute of Diaper Services, Inc., asked that the cost of 'antiseptic diaper service' be made a tax deductible expense.[6]

After the end of the hearings the Finance Committee devoted five weeks to its consideration of the bill, and proposed numerous amendments,[7] none of economic significance in their effect on the revenue. Introducing the bill in the Senate of 28 June 1954 Senator Millikin declared that the bill would go part of the way towards

[1] Representatives Abitt, Gary, Hardy, Harrison, and Tuck. Smith voted against the motion to recommit and against the passage of the bill.

[2] See the arguments used in his speech; *Congressional Record*, Vol. C, p. 3518.

[3] *Congressional Record*, Vol. C, p. 3420.

[4] Senate, Committee on Finance, *Hearings on H.R.8300*, pp. 1924–33.

[5] Ibid., p. 820.

[6] Ibid., pp. 689–91 (written statement).

[7] The Committee's amendments are printed in the *Congressional Record*, Vol. C, pp. 8999–9045.

restoring 'normal economic incentives', which was essential since the stimulus given to the economy by abnormal military expenditure was fast disappearing. He emphasized the by then apparent fact that the decline had come to an end, arguing that as a result further tax reduction was not necessary to bring about recovery.[1]

Senator George agreed that the recession had not got as bad as had at one time seemed likely; he therefore proposed an amendment to increase the individual exemption from $600 to $700, instead of to $800 as he had suggested earlier. Although his proposal would increase the deficit in the immediate future, he maintained that 'There will be a greater deficit if we do not sustain the principles of a sound and expanding economy' and that it was more important to balance the 'home budget' than to balance the budget of the Federal government.[2] Douglas argued powerfully that the main economic problem at the moment was not lack of productive capacity but lack of effective consumer demand, and that no tax concessions to investment would achieve results if there was no market for the output from the increased capacity. The reasoning which underlay the bill was therefore fallacious; it would add to private savings, but would do nothing to add to investment, which was being held back by lack of markets.[3]

Millikin moved an amendment to provide for a reduction of tax of $20 in tax liability for each taxpayer, a slightly less costly substitute for George's proposal; it was ill received by George and his supporters and was rejected by 49 votes to 46, the vote being on party lines except that Langer voted with the Democrats. George's amendment to increase the individual exemption was rejected by 49 to 46, the margin of defeat being supplied by the four Democrats voting against it, Byrd, Robertson, Johnson of Colorado, and Holland. No general tax reduction was thus enacted.

The hostility to the dividend credit made its impact, however. Millikin himself moved an amendment, which was carried without a division, to reduce the credit to 5 per cent and to limit the exclusion of dividends from taxable income to $50 in all years. A further amendment, moved by Johnson of Colorado, to eliminate the dividend credit altogether, was carried by 71 votes to 13. The bill was passed by the Senate on 2 July 1954, shorn of all the provisions for relief of tax on dividends other than the exemption from tax of the first $50 of income from dividends.

[1] Ibid., p. 9063.   [2] Ibid., p. 9298.   [3] Ibid., p. 9168.

The Conference Committee restored a credit against tax liability of 4 per cent of income from dividends. The estimated cost of the changes made by the bill was $1,363 million in a full year. The House gave final approval on 28 July and the Senate on 29 July. The President signed the bill on 16 August, whereupon it became the Internal Revenue Code of 1954.

It is difficult to assess the effectiveness of the provisions for more rapid depreciation as a stimulant to investment. The difference made to the profitability of investment was not great, only about 5 per cent in many cases (i.e. if the rate of return was previously 20 per cent it would be increased to 21 per cent).[1] However, the Administration looked for results from the changes through their impact on business attitudes rather through the mathematical difference they made.[2] One would expect that the growing technical skill of business managements and precision in costing would increase the importance of mathematics relative to attitudes. Some support for this view is found in a paper 'The Effect on Business Decisions of Changes in Tax Depreciation Policy[3] by William J. Edmonds, discussing the results of a survey conducted by the National Society for Business Budgeting. Of the seven firms with net worth under $25 million that took part in the survey, four replied that they expected that their programme of capital expenditures would be accelerated as a result of the changes in depreciation allowances, whereas of the other twenty-seven, only five said that it would. The writer's conclusion was 'the method of depreciation employed would not often be material in the selection of specific projects for investment where a high rate of return is the principal criterion'. On the other hand, the work of Meyer and Kuh[4] suggests another means, perhaps more important, whereby the change in depreciation allowances could have stimulated business investment; of the variables studied, undistributed profits plus depreciation allowances appeared to exert the strongest influence on investment. An increase in the depreciation allowances granted in the early years of the 'life' of an asset increases the 'cash

[1] For a full account, see E. C. Brown, 'The New Depreciation Policy under the Income Tax: An Economic Appraisal', *National Tax Journal*, 1955, pp. 82–94.

[2] D. T. Smith, 'Two Years of Republican Tax Policy', *National Tax Journal*, 1955, p. 8. Dr. Smith was at the time Special Assistant to the Secretary of the Treasury.

[3] *National Tax Journal*, 1955, pp. 95–108.

[4] J. R. Meyer and E. Kuh, *The Investment Decision* (Cambridge, Mass., 1956).

throw-off'[1] of a firm which is doing any investing at all and so increases its internal supply of investible funds. The rapidity of the rise in orders for machinery after September 1954 and of the rise in business investment in fixed capital that began in the second quarter of 1955 is consistent with the view that changes in depreciation provisions enacted by the Internal Revenue Code had a significant effect.

PUBLIC WORKS POLICY

The Administration did not initiate any major programmes of public works for the purpose of counteracting the recession in 1954, though preparations were made to do so. These included the planning done in the Bureau of Reclamation and the Corps of Engineers,[2] and the planning of road construction by the Bureau of Public Roads and state Highway Departments which was embodied in the plans for a new Interstate road system which were presented by the Administration in 1955. A public works coordinator was appointed to the staff of the Council of Economic Advisers to keep a check on the public works programmes of the Federal agencies and of the state and local governments.[3]

Although on one occasion the President expressed opposition to the launching of a 'slam-bang' public works programme,[4] this was not on account of any opposition to the principle. At a Cabinet meeting on 15 February he said that he was willing to ask the Congress for additional appropriations, and set 1 July as the tentative date for action if there was not clear evidence that the decline had come to an end. Even Humphrey gave his approval to a public works programme if other measures did not prove adequate.[5] Well before the tentative date for launching a public works programme, the decline had come to a halt. Conditions in the building and construction industry remained fairly good throughout the recession, partly be-

---

[1] I.e. undistributed profits plus depreciation allowances.

[2] See p. 216 supra. The budget submitted in January 1954 estimated that projects amounting to $1·2 billion were planned to a stage where construction could be started by the end of fiscal 1954, and another $1·7 billion worth would have reached that stage by the end of fiscal 1955. *Budget of the United States for the year ending 30 June 1955*, p. 1142.

[3] Joint Committee on the Economic Report, *Hearings on the Economic Report of the President*, 1955, p. 23

[4] At his Press conference on 24 March 1954. Reported in the *New York Times*, 25 March 1954.

[5] Donovan, op. cit., pp. 213–4.

cause of the success of the measures taken to stimulate house building and partly because commercial building declined much less than
did investment in producers' durable equipment. Nevertheless, the
Administration's preparations for a programme of public works
looked sufficiently realistic to cause disquiet among those who
distrusted this means of coping with a recession.[1]

RECOVERY, SEPTEMBER 1954 TO EARLY 1955

On 23 July 1954 Dr. Burns told the Cabinet that all the indicators
pointed to the conclusion that the decline was over,[2] and during
the last quarter of 1954 it became apparent that the 'saucer' movement
of the principal economic indices had given way to a rapid recovery.
Inventory liquidation had come to an end and consumption was
rising strongly. The sequence of events expected by the Administration in the early part of the year had come to pass. The authorities
considered that no further measures of stimulation were called for.
In December 1954 the Federal Reserve System abandoned the policy
of 'active ease' and limited its purchases of securities to an amount
slightly smaller than that needed to meet the seasonal demand for
currency.[3] At this stage the policy was one of withdrawal to a more
'neutral' position rather than one of active restraint. The view was
taken in the Economic Report of the President in January 1955 that
the recovery had sufficient strength as to make it desirable for policy
to be directed to long-term growth rather than bringing about an
'immediate upthrust'.[4] Members of the Administration were once
more talking about the dangers of inflation and the elimination of
deficits. In an article published in January 1955 Secretary Humphrey
stated that the prevention of inflation would be one of the most
important objectives for the year, and would be achieved by a continuation of sound money policies.[5]

The Budget for fiscal 1956, submitted in January 1955, estimated
that there would be a deficit of $2·4 billion in the conventional budget

---

[1] See, for example, the comments in the *National City Bank Monthly Letter*,
February 1954.

[2] Donovan, op. cit., p. 222.

[3] Chairman of the Board of Governors of the Federal Reserve System to
Senate Finance Committee; Senate, Committee on Finance, *Hearings on the
Financial Condition of the United States*, August 1957, p. 1253.

[4] *Economic Report of the President, 1955*, p. 48.

[5] *Nation's Business* (organ of the U.S. Chamber of Commerce) January 1955,
p. 29.

and an almost exact balance in the cash budget. Receipts were estimated to be $1 billion greater than in the current year, and expenditures $1 billion less. This reduction in expenditures was to be achieved almost entirely through an expected fall in outlays for supporting farm prices and through a reduction in purchases and increase of sales of mortgages by FNMA. It was not a budget which sought to reduce demand by sharp cuts in public expenditure.

The VA took steps to moderate the housing boom; in February it issued regulations requiring the 'closing costs' (i.e. legal fees) to be paid in cash and not included in mortgages guaranteed by the VA, and in April required a deposit of 2 per cent (in the previous year about 25 per cent of VA-guaranteed mortgages had required no deposit at all).

In the Budget Message the President opposed any reduction of tax rates in 1955, but expressed the hope that reduction would be possible in 1956,[1] a qualification inserted somewhat reluctantly at Secretary Humphrey's behest.[2] Since the Excise Tax Reduction Act and the Internal Revenue Code had extended the remainder of the 1951 increases in excise tax rates and the increase in the rates of the corporation profits tax for one year only, fresh legislation had to be passed to extend them, and a bill (H.R.4259) was accordingly on its way through the Congressional machinery.

From a meeting between Speaker Rayburn and the senior Democratic members of the Ways and Means Committee on 19 February 1955 there emerged a proposal to attach to H.R.4259 provision for a reduction of tax liability of $20 for each taxpayer and each of his dependents.[3] Two days later it was formally approved by the Ways and Means Committee. On 23 February the President declared that it would mean a return to inflationary deficit financing, and described it as 'the height of fiscal irresponsibility'.[4]

From the debate on the bill in the House of Representatives on 25 February 1955 it appears that the Democrats' move was inspired mainly by considerations of equity, in particular that tax reduction ought to be provided for those who received no benefits from the Internal Revenue Code of 1954,[5] though it was contended too that far from being inflationary, it would be beneficial through bringing

[1] *Budget of the United States for the year ending 30 June 1956*, p. M13.
[2] Donovan, op. cit., p. 314.
[3] *New York Times*, 22 February, 1955.
[4] Transcript of the Press conference in *New York Times*, 24 February 1955.
[5] E.g., Rep. Patman; *Congressional Record*, Vol. CI, p. 2165.

into use resources which at the moment were unemployed.[1] Since the proposed tax reduction, if enacted, would not come into effect until 1 January 1956, there can be little doubt that the main purpose was to beat the President to the punch with tax reduction in 1956 in order to enact a reduction that was more in line with the majority of Democrats' ideas of equity than the reduction the President was expected to propose. If the principal purpose was to stimulate more rapid recovery it is reasonable to suppose that an earlier effective date would have been provided. No argument was presented to show that if addition to effective demand was needed the need would be greater early in 1956 than in 1955. To the extent that some people might spend in 1955 the tax reduction they were going to receive in 1956 there would be some stimulating effect in 1955, but surely not as much as if an earlier effective date had been provided. It was opposed as being inflationary, leading to deficits, and exempting too many people from liability to income tax altogether.[2] The motion to recommit was rejected by 210 votes to 205, with six Republicans voting for the tax reduction and eighteen Democrats, including the Virginia delegation, voting against it.

When the Finance Committee held hearings on the bill, Secretary Humphrey stated that passage of the tax cut would 'start us right back on the reckless road of inflation'.[3] Dr. Keyserling supported the tax cut, and recommended an even larger one to remove the condition of 'severe slack' from the economy.[4] Senators Byrd and George voted with the Republican members of the Committee to reject the proposed tax cut. A compromise, supported by the other six Democratic members of the Committee and reputedly devised by Senator Johnson, provided for a reduction of $20 for a head of household and $10 for each dependent except his wife, on condition that the taxpayer waived his right to use the 'income splitting' provision of the income tax law; the revenue loss was to be recouped by repealing the dividend credit and the accelerated depreciation provisions of the Internal Revenue Code of 1954.[5]

[1] Among others, by Rep. McCarthy, who presented this argument very capably. *Congressional Record*, Vol. CI, p. 2046–7.

[2] In this respect its effect would be the same as the increase in the exemption to $700 that was proposed in 1954.

[3] The text of his statement is printed in the *Annual Report of the Secretary of the Treasury for the year ending 30 June 1955*, pp. 226–7.

[4] *New York Times*, 2 March 1955.

[5] The proposal is described in a statement by Senators Kerr, Frear, Long, Smathers, Johnson, and Barkley in the *Congressional Record*, Vol. CI, p. 2596.

As in the House, most of the supporters of the tax reduction in the Senate based their case on equity rather than on the need to add to effective demand.[1] Senator Neuberger said: 'I fail to understand how tax reductions granted in 1954, when there was a substantial deficit, were evidence of statesmanship, while different kinds of tax reduction in 1955, when there is still a deficit, are called fiscal irresponsibility by Republicans'.[2] The proposed tax reduction was opposed on the ground that it would lead to deficit financing, which is undesirable because, among other things, 'it leaves out the human equation and the spiritual drives that are our greatest resources'.[3] Not all the debate was on this level; Senator Flanders took care to point out that he did not believe that the budget should be balanced under all circumstances, but that it would be sound policy to balance it at that time.[4] Senator Robertson noted that there were 'valleys' in the economy, but held that tax reduction to eliminate these involved too great a risk of inflation; it would be better, he said, to wait until 1956 and see if stimulation really was required then.[5]

The amendment to strike out the $20 a head tax reduction was carried by 61 votes to 31, and Johnson's compromise proposal was defeated by 50 votes to 44, the margin of defeat being supplied by four conservative Democrats, Byrd, Robertson, Holland, and George The last dispute over fiscal policy in connection with the recession of 1953–54 thus ended with the Administration's view, that the risk of fresh inflation outweighed the risk of slower recovery, carrying the day.

CONCLUSIONS ON THE USE OF FISCAL POLICY IN THE RECESSION OF 1953–5

The Eisenhower Administration's handling of the recession was sound if judged by the standards of counter-cyclical policy, though it was extremely cautious in its unwillingness to run much of a risk of inflation in order to speed recovery. The analysis of the state of consumption demand and the consequent unwillingness to support further reduction in income tax rates to stimulate consumption were well-founded. Had the speed of the decline in defence expenditure been more accurately foreseen, it is possible that a further general

---

[1] Senator Humphrey did argue for it on this ground, however; *Congressional Record*, Vol. CI. p. 2725.

[2] Ibid., p. 2901.   [3] Senator Bennett, ibid., pp. 2798–9.

[4] Ibid., p. 2887.   [5] Ibid., pp. 2882–3.

tax reduction might have been approved, bringing about earlier recovery through cleaning out the excess inventories more quickly. But by the time the speed of the decline in defence expenditure became apparent, the downward phase of the recession was over and there were good prospects of recovery even without additional stimulation. The forecast that recovery would proceed sufficiently strongly on 1955 without the stimulus of a further tax reduction proved to be correct also.

The administration was widely criticized, however, for complacency and for timidity. Senator Douglas and Representative Bolling in their supplementary statement of views in the report of the Joint Committee on the Economic Report in 1954 attacked the Administration vigorously for having a 'Pollyannish'[1] approach[2] to the recession, and similar views were expressed in practically every speech by a trade union leader during the period. The executive Board of the C.I.O. stated: 'The Washington do-nothing, look-the-other-way is both dangerous and disgraceful'.[3] Senator Douglas became prominent as the leading spokesman among Congressional Democrats for the view that more drastic measures should be taken[4] and for his pains was attacked as 'a prophet of gloom and doom'.[5] Among the specific policies advocated by the Administration's critics, in addition to the increase in the individual exemption from income tax, were further tax reduction and increases in Federal expenditure[6] and ex-President Truman's suggestion that government action should be taken to double the number of houses built.[7] Some of these proposals amply justified the reproof in the Economic Report of the President of 1955 to those who advocated massive expenditures with little regard to the size of the deficiency of demand

[1] I.e. expressing sweetness and light in complete disregard of the adverse factors in the situation. cf. the film, *Pollyanna*.

[2] *H. Rept. No. 1256*, 83rd Cong., 2nd Sess., p. 21.

[3] *C.I.O. News*, 29 March 1954, p. 1.

[4] Note, for instance, his public letter to the President on 19 February 1954; its text is printed in the Congressional Record, Vol. CI. pp. 2806–7.

[5] Leonard W. Hall, Chairman of the Republican National Committee; naming Douglas, Stevenson, Morse, and Reuther, he said: 'This quartet rides like the four horsemen over all the country, spreading gloom and doom across the land.' *New York Times*, 6 February 1954.

[6] This was the recommendation of the Conference on Economic Progress, of which Dr. Keyserling was a leading member. *New York Times*, 1 August 1954.

[7] Speech to the Convention of the Amalgamated Clothing Workers of America, C.I.O. at Atlantic City, N.J., on 13 May 1954, of which the text is printed in the *New York Times*, 14 May, 1954.

to be filled.[1] None the less the actions of the Opposition during the recession had a salutary effect in increasing the pressure upon the Administration to take prompt and effective action. Such had been the amount of *laissez-faire* dogma that had been heard from Republicans during the preceeding twenty years that the more political pressure there was for energetic action against the recession, the better.

The fear of future inflation clearly weighed more heavily with the Administration than it did with certain Congressional Democrats and the trade union leaders. In 1955 the Democratic members of the Joint Committee on the Economic Report charged: 'Emphasis on fighting an inflation "straw man" at the expense of what should be the primary objective of economic policy—maximum employment and purchasing power—accounts in large part for the disturbing level of unemployment.[2] Mr. Reuther in his statement to the Joint Committee on the Economic Report strongly criticized 'the banker mentality reflected by Mr. Humphrey and his associates' who 'move in and put the brakes on long before we have reached any recovery in proportions that would create inflationary threats'.[3] It does seem, however, that the complaints about 'putting on the brakes' were disproportionate to the measures actually taken, which were little more than a withdrawal from the policy of active stimulation of the economy. It was not until about the middle of 1955 that the Federal Reserve System became concerned that inflation was emerging.[4]

While neither the Secretary of the Treasury nor the Director of the Bureau of the Budget thought of public finance in compensatory fiscal terms,[5] this did not lead to any general disposition in the Administration to let the recession run its course. Eisenhower in particular was constantly concerned about whether the Administration was doing enough, and maintained that it would be better to err

---

[1] *Economic Report of the President*, 1955, p. 2.

[2] *S. Rept. No. 60*, 84th Cong., 1st Sess., p. 10.

[3] Joint Committee on the Economic Report, *Hearings on the Economic Report of the President*, 1955, p. 1153.

[4] Chairman of the Board of Governors to Senate Finance Committee. Senate, Committee on Finance, *Hearings on the Financial Condition of the United States*, August 1957, p. 1304.

[5] This is apparent from numerous remarks: for instance, in reply to a question about the stimulating effects of a tax reduction, Humphrey said: 'To borrow for the payment of current expenses in your home, your business, in your Government, I think it is wrong'. Senate, Committee on Finance, *Hearings on H.R.8224*, 1954, p. 227.

on the side of doing too much rather than too little.[1] Thanks to the confidence he placed in the Council of Economic Advisers, sound economic advice was available to the Administration. It became apparent that the Administration was not rigidly bound to the dogmas that Republicans had expounded while in opposition; Donovan, who had access to Cabinet minutes in writing his book, wrote as follows: '. . . with the fate of the economy in the balance it (i.e. the doctrine of the balanced budget) was submerged under the determination of the President and of the Cabinet to undertake an expansive public works program if necessary and to prevent a serious recession at any cost.[2] The editors of *Fortune* agreed with this judgement; they wrote: 'When the choice lay between producing a balanced budget and supporting a balanced economy, the Treasury winced slightly but chose the second course'.[3]

Likewise, the balanced budget doctrine did not determine major policy in Congress, although it played an important part in the thinking of many Members, as the quotations elsewhere in this chapter show. There was no drive to cut expenditure in order to balance the budget despite the recession, as in 1949 and 1950. The following unanimous statement by the Joint Committee on the Economic Report is worthy of note: 'if economic conditions deteriorate much below present levels the Federal government may be called upon to act promptly and vigorously, accepting a deficit as an unfortunate necessity but none the less the most appropriate fiscal policy'.[4]

The good fortune that attended the conduct of American economic policy since the war was not lacking in 1953–4, especially in the administrative circumstances that brought about a large tax cut so early on in the recession. But the policies pursued were generally sound, though very cautious. It was not so much that 'Republican economics work', as the editors of *Fortune* exulted;[5] it was rather that a Republican Administration realized that in spite of the political history, the economics of stabilization policy is not the private doctrine of New Dealers but is sound policy under a Republican Administration as well.

[1] Donovan, op. cit., p. 221.   [2] Donovan, op. cit., p. 214.
[3] *Fortune*, July 1954, p. 66.
[4] *H. Rept. No. 1256*, 83rd Cong., 2nd Sess., p. 6.
[5] *Fortune*, August 1954, p. 66.

CHAPTER XII

EXPANSION, INFLATION, AND THE PRE-EMINENCE OF MONETARY POLICY, 1955–1957

IN most respects 1955 was an economic 'golden year'. Recovery from the recession was completed, and production and real income rose far beyond the previous high points of 1953. This expansion was achieved without any stimulus from increased military expenditure, and most noteworthy of all, was accompanied by only a slight increase in prices.[1] But in 1956 the situation deteriorated; a general increase in the price level began, and the rise in real income came almost to a stop. This trend continued until the autumn of 1957, with prices rising steadily while output rose hardly at all. The following table shows the contrast clearly:

TABLE 30

Increase in G.N.P. at Current and Constant Prices, 1955–7

	At Current Prices	At Constant Prices
From 4th Quarter 1954 to 4th Quarter 1955	10·3%	8·4%
From 4th Quarter 1955 to 4th Quarter 1956	5·3	1·5
From 4th Quarter 1956 to 3rd Quarter 1957	3·5	0·5

Source: Department of Commerce, *U.S. Income and Output,* 1959, Tables I–3 and I–5.

The rate of increase of prices varied markedly between sectors. The increase was greatest in the prices of producers' durable goods (16·0 per cent between the fourth quarter of 1954 and the third quarter of 1957),[2] and in the price of construction (13·6 per cent). The rise in the price of consumers' goods and services, as measured by the deflator implicit in the estimates of G.N.P. and its components at constant prices, was 5·7 per cent over the period, of which 5·1 per cent occurred between the fourth quarter of 1955 and the third quarter of 1957. The Consumer Price Index rose by 6·0 per cent

---

[1] The price of consumer goods, measured by the 'implicit deflator' rose by only 0·6 per cent. *U.S. Income and Output,* Table VII–3.

[2] Ibid.

between January 1955 and August 1957; of this 5·6 per cent occurred after January 1956. The stability of the Consumer Price Index in 1955 was the result of a decline in the price of food (1·3 per cent) and a smaller decline in the prices of other commodities offsetting a rise (about 2·0 per cent) in rents and in the prices of other services.[1] The wholesale price of finished consumers' durable and non-durable goods began to rise in the second half of 1955,[2] which was followed by a rise in their retail prices in 1956. In the spring of 1956 the slow decline in the price of food ceased and thereafter food prices rose. The price of services rose at an accelerated rate.

During 1955 the boom in house building, which had played such a prominent part in the recovery, reached its peak. Consumption expenditure rose rapidly, especially for durable goods; output of cars in 1955 was greater than in any previous year, financed in large part by a rapid increase in instalment credit; the amount of instalment credit extended for the purchase of cars in 1955 was $4·9 billion greater than in 1954, and the amount of such credit outstanding at the end of 1955 was $5·5 billion greater than at the end of 1954[3] (the increase in 1954 had been only $0·5 billion). Inventory accumulation throughout the year was at average annual rate of $5·5 billion.[4] In addition to these other sources of demand, investment by business in fixed capital began a rapid rise in the second quarter as the increase in orders noted above[5] was reflected in the amount of equipment installed; private domestic investment in producers' durable goods rose from a seasonally adjusted annual rate of $20·5 billion (at current prices) in the first quarter of 1955 to $25·4 billion in the fourth quarter.[6] The number of wage and salary earners employed in manufacturing industry rose by 971,000 between December 1954 and December 1955.[7] The average number of hours worked per week in manufacturing industry also rose in 1955, and in the last three months of the year exceeded 41·0, higher than the average for any year since 1945.[8] The ratio of corporate profits

[1] Bureau of Labor Statistics, monthly statistics published in *Monthly Labor Review* and elsewhere.
[2] Bureau of Labor Statistics, monthly statistics.
[3] Board of Governors of the Federal Reserve System, monthly statistics, published in the *Federal Reserve Bulletin*.
[4] *U.S. Income and Output*, Table I–3.   [5] See p. 235 supra.
[6] *U.S. Income and Output*, Table I–3.
[7] Bureau of Labor Statistics, monthly statistics published in *Monthly Labor Review* and in *Economic Report of the President*, 1957, Table E–22.
[8] Ibid.

before tax to national income rose steadily quarter by quarter in 1955.[1] There was thus good reason for regarding the increases in wholesale prices that appeared in the autumn of 1955 as being attributable to excess demand. This was clearly true of the increases in the price of investment goods.

The situation changed in 1956. Expenditure for house building began to decline in real terms in the third quarter of 1955 and the decline was accelerated in 1956. Expenditure on cars declined very sharply, as it had to after the abnormally high expenditure in 1955. Consumers' purchases of cars (at current prices) declined from an annual rate of $19·7 billion in the third quarter of 1955 to $15·0 million in the third quarter of 1956.[2] The rate of inventory accumulation slackened after the first quarter of 1956. Only business investment in fixed capital continued to expand apace, and it was described in the Economic Report of the President as being 'foremost among the sources of strength in 1956'.[3] The rise in business investment approximately offset the declines in other sectors. The number of wage and salary earners employed in manufacturing industry rose by only 113,000 between December 1955 and December 1956, and the average numbers of hours worked per week in manufacturing industry through most of 1956 was appreciably below the level of 1955. The ratio of corporate profits before tax to national income declined in 1956. Most of the factors pointing to the existence of general excess demand towards the end of 1955 were thus no longer operative in 1956. The trends outlined above continued during the first three quarters of 1957; house building and the rate of inventory accumulation declined still more, business investment in fixed capital reached its peak, while consumption of non-durable goods and services rose very slightly. Both the number of wage and salary earners employed in manufacturing industry and the average number of hours worked per week declined slightly in the first three quarters of 1957. There were thus few signs of *general* excess demand in 1956, and hardly any in 1957. Such information as is available about productive capacity[4] suggests that it grew much more rapidly between 1955 and 1957 than did output, as might be expected in view of the size of the investment boom.

[1] *U.S. Income and Output*, Table I–9.

[2] *U.S. Income and Output*, Table II–6.

[3] *Economic Report of the President*, 1957, p. 21.

[4] Estimates are made by the Department of Economics of the McGraw-Hill Company and by *Fortune*.

There are thus grounds for believing that the inflation experienced after 1955 differed in important respects from that experienced from 1945 to 1948 and from 1950 to 1951. In both these cases there is not much doubt that effective demand exceeded capacity to supply in all or nearly all sectors of the economy, whereas in 1956, and even more so in 1957, there was little evidence of excess demand outside the capital goods sector. The inflation was the subject of much debate in political, business, and academic circles. On one hand was the view widely held in official Washington, especially in the Federal Reserve System, that the inflation was the result of demand exceeding capacity to supply at prevailing prices, which regarded the inflation as similar, in those aspects relevant to public policy, to the other instance of inflation in the United States since the war.[1]

On the other hand there was increasing support for the view that the principal cause of the inflation was not general excess demand but excess income claims, either in the form of demands for wage increases well in excess of increases in productivity or of attempts by firms to raise their *ex ante* profit margin. The spokesmen for the trade unions naturally tended to blame business managements for raising 'administered prices', and conversely many businessmen presented the problem as trade union-induced cost inflation. There has been a growth of academic support for the view that pressures on costs were an inflationary force separate from general excess demand in 1956–7; though there was little disposition to express opinions about the relative responsibilities of trade unions and business managements for it.[2]

In view of the paucity of evidence for the existence of any general excess demand in 1956 and 1957, there are grounds for regarding cost-determined price increases as being an important factor in the inflation. Two separate effects have been distinguished; the first was a by-product of the excess demand for capital goods and the second the increase in 'indirect' labour costs relative to 'direct' labour costs. The increase in demand for capital goods added to demand for materials used in their production and for labour; the increased prices of the materials concerned, which are used in other industries

[1] For analysis of the situation in these terms, see R. T. Selden, 'Demand-Pull versus Cost-Push Inflation', *Journal of Political Economy*, Vol. LXVII (1959), pp. 1–20.

[2] See the papers by Lerner, Eckstein, and Ackley in *The Relationship of Prices to Economic Stability and Growth*, compendium of papers submitted by panellists appearing before the Joint Economic Committee, (Washington, 1958).

as well, represented increased costs to these industries; likewise, with wages rising in the capital goods industries there would be a tendency for other industries to follow suit, after various time lags, even if demand for their products was not excessive at the prevailing prices. The contention that excess demand in one sector could lead to price increases in this way in sectors where demand is not excessive depends on prices of final products being determined to a substantial degree on the basis of costs, and there is much evidence that this is so. The consequence of a rising proportion of indirect labour is that if profit margins are to be maintained the 'costing margin' by which price exceeds direct cost per unit of output must be raised, which means that either the price must be increased or else wages of direct labour (the 'trade union' group) must rise more slowly than output per head. There is evidence that indirect labour costs rose relative to direct labour costs between 1955 and 1957.[1] In such a situation an increase in wages of direct labour which did not exceed the increase in output per head of such workers would raise total costs unless the salaries of 'overhead' workers rose correspondingly more slowly.

There are important implications for policy if the above analysis is substantially correct. If the prices of many categories of goods and services are cost-determined then a moderate cut in demand will lead to a fall in output and employment rather than a fall in prices, and if in a situation like that of 1956–7 general deflationary policy is pressed far enough to eliminate the excess demand in all sectors, then demand in those sectors where there was no excess demand in the first place is likely to be pushed well below the capacity to supply. And all the time there is excess demand in particular areas, there will be forces at work to push up prices in other sectors. The increasing prevalence of cost-of-living 'escalator' clauses in wage agreements reinforces this. In short, therefore, unless there is a fortuitous factor such as a fall in agricultural prices or a fall in import prices (which would have to be enormous to make much of a mark on the general price level in the United States) the degree of deflation needed to put an end to rising prices might be high. The existence of a possible conflict between the objectives of full employment and price stability had long been recognized, but the analysis of cost-determined prices and wages, insensitive to quite large reductions of demand, poses the

[1] C. L. Schultze, *Recent Inflation in the United States*, Study Paper No. 1 for the Joint Economic Committee, 1959, Chapters 4 and 5. The analysis in the foregoing paragraphs owes much to Professor Schultze's paper.

dilemma in a much more acute form. Needless to say, much of this only became apparent as the inflation proceeded, and was organized into an analytical framework *ex post*. It would be unreasonable therefore to criticize the authorities in the United States for not having pursued a policy based on the cost-inflation analysis. It was the failure of the inflation of 1956–7 to behave as its predecessors had done which provided the stimulus to the work that has added so much to understanding of the nature of inflation.

MONETARY RESTRAINT AND AUTOMATIC STABILIZATION, 1955

The growth of the prominence of monetary policy among the techniques of economic control that had been apparent in the first two years of the Eisenhower Administration continued in 1955 and later. Monetary policy was the main technique which was used in a discretionary way to restrain the growth of demand in 1955. The fiscal system made a significant contribution, but through its property of automatic stabilization, not through changes in tax rates or in government expenditures for the purpose of restraining demand.

The following table gives an indication of the stabilizing effect exerted by the budget:

TABLE 31

Federal Receipts and Expenditures as shown in the National Income Accounts, 1954–5

	1954		1955	
	First Half	Second Half	First Half	Second Half
Receipts				
Personal tax and non-tax receipts	29·0	29·3	30·9	32·1
Corporate profits tax accruals	16·3	17·0	19·4	21·7
Indirect business tax and non-tax accruals	10·2	9·9	10·9	11·2
Contributions for social insurance	7·10	67·9	68·5	69·3
	8·1	8·1	9·1	9·6
Total	63·7	64·3	70·5	74·6
Expenditure	71·0	67·9	68·5	69·3
Surplus or Deficit (−)	−7·3	−3·6	1·9	5·3

Amounts in $ billion at seasonally adjusted annual rates; detail does not always add to totals because of rounding.
Source: Economic Report of the President, 1958, Table F–53.

In a year such as 1955 in which corporate profits are rising, receipts from the corporation profits tax and hence total revenue and the surplus as shown in the national income accounts are greater than those shown in either the administrative budget or the cash budget, since receipts from the corporation profits tax are shown in the national income accounts as liability accrues and not when the tax is paid. The emergence of a substantial surplus in the second half of 1955 is almost a 'text book' example of the working of automatic stabilization. The decline in expenditures that might be expected to occur in times of high activity did not appear because of the increase in expenditure for subsidies to maintain agricultural prices and to the increase in the rates of Social Security benefits.

The Treasury's review of the budget outlook, published in August 1955, showed a net increase in estimated revenue for fiscal 1956 of $2·1 billion over the January estimate, as against a net increase of $1·1 billion in expenditure. It touched off a wave of speculation about the possibility of a tax cut in 1956, as the President had hinted in the Budget Message in January. Discussing the budget review at his press conference, Secretary Humphrey insisted that any tax cut must leave the budget in balance: 'if ever there was a time when the budget should be balanced, it is now', adding: 'I don't believe in cutting taxes out of borrowed money'.[1] Senator George remarked: 'whether one approves of it or not, Congress is going to cut taxes next year';[2] Millikin, the senior Republican member of the Finance Committee, also expected a tax cut in 1956, but Byrd, now Chairman of the Finance Committee[3] expressed misgivings lest a tax cut should unbalance the budget. But others warned about the inflationary dangers of such a tax cut; Representative Reed called talk of a tax cut 'premature', and said: 'When the economy is operating at record-breaking levels the inflationary impact of tax reduction should be carefully appraised. Inflation is a more deadly enemy of the nation's security than taxes ever will be'.[4] Dr. Ensley, Staff Director of the Joint Committee on the Economic Report, argued in a speech to the annual conference of the National Tax Association that a tax cut in the existing state of boom would be inflationary, and warned against over-confidence in the power of monetary policy leading to the belief that it could contain inflationary pressure despite a tax cut.[5] It was

[1] *New York Times*, 26 August, 1955.   [2] Ibid., 27 August 1955.

[3] When the Democratic majority 'organized' the Senate at the beginning of 1955, George's seniority entitled him to the Chairmanship of either the Foreign Relations Committee or the Finance Committee. He chose the Foreign Relations Committee.   [4] *New York Times*, 4 September 1955.

[5] Text printed in Joint Committee on the Economic Report, *Hearings on the Economic Report of the President*, 1956, pp. 680–3.

overlooked by none that 1956 was an election year, so that the purely political inducement to take the risk of tax reduction was greater than in a 'normal' year.

The increase in the national debt limit from $275 billion to $281 billion that was enacted in1954 was due to expire on 30 June 1955. The bill to extend it for a further year (H.R.6992) was passed without much opposition, but the rumblings from both sides of the aisle[1] were portents of the trouble over the debt limit that was to come later.

The policy of the Federal Reserve System became steadily more restrictive in 1955. From a policy of withdrawal from 'active ease' the Federal Reserve System swung to a policy of active restraint. The rediscount rate was raised four times during the year. By the autumn of 1955 member banks' borrowing from the Federal Reserve Banks was greater than their excess reserves for the first time since May 1953, and by the end of the year short-term interest rates had risen above the 1953 peaks. The decline in house building which began in mid-1955 was probably a consequence of the monetary policy, though the restriction imposed by the VA[2] doubtless contributed. In view of the sharp rise in house building that took place in 1958, it is unlikely that demographic factors were responsible for the decline that began in 1955 and continued through 1956 and 1957. The Chairman of the Board of Governors of the Federal Reserve System later stated that it was about the middle of 1955 that the Board began to get worried about inflation.[3] If the argument above is correct in attributing to monetary policy a major share of the responsibility for bringing about the decline in house building, then the use of monetary policy achieved a restraint on one sector of demand with speed and despatch. That more than this was needed to prevent inflation was soon to become clear.

BUDGETARY POLICY AND AUTOMATIC STABILIZATION, 1956

The questions raised in 1955 about whether the Administration would support a tax cut in 1956 were answered when in the State of the Union and Budget Messages the President expressed opposition

[1] Byrd remarked that the temporary extension should be taken as 'Congressional notice that it should not be repeated again' *Congressional Record*, Vol. CI, p. 9753.

[2] See p. 237 supra.

[3] Senate, Committee on Finance, *Hearings on the Financial Condition of the United States*, 1957, p. 1304.

to any tax reductions. He recommended that the reductions in the corporation profits tax and certain excise taxes that under existing law would go into effect on 1 April should be postponed for a further year. The loss of revenue in fiscal 1957 if these reductions were to go into effect was estimated at $2·3 billion.[1] The extension required the full support of Congress, not just the support of enough Members to sustain a veto as in 1947. If the bill to extend these tax rates were to have attached to it provisions making other reductions, the President would be compelled to accept it, since a veto would mean an even greater loss of revenue.

The Budget for fiscal 1957, published on 16 January 1956, estimated that revenue would be about $1·8 billion greater than in fiscal 1956, and expenditures $1·6 billion greater. The estimates showed a surplus of $435 million, on the assumption that the Congress passed the legislation recommended by the President to increase postage rates to yield an additional $350 million. If this were not enacted, $225 million would be covered by the 'contingencies' item in the estimates of expenditure, in which case there would be a surplus of $310 million. This was the first time since January 1948 that the budget estimate for the coming fiscal year had shown a surplus; the Administration was obviously pleased at this, as were the Republican Members of Congress.

The increases in estimated expenditure fell under the heads of 'major national security', 'labor and welfare', 'commerce and housing' and 'general government'. The increases in the last category were the result of increases in Civil Service salaries and in interest on the national debt, and were for all practical purposes automatic. Defence expenditure was estimated to rise by $900 million, most of which was for aircraft and guided missiles. Expenditure for welfare was estimated to rise by $230 million, made up of three main items, of which the largest was the programme of grants-in-aid to states for the building of schools, which was estimated to cost $150 million in fiscal 1957; in addition there was an increase in funds for medical research and the cost of the scheme to provide Federal reinsurance for certain types of health insurance which private firms were unwilling to undertake. The largest part of the increase of $250 million in estimated expenditure for 'commerce and housing' (excluding the Post Office) was for grants-in-aid for road building; there were also

[1] *Budget of the United States for the Year ending 30 June 1957*, p. M16 and tables.

increases for many other purposes, including subsidies to shipbuilding and the provision of control towers at airports.

In recommending the expenditure of Federal funds for school
building and for the extension of health insurance to people hitherto
unable to obtain coverage (though by the most cautious and in-
expensive way which would interfere least with the existing system of
private finance of medical care) President Eisenhower was pursuing
a policy which bore a considerable resemblance to that of President
Truman in 1949 and after. In addition the President renewed his
recommendation for legislation to provide for the building of the
Interstate trunk road system. Though this was to be financed by
'earmarked' taxes on petrol and tyres and on lorries and buses,
through a trust fund outside the budget, it would increase substantially the total expenditure of the Federal government for domestic
civil purposes. This was an ambitious programme of social welfare
and public investment; in this respect 1956 marked the zenith of the
influence of 'modern Republicanism' in the Eisenhower Administration.

The Administration's policies with respect to government expenditures were thus determined almost exclusively by judgements
about the needs of national defence and the provision of public
services. The ideas of the previous autumn of cutting government
expenditure for disinflationary purposes[1] had been abandoned. The
most significant budget recommendation, from the economic point
of view, was that the tax reductions scheduled under existing law
should be postponed for another year. The President explained the
policy in the following terms:

'Under conditions of high peacetime prosperity such as now exist
we can never justify going further into debt to give ourselves a tax cut
at the expense of our children. So in the present state of our financial
affairs I earnestly believe that a tax cut can be deemed justifiable
only when it will not unbalance the budget, a budget that makes
provision for some reduction, even though modest, in our national
debt. In this way we can best maintain fiscal integrity. . . .

'Over the long term, a balanced budget is a sure index of thrifty
management—in home, business, or in the Federal government.
When achievement of a balanced budget is for long put off in a
business or at home, bankruptcy is the result. But in similar circum-

---

[1] This had been considered by the Cabinet, but no detailed programme of
reductions was drawn up.

stances a government resorts to inflation of the money supply. This inevitably results in a depreciation of the value of money and an increase in the cost of living.'[1]

The argument here comes close to being pure 'balanced budget' doctrine. But for the inclusion of the qualifying phrases 'in the present state of our financial affairs' and 'over the long term', the impression given by the Message would have been that the concept of a counter-cyclical fiscal policy formed no part of the Eisenhower Administration's approach to public finance. In particular the argument cited here implies that the most appropriate time for a tax reduction is when it would be consistent with a small surplus rather than when it would help to keep aggregate demand in line with the capacity of the economy to supply.

This recrudescence of the older approach to public finance attracted comment and criticism. Economists appearing before the Joint Committee on the Economic Report stressed the point,[2] and the Committee in their report[3] drew attention to it. The Committee's report stated that a 'basic guide' to fiscal policy in the coming year should be the state of the economy, and that the maintenance of high tax rates in times of boom was a corollary of the principle that deficits could not be avoided in times of recession.[4] This implied criticism of the Administration's view was expressed much more sharply in a statement of views by the Democratic members, in which they said that in the absence of a clear statement that the same principle which indicates a budget surplus at a time of prosperity and inflation indicates a tax reduction in time of recession, the President's remarks about fiscal integrity were 'grossly misleading'.[5]

These well-taken criticisms of the President's statements of policy did not, however, challenge the soundness of the policy he recommended. The Joint Committee on the Economic Report held the immediate outlook to be one of boom and inflation, in which a tax cut would almost certainly make the inflation still worse, They therefore approved the retention of all taxes at existing rates, adding that the economic situation was liable to change quickly and that

[1] The text of the Message is printed in the *New York Times*, 6 January 1956, and in the Congressional Record, Vol. CII, pp. 137–43. The quotations are on p. 140.

[2] See the statements of G. Colm and R. E. Paul in Joint Committee on the Economic Report, *Hearings on the Economic Report of the President*, 1956, especially at p. 230.

[3] *S. Rept. No. 1606*, 84th Cong., 1st Sess.   [4] Ibid., p. 3.   [5] Ibid., p. 32.

should economic activity decline seriously a tax reduction might be necessary.[1] It was not the specific measures recommended by the Administration which were criticized, but the reasoning which appeared to underlie them; although it had given rise to recommendations which were sound enough under the generally held assumptions about the economic outlook, it might give rise to an unsound policy in the future when there was either a recession or a large surplus in time of inflation.

From the estimates presented in the budget document the Administration appeared to be proposing another 'carry-on' budget, neither reinforcing nor diminishing the restraining effect of the surplus that had developed during 1955 through the operation of the automatic stabilizers. But the revenue estimates were open to question as to whether they were unduly low, being based on the assumption that personal income in the calendar year 1956 would be $312·5 billion and corporate profits $43 billion.[2] In the third quarter of 1955, the last quarter for which estimates were available when the budget was being prepared, personal income was at a seasonally adjusted annual rate of $313·8 billion.[3] Since production was still rising, it was clear that personal income would be even higher in the fourth quarter; even allowing for a margin of error in the estimates, the Treasury was in effect assuming that personal income in 1956 would not rise beyond the level reached at the end of 1955. In this there was an implicit assumption that there would be no growth of real output,[4] which contrasted sharply with the statements about the economic outlook made in the Economic Report.

Members of the Joint Committee on the Economic Report had no difficulty in establishing this point in the course of the hearings, and gave the Director of the Bureau of the Budget and the Secretary of the Treasury an uncomfortable time in defending the reasonableness of the revenue estimate while contending that no rise in unemployment was expected. For it was argued[5] that if total output

---

[1] *S. Rept, No. 1606*, 84th Cong., 2nd Sess., p. 3.

[2] Letter from Secretary Humphrey to Senator Douglas, printed in Joint Committee on the Economic Report, *Hearings on the Economic Report of the President*, 1956, p. 82.

[3] *U.S. Income and Output*, 1959, Table II–2.

[4] An absence of growth in personal income implies an absence of growth in G.N.P., unless the ratio of corporate savings to G.N.P. rises or transfer payments fall, neither of which occurred in 1956.

[5] Joint Committee on the Economic Report, *Hearings on the Economic Report on the President*, 1956, p. 88ff.

did not rise, unemployment would increase, since the labour force was growing and it was reasonable to assume that productivity would continue to rise. In reply to this the Director of the Bureau of the Budget and the Secretary of the Treasury could only emphasize the importance of conservatism in estimating revenues.

The estimate of $43·0 billion for corporate profits in 1956 proved to be correct,[1] but the estimate for personal income turned out to be very low. The final estimate was $330·5 billion;[2] if allowance is made for price changes by deflating the estimate of personal income by either the implicit deflator for G.N.P. or that for personal consumption expenditure,[3] then personal income in 1946 measured at 1955 prices can be estimated at about $321 billion (using the deflator for G.N.P.) or $324 billion (using the deflator for personal consumption expenditure).

From this it follows that had the revenue estimates published in January 1956 been based on an estimate of personal income that accorded more closely with the amount actually recorded, a substantially greater budget surplus would have been shown. In fact, Federal expenditures would have been budgeted to rise more slowly than G.N.P., whereas revenues would rise at least at the same rate, and probably slightly faster because of the progressive features of the Federal tax structure.[4] The estimate of expenditure also proved to be low, mainly because of increases in the cost of supporting farm prices and in defence expenditure.

Despite the talk during the previous year about tax reduction in 1956, the bill to continue the existing rates of the corporation profits tax and the excise taxes for a further year was passed with remarkably little controversy. There was no repetition of the previous year's attempt to attach to it provisions for tax reduction. The political attractiveness of tax reduction in an election year had to yield to considerations of sound fiscal policy, interpreted either as the need to avoid tax reductions which would increase the risk of inflation or the need to make some provision for reducing the national debt

---

[1] The final estimate was $42·9 billion. *U.S. Income and Output*, 1959, Table I-8

[2] *U.S. Income and Output*, Table I–17.

[3] *U.S. Income and Output*, Table VII–2.

[4] Principally the personal income tax; in all cases except that of a taxpayer with an income sufficiently large to benefit from the limitation of the maximum effective rate of 87 per cent, the marginal rate of tax is higher than the average rate (except in the case of someone who pays no tax at all), so increasing the ratio of tax payments to total income as income rises.

rather than throw the budget into deficit by cutting tax rates. Both concepts of 'sound fiscal policy' indicated much the same course in the circumstances of early 1956.

There was no attempt to cut the budget to 'pay for' tax reduction. Although Senators Byrd and George expressed disquiet at the increases in expenditure, most of the appropriations were passed with only minor cuts and little controversy. Even the U.S. Information Agency was treated fairly liberally. The two leading controversies over appropriations in 1956 were both about increases. The more prominent one concerned the Air Force appropriation. After expression of concern in both House and Senate about the growth of Russian air power and demands for more energetic action to build up American air strength, the Senate Appropriations Committee voted by 13 to 12[1] in favour of an amendment to add $800 million for the purchase of aircraft and $200 million for the construction of bases, despite a special request from the Administration not to appropriate these additional funds. On the Floor of the Senate the additional funds for the construction of bases were deleted; but the additional appropriation for the purchase of aircraft was retained, and, because of the persistence of the Senate conferees, accepted by the Conference Committee. President Eisenhower declared that existing plans for the Air Force were adequate and that the additional funds would be placed in reserve and not spent. The other controversy was over the appropriation for the National Institutes of Health;[2] the House voted an increase of $9 million over the Administration's request, but the Senate increased it by a further $48·9 million, which the House conferees accepted with considerable complaint.

Not all of the President's recommendations for new programmes requiring additional public expenditure were enacted. The Interstate and Defense Highways Act was passed, providing for the construction of a national system of 'super-highways' to be financed through a separate trust fund;[3] the extension of Social Security was enacted, increasing both the benefits and the contributions; and the

---

[1] Ten Democrats and three Republicans (McCarthy, Young and Mrs. Smith) voted in favour; nine Republicans and three Democrats against).

[2] Semi-autonomous bodies which administer grants for medical research in several fields, notably cancer and heart disease.

[3] The receipts from the existing Federal taxes on motor fuel and tyres were also transferred to this trust fund, and from it all Federal expenditure for roads was to be financed except for a few minor programmes such as the building of forest roads and trails.

'Soil Bank'[1] was set up. On the other hand, nothing came of the plan for Federal re-insurance of certain private medical insurance contracts; and the bill providing for Federal grants-in-aid for school building came to grief in the House as a result of the success of Representative Powell in attaching to it an 'anti-segregation' amendment.[2]

The Federal finances exerted a further stabilizing effect on the economy in 1956, as the following table shows:

TABLE 32

Federal Receipts and Expenditures as shown in the National Income Accounts, 1955–7

	1955	1956		1957
	Second Half	*First Half*	*Second Half*	*First Half*
Receipts	75·0	77·7	79·8	83·0
Expenditures	69·4	70·2	73·6	78·9
Surplus	5·6	7·5	6·2	4·0

Amounts in $ billion at seasonally adjusted annual rates. Detail does not add to totals because of rounding.
Source: Economic Report of the President, 1959, Table D–53.

But while the Federal finances were having a general restraining effect on demand, one feature of the fiscal system was working to strengthen the investment boom. This was the procedure whereby investment adjudged by the Office of Civilian and Defense Mobilization to be essential on strategic grounds qualified for 'accelerated amortization', that is to say, a specified proportion of the cost could be written off for tax purposes in five years, whatever the normal accounting life of the asset. Similar to a selective 'initial allowance', it was introduced in 1950[3] to stimulate the building of capacity needed for the defence effort. The value of such investment rose rapidly in 1955 and the first half of 1956; between 1 July 1955 and 18 April 1956 $4,888 million of investment was certified for acceler-

---

[1] A programme under which a farmer received payment for withdrawing part of his land from cultivation with commercial crops, subject to his planting it with certain 'soil-conserving' crops.

[2] It is safe to assume that some of those voting for this amendment did so in the belief that it would force Southerners who supported the principle of Federal grants-in-aid for school building to vote against the bill.

[3] A similar scheme had been in operation during the Second World War.

ated amortization compared with $2,949 million in the eighteen months between 1 January 1954 and 30 June 1955.[1]

Investment in manufacturing industry during the period of the investment boom received little direct stimulus from the accelerated amortization scheme, for most of the investment certified was for other purposes; of the $2¼ billion certified in January to April 1956, electric power accounted for $750 million, railways for $576 million, and air transport for $510 million, these 'utilities' thus accounting for four-fifths of the total. 'Defence' appeared to have been interpreted very broadly, which led to the end of the scheme. After the bill providing for the construction by the Federal government of a hydro-electric power dam at Hells Canyon, Idaho, had been rejected, it transpired that the Idaho Power Company, which was undertaking the development of the hydro-electric power potential at Hells Canyon, had received an 'accelerated amortization' certificate for its investment there. The combination of supporters of Federal development of Hells Canyon and those such as Senator Byrd who objected to the loss of revenue caused by 'accelerated amortization' was able to pass legislation to bring the system to an end.

Because of the small extent of the assistance given to manufacturing investment it seems that the contribution of the accelerated amortization scheme to the investment boom was small in the aggregate, though perhaps important to the public utility sector. It had the effect of offsetting at least part of the impact of general restraints on those sectors of investment demand which received its benefits, and to that extent impaired the effectiveness of the anti-inflationary measures; but if the investment were deemed essential this would be inevitable, just as the indispensability of much of government expenditure prevents its being cut for anti-inflationary purposes.

The economic situation in 1956 had several perplexing aspects. A considerable amount of 'readjustment' was going on in that house building and output of cars were declining while business investment in fixed capital was rising. Under the influence of these mutually offsetting forces real output was not rising. If the behaviour of real output were taken as the criterion, it would be very doubtful if intensification of restrictive measures was called for; but price increases were spreading and the rate of increase of those that were

[1] Report of the Staff of the Joint Economic Committee, inserted in the Committee's *Hearings on the Economic Report of the President*, 1957, p. 772.

already rising (prices of capital goods) appeared to be gathering momentum. In April 1956 the Federal Reserve System raised the rediscount rate, clearly directing its policy to the rise in prices rather than the stability of total output. There was disagreement with this step from within the Administration. Secretary Humphrey thought the situation was 'in balance' without the increase,[1] and Burns thought that in view of the divergent trends in the various sectors the timeliness of the Federal Reserve's action was very doubtful.[2] It appears that the Administration would have preferred to wait and see what happened to output before taking further restrictive measures.

FURTHER INFLATION AND THE STRUGGLE OVER THE BUDGET, 1957

The economic outlook as seen by the Administration at the beginning of 1957 was for further growth, stimulated by a continuation of the rise in business investment, increasing expenditures by state and local government on both current and capital account, a continued high level of exports and continued high expenditure for consumption.[3] Inflation was seen as the main problem; taxes should be maintained at their existing rates, and Federal expenditures 'strictly limited'. An interesting and possibly important innovation was the exhortation to managements and trade unions to conduct their price and wage policies in a way that was compatible with the public interest in price stability.[4] The President stated that fiscal and monetary policy by themselves could not do the whole job of maintaining price stability, and that managements and trade unions must do their share; if they did not, it would lead to demands that their responsibility for conducting their wage and price policies in a way which did not aggravate the inflation be assumed by the government.[5]

The Administration did not attempt to exert any intensified deflationary influence by fiscal means in 1957. Both revenues and expenditures were estimated to rise, as the following table shows.

[1] *Conflicting Official Views on Monetary Policy*, Hearings before the Economic Stabilization Subcommittee of the Joint Committee on the Economic Report, 12 June 1956, p. 7.
[2] Letter to Representative Patman, Chairman of the Economic Stabilization Subcommittee, inserted in the *Hearings* at p. 6.
[3] *Economic Report of the President*, 1957, p. 45–6.
[4] Ibid., p. iii–iv, 3.   [5] Ibid., p. 3.

The conventional budget totals have been adjusted to allow for the exclusion of highway expenditures (now in a separate Trust Fund) and the recommended increase in postage rates, which was the basis of the official estimate of expenditures for postal service but which was not passed by the Congress till 1958.

TABLE 33

Estimates of Total Receipts and Expenditures

	Fiscal Years	
	1957	*1958*
Administrative Budget plus Highways: ($ million)		
Receipts	72,167	75,677
Expenditure	70,050	74,077
Surplus	2,117	1,600
Cash Budget: ($ billion)		
Receipts	81·7	85·9
Expenditure	78·2	82·9
Surplus	3·5	3·0

Source: Budget of the United States for the year ending 30 June 1958.

At first sight it appears that the Administration was recommending a 'balanced budget' increase in revenue and expenditure as it had done the previous year. But the estimate of revenue for fiscal 1958 was based on the assumption that in the calendar year 1957 personal income would total $340 billion and corporate profits $44 billion.[1] This in turn was based on the assumption that G.N.P. in 1957 would be three to three-and-a-half per cent greater than in 1956,[2] in real terms, not in money terms. The 'conservatism' of the previous year had not been repeated. The fact that expenditures were budgeted to increase as much as revenues when the revenue estimate assumed growth that was more rapid than in the preceding year, and as rapid as that achieved in any year when the starting point was not one of recession-induced unused capacity, clearly meant that no further disinflationary effect was to be exerted through the budget.

The reason was not that a more disinflationary policy was thought inappropriate. Dr. Saulnier (Chairman of the Council of Economic Advisers), told the Joint Economic Committee: 'In the present

[1] Letter from Secretary Humphrey to Senator Douglas, inserted in Joint Economic Committee, *Hearings on the Economic Report of the President*, 1957, p. 19–20.

[2] Dr. Saulnier, ibid., p. 32.

circumstances I would prefer a larger budget surplus than is contemplated.'[1] The Chairman of the Board of Governors of the Federal Reserve System agreed; he told the Senate Finance Committee in August 1957 that the budget submitted in January was inflationary and that a larger surplus was called for at the time of speaking.[2]

A more disinflationary fiscal policy was not pursued because the increases in expenditure were considered to be essential on grounds other than economic stability, and because of the widespread opposition to an increase in tax rates. The President said in the Budget Message: 'While taking economic conditions into consideration, the budget must also reflect the general responsibilities of a government serving 172 million people . . . the needs for schools, highways, and homes are so urgent that I am proposing to move ahead with programs to help our states, cities, and people undertake such construction at a prudent rate'.[3] In the Budget Message and the Economic Report the President did not discuss the role of taxation beyond recommending that the reductions due on 1 April should be postponed for yet another year. But Secretary Humphrey told the Senate Finance Committee in June 1957 that to achieve a larger budget surplus through raising tax rates 'would have required the imposition of additional taxes on top of our present heavy load, which would not have been acceptable'.[4] Further evidence of the extent to which the Administration treated the existing tax rates as a 'ceiling' is given by the position taken by the President in November when increases in military expenditure were being called for in consequence of the shock caused by the launching of 'Sputnik'. In a speech at Oklahoma City he said that it would be the task of the Congress to cut out or defer 'whole categories' of Federal civil expenditure to offset the increase in military expenditure, and that to the extent that the cuts in civil expenditure did not cover the increase in military expenditure a budget deficit would ensue, which would have to be accepted as part of the cost of military preparedness.[5] Even when a tax increase could be presented as being needed

---

[1] Ibid., p. 30

[2] Senate, Committee on Finance, *Hearings on the Financial Condition of the United States*, August 1957, p. 1308.

[3] *Budget of the United States for the year ending 30 June 1958*, p. M6.

[4] Senate, Committee on Finance, *Hearings on the Financial Condition of the United States*, 1957, p. 20.

[5] Speech on 13 November 1957, of which the text is printed in the *New York Times*, 14 November 1957.

to 'pay for' strengthening the national defence, the disadvantages of higher tax rates were held to outweigh the advantages of a surplus (or smaller deficit) for economic stability. If a tax increase was considered undesirable or politically impossible even after 'Sputnik', it was all the more so early in 1957.

The immediate Congressional reaction to the budget was in no way unusual. But there soon arose a storm of criticism, the most violent since the 'cut-the-budget' drives of 1951 and 1952, only this time it was a Republican Administration's budget that was under attack. There is little doubt that Secretary Humphrey's remarks at his press conference on 16 January contributed to the emergence of the 'cut-the-budget' drive. He was reported as saying that 'there are a lot of places where the budget can be cut' and that if the 'terrific' tax burden was not reduced 'I predict you will have a depression which will curl your hair'.[1]

It was a long time before the President took vigorous action to defend the budget. At his first press conference after the storm had arisen, he said that since the budget contained so many items and a long time had to be taken in preparing it, it was likely that some items which were desirable when included had since become less necessary; if Congressional experts could eliminate them, so much the better.[2] But the reductions achieved in this way would be very small compared with the demands being made in the Congress in the country for reductions ranging up to $6 billion or even $8 billion. The President went as far as declining to rebuke in public a subordinate member of his Administration for saying in public that the budget could be cut.[3]

The struggle in the Congress over appropriations was prolonged and at times acrid, having on occasions an immediate impact in the country. One such impact arose from the decision of the House Appropriations Committee to allow a supplemental appropriation for the Post Office of $17 million only instead of the $47 million requested. The Postmaster-General replied by ordering the number of deliveries to be reduced and the post offices to be closed on Satur-

---

[1] Reported in the *New York Times* 17 January 1947. The partial transcript of the press conference is printed in the *Congressional Record*, Vol. CIII, pp. 884–7.

[2] Reported in *New York Times*, 24 January 1957.

[3] W. Randolph Burgess, Deputy to the Secretary of the Treasury, who told the Senate Finance Committee on 3 April that the budget should be cut by $2 to $3 billion, which would be 'a sound thing to do' since it would make possible a tax cut. *New York Times*, 4 April 1957.

days, on the ground that only by such means could the Post Office get to the end of the fiscal year with the funds available. In face of this the Committee yielded, though not with good grace. The appropriation for the U.S. Information Agency was cut severely,[1] and several large 'phony' cuts were made in the appropriations for ex-servicemen's pensions and grants-in-aid to the states for public assistance. The votes on the Floor of the House of Representatives on the Labor-H.E.W. appropriation bill[2] marked a turning point. On 27 March an amendment to reduce the appropriation by a total of $442 million was approved by 126 to 104 in a non-record vote;[3] on 4 April in a series of roll-call votes the House voted to restore all but $15 million of the cuts, even the funds for grants to state and local governments for the construction of sewage works being restored. It was clear that however much members of the House of Representatives might favour drastic reductions in Federal expenditures in general, a majority felt that to take public responsibility for reducing domestic civil expenditures which benefit large numbers of people was a different matter altogether.

When the House of Representatives made a large cut in the appropriations for defence and for foreign aid the President reacted more strongly, declaring that the cuts would weaken the defence of the United States. As a result, the Senate restored part of the cut. But not long afterwards the Administration began its own internal economy drive,[4] which was mainly at the expense of the defence establishment. There was a sharp drop in the value of military contracts let, the amount falling from $9·9 billion in the first half of 1957 to $7·9 billion in the second half.[5] The immediate reason for this was not any change in the international situation or even in military technology, but the national debt limit. The Act passed in 1956 had

---

[1] In part this was due to personal hostility to the Agency's Director, Arthur Larson, who had made himself unpopular with the Right-wing Republicans by his writings and speeches on 'modern Republicanism' and had antagonised the Democrats by saying that in the 1930's the United States was under the government of 'a somewhat alien philosophy'.

[2] I.e. the appropriation for the Department of Labor and the Department of Health, Education, and Welfare.

[3] A vote in which the names of the members voting on a motion are not recorded.

[4] The President had already proposed reductions in appropriations for fiscal 1958 of about $1·8 billion, in a letter to Speaker Rayburn on 18 April. Hardly any of these would bring about genuine cuts in expenditure, however.

[5] Economic Statement and 'Fact Paper' issued by the White House, 12 February, 1958, reported in the *New York Times*, 13 February 1958.

raised the limit from its permanent level of $275 billion to $278 billion for one year only, expiring on 30 June 1957. The President did not request an extension of the increase in his Messages to the Congress at the beginning of the year, and did not subsequently press, in the teeth of the economy drive, for an increase in the limit after it became known that military expenditure had been rising faster than expected. As a result the Treasury was placed in serious difficulty during the early autumn when receipts are low because of the timing of tax payments. Recourse was had to such expedients as running down the Treasury's cash balance and borrowing outside the debt limit through the sale of FNMA debentures,[1] but despite this the U.S. Government was driven to postponing briefly certain payments on account to military contractors. At no other time since the War had the debt limit and the political inhibitions associated with it interfered so seriously with financial management.

Another consequence of the economy drive was the defeat once more of the bill to make grants to the states for the building of schools. Its prospects had appeared good, for a number of liberal Democrats and their Republican allies had agreed to vote against the 'anti-segregation' amendment which had led to the bill's defeat in the previous session. But powerful conservative organizations, notably the U.S. Chamber of Commerce, waged a vigorous campaign against it, and it was narrowly defeated in the House of Representatives. Although the President had strongly supported the bill at the beginning of the Session, at the critical time he did not even make a speech in favour of it.

The President's budget was attacked both by a considerable section of his own party and by a large number of Democrats, including the 'middle-of-the-road' group who were the strongest supporters of their party's Congressional leaders, Senator Lyndon Johnson and Speaker Rayburn. The Right-wing Republicans and the conservative Southern Democrats opposed Eisenhower's budget in 1957 for the same reasons as they had opposed Truman's and Roosevelt's budgets. Senator Knowland told a Republican dinner at Hollywood, Calif.: 'A tax system under which the Federal government taxes personal

---

[1] These securities are obligations of FNMA, not of the U.S. Treasury, and legally are not part of the national debt. With the funds received from the sale of these debentures FNMA repaid to the Treasury part of the funds borrowed from it previously. This was a receipt for the Treasury from the accounting points of view, reducing its need to borrow.

incomes at rates varying from 20 to 91 per cent and corporate income at 52 per cent is simply too burdensome. It will ultimately destroy our free enterprise system.'[1] The first three budgets submitted by the Eisenhower Administration had shown a reduction in expenditure, and tax rates had been reduced in 1954, so that the Right was reasonably satisfied. Most of the reduction had however been in military expenditure, so that when the stage was reached in 1955 that the reduction in military expenditure could go no further without a drastic revision of the American defence system and foreign policy, the decline in total expenditure came to a halt. The forces that had made for an expansion of civil expenditure under previous Administrations, such as the expanding population and the growing need for public services, then brought about an upward trend in total expenditure, which was reinforced by developments of military technology that necessitated the purchase of weapons which were ever more intricate and expensive. Given the international situation, which precluded large cuts in defence expenditure, and given the unwillingness (in the Administration, in the Congress, and in the country) to go back to the 1890's[2] in the services rendered by the Federal government, total expenditures remained high and rising and general tax reductions seemed as remote under President Eisenhower as it had done under President Truman. Small wonder, therefore, that many on the Right were disillusioned.

The reasons for the support of the 'budget-cutting' drive by Democrats other than the extreme conservatives of the Byrd school are more obscure, for the Democratic moderates had not in the past opposed the assumption by the Federal government of the functions responsible for the high level of Federal civil expenditures, nor were they opposed to the foreign policy which necessitated the heavy defence expenditure. The most probable explanation is in terms of short-run politics. There was generally believed to be much stronger than usual support in the country for cuts in Federal expenditure,[3] though of course it is hard to tell whether this reflected a real spread of support for drastic reduction in Federal government services or

---

[1] Reported in the *New York Times*, 24 April 1957.

[2] The phrase was used in the context of the debate over the budget by President Eisenhower at his press conference on 10 April 1957. Reported in *New York Times*, 11 April 1957.

[3] Senator Johnson said on 29 April: 'I have never in my long service seen such strong public demand for economy'. Reported in the *New York Times*, 30 April 1957.

for a change in foreign and defence policy,[1] or whether the explanation was merely that those who had always wanted reductions in Federal expenditure were more vocal and better organized than usual. But there were widespread reports of extreme conservatives who had supported Eisenhower withdrawing their support because of his failure to reverse the domestic policies of previous Administrations;[2] the more the Democrats could emphasize the 'economy' issue, the more serious the defection of Right-wing Republicans was likely to be.

Many of the policies supported by the Democratic Left (some of them supported by the Centre too), such as Federally-financed development of hydro-electric and nuclear power, grants-in-aid to states for education, increased grants for public health and medical education, would if adopted result in a permanent increase in Federal expenditure. In most instances the Left-wing Democrats remained silent while their colleagues of the Right and Centre made the running, though they played an important part in reversing the cuts made in the Labor-H.E.W. appropriation.[3]

One of the problems of this political explanation of the causes of the struggle over the budget in 1957 is that expenditures rose in 1956 also, yet not only was there then no economy drive but the Congress attempted to force on the Administration unwanted appropriations. The most important of the probable explanations is the greater concern over inflation in 1957, when the Consumer Price Index had been rising for nearly a year. A rise in the price level generates support for reduction in government expenditure through processes of thought quite different from the theory of compensatory fiscal policy. It was a common belief that too much 'spending' causes inflation, hence government expenditure should be cut down, both to reduce 'spending' directly, and so that the government could be seen to be practicing what it was preaching to consumers and private investors.

Supporters of the budget-cutting drive were after a tax reduction,

---

[1] It is most unlikely that those supporting economy wanted a reduction in military expenditure to be made possible by a less determined policy towards Russia. The far Right wing on economic issues in the United States since the War has always, with the rarest of exceptions, been the strongest supporter of a less cautious policy towards the communist powers, at least in general terms.

[2] *New York Times*, 5 and 6 June 1957.

[3] See p. 263 supra.

however, not an anti-inflationary surplus.[1] If the cut in expenditure
were balanced by tax reduction there would probably be a small
reduction in aggregate demand through the 'balanced budget
multiplier' effect. If a cut in government expenditure were deemed
practicable as a means of countering inflation, there were strong
arguments against 'wasting' it through tax reduction. But the supporters of the drive to cut the budget did not think in these terms
at the time; any contribution to the control of inflation through
reduction in aggregate demand would be merely a side-effect of a
drive of which the purpose was tax reduction.

CONCLUSION: THE LIMITED USE OF FISCAL POLICY AND
THE PRE-EMINENCE OF MONETARY POLICY

In this chapter stress has been laid on the importance of the needs
of defence and of the civil public services in determining the level of
Federal expenditures and on political attitudes towards taxation
and the debt limit. There can be no doubt that the main reasons why
fiscal policy was not used in a more disinflationary way in 1956–57
were that the level of expenditure was regarded as 'given' by considerations other than the need to maintain price stability and that
existing Federal tax rates were treated as being a 'ceiling' which
could not be raised. Though it is clear that the Administration regarded an increase in tax rates as unacceptable, the temper of the
Congress as revealed in the 'battle of the budget' in 1957 meant that
politically speaking an increase in tax rates was not 'on', even had
the Administration been prepared to support it.

A further problem is posed by the apparent recrudescence of the
'balanced budget' doctrine as the guiding principle of American
public finance.[2] During the Senate Finance Committee's hearings
Senator Williams put the following proposition to Secretary Humphrey: 'I think we would be in agreement that taxes in themselves
should not be utilized as a source of siphoning of (sic) the money of

---

[1] On 10 April Speaker Rayburn indicated that the Democratic leaders had
made tentative plans for a tax cut to take effect on 1 January 1958, provided that
a large enough cut could be made in the budget. Reported in the *New York
Times*, 11 April 1957.

[2] In a statement submitted to the Joint Economic Committee, Professor Sey-
mour Harris wrote: 'the administration has not shown a grasp of modern fiscal
theories ... Secretary Humphrey, early in 1957, confirmed the ascendancy of
folklore and mythology over arithmetic'. Joint Economic Committee, *Hearings
on the Economic Report of the President*, 1957, p. 489.

the people just to curb inflation', to which Humphrey replied 'I agree'.[1] Discussing the question of a reduction in the income tax, Humphrey said: '. . . that will depend on when money is available, when a surplus is available for tax reduction'.[2] The possibility exists, therefore, that even had it been deemed possible to reduce Federal expenditures the disinflationary effect might have been offset in large part by tax reduction, despite the views of Saulnier and Martin about the need for a larger surplus.[3] Since the reduction in expenditures achieved was not large enough this remains a hypothetical question.

Given the circumstances which made the achievement of a larger budget surplus impossible, the share of the responsibility for the restraint of demand that was placed upon monetary policy was perforce increased. From early 1955 onwards the policy of the Federal Reserve System became more and more stringent, except from May to August 1956. An indication of the vigour with which the Federal Reserve System pursued its policy is the fact that, for the twenty-nine months from August 1955 to December 1957 inclusive members banks' excess reserves were less than their borrowings from the Federal Reserve Banks; by 1957 interest rates had risen to the highest levels since 1933. Tight control was kept over the supply of money; demand deposits plus currency in circulation outside banks (seasonally adjusted) in June 1955[4] amounted to $132·0 billion; in August 1957 the corresponding figure was $134·7 billion, an increase of only 2·0 per cent. In contrast, G.N.P. at current prices, measured at seasonally adjusted annual rates, rose by 13·4 per cent in the same period (second quarter 1955 to third quarter 1957) and G.N.P. at constant prices rose by 5 per cent.[5] Despite this apparent stringency of monetary policy, bank lending increased very rapidly in 1955 and 1956. Total bank loans increased from $70·6 billion at the end of 1954 to $90·3 billion at the end of 1956, of which increase loans to business accounted for $11·8 billion;[6] not until the summer of 1957 did the rise in business loans come to a halt.

The banks were able to finance this increase in their loans to

[1] Senate, Committee on Finance, *Hearings on the Financial Condition of the United States*, June 1957, p. 319.
[2] Ibid., p. 317.   [3] See p. 260–1 supra.
[4] *Federal Reserve Bulletin*, Vol XLIII (1957), p. 825; and monthly statistics in subsequent issues.
[5] *U.S. Income and Output*, 1959, Tables I–3 and I–5.
[6] *Economic Report of the President*, 1958, Table F–41.

business at a time when the monetary authorities were pursuing a disinflationary policy through reducing their holdings of U.S. Government securities. Between the end of 1954 and the end of 1956 the commercial banks reduced their holdings by $10·4 billion.[1] The rise in interest rates evidently did not prevent banks from selling 'Governments' in order to increase their loans, nor did it prevent insurance companies from reducing their holdings of 'Governments' while adding substantially to their holdings of corporate bonds.[2]

The monetary policy pursued in 1956–57 aroused much controversy. It clearly did not prevent rise in prices; in the late summer of 1957 there was still no sign of an end to the upward drift in prices, although a restrictive monetary policy had been in effect for two years. The growth of real output had been very slow after the end of 1955. It was not surprising that the combination of rising prices and very slowly rising real output led to much criticism of official policy. In view of the prominence given to monetary policy by all concerned in the Administration, it was monetary policy and the Federal Reserve System that bore the heaviest weight of criticism. It was further charged that the restrictive policy was discriminatory in its incidence, that it bore with greater severity on housing, on state and local governments, and on small businesses, because of their greater dependence on borrowing for finance; the first two being especially vulnerable because the borrowing is long-term and thus more open to the effect of increasing interest rates.

It was the generally held view of the Federal Reserve System that one of the most important reasons why it took so long for the restrictive policy to really 'bite' was that the pursuit of the policy of 'active ease' during the recession had been too vigorous and had added to the liquidity of the banking system so much that the absorption of the excess liquidity took an appreciable time; the commercial banks had increased their holdings of 'Governments' by $10·7 billion between May 1953 and December 1954, which they could sell in subsequent years to finance additions to their loans. The Chairman of the Board of Governors of the Federal Reserve System stated that in retrospect it seemed to him that the Federal

[1] Ibid.
[2] Board of Governors of the Federal Reserve System, Flow-of-Funds series, in *Federal Reserve Bulletin*, Vol. XLV (1959), pp. 1046–62; Table 8 (II–2) lines D and I.

Reserve delayed too long before instituting a restrictive policy in 1955.[1]

Several points deserve comment. Although the criticism of the discriminatory effects was specific to monetary policy (that insofar as it restricted at all it restricted the wrong things), the more general criticism, that the policy of restraint had checked the rise in real output but not the rise in prices, applied equally to fiscal policy or any other technique for the restraint of aggregate demand. Although monetary policy was the more prominent, partly because of the obstacles to a restrictive fiscal policy discussed above,[2] and partly because of the views of members of the Administration, especially Secretary Humphrey, who took every opportunity to stress the importance of monetary policy,[3] the role played by fiscal policy should not be overlooked. An element of discretion was involved, since the maintenance of existing tax rates required the passage of legislation each year. Despite the political incentive to reduce tax rates in 1956, the considerations of economic policy were accorded priority. The important point about tax policy in 1956 was not what changes were made but what were not made.[4]

The major problem of the years 1956 and 1957 was what policy should be pursued to cope with a rise in prices which stemmed at least in part from pressures on costs. It was a problem which came to be appreciated only gradually, as evidence accumulated that output was running at well below capacity levels, although prices continued to rise. If the 'cost-inflation' analysis had validity, restraint of aggregate demand alone was not enough unless the objectives of maximum employment and production were to be laid on one side and deflation pursued to whatever degree needed to overcome the rigidities of costs and prices. The Federal Reserve System in 1956–57 adhered strongly to the view that the demand factors were the im-

---

[1] Senate, Committtee on Finance, *Hearings on the Financial Condition of the United States*, 1957, p. 1305.

[2] See p. 267 supra.

[3] See his statement to the Senate Finance Committee, in which he said that the abandonment of the policy of 'pegging' the long-term Government bond market was 'the most effective single action in the battle against inflation', and treated the limitation of demand as being a matter of controlling the quantity of money and credit, and therefore a matter for which the Federal Reserve System was responsible. Senate, Committee on Finance, *Hearings on the Financial Condition of the United States*, 1957, pp. 11 and 13–4.

[4] Cf. Sherlock Holmes: 'The significant thing, Watson, is that the dog did not bark'.

portant ones and that accordingly the way to end the inflation was to exercise restraint over demand.[1] Despite this, Chairman Martin did concede under questioning in August 1957 that there were few instances in which it could be shown that the economy was being strained by excess demand. Since the end of 1956 the Index of Industrial Production, employment in manufacturing industry, and the average number of hours worked per week had drifted irregularly downward; new orders for capital goods began to decline at the end of 1956; and the survey of business investment plans in the spring of 1957 indicated that the rise in business investment in fixed capital was coming to an end.[2] Despite these indications of an emergent deficiency of effective demand, prices were still rising, and in August 1957 the rediscount rate was raised again, clear evidence of a restrictive monetary policy. Policy appears to have been influenced by the trend of prices almost exclusively, to the disregard of indicators showing that output was well below capacity. It is of course, easier to find signs of a coming recession with the benefit of hindsight, but even allowing for this it is reasonably clear that it was the behaviour of the price level that was the predominating factor in Federal Reserve policy in 1957.

The Council of Economic Advisers' forecast at the beginning of 1957 for the year was one of continued growth in real income. This turned out to be erroneous, and had it been possible to achieve the larger surplus recommended the result would almost certainly have been to aggravate the early stages of the recession. There is considerable similarity to events at the end of 1948; then also short-term general economic policy had for more than two years been directed to fighting inflation, and then also developments which in retrospect appeared as indicators of an emergent deficiency of aggregate demand were given less weight than they would had attention been less concentrated on inflation. With the rise in prices still continuing in the autumn of 1957, the authorities were not disposed to take the risk of relaxing the anti-inflationary measures in order to pay more attention to real output; whether deliberately or not they were taking

---

[1] Chairman Martin told the Senate Finance Committee in August 1957 'Our problem at the moment is overspending, too much spending in relation to available saving'; Senate, Committee on Finance, op. cit., p. 1306; previously he had said: 'Inflation comes from demand, not from costs, you see'; Economic Stabilization Subcommittee of the Joint Economic Committee, *Hearings*, December 1956, p. 75.

[2] Department of Commerce, *Survey of Current Business*, June 1957, p. 2.

the risk of further stagnation of real output and even of a recession in order to take more vigorous measures to deal with inflation.

The trends of prices and output in 1956–57 raised far-reaching problems of policy. If orthodox deflationary measures would hold down the growth of output without checking inflation unless pushed to lengths which would generate a recession, it became at least arguable that cost-induced inflation, if it could be kept to a slow rate, should be accepted as a lesser evil than the unemployment and loss of output caused by measures to stop it. Even on the assumption, which was open to dispute, that such an inflation would not accelerate to an extent clearly intolerable, such a policy would involve important issues of social justice, as grave as those involved in the alternative policy. Even wider in their implications were the proposals for dealing with the problem by methods aimed at eliminating or mitigating the pressures on costs. On one hand were price- and wage-controls, either formally enforced by statute or informally enforced through fact-finding bodies which would rely on weight of public and political opinion to ensure that due notice of their findings was taken by the managements and unions concerned; on the other hand were measures intended to remove those features of the product and labour markets which permit prices in those markets to be cost-determined over wide ranges of demand. This was obviously a long-term policy, and since for fulfilment it would require the abolition of large firms and effective trade unions, it was open to attack as being likely, if pushed far enough to do any good in the direction of cost-inflation, to have side effects which were more costly and disagreeable than inflation. The questions of political principle and administrative practicality of price- and wage-control in the United States are important and well known. This is a problem which has plagued nearly every country; although recognized earlier in other countries, it took the inflation of 1956–7 to thrust it among the urgent issues of American public policy. It will be discussed further in the concluding chapter.

CHAPTER XIII

RECESSION AND RECOVERY, 1957–1959

IN the late summer and early autumn of 1957 there began the third
recession in the United States since the end of the Second World
War. After being approximately stable in the first three quarters of
the year real G.N.P., measured on a quarterly basis, fell sharply in
the fourth quarter. In the Index of Industrial Production the decline
began in September and became steeper in October. The turning
point in the National Bureau of Economic Research's 'reference
cycle' has been located in July 1957.

The recession was more severe than either of its two predecessors.
The fall in quarterly G.N.P. at constant prices from the pre-recession
peak to the 'trough' quarter was 2·4 per cent in 1948–9, 3·7 per cent
in 1953–4, but 4·7 per cent in 1957–8.[1] The following tables give
an indication of the nature and magnitude of the recession:

TABLE 34

Indicators of the Magnitude of the Recession, 1957–8

	G.N.P. ($ billion at 1954 prices)	Industrial Production	Production of Durable Goods	Unemployment (% of civilian labour force)
1957 Peak	411·0	154	166	4·2
	(3rd Quarter)	(August)	(August)	(August)
1958 Trough	391·6	132	129	7·5
	(1st Quarter)	(April)	(April)	(August)

Note: the months designated 'peak' and 'trough' are those followed by a continuous decline or an almost continuous rise. There was an irregular downward
trend in industrial production in the first half of 1957 (see p. 271 supra),
with the result that the Index of Industrial Production was higher and the
unemployment percentage lower in certain months early in 1957; these months
were not designated as 'peak' because they were not followed by a continuous
or near-continuous decline.

Sources: G.N.P. at constant prices: Department of Commerce, *Survey of Current
Business*, July 1960, Table 5.

Industrial Production and Production of Durable Goods: Federal Reserve
revised seasonally adjusted indices, published in *Federal Reserve Bulletin*,
December 1959, pp. 1469–71.

Unemployment: Seasonally adjusted series, published in *Survey of Current
Business*, April 1960, p. 22.

[1] *U.S. Income and Output*, 1959, Table I–5; and *Survey of Current Business*,
July 1960, Table 5.

T

TABLE 35

Changes in Components of G.N.P.

	Change from 3rd Quarter of 1957 to:	
	1958 1st Qtr.	1958 4th Qtr.
Personal Consumption	−4·4	+6·0
Durable Goods	−4·1	−1·4
Other Goods and Services	−0·3	+7·3
Non-farm Housing	+0·2	+2·5
Other Private Domestic Gross Fixed Capital Formation	−5·4	−7·4
Inventory Accumulation	−8·5	+0·6
Net Exports	−3·5	−4·9
Government Purchases of Goods and Services:		
Federal	+0·4	+2·5
State and Local	+1·9	+5·0
Total G.N.P.	−19·4	+3·3

Amounts in $ billion at constant (1954) prices. Detail does not always add to totals because of rounding.
Source: Survey of Current Business, July 1960, Table 5.

The decline was thus concentrated in inventories, fixed capital formation by business, consumers' purchases of durable goods, and exports. A further factor which was probably of some importance but which is not shown in the above figures was the cut in defence contracts let in the second half of 1957[1] as a result of the Administration's drive to hold down Federal expenditure.

The drop in fixed capital formation by business in 1957–8 was much more severe than in either 1948–9 or 1953–4, and the swing in inventory accumulation, measured as a percentage of G.N.P., was about as great in 1957–8 as in 1953–4, though slightly smaller than in 1948–9.[2] In the drop in exports in 1957–8 there was a source of instability not present in either of the previous recessions.

It was significant that the recession of 1957–8 could not be ascribed to an exceptional cause in the way that the recession of 1948–9 could be ascribed to the making good of the backlogs of demand left from the war and the recession of 1953–4, at least in part, to the reduction in defence expenditure. The 'special' features of the recession of 1957–8, the reduction in defence orders and the

[1] See p. 263 supra.
[2] Data taken from *U.S. Income and Output*, 1959, Table I–5; and *Survey of Current Business*, July 1960, Table 5.

fall in exports, accounted for a much smaller proportion of the drop in total demand than did the fall in defence expenditure in 1953–54. In the sharp fall in business investment in fixed capital and the heavy swing to liquidation of inventories the recession of 1957–8 resembled the 'text book' cyclical movement originating in the private investment sector of the economy, the principal source of instability in capitalist economies in the days before the vagaries of defence expenditure made the public sector of the economy a source of instability. It was even suggested that the recession was in fact the beginning of the return of depression that had been expected after the end of World War II but held off by a succession of temporary circumstances. The fact that the recovery of 1958–9 proved this fear to be unfounded does not contradict the view that the recession was a more important test of the inherent stability of the American economy, the effectiveness of the built-in stabilizers, and of how feasible discretionary measures of stabilization are under American conditions than the two previous recessions had been.

Two possible causes of the drop in investment in inventories and in fixed capital by business can be suggested. Firstly, the fact that this drop in investment came after two years of deflationary monetary policy could be taken to indicate that the restriction of the quantity of credit and the rise in interest rates at last brought about that check to investment which is their purpose. Secondly, the drop in investment could have been caused by 'over-building' of capacity relative to current demand in the investment boom of 1955–7; since real output rose so slowly in 1956 and 1957, the drop in investment resembles an 'acceleration principle' effect. Similarly, it was likely that an important cause of the liquidation of inventories was the cessation in 1957 of the growth of total sales, the more so if the previous accumulation had been based on the expectation of continued growth. The Federal Reserve System's success in weakening the 'inflationary psychology' must also have weakened the expectation of continued growth in the near future.

It was also commonly asserted that the recession was an aftereffect of the previous inflation in that labour and business had 'priced themselves out of the market'. Since higher prices must be matched by higher incomes for somebody, American producers aggregated together could not have 'priced themselves out of the market' to an extent greater than that reflected in the fall in the export surplus unless adverse reactions of consumers to higher prices led them to save a larger proportion of their incomes.[1] Since the ratio of gross corporate profits to G.N.P. fell slightly in 1957, there could be no question of a swing in the distribution of the national income away from consumers, which was at least arguable as a contributory cause of the recession in 1948–9. The evidence to support the contention that a rise in American prices relative to foreign supply prices of internationally traded goods was an important cause of the recession is very sketchy. Part of the fall in exports in the second half of 1957 was merely the effect of the disappearance of special factors (such as the closing of the Suez Canal) which had made certain exports rise abnormally at the end of 1956 and early in 1957. The greater stability of imports despite the fall in income is stronger evidence for some goods being 'priced out of the market' at the margin, but even here the picture is complicated by an apparently autonomous change in consumers' tastes leading to a doubling of the number of foreign cars imported. The order of magnitude of that part of the decline in the export surplus attributable to substitution of foreign for American goods and services for reasons of price was small relative to the drop in other components of demand. The timing of the drop in investment relative to the drop in the export surplus differs markedly from what would be expected if the former were an 'accelerator' effect of the latter.

The importance of the opinion that business and labour had brought the recession upon themselves through over-pricing lay in the inference as to policy, namely that the way to deal with the recession was for the mistakes of price and wage policy to be corrected, rather than use the conventional means of expanding demand to validate *ex post* price and wage levels that were unduly high originally.

THE INITIAL REACTION TO THE ONSET OF THE RECESSION

The way in which the Federal Reserve System maintained its restrictive monetary policy into the late summer of 1957 despite accumulating evidence that the capital goods boom was coming to an end was outlined in the preceding chapter.[2] Not until late October did the System's open market operations relax the degree of restraint

---

[1] There is no evidence of this in the estimates of aggregate disposable income and saving. Moreover, if consumers did behave in this way, the fear that a slow inflation would accelerate because of people being less willing to save would be baseless.

[2] See p. 271 supra.

exerted by monetary policy; and on 15 November the rediscount rate was reduced, giving a public sign that the Federal Reserve System had discerned a change in the economic outlook which made necessary a change in its policy. This was four months after the turning point of the National Bureau's 'reference cycle'.

The Administration proper took longer to redirect its policy towards dealing with deflation. The policy recommended by the President in his speech on 13 November,[1] reduction of civil expenditure to offset an increase in defence expenditure, would contribute to economic stability in the short run only if the immediate outlook was for further inflation.

This policy was embodied in the Budget transmitted to Congress on 13 January 1958. Expenditure for defence (including the 'defense support' category of foreign aid) was budgeted to rise by $965 million above the estimate for the current year (fiscal 1958). The increase in expenditure recommended for education was $100 million, to help finance the improvements in the quality of education that were so widely demanded after the Russians' scientific success. The Budget contained a series of recommendations for reducing Federal expenditures, some of which would make their impact only in ensuing years. The most important of the measures which would take immediate effect was the proposed increase in postage rates, an increase large enough to replace the existing postal deficit of $680 million by a small surplus. In addition the President recommended that the grants made under the programme of aid to 'Federally impacted'[2] school districts should be reduced and then ended; that the grants-in-aid to states for public assistance should be revised to increase the states' share of the cost; that grants-in-aid for the building of hospitals should be restricted to meeting the most urgent needs; and that certain economies should be made in services to veterans and in the grants to farmers for approved soil conservation work.

No changes in tax rates were recommended. Revenue was estimated at $74·4 billion, giving a surplus in the 'administrative' budget of $466 million. The estimate was based on the assumption that corporate profits in the calendar year 1958 would be $42 billion and

---

[1] For details, see p. 261 supra.

[2] I.e. districts in which there are large Federal installations which add to the number of children to be educated but without adding to the local tax base (Federal property is exempt from local taxation).

personal income $352 billion,[1] that is to say, corporate profits would continue at the same level as in 1957 and personal incomes would rise by 2 per cent. This estimate obviously presupposed that any decline in income in the early part of 1958 would be made up later in the year. No recession of any size was anticipated, and the budget recommendations were in no sense part of an anti-deflationary fiscal policy.

In both the Budget Message and the Economic Report of the President it was stated that the Administration was confident that the 'adjustment' would be short-lived and expansion would soon be resumed.[2] The main factors cited to support this conclusion were the increase in defence expenditure and the acceleration of the placing of orders on defence account; increased expenditure by state and local governments; signs that fixed capital investment would not fall much further; and the fact that consumers' purchases had fallen but little while a considerable reduction in inventories had been achieved, which made it likely that the inventory liquidation would soon come to halt.[3] Although the Economic Report stated that government policies would be directed towards bringing about a resumption of expansion, the only such policy to be discussed in detail was the reduction in minimum deposits on mortgages insured by FHA. Indeed, it was stated that a fiscal policy was recommended which would meet the nation's need for strengthened defences and improvements in science and education 'within the framework of a budget in which expected revenues are adequate to cover projected expenditures'.[4]

There is a striking contrast between the tone of the *Economic Report* of 1958 and that of the *Economic Report* of 1954. Whereas the latter had listed the 'formidable arsenal of weapons' available to deal with recession and emphasized that there would be no hesitation about using any or all of them if the situation should require,[5] no such assurance was given in the 1958 Economic Report; its whole theme was that the economy would recover without any special action to this end by the Federal government. The Administration was relying on the automatic stabilizers to maintain consumption

[1] Secretary of the Treasury (Robert B. Anderson) to Joint Economic Committee; *Hearings on the Economic Report of the President*, 1958, p. 416.
[2] *Budget of the United States for the year ending 30 June 1959*, p. M9–10; and *Economic Report of the President*, 1958, pp. iii–iv and 49–50.
[3] *Economic Report of the President*, 1958, p. 49–50.
[4] Ibid., p.v.   [5] See p. 217 supra.

and so permit inventories to be run down expeditiously, after which inventory liquidation would have to stop and output rise to the level of current sales; the deflationary consequences of the fall in business investment in fixed capital were expected to be offset by the increase in expenditure by state and local governments, especially for road construction, the increase in defence orders, and by the expected increase in house building.

In the light of the information available at the beginning of 1958 this was not an unreasonable forecast. But such a cautious policy implied serious risks; in the first three months of 1958 output and employment were still declining rapidly, and all the time this was happening there was a danger that a deflationary spiral might develop through falls in income and therefore of consumption frustrating the attempt to liquidate inventories, and so leading to further rounds of cuts in production, employment, incomes, and expenditures.

CONGRESSIONAL ACTION AND PRESSURE FOR MORE VIGOROUS REFLATIONARY POLICY

Although the Administration appeared to be convinced that the recession would be overcome without special measures being taken, considerable sections of opinion in the Congress and in the country did not share this conviction. Soon after the beginning of the Session demands for more vigorous action were heard; the principal measures suggested were tax reduction and a variety of proposals for increasing expenditures.

The proposals for increases in expenditures were the more widely supported in the Congress. The Joint Economic Committee in their report on the Economic Report of the President recommended that expenditures should be increased, especially for projects that could be completed quickly; tax reduction was called for if the situation should worsen, but was not recommended for immediate action.[1]

The most prominent Congressional supporter of tax reduction was Senator Douglas. He attempted to meet the objection that a tax reduction made to deal with the recession would in practice prove irreversible and so would cause inflation when recovery had taken place by so drafting the tax reduction bill that tax rates would revert automatically to their previous levels at the end of a year unless new legislation were passed to postpone this; the restoration of the rates in force before the cut would require only enough Con-

[1] *H. Rept. No. 1409*, 85th Cong., 2nd Sess., p. 4.

gressional votes to sustain a Presidential veto. Such a tax reduction was open to criticism on the ground that consumers would spend a smaller proportion of the additional disposable income that resulted from a tax reduction that they knew was only temporary. In the absence of any prior experience no conclusion was possible on this point.

There was considerable support outside the Congress for a tax reduction as an anti-recession measure. Among those in favour were Dr. Arthur F. Burns,[1] the committee that drafted the Rockefeller Brothers' Fund report on economic policy,[2] and on the Left, Mr. Walter Reuther. Studies were made in the Treasury and the Federal Reserve System on the economic effects and cost to the revenue of various possible types of tax reduction, and it is generally believed that around March and April, when the recession was at its worst, at least Vice-President Nixon and the Secretary of Labor, Mr. James Mitchell, were in favour of tax reduction. But the Secretary of the Treasury, Mr. Anderson, was opposed at the time, both because of concern lest the loss of revenue prove permanent and because on ground of general principle he had stronger reservations about large scale government action to influence the level of economic activity.[3] Secretary Anderson had reached an understanding with the Democratic leaders in Congress, Speaker Rayburn and Senator Johnson, that no measures to reduce tax rates should be taken up except after full consultation between them. While this gave the best prospect that if tax reduction were resorted to it would be in a form which corresponded to economic criteria rather than being the partly fortuitous outcome of a political struggle, it also had the effect of ensuring that the Congressional Democrats would not force the issue for the time being.

While the decision on tax reduction was deferred, there was no lack of action on expenditures. Appropriations were handled in a way that was in complete contrast with the previous year. The regular appropriation bills were passed with abnormally small cuts and with unusual speed. The Administration decided to expedite work on projects for which funds were already available and to bring forward into fiscal 1958 some work which was not scheduled until fiscal 1959. In a letter to the Republican leaders in the House of Representatives and the Senate on 8 March 1958 the President

[1] Reported in the *New York Times*, 23 March 1958.
[2] The report was published on 20 April 1958. Summarized in the *New York Times*, 21 April 1958.   [3] See p. 306 infra.

recommended an additional appropriation of $186 million for this purpose; he also recommended the amendment of the Highway Act to suspend certain limitations on allotment of funds from the high-way trust fund, and recommended an extension of the period for which unemployed insurance benefit was payable. In the same letter he announced the release of additional funds to FNMA and the channelling of government contracts to areas in which unemployment was especially severe.

Quite a lot was done to speed up government purchases of goods for ordinary operations. By Joint Resolution approved on 21 April 1958 the Congress authorised the expenditure forthwith of $820 million appropriated for the purchase of goods in fiscal 1959, which did not begin until 1 July. Extensive use was made of this by the Veterans' Administration, General Services Administration, and the Post Office.[1] The appropriation of supplemental funds as requested by the President made possible an acceleration of work on water-resource projects that had already been started. Allocation of grants to states for hospital building, medical research, and airports was accelerated in March and April 1958, and the Internal Revenue Service accelerated refunds of taxes over-paid; payments in the first five months of 1958 exceeded the amount in the corresponding period of 1957 by $700 million.[2]

Congressional action went further than the President had requested. The first measure was the Emergency Housing Act (P.L.364) which became law on 1 April. It reduced the minimum deposit on FHA-insured mortgages from 3 per cent of the first $10,000 to 3 per cent of the first $13,500, provided to FNMA $1 billion for the purchase at par of FHA- and VA-insured and guaranteed mortgages of $13,500 or under and $50 million for purchases of mortgages on special types of houses, and provided to VA for direct loans to finance house building $150 million annually in fiscal 1959 and 1960 and $50 million for the remaining part of fiscal 1958. When signing this bill President Eisenhower expressed misgivings on the ground that it placed burdens on the Treasury which should be borne by private investors. However, he promptly authorized the expenditure of the funds carried by the Act.

In the Highway Act (P.L.381) which became law on 16 April 1958 the 'pay-as-you-go' limitation on the allocation of grants to states from the highway trust fund was suspended, as the President had

[1] *Economic Report of the President*, 1959, p. 41   [2] Ibid.

requested. In addition it authorized the payment of an additional $200 million in fiscal 1959 and $300 million in fiscal 1960 and 1961 to states for the Interstate road system, and an additional $400 million in fiscal 1959 for other Federally-aided highway construction. Instead of the usual dollar for dollar the states were required to spend only one dollar of their own funds for every two dollars of the Federal grant; moreover, the states were empowered to borrow from the Federal government up to $115 million in order to finance their matching payments. This was explicitly an anti-recession 'spending' bill, and was passed by large majorities; on signing it the President again expressed misgivings.

In a Message on 25 March the President gave specific form to his recommendation for an extension of the period for which unemployment insurance benefit is payable. He recommended that the maximum period for payment of benefits should be extended by one-half of the period then in effect under state law; the states were to borrow the funds to finance this from the Federal Treasury and to repay it from an increase in the employment tax; it was recommended that the programme should be made operative from 1 July 1958 and last for one year. The bill reported by the Ways and Means Committee (H.R.12065), was more drastic, providing for the extension of unemployment insurance benefit for 16 weeks in all cases, plus benefits for 16 weeks for those unemployed ineligible for benefit under the existing state laws, all to be financed by direct grants to the states. The President opposed this, and on the Floor of the House it was replaced, by a vote of 223 to 163, by a measure similar to that recommended by the Administration except that the states were given the option of participating, whereas under the President's original proposal no such option was allowed. The substitute was moved by Representative Herlong and passed by the combined votes of the Republicans and conservative Southern Democrats. The Senate made no changes, and it became law on 4 June. Fifteen states,[1] Alaska, and the District of Columbia took part in the programme, and five more[2] provided extended unemployment insurance benefits from their own funds.

[1] Alabama, Arkansas, California, Delaware, Indiana, Maryland, Massachusetts, Michigan, Minnesota, Nevada, New Jersey, New York, Pennsylvania, Rhode Island, and West Virginia.

[2] Colorado, Connecticut, Illinois, Ohio, and Wisconsin. These states, together with the fifteen listed above, accounted for 70 per cent of the total unemployment covered by insurance schemes (*Economic Report of the President*, 1959, p. 87.)

Two further pieces of 'spending' legislation, the bill to provide additional grants-in-aid for the construction of municipal airports (S.3502) and the bill to provide Federal loans to depressed areas (S.3683) were prevented from becoming law by the President's use of the 'pocket veto'. He also vetoed a Rivers and Harbors bill on the ground that some of the projects it authorized were not necessary, but signed it when it was passed again in a modified form. Two further bills which would have led to a substantial increase in Federal expenditures were passed by the Senate but failed to pass the House. They were the 'omnibus' housing bill providing additional funds for slum clearance and subsidized housing, and the Community Facilities bill, which would have provided loans to local governments for public works of all kinds at low rates of interest.[1]

The President's veto, exercised with vigour after June when it became apparent that the economic decline had halted, and the strength of the conservative coalition of Republicans and Southern Democrats in the House kept down the amount of new expenditures authorised under the spur of the recession, but the amount was none the less substantial. The table on the following page compares estimates of expenditure in fiscal 1959 submitted in January 1958 with the estimates for the same year submitted in January 1959, the 1959 estimates taking into account increases resulting from anti-recession measures.

The subscription to the International Monetary Fund was budgeted for as a result of the successful conclusion of the negotiations to increase the Fund's resources and was in no sense part of the measures taken to deal with the recession. Not all of the remainder of the net increase in estimated expenditure was the result of decisions by the Administration or the Congress to adopt reflationary policies; part was the automatic result of the recession, and still more was autonomous with respect to the economic situation even if its timing did turn out to be helpful. A classification of increases in expenditure as between automatic, autonomous, and discretionary can only be approximate; moreover, the distinction between autonomous and discretionary expenditure is subject to the conceptual consideration that assuming a given change (or no change) in tax rates the greater the increase in expenditure occurring autonomously, the smaller will be the discretionary increase needed to bring about a given volume of aggregate demand.

[1] In the Senate bill (S.3497), the authorization was for $1 billion at $3\frac{1}{2}$ per cent interest.

TABLE 36

Estimates of Expenditure in the Fiscal Year 1959

	Jan. 1958 (est.)	Jan. 1959 (est.)	Change
National Defence (a)	44,951	46,120	+1,169
International Affairs and Finance			
Additional I.M.F. Subscription (b)	Nil	1,375	+1,375
Other	2,197	2,333	+ 136
Veterans' Services and Benefits	5,012	5,198	+ 186
Labour and Welfare	3,643	4,380	+ 737
Agriculture	4,601	6,775	+2,174
Natural Resources	1,492	1,708	+ 216
Commerce and Housing	1,627	3,509	+1,882
General Government	1,403	1,671	+ 268
Interest	7,869	7,601	− 268
Contingencies and Proposed Legislation (c)	1,139	200	− 939
Total	73,934	80,871	+6,937

(Amounts in $ million.)

Notes: (a) The 'defense support' category of foreign aid was included under 'major national security' in the January 1958 estimates and under 'international affairs and finance' in the January 1959 estimates. The 1959 classification has been used in this table.

(b) A non-recurring item recommended by the President to the 1959 Session of Congress.

(c) Includes $339 million for proposed increases in civil service and Post Office salaries.

Source: Budget of the United States for the year ending 30 June 1959, and for the year ending 30 June 1960.

The increased expenditures for defence and foreign aid can be placed in the autonomous category, as can the 'post-Sputnik' increase in expenditure for education, the increase in civil service salaries, and the Post Office deficit that arose from the salary increase being larger and the increase in postage rates smaller than had been assumed in January 1958. Most of the increase in expenditure for agriculture was accounted for by extra outlays for price supports, caused partly by the abnormally large wheat harvest and partly by the downward pressure on price arising from the recession: it cannot be allocated between the autonomous and automatic categories, therefore.

Attributable to discretionary anti-recession policy were the increase in 'labour and welfare' expenditure due to the extension of unemployment benefit ($400 million); the increase in expenditure for natural resources ($216 million) and the increase in expenditure for 'commerce and housing' apart from the postal deficit ($1,114 million). Allowing for the fact that a slight increase in expenditure for both natural resources and housing might have resulted merely from the lack of absolute precision in the original estimates, the 'discretionary' increase in expenditure can be put at about $1·7 billion.[1] Outside the budget proper, the January 1959 estimate of expenditures from the Highway Trust Fund did not exceed the January 1958 estimate despite the additional payments voted by the Highway Act of 1958; the lag between the authorization of expenditure and payments for road construction is often long; and it is possible that payments would not have come up to the increases originally scheduled but for the additional grants voted.

A substantial drop in revenue occurred. The January 1959 estimate was $6·4 billion less than the January 1958 estimate, accounted for by a drop of $3·4 billion in the expected yield of the corporation profits tax, $1·6 billion from the personal income tax, $840 million from excise taxes, and the rest from miscellaneous receipts. The drop in receipts was entirely automatic except for the repeal of the tax on the carriage of goods,[2] which was estimated to cost about $460 million in a full year, and the 'small business' reliefs from the corporation profits tax. The increase in expenditures and fall in revenue replaced an estimated surplus of $500 million by an estimated deficit of $12·9 billion; the swing in the cash budget was even greater, from an estimated surplus of $600 million to a deficit of $13·2 billion.[3]

By the end of May it became apparent that a large deficit was in prospect even if existing tax rates were retained, which together with the signs that the decline in the economy was coming to a halt were the main reasons why the Administration finally decided to oppose tax and reduction and why the Congress concurred. On 26 May the President formally recommended the passage of legislation to postpone for a further year the reduction in the corporation profits tax and certain excise taxes scheduled for 1 July. The House passed the necessary bill without any provisions for tax reduction at all. The Senate inserted provisions to repeal the tax on the carriage of goods (3 per cent) and on the transport of passengers (10 per cent), primarily to aid the railways, whose long-term difficulties were

[1] The Secretary of the Treasury put the amount at $2 billion. Joint Economic Committee, *Hearings on the Economic Report of the President*, 1959, p. 400.

[2] See p. 286, infra.

[3] In the final out-turn the deficits proved to be $12·5 billion and $13·0 billion respectively.

aggravated by the fall in receipts from goods traffic caused by the recession. Senator Douglas's proposal that hearings should be held on general tax reduction was rejected by the Senate Finance Committee; when he moved his proposed tax reduction[1] as an amendment to the tax rate extension bill it was rejected by 65 votes to 23. The Conference Committee deleted the repeal of the tax on the transport of passengers, but approved the repeal of the tax on the carriage of goods. The President signed the bill into law on 30 June.

The debt limit was twice raised in 1958: in February there was enacted a temporary increase of $5 billion, and by P.L.912, which became law on 2 September, the permanent debt limit was raised by $8 billion in addition to the temporary increase enacted in February, making an increase of $13 billion in all over the limit in force at the beginning of 1958. There was some criticism of the first increase, though not enough to delay its passage. Opposition to the second increase in the debt limit was slight.

The fall in personal income from production was offset to a substantial extent by the fall in tax payments and the rise in transfer payments. Personal income before tax, payment of social security contributions, and transfers fell from a seasonally adjusted annual rate of $340·4 billion in the third quarter of 1957 to $335·4 billion, a drop of $5·0 billion, while disposable income fell by $1·3 billion only. The changes in tax and transfer payments bringing this about are shown in the following table:

TABLE 37

Changes in Personal Income, Tax Payments, and Transfers, 1957–8

	Change from 3rd Qtr. 1957 to	
	1958 1st Qtr.	1958 2nd Qtr.
Personal income before tax, payment of social insurance contributions, and transfers	−5·0	−4·6
Federal personal tax payments	−1·4	−1·3
State and local personal tax payments	+0·2	+0·3
Contributions for social insurance	0	−0·1
Transfer payments	2·6	4·8
Disposable income	−1·3	1·3

Amounts in $ billion at seasonally adjusted annual rates.
Detail does not always add to total because of rounding.
Source: Survey of Current Business, July 1960, Table 4.

[1] A reduction in personal income tax of $50 for each taxpayer and each of his dependents, together with certain reductions in excise taxation. The estimated cost in a full year was about $6 billion.

The decline in tax payments and the rise in transfers thus offset three-quarters of the decline in personal incomes from production between the third quarter of 1957 and the first quarter of 1958. The further rise in transfer payments in the second quarter was sufficient to raise disposable income above its pre-recession level, although income from production was still over $4 billion down and no reduction had been made in personal income tax rates. Of the increase in transfer payments between the third quarter of 1957 and the second quarter of 1958, $2·5 billion arose from state unemployment insurance, $1·1 billion from benefits under Old Age and Survivors Insurance, $0·3 billion from ex-servicemen's benefits, and the remainder from other sources (including payment by states to old people, dependent children's allowances, and ordinary poor relief).[1] The maintenance of personal disposable income through the automatic stabilizers sustained consumption expenditure and thus facilitated the liquidation of inventories quickly.

RECOVERY, 1958–9

Recovery began almost immediately the decline had come to a halt; there was no 'saucer' movement as in 1954. In December 1958 the seasonally adjusted index of industrial production reached the level of September 1957, and in March 1959 the index rose above the pre-recession peak. In the fourth quarter of 1958 real gross national product slightly exceeded that recorded for the third quarter of 1957, the highest quarter before the recession. In the second quarter of 1959 gross national product (measured at constant 1954 prices) was estimated at $434·2 billion (at a seasonally adjusted annual rate),[2] $5\frac{1}{2}$ per cent above the pre-recession peak. Employment was slower to recover, and the persistence of high unemployment in the autumn and winter despite the rise in output caused considerable disquiet. The situation improved in the spring of 1959, and in May and June unemployment was estimated at 4·9 per cent of the civil labour force.[3] Even this was still about $\frac{3}{4}$ per cent higher than the average of mid-1955 to mid-1957, and $1\frac{1}{2}$ per cent above the average in 1951–3.

The expansion in demand occured mainly in consumption, inventory accumulation, house-building, and government purchases of goods and services. Consumption, measured at seasonally adjusted

---

[1] *Survey of Current Business*, July 1960, Table 4.   [2] Ibid., Table 5.
[3] *Survey of Current Business*, April 1960, pp. 22–3.

annual rates, rose from $269·0 billion in the first quarter of 1958 (the 'trough' quarter) to $290·0 billion in the second quarter of 1959. Inventory investment swung from liquidation at an annual rate of $6·2 billion to accumulation at an annual rate of $10·1 billion, partly because of stocking-up in readiness for the expected steel strike. Purchases of goods and services by Federal, state, and local governments rose by $4 billion over the period. The value of work done in non-farm residential building rose by $5·0 billion.[1] Business investment in plant and equipment was slower to recover; the decline in 1958 went further than the surveys of investment plans had indicated,[2] but in 1959 a recovery began, which accelerated in the second half of the year; even so, at the end of 1959 fixed capital formation by business remained below the peak in 1957.

The extent to which the recovery was based on consumption and inventory accumulation gave rise to doubts about its further progress. Inventory accumulation was at the highest rate reached except during the rush to build up stocks following the outbreak of the war in Korea, and so little further addition to demand could be expected from it. The expansion of consumption was financed to a considerable degree by credit: instalment credit outstanding rose by $2·4 billion in the first six months of 1959,[3] more than the total increase in the whole of 1957 and only $400 million less than the increase in 1956. The number of houses started began to decline in May 1959; and the Administration's statements of policy rendered unlikely a further rise in purchases of goods and services by the Federal government. In the second half of 1959 output was depressed by the steel strike; and in the first half of 1960 output recovered to the levels reached before the strike, but made little further progress.

Within three months of the beginning of the recovery the authorities had moved from a policy of stimulation to one of 'neutrality'; and well before the end of the year this had become a policy of active restraint. The President's veto of two 'spending' bills at the end of the Congressional session was noted above;[4] in August the Federal Reserve System began to reverse the easy money policy which had been in effect since November 1957. In June and July

---

[1] Data taken from *Survey of Current Business*, July 1960, Table 5.

[2] *Survey of Current Business*, September 1958, p. 5; December 1958, p. 2; and March 1959, p. 11.

[3] Board of Governors of the Federal Reserve System, monthly statistics published in the *Federal Reserve Bulletin*.

[4] See p. 283, supra.

1958 interest rates rose sharply as purchasers of 'Governments' who had bought in the expectation of a continued easy money policy hastily unloaded them when it became realized that the decline in the economy had come to a halt and that the easy money policy would therefore soon be reversed. At this time too the size of the prospective Federal deficit for fiscal 1959 became apparent, portending a heavy demand by the Treasury for loanable funds at a time when demands by business would be increasing. On 18 July the Open Market Committee of the Federal Reserve System authorised operations in securities other than Treasury bills in order to steady the market.[1] The Federal Reserve Banks raised their rediscount rates in August–September and again in October–November; by the beginning of November interest rates on U.S. Government securities had risen above the previous high point reached in October 1957. In December 1958 member banks' free reserves (excess reserves minus borrowing from Federal Reserve Banks) became negative again. In 1959 monetary policy became progressively more stringent, as is indicated by the continued rise of member banks' borrowing from the Federal Reserve Banks relative to excess reserves (in June 1959 free reserves were minus $513 million). Rediscount rates were raised in March and again at the end of May, and in September were raised to 4 per cent. The Chairman of the Board of Governors of the Federal Reserve System in his statement to the Joint Economic Committee in February 1959 reiterated his view that in 1954–5 'we maintained the policy of ease too long'.[2] It was evident that the Federal Reserve System was intent on not repeating this mistake[3] in 1958–9.

The Administration endorsed this policy, and attempted to reinforce it through budgetary policy. In the election campaign of 1958 President Eisenhower reverted to the orthodox Republican approach to anti-deflationary fiscal policy, to attack the Democrats for supporting excessive expenditures. He said in a speech at Los Angeles: 'One after another Administration bills were mangled or mushroomed by extremists pursuing economic and political goals at odds with the

---

[1] For an account of this episode, see *Federal Reserve Bulletin*, Vol. XLV (1959), pp. 860–9.

[2] Joint Economic Committee, *Hearings on the Economic Report of the President*, 1959, p. 482.

[3] If delaying anti-inflationary measures at a time when prices are still stable in order not to risk interfering with the growth of output can be considered a 'mistake'.

6345

U

American tradition. We saw this in housing and public works, in agriculture and unemployment benefits, in urban redevelopment, and in Federal-state community development'.[1] There is no evidence that the President's reversion to this theme did his party's Congressional candidates any good; the Republican strength in both House and Senate after the 1958 elections was lower than it had been at any time since 1938. The Right-wing Republicans suffered most severely, several of the 'Class of '46'[2] losing their seats.

After the 'spenders' (or rather the party so described by their opponents) had won the election, President Eisenhower's principal aim in domestic politics was to prevent the Democratic majority in the Congress from embarking on policies which would increase the danger of inflation. The strengthening of the 'liberal' group in the Congress aroused fears (and hopes) of expansion of services rendered by the Federal government which would lead to large increases in government expenditure; both the fears and the hopes proved exaggerated, in part because the influence still wielded by the Southern conservatives whose seniority placed them in strong positions had been under-estimated.

The Administration believed that the recovery was strongly based and would continue without further stimulation from Government policy, and regarded the prevention of inflation as the most pressing task of short-term economic policy. Accordingly a balanced budget was submitted for fiscal 1960. Revenues were estimated at $77·1 billion, on the assumption that personal income in 1959 would be $374 billion, corporate profits $47 billion, and G.N.P. 'somewhat more than' $470 billion.[3] Expenditures were to be held down to $77·0 billion, giving a surplus of $100 million. The reduction in estimated expenditures below the estimate for fiscal 1959 was $2.9 billion, of which $1,375 million was accounted for by the subscription to the International Monetary Fund, a non-recurring item of expenditure which fell in fiscal 1959. The temporary extension of unemployment benefit undertaken as an anti-recession measure in 1958 was not to be continued, a fall in expenditure for supporting the price of agricultural products was expected, and reduced purchases and increased sales of mortgages by FNMA were expected

[1] 20 October 1958. Text printed in the *New York Times*, 21 October 1958.
[2] See p. 59, supra.
[3] The out-turn was: G.N.P., $482·1 billion; personal income, $383·3 billion; corporate profits, $46·6 billion. *Survey of Current Business*, July 1960, Table 3.

to reduce expenditure on housing by $900 million compared with fiscal 1959. Apart from the discontinuance of the 'emergency' increases in expenditure, the budget did not attempt to enforce cuts in real expenditure that were large enough to be economically significant. The importance of the budget lay in the effort to prevent any increase in expenditures; the symbolic effect of budget estimates that balanced (albeit through limiting the item for contingencies to $100 million instead of the customary $400 million) was expected to be useful as a restraint on the Congress.[1]

Despite fears expressed after the elections, the 86th Congress did not enact measures requiring large increases in Federal expenditures. The President let it be known that he would use his veto to prevent the passage of bills which would increase Government expenditures, and his use of the 'pocket veto' in 1958 showed that this was no idle threat. The conservative coalition in the Congress had more than enough votes to sustain a veto, and the Democratic leaders were reluctant to push forward measures as gestures which they knew in the end would come to nothing. Only three important vetoes were overridden, that of the public works appropriation bill in 1959, and in 1960 those of bills to increase the salaries of certain Federal employees and to curtail the authority of the Secretary of Agriculture over expenditure for rural electrification. The cuts recommended by the Administration in 1959 in appropriations for medical research and hospital-building were rejected by the House Appropriations Committee.[2] The measures which would have required really large increases in expenditure, such as Federal grants-in-aid for school building and teachers' salaries, and medical care for retired people, were not passed either in 1959 or in 1960. In 1959 the tax on motor fuel was increased, as the President requested, so as to keep the Highway Trust Fund from having to borrow, and the corporation profits tax and the excise taxes were extended at their existing rates for a further year.

On the other hand, the Congress did not accede to the President's request for the repeal of the maximum limit of $4\frac{1}{4}$ per cent to the interest rate on Government bonds with a maturity of five years or more. This limit, imposed by legislation passed in 1918, became a

[1] According to preliminary estimates, the out-turn was a surplus of $1·1 billion.
[2] In large part because the chairman of the sub-committee concerned, Representative Fogarty, was a strong supporter of higher Federal expenditure for medical research.

serious problem in 1959 as interest rates rose under the influence of the Federal Reserve System's restrictive policy and fears about further inflation. Its effect was to confine Federal debt issues to maturities of under five years, thus aggravating the problem of managing the debt in a way which does not make the task of monetary control more difficult by making the private sector more liquid. The difficulty of conducting a restrictive monetary policy when large amounts of public debt must be re-financed at short intervals became prominent in 1959, leading to an increase in the emphasis placed on the importance of a budget surplus for the control of inflation. In the Budget for fiscal 1961 the President estimated that there would be a surplus of $4·2 billion, to be achieved by holding the rate of growth of Federal expenditure below the rate of growth of revenue.

CONCLUSION ON THE 'SECOND EISENHOWER RECESSION'

Changes in Federal expenditures and tax receipts made a major contribution to limiting the extent of the decline. The effectiveness of the 'automatic stabilizers' in offsetting declines in personal income from production was demonstrated once more. The discretionary increase in Federal expenditures for anti-recession purposes was greater than in either of the two previous post-war recessions; and as in 1949–50 the timing of substantial 'autonomous' increases in Federal expenditure, especially for defence, proved to be helpful.

As in 1949 the authorities were slow in swinging from fighting inflation to fighting deflation; although signs of a coming recession were increased in the summer of 1957 and by November it was quite evident that a decline had begun, the Budget submitted in January took no account of this, and it was not until until March 1958, six months after the recession had begun and four months after it had become quite visible, that the Administration submitted recommendations for fiscal measures to deal with it; even these were far from drastic. Once recovery was under way the attention of the Administration and the Federal Reserve System was directed once more to checking inflation. While in 1957 they were unwilling to take expansionary measures before the decline was clearly under way, when the question arose of taking anti-inflationary measures before recovery had gone far enough to approach full capacity output, there was no disposition to wait until inflation was beginning again before taking action.

This greater readiness to take anti-inflationary measures than to take expansionary measures and to take them sooner arose in large part from the fear of renewed inflation. Since prices continued to rise despite the recession, this was no groundless fear; between September 1957, the month in which the decline was beginning, and May 1958, at the bottom of the decline, the Consumer Price Index rose by 2·1 per cent; the price of commodities other than food did not decline, and the price of food and services continued to rise. The effect of this in a situation where the steady rise in the price level in the eighteen months before the beginning of the recession had caused widespread concern and made large numbers of people, not least in the Administration and the Federal Reserve System, 'inflation-conscious' was to increase the reluctance to take measures which might make it more difficult to get inflation under control when the recession had been reversed.

This reluctance to take inflationary risks in order to take prompt and effective action against the recession was strengthened by the confidence felt by many members of the Administration in the 'inherent resilience' of the private economy. In his letter of 8 March 1958 outlining his programme of anti-recession measures the President expressed concern over 'the upsurge of pump-priming schemes' that showed 'lack of faith in the inherent vitality of our free economy' and in the American as an individual'.[1] Secretary Anderson, discussing the subject before the Joint Economic Committee in February 1959, said: 'Had we resorted to a tax cut we would not have had this demonstration of the economy's inherent recuperative powers. We would have helped develop a philosophy that tax relief was necessary to pull us out of the downturn'.[2] This amounts to preferring a later recovery brought about by 'inherent' factors to a prompter recovery brought about by reflationary fiscal policy, on grounds of 'free enterprise' doctrine. There was little sign of this in 1954; a probable reason is that then Republican survival as an effective party depended on being able to prevent a depression; the spectre of 'those Hoover years' had to be exorcized at almost any cost. The successful handling of the recession in 1954 without resort to the drastic measures that

[1] Text printed in the *New York Times*, 9 March 1958.
[2] Joint Economic Committee, *Hearings on the Economic Report of the President*, 1959, p. 400.

the Administration was prepared to use if need be increased the Administration's confidence in the 'inherent vitality' of the private economy; the stronger this confidence, the greater the equanimity with which anti-inflationary measures could be pressed despite signs of decline.

A further factor making for reluctance to press reflationary measures which was absent in 1954 was the balance of payments deficit. For the first time for many years there was talk in international financial circles about the 'weakness of the dollar'.[1] There can be little doubt about the concern this caused in the United States. Among the reasons Secretary Anderson gave for the practice of 'sound fiscal policies' in 1959 was the need to maintain prestige abroad,[2] though the loss of gold itself was not cited as a reason for deflationary measures. In addition to 'prestige', the main argument cited has been the danger that the United States would 'price herself out of world markets', which is basically an employment argument.

For all these reasons the Administration was more reluctant than in 1953–4 to take vigorous anti-deflationary measures. But this reluctance was offset in part by 'autonomous' increases in expenditure which in addition to their main purpose had a beneficial side-effect on aggregate demand, and in part by the strength of support in the Congress for more drastic measures. In complete contrast to 1949 the majority in Congress was intent on more drastic reflationary measures than the Administration was willing to support. Among the reasons for this was that the Democrats were in control of the Congress but not the Presidency, and more vigorous action to deal with unemployment was the 'natural' policy for them in such a situation; the liberal Republicans, especially those representing cities and states containing large industrial populations, were willing to support 'spending' measures for the relief of unemployment. Not to be overlooked is the gradual but none the less real increase in the familiarity of Members of Congress with economic problems, especially the problem of dealing with recessions. For the first time

[1] It is somewhat ironic that the United States should have been criticized on this score, for among the reasons for the deficit was the stability of American imports despite the recession, which greatly limited the effect of the American recession on other countries; it had been the tendency of American imports to decline and of her balance of payments surplus to increase in time of recession that had previously been the subject of foreign criticism.

[2] Joint Economic Committee, *Hearings on the Economic Report of the President*, 1959, p. 401.

since 1932 the United States had the experience of the President resisting Congressional pressure for expansionary measures.

The recovery in the latter months of 1958 and the first half of 1959 removed the argument of dealing with the recession from the supporters of increased Government expenditure, and the President's position became tenable politically as well as economically (on the assumption that in order to guard against inflation it was worth risking a slower growth of output and employment, at any rate in the short run). A permanent and substantial increase in Federal expenditure in 1959 meant an increase in tax rates unless inflation was to be deliberately risked in order to attain other social aims; and reluctance to take responsibility for an increase in tax rates was as strong among 'liberals' in 1959 as it was in other sections of opinion.

CHAPTER XIV

CONCLUSIONS

ALTHOUGH by the end of the Second World War economic analysis provided guides to policies which offered better hopes than ever before of preventing deep or prolonged recessions, the ability and willingness of the United States to put these policies into effect if the need should arise was open to legitimate doubt. The Federal system and the separation of powers raised obstacles to quick and effective action not present in other forms of democratic government; and the structure of political opinion in the United States, deeply influenced by the events of the 1930's, made it at least possible that the onset of a recession might be met by inaction or even by measures that would make the situation worse. But in the event, the conduct of general economic policy in the United States between 1945 and 1960 belied the worst of the fears, although the conditions experienced differed substantially from what had generally been expected and the effectiveness of American counter-cyclical policy on really unfavourable terrain remained untested. Several problems which had not in 1945 appeared very pressing had by 1960 emerged as major economic problems for the United States as for other Western countries. Prominent among these problems were the structural features of the economy making for inflation. Steady economic growth had been added to the original objectives of full employment and price stability. In this concluding chapter each of the points mentioned above will be considered in turn in more detail.

STABILIZING FISCAL POLICY IN PRACTICE PART OF THE 'AMERICAN CONSENSUS'

Although support for the old orthodoxy continued among important sections of American opinion, there were no cases of fiscal measures being taken which were demonstrably in the 'wrong' (i.e. de-stabilizing) direction. In none of the three recessions between 1945 and 1960 were tax rates increased or expenditures cut in an attempt to eliminate a recession-induced deficit, though in 1949 it was 'a damned close run thing'. In 1950 an expenditure-reducing amendment was attached to the Omnibus Appropriation Bill, but action on it was not completed until the outbreak of the Korean war had changed the economic outlook completely. In neither 1954 nor 1958 did an economy drive develop in the Congress. The same Congress which in 1957 had undertaken a vigorous economy drive was pressing the Administration to 'spend' in the spring of 1958. Part of the explanation is that in both 1954 and 1958 a Republican Administration was in office. When a Republican Administration is in office during a recession, it is the obvious strategy for the Democrats to attack their opponents for not doing enough to bring about recovery and so revive the image of the Republicans as the party which did nothing while recession turned into depression. But even among Republican Members of Congress there were few supporters of drastic cuts in expenditures to eliminate the deficit in 1954 and 1958.

In reports of the Joint Economic Committee and its sub-committees from 1954 onwards there was general agreement that the state of the economy is the primary consideration in deciding whether or not attempts ought to be made to balance the budget, and that to try to offset the automatic decline in revenues and increase in social welfare expenditures during a recession by raising tax rates or cutting other expenditure is unsound. Individual dissents from this view have been few, in marked contrast to the united statements of minority views by the Republican members in 1949 and 1950.

At no time did the Administration propose measures intended to eliminate the deficit during a recession. President Eisenhower was asked at his press conference on 15 January 1958 whether he was in favour of tax increases to prevent the emergence of a deficit; he replied that he was not, for the economy needed 'to have a little needle, some needle rather than a check-rein on it'.[1]

The experience of the recessions of 1949, 1954, and 1958, especially the last two, indicates that the danger of the working of the automatic stabilizers being impeded by unwise measures intended to balance the budget is remote. The recommendation of economic theory on this point is clear cut, and has been followed by both Republican and Democratic Administrations and Congresses with both Republican and Democratic majorities.

There also existed the possibility that inflation might be aggravated

[1] The transcript of the press conference is printed in the *New York Times*, 16 January 1958.

by a tax reduction which 'gave way' the surplus produced by rising revenues and more slowing rising expenditure, a contingency that proved to be of more practical importance than had seemed likely in 1945. Such a tax cut was made much less likely by the existence of a large national debt, which according to classical principles it would be prudent to reduce before using the surplus for tax reduction. The one instance of tax reduction at a time when most of the indications were that inflation was still serious was the Revenue Act of 1948. Fears of recession in 1947 and 1948 would have provided grounds for tax reduction had it been preferred to risk inflation deliberately rather than a recession, but there can be little doubt that it was for reasons unconnected with economic stability in the short run that the Republicans sought to push through tax reduction in 1947 and succeeded in the following year.[1]

The next occasion on which there was the possibility of an inflationary tax reduction was in 1956. A budget surplus was in sight for the first time since fiscal 1951, and in an election year the purely political inducement to 'give away' an expected surplus was more than usually strong. Although the maintenance of existing tax rates required affirmative legislation, this was achieved without difficulty. The probable inflationary effect of a tax cut was evidently the principal reason why the Administration recommended that existing tax rates be continued, and why Congress concurred.[2]

The fear that the Administration or the Congress, especially the latter, might react to deflation-induced deficits or inflation-induced surpluses by positive action of the wrong kind, had up to 1960 proved largely groundless. For this a steady increase in familiarity of men in public life with the elements of counter-cyclical fiscal policy is partly responsible.[3] Acceptance of the fiscal automatic stabilizers as useful features of the economy is common ground among almost all who have any practical responsibility for the conduct of public affairs. No great departure from a policy of non-intervention is really implied: once the stabilizers have been built into the system[4] the action required is less than under the principle of the

---

[1] For the circumstances of the Revenue Act of 1948, see Chapters V and VI, supra.

[2] See pp. 249–54, supra.

[3] A comparison of Congressional discussion of the economic situation in 1949 and 1958 would demonstrate this growth in knowledge.

[4] See pp. 11–12, supra, for the origins of the automatic stabilizers.

balanced budget, which in a recession requires positive action of a politically unpleasant kind.

Positive counter-cyclical fiscal measures remain more controversial. Criticism of such measures in the United States falls under two distinct heads, which are not always kept as separate as would be desirable. The first criticism is ideological, based on a belief in the self-equilibrating private economy; the second accepts compensatory measures when presented in analytical terms, but holds that an attempt to apply them in American political conditions would impart a significant inflationary bias to the economy. Quite early it was held that the use of compensatory fiscal policy, however faultless in principle, would in practice not be applied symmetrically and would maintain full employment only at the cost of more or less continuous inflation. Both the Administration and the Congress, conscious of the unpopularity of tax increases and of cuts in government expenditure, would be eager to take compensatory action when deflation threatened, but would be unwilling to take the disinflationary measures needed to prevent recovery from turning into inflation.

Up to 1960 fears of Administrations and Congresses straining at the leash to launch massive reflationary policies at the first sign of deflation had proved groundless. The Truman Administration's handling of the 1949 recession is especially significant in this context. It was slow to abandon the position that inflation was the more pressing danger than deflation, and the reflationary measures when taken were very cautious.[1]

The fiscal policies of the Eisenhower Administration in the recessions of 1953–4 and 1957–8 were certainly not hasty or rash. The interval between the onset of the recession in 1957 and the initiation of positive measures to deal with it was very long. The 'reaction-time' in 1953–4 was shorter, but mainly because the tax reduction made on 1 January 1954 were automatic under existing law, a fortuitous factor in the timing of counter-cyclical measures.[2]

Although the handling of recessions by post-war Administrations was very cautious both in the timing and in the magnitude of the steps taken, there is little reason to doubt that more drastic measures would have been taken had the recessions proved more severe or prolonged. The declarations of policy in the Economic Reports of the President in July 1949 and January 1954 are forthright enough on this point, and from what is known about the planning that was be-

[1] See Chapter VII, supra.   [2] See p. 215, supra.

ing undertaken there is no reason for doubting the sincerity of the statements of policy. How far the situation would have had to deteriorate in 1949, 1954, or 1958 before measures such as substantial reductions in tax rates or large programmes of public construction would have been undertaken cannot be known for certain, for statesmen are wisely reluctant to express opinions on hypothetical contingencies.

On the other hand, the fear that a compensatory fiscal policy would be inhibited by the practical difficulties of increasing tax rates or making economically significant reductions in government expenditures has been shown to be justified. On all occasions when 'economy' drives have been attempted, the gap between the cuts actually achieved and the amounts desired, promised, or threatened has been large. 'Expenditure depends upon policy', and given unwillingness to make major alterations in policies about defence, social security, and other public services solely in order to restrain inflation more effectively, the usefulness of reductions in government expenditure as a disinflationary measure has proved to be very small.

Resistance to increases in tax rates has further restricted the use that could be made of fiscal policy as an anti-inflationary technique. Between 1945 and 1960 there was no general increase in Federal tax rates for the express purpose of providing for an anti-inflationary budget surplus or for making possible an increase in government civilian expenditure without inflation.[1] When fiscal policy was used most effectively for the control of inflation, after the outbreak of the war in Korea, tax increases could be and were supported as being necessary to 'pay for' the war and rearmament. Even so, the increases in tax rates in 1951 were enacted only after a bitter and prolonged struggle. The fate of the Revenue Act of 1951 demonstrated that it was the general opinion in the Congress that further increases in tax rates were not acceptable in circumstances short of general war. None of the important economic interest groups was willing to acquiesce publicly in substantial increases in the tax burden borne by its members, even if the burdens of other groups were being increased too. A political upper limit to tax rates had evidently been reached.

The same state of affairs persisted under the Eisenhower Administration. There is strong evidence that the existing tax rates

[1] For a discussion of the increases in the rates of the taxes paid to the O.A.S.I. and highway trust funds, see p. 306, infra.

were taken by many, including members of the Administration, as 'given', capable of being exceeded only in circumstances much graver than those following the launching of 'Sputnik', when the argument of 'national defence' could have been invoked to support an increase in tax rates to accompany the increase in military expenditure. The drive to cut the budget in 1957, which had tax reduction as its aim, was a further indication of the strength of support for tax reduction and hence of resistance to further increases.

It thus appears that given these political attitudes and the need to spend \$40–45 billion a year on defence, the only way in which fiscal policy could be used to exert a disinflationary effect would be to hold the rate of increase of government expenditure below the rate of increase of G.N.P. But this would impose narrow limits on improvements in public services rendered by the Federal government, and there are many Americans, not confined to the Democratic Left, who are not willing to treat public goods and services and transfer payments as the 'residuary legatee' in this way. This effective upper limit to tax rates is of great importance and will be discussed further in a later section of the chapter where attention is turned to unsolved problems which in 1960 remained for the future.

The record of the fiscal policies pursued from the end of the Second World War to 1960 was thus one of the unhampered working of the automatic stabilizers, which proved very efficient in insulating personal disposable income and hence consumers' expenditure from declines in output and income from production. The automatic effects were supplemented by discretionary measures which were very cautious both in magnitude and in timing. At practically all times[1] the policies were in the right direction, even if questions can be raised about the timing and the magnitude.

If this is a generally correct picture of the fiscal policies pursued in the United States after 1945, there remains the question of how this came about when many of those concerned with the making of fiscal policy appeared, insofar as their opinions can be discerned in their statements and writings, to be opposed to counter-cyclical fiscal policy as a matter of principle. Throughout the years of the Truman Administration 'down with deficit financing' and 'balance the budget by cutting expenditures' were recurring themes of Republican

---

[1] This must be qualified in respect of the tax reduction attempted in 1947 and enacted in 1948 which then appeared 'wrong' *ex ante*, and the tax increase proposed by the Truman Administration in January 1949, but not enacted.

statements of policy in the Congress and in the country. In 1951 this took the form of hostility to increases in tax rates, government expenditures, and deficits alike. Not only was compensatory policy as applied to deflation bitterly attacked, but few people in public life, as distinct from professional economists, thought it necessary or expedient to repudiate the older doctrine.

The deference to the precept does not necessarily imply rigid adherence to the practice. It is apparent to those who have to deal with the problem and are responsible for the consequences, that the cuts in expenditure and increases in tax rates that the balanced budget doctrine prescribes in cases of deflation are harmful rather than helpful, as well as being politically difficult to achieve. The record of the Eisenhowever Administration illustrates the point clearly; in early 1953, from 1955 to 1957, and again in 1959–60, when a policy of risking slower recovery and growth in order to keep the risk of inflation to a minimum indicated disinflationary measures, the balanced budget doctrine was proclaimed in something like its pristine purity; on the other hand, expressions of devotion to the doctrine were few and far between in 1954 and 1958 when the situation required measures incompatible with the balanced budget principle. This is not to impute insincerity to President Eisenhower and others who in 1955, 1956, and 1957 spoke of a balanced budget as being the sound policy and a sure sign of good management in government as in a business or a household.[1] The balanced budget can be regarded as a goal which is always desirable because of its effects in restraining inflation and limiting irresponsibility in government expenditures, but at the same time it can be recognized that the goal of a balanced budget, like other goals, cannot safely be pursued with equal zeal all the time. When deflation is the pressing problem, the balanced budget has to yield to the more urgent goal of checking the decline and bringing about recovery, both out of common humanity to keep suffering and loss to a minimum and to avoid the fate that the recent historical record suggests awaits parties that allow serious recessions to develop. The precept of the balanced budget is not explicitly renounced in time of deflation, but it is quietly disregarded. It comes back into its own when the economic situation renders it safe.

[1] The continued use of this traditional expression is noteworthy in view of the rapid increase of private debt, both corporate and individual. Between the end of 1948 and the end of 1958 total net corporate debt rose from $118 billion to $236 billion, and individual and other private non-corporate debt rose from $72 billion to $216 billion (*Economic Report of the President*, 1959, Table D–47).

In view of the policies pursued during the recessions of 1953–5 and 1957–9 it is reasonable to conclude that that government action including fiscal measures, to deal with economic instability, including deflation, has become part of the generally accepted practice of American politics and government. The Eisenhower Administration's handling of the recession of 1953–5 was particularly important in clearing the air on this point. After nearly two decades of Republican condemnation of the measures which modern economic analysis suggests are the best ways of dealing with a deficiency of effective demand, it was permissible to have doubts about whether a Republican Administration would or would not place ideology above economics, despite Eisenhower's pledges in the closing stages of the campaign. When it came to the point the recession was handled in accord with capable economic advice and in a manner not notably different from that in which the Truman Administration handled the recession of 1949. There was thus strong evidence that counter-cyclical fiscal policy is part of the so-called 'American Consensus',[1] the broad areas of agreement between all except the 'outside-Right' that on economic issues amounts to approval, *de facto* if not quite *de jure*, of the 'mixed economy'.

It is of course true that there still existed in the United States in 1960 a significant group that was out to the Right of this 'Consensus'. The National Association of Manufacturers was still assailing deficit financing and warning, as it had done year in and year out, of the unchecked drift to socialism, as did organizations whose interests were threatened by the policies advocated at the Left edge of the consensus or outside it, such as the private power companies and the American Medical Association. Among those who held these views in the 1940's and 1950's were prominent Members of Congress and numerous owners of newspapers, who between them managed to give the impression of the existence of a powerful group which had learned nothing about economic policy since the days of Andrew Mellon.[2]

[1] The term is quite a common one and is given much the same content by both Democratic and Republican writers. Take for example the discussion in A. Larson, *A Republican Looks At His Party* (New York, 1956), and C. Bowles, *American Politics in A Revolutionary World* (Cambridge, Mass., 1956). Both Larson and Bowles argue that the idea that the Federal government should take fiscal action to deal with recessions is part of the 'consensus', and Bowles cites the practice of the Eisenhower Administration in 1953–4 as proving this.

[2] It is customary to take President McKinley in making this kind of comparison, but it does him an injustice in that he was far from being a doctrinaire, and by the standards of his time was something of a 'progressive' on social policy.

It is fairly clear that the mass support enjoyed by this group in the United States came not from real approval by substantial sections of the electorate of its economic policies, but from grievances over going to war again against Germany on the side of Britain and the politically related grievances over foreign and domestic communism, which for historical reasons were channelled into support for men holding extreme Right-wing economic views. With the waning of alarm over domestic communism and the end of the Korean war support for the extreme Right ebbed a long way, as the results of the Congressional elections of 1958 made clear.

The existence of this 'outside-Right' group which feels very strongly about *laissez-faire*, balanced budgets, and disapproval of the national debt, cannot be written off as having no impact at all on the conduct of affairs, for these precepts, in a rather vague way, are part of the American national orthodoxy that is taken more or less for granted by most people who do not approach these issues as professional economists or as deliberate critics of contemporary society. The view that a predominantly private enterprise economy and political and civil liberty are so closely inter-related that private enterprise and *laissez-faire* are just as much the values which must be preserved as are democracy and liberty[1] is widely, if diffusely, adhered to outside of groups that support the extreme Right. It is held as a dogma, supported by weight of rhetoric (generally of a 'patriotic' flavour) rather than by evidence, and such evidence as is presented is almost always drawn from Hitler's Germany or, more commonly, the communist countries, rather than from such examples as Britain, New Zealand, or Scandinavia. When practical problems of sufficient urgency force the issue, dislike of intervention by the Federal government has to yield to the need to get the job done, of course, but the residue of sentiment against the use of the Federal government is still a force to be reckoned with.

The political conflicts of the 1930's made the principle of the always balanced budget a symbol of 'private enterprise', so that until time

---

[1] The ferocity with which this view is sometimes put forward can be startling to someone who is not used to the linguistic usages of American political debate and invective. For example, take the following statement made by Senator (later Secretary of State) Dulles in a broadcast concluding his campaign for election as Senator from New York in 1949: 'He (Herbert H. Lehman, Dulles's opponent) knows that the so-called Welfare State sought by the Democratic Administration with the help of a posse of left wingers and communistic elements means state socialism and an end to liberty' (*New York Times*, 8 November 1949).

erodes the efficacy of this symbol (the process had already gone some way by 1960), the support felt for 'private enterprise' strengthens reluctance to take anti-deflationary measures. It probably lengthens the period that must elapse between the emergence of deflationary trends and the decision to take reflationary action, and is a force for caution about the scale of the measures taken. The stronger the faith in the 'free enterprise system' the greater the inducement to refrain from drastic measures in the expectation that the self-equilibrating forces in the 'system' will do their stuff. President Eisenhower's rebuke in March 1958 to supporters of increased public expenditures for their 'lack of faith in the inherent vitality of our free economy and in the American as an individual'[1] is an example of this.

The survival of the older doctrine is part of the reason why the degree of unemployment that is necessary to call forth reflationary measures is higher in the United States than in Britain. Just how much higher cannot be specified with precision, for, as is well known, the methods used to compile the monthly statistics of unemployment in the United States and Britain tend to understate the level of unemployment in Britain[2] relative to that in the United States; also, the very size and diversity of the United States makes possible a greater amount of structural unemployment even with a 'full employment' level of effective demand. Notwithstanding these qualifications, it is clearly politically possible in the United States to swing from reflationary to disinflationary policy when unemployment is still high by British standards, as in the second half of 1958. President Truman's view in 1950 of what constituted a tolerable level of unemployment[3] also merits note; one can hardly imagine a Prime Minister or Chancellor of either party in Britain saying that 'from a million to one-and-three-quarter million unemployed can be supported,[4] or even half as many. The difference in emphasis on full employment as a preferred objective of economic policy was evident in the Anglo-American negotiations on trade relations in 1945–6.[5]

The imprint of the 'free enterprise' doctrines can be further seen

[1] See p. 293, supra.

[2] See H. A. Turner, 'Employment Fluctuations, Labour Supply, and Bargaining Power', *Manchester School*, May 1959, pp. 177–89.

[3] See p. 130, supra.

[4] These figures bear approximately the same relation to the total civilian labour force in Great Britain as the figures cited by President Truman bore to the total civilian labour force in the United States in 1950. Even one-half of the above figures (500,000 and 875,000) would seem unacceptably high for Great Britain.

[5] R. N. Gardner, *Sterling Dollar Diplomacy* (Oxford, 1956), pp. 271–80.

in the fact that when a disinflationary fiscal policy is desired it was still usual to talk about it in traditional terms rather than in terms of anti-inflationary surpluses. Examples are many, including President Eisenhower's description of the balanced budget as 'a sure index of thrifty management'[1] and Secretary Anderson's assertion that it would be immoral to leave the national debt to the future without reducing it.[2] Contrast the following remarks by Mr. R. A. Butler, introducing his 1954 'carry on' budget in circumstances in some respect similar to those in the United States in 1956 and 1959: 'The aim of the budget must always be to maintain the balance of the economy as a whole, whatever the mathematics above or below the line. . . . The realities of our situation may thus call for a surplus or a deficit on the conventional budget'.[3] The impression that the theory of compensatory fiscal policy had had little impact on American public finance is therefore strengthened.

Likewise, uneasiness persists about even unavoidable increases in Federal civil expenditure. The Federal share of the cost of the construction of the Interstate highway system is being financed through a trust fund separate from the budget instead of being treated as an ordinary expenditure, an economically meaningless distinction explicable only by sensitivity to increase in the administrative budget as such and lesser resistance to a levy which appears different in some ways from ordinary taxation. In the same vein is the 'lease-purchase' scheme, under which a Federal agency contracts with a private firm for the latter to build the premises which the agency requires and for the agency to rent them for a specified period, at the end of which they will be sold to the government for a nominal price. Under this system the expenditure shown in the budget in the year of building is much less than if the premises were built on government contract in the ordinary way, though the demand for real resources is just the same.[4] The tendency to subsume as much as possible of Federal expenditure under the head of national defence (e.g. the Interstate *and Defense* Highways Act of 1956 and the *National Defense* Education Act of 1958) is a bow in the direction of that part

---

[1] See p. 252, supra.   [2] *New York Times*, 21 April 1959.

[3] *House of Commons Debates*, Vol. 526, col. 207.

[4] Though the amount of Federal borrowing is reduced (or the amount of debt repayment increased) which may facilitate the conduct of a restrictive monetary policy unless the finance of the lease-purchase transaction absorbs funds which otherwise would have been available for the purchase of U.S. Government securities.

of the traditional doctrine which casts doubt on the status of Federal expenditures for civil purposes. The statutory limit to the national debt and the expressions of regret and misgiving when the limit has to be raised are still further testimony to the persisting effect of the doctrine of the self-equilibrating private enterprise economy on American fiscal usages.

In the foregoing paragraphs the survival of support for the *laissez-faire* principles of public finance has been depicted merely as a cause of half-heartedness and delay in measures to guard against deflation. But it has doubtless had some advantages, given the assumption that inflation would have remained a danger in the post-war years even in the absence of a stabilization policy. It is at least part of the reason why fears of asymmetrical use of compensatory policy leading to severe inflation proved groundless. Its undoubted effect in strengthening responsibility in the handling of government finances ruled out any danger of the Federal finances becoming an engine of inflation through excessive resort to the printing press in the manner of the Continental Congress in the 18th century or certain South American countries in the 1950's. In any democracy there is need for some kind of 'public philosophy' to provide safeguards against irresponsible use of the sovereign power to create money and spend it. In the United States, where the system of government provides less scope for the government of the day to take measures that are unpopular in the short run than does the Cabinet system where there is a solid parliamentary majority, the carry-over of *laissez-faire* sentiment has fulfilled this function well.

SOME UNRESOLVED ISSUES FOR THE FUTURE

The experience in the United States in the maintenance of economic stability since 1945 raised several important problems which remained unresolved at the end of 1959. Some of these problems related to the means of controlling aggregate demand, but over-hanging them was the deeper question of whether there does exist any relationship between aggregate demand and the capacity of the economy to supply which will maintain price stability and at the same time maintain a satisfactory rate of growth of real income and avoid other than short departures from 'maximum' employment, without the use of direct controls. These problems will be considered briefly in turn.

Mention was made above of the apparent existence of a 'ceiling' to Federal tax rates, which, in view of the urgency of the needs for

Federal expenditure for defence and an increasing array of public services, limited severely the extent to which fiscal policy could be used to control inflation. This resistance to increases in tax rates and support for reductions in existing tax rates also increased the obstacles to the use of tax reduction as a means of dealing with deflation, for should such a tax reduction prove irreversible when the recession was over, the inflationary effect would be obvious. Since policy makers cannot be indifferent to future inflationary effects of remedies for recession, tax reduction is less readily available as an anti-deflationary weapon. If tax reduction is not the flexible, reversible measure depicted in the text-books but an irreversible once-and-for-all measure, the inducement to try to ride out the recession without using the weapon which might bring it to an end quickly is increased. The Administration's policy in 1958 appears to be an instance of this.

A brief examination of this 'ceiling' is relevant here. The rates of the personal income tax in force in 1960 were those set by the Revenue Act of 1950, and those of the corporation profits tax were set by the Revenue Act of 1951, extended after 1954 by annual legislation; the Federal excise tax rates (except those on motor fuels and tyres) remained as fixed by the Excise Tax Reduction Act of 1954. The ratio of Federal receipts other than contributions to social insurance, as shown in the national income accounts, amounted to 19·5 per cent and 19·3 per cent of national income in 1956 and 1957 respectively, the percentage in the latter year being almost exactly the same as that for 1947.[1] But the burden of the social security taxes and state and local taxes increased over the same period; contributions for social insurance paid to the Federal Government amounted to 2·6 per cent of national income in 1947 but 3·4 per cent in 1957;[2] and state and local taxes amounted to 6·4 per cent of national income in 1947, but 8·4 per cent in 1957.[3] All taxes taken together thus amounted to 28·3 per cent of national income in 1947, and 31·1 per cent in 1957; by way of comparison, taxes (similarly

[1] *U.S. Income and Output*, 1959, Tables I–17 and III–1. 1947, 1956, and 1957 are taken as being years when employment was fairly 'full'. The principal reason why the ratio was no higher in 1957 than in 1947 despite the increases in tax rates in the interim (notably in the corporation profits tax) is that the ratio of corporate profits to national income was substantially lower in 1957 than in 1947.

[2] *U.S. Income and Output*, 1959, Tables I–17 and III–1.

[3] Ibid., Tables I–17 and III–2. 'State and local taxes' are defined as Table III–2 line 1 *minus* lines 8, 21, and 22.

defined) in the United Kingdom in 1957 amounted to 35·2 per cent of national income.[1] The point is not that the social services in the United States have been starved through complete rigidity in tax rates, but rather that the increases have been in the rates of state and local taxes and social security taxes, which are not 'available' for economic control. Partly as a result of increases in other taxes, Federal tax rates have come to appear flexible downwards but inflexible upwards.[2] There is very little to suggest that this political limit coincides with any economic limit to taxable capacity; despite oft-expressed fears about the effect of post-war tax rates on incentives to work and the inducement to invest, recent experience provides no evidence of these factors being strong enough not to be swamped by others. For instance, the very size of the investment boom of 1955–7 indicates that the effect of the corporation profits tax on inducements to invest could not have been great in the circumstances then prevailing.

This politically-induced rigidity in tax rates is probably one of the reasons for the more extensive use made of monetary policy in the 1950's than economic thinking at the end of the War would have indicated. Other probable reasons are that the situation was inflationary more often than not, contrary to expectations in 1943–5; and a political factor: the survival of support for the principle of the self-equilibrating private enterprise economy that militates against the effective use of fiscal policy imposes far fewer obstacles to monetary policy. The last distinction is one of politics rather than logic, for monetary policy too is a form of 'intervention'; but it does not have the lingering association with the New Deal that fiscal policy does, and its acceptability in conservative circles is thereby enhanced.

But the belief that monetary policy alone provides a way of controlling inflation without recourse to such intrinsically disagreeable

---

[1] *National Income and Expenditure*, 1959, Tables 1 and 40. Tax receipts include national insurance and health contributions. In comparing American and British tax ratios allowance should be made for the purchase by consumers in the United States of medical goods and services which in the United Kingdom are supplied through the public sector. In 1957 such purchases amounted to 4·1 per cent of national income (*U.S. Income and Output*, Table II–4 line 42 *minus* line 50); this overstates the allowance, since consumers in the United Kingdom buy an appreciable quantity of medicinal preparations, in addition to private purchase of medical care.

[2] This state of affairs is in no way unique to the United States. The presentation of tax reduction in 1953 and 1959 as lasting reductions in the burden of taxation rather than short-term reflationary measures and their popular acceptance as such gives ground for belief that similar conditions exist in the United Kingdom.

measures as higher tax rates or cuts in public services is unfounded in an economy such as that of the United States where there is a substantial short term national debt which must be periodically refinanced. In such a situation the private sector can obtain the finance to make its demands effective merely by subscribing for less of the fresh issue of government debt than it holds of the maturing issue. The government must finance itself somehow, and the monetary authorities have no choice but to relax their restraint sufficiently for the Treasury's issue to be taken up. Despite the Federal Reserve System's independence of the Administration proper, it cannot conduct its policy without regard for the Treasury's needs; in 1957 the increase in the rediscount rate was delayed for several months in order not to embarrass the Treasury in its re-financing.[1]

The urgency of this problem is much less if a revenue surplus reduces the amount of fresh borrowing needed; then no embarrassment is caused if private investors do let some of their holdings of government securities run off. But of course, whether the surplus is looked on as a means of facilitating a restrictive monetary policy (or of keeping hold over the quantity of money despite forces in the private sector pressing to increase it) or in conventional 'compensatory' terms, the difficulty of achieving it is the same. Tax increases are no more acceptable if presented as being necessary to permit a restrictive monetary policy, and despite the much-criticized tendency of substantial sections of American opinion to attribute to private goods and services a doctrinal superiority over public goods and services, there has been no disposition to treat the public sector as a mere 'residuary legatee', even in the heat of the economy drive of 1957.

Monetary policy was used as a supplement to fiscal policy in the United States and not as a deliberately chosen substitute (if the above argument about the limit to tax rates is correct). There was no instance in American financial policy in the 1950's of such overconfidence in the potency of a restrictive monetary policy as the reduction in tax rates made in the United Kingdom by the Budget of April 1955.[2]

[1] C. C. Balderston in *Inflation*, Vol. 326 of the *Annals* of the American Academy of Political and Social Science, 1959, p. 124. Mr. Balderston was Vice-Chairman of the Board of Governors of the Federal Reserve System.

[2] Tax rates were reduced 'taking into account the resources of flexible monetary policy'. Committee on the Working of the Monetary System, *Report* (Cmnd. 827 of 1959), para. 418. See also Sir Anthony Eden, *Memoirs* (London, 1960), pp. 277–8.

But over and above the problems of how to control aggregate effective demand by the means that the American political situation allows to be used is the wider problem of whether control of aggregate demand, given the existing structure of product and labour markets, can maintain price stability combined with high employment and growth. Not much attention was given to this question at the end of the war beyond noting that full employment and sellers' markets would strengthen the power of unions and would allow employers to recoup the cost of higher wages by higher prices; from there few American economists went further in the direction of the formulation of policy than exhortations to responsible behaviour. Not until the inflation of 1956–7 demonstrated its intractability to monetary policy did concern about the possibility of 'creeping' inflation in the absence of general excess demand become widespread; but when prices did not cease to rise despite the onset of a recession that was more severe than either of its two post-war predecessors, concern became much more general. Specifically, the problem is one of the existence of a zone within which prices are insensitive to reductions in demand; within this zone, therefore, a reduction in demand cuts output and employment rather than prices. If the pattern of demand is changing, such that demand in a particular industry or sector is excessive until sufficient additional factors of production have been brought into this industry or sector, and prices rise there, either in direct response to higher demand for the product or through the effect on costs of bidding for additional labour, then in an economy where prices are flexible declines in prices in the areas of declining demand would offset the increases, leaving the *general* price level more or less the same. But where prices are inflexible downwards this no longer follows; the change in the pattern of demand has a net inflationary effect, and general disinflationary measures check inflation only to the extent that they cut into the excess demand in the particular sector; at the same time they are cutting output and employment in the other sectors. If the deflationary policy is pressed far enough to eliminate excess demand in all sectors, then in some demand will be far below the level required for full employment output. If the rigid price zone is wide, price stability will have been achieved only at the cost of severe unemployment.

The existence in the American economy of many prices which are cost-determined over significant ranges of demand seems well established; the index of retail prices of commodities other than food was higher at the trough of the recession in 1958 than in August and September of 1957, when the recession got under way. If prices tend to rise in periods of boom, though only mildly, and do not decline significantly in recessions (and *a fortiori* if they rise) a secular inflationary trend is present in the system provided that stabilization policy is conducted with sufficient skill to prevent depressions severe enough to break through the price rigidities.

The problem of the relationship between aggregate demand and changes in the price level has important implications for the choice of policies to achieve substantial economic growth combined with price stability. Economic growth has always been implicit in the objective of full employment in the United States because of the increase in the labour force arising from demographic causes and of increases in productivity; but in the post-war years the analysis of economic growth has been more carefully developed, and by 1960 growth had come to be regarded by most people in the United States (except for Professor Galbraith in *The Affluent Society*) as an objective of policy equal in importance to full employment and price stability. The need for economic growth became part of Galbraith's 'conventional wisdom'. The reasons for wanting growth are many and various. In an economy where the labour force is growing and technical progress continuing, growth is essential to maintain full employment, unless something startling happens to hours of work or to participation in the labour force; the American trade unions have in consequence been strong supporters of the principle of economic expansion. Growth reduces the urgency of redistribution of income, which makes it attractive to the political Right, as does the emphasis placed on innovation, entrepreneurship, and saving, the long-established virtues of the private economy which the 'full employment' economics of the 1930's was thought to have relegated to a second order of importance. To the Left economic growth has the advantage of making possible the provision of expensive additions to public services without having to raise the tax rates. Finally, the rapid rise in real output per head in Russia led to demands that output per head in the United States ought to be made to rise rapidly too, both to provide the wherewithal for extra military and other 'Cold War' expenditure and also to impress third parties who have to choose between the Russian and the Western approaches to economic development.

Although all parties of opinion are agreed on the advantages of economic growth, there is, as of 1960, no consensus of opinion about policy to achieve it, even among economists. There are no generally agreed ready-to-hand guides to policy for growth as there are for maintaining stability in the short run. Instead, there are two distinct streams of thought, both of which are becoming more closely articulated and their implications more thoroughly explored. The two streams may be labelled 'Left' and 'Right' or 'high pressure' and 'low pressure'.[1] The 'Left' or 'high pressure' approach relies heavily on a rising volume of aggregate demand, to be maintained by heavy Federal civil expenditure where required. The high level of aggregate demand thus achieved is expected to provide the necessary inducement to invest in the private sector. Most formulations of the 'high pressure' approach assign a small role to monetary policy, on the ground that high interest rates restrict investment more than do tax increases, which can be made to fall primarily on consumption. Five per cent a year is the rate of growth of real G.N.P. that by the end of the 1950's had come to be recommended as a goal of policy by supporters of the 'high pressure' approach.

From the economic point of view the critical question about such a policy is whether the expansion of demand would cause large increases in the price level, for the risks of generating excess demand by such a policy are obvious. On the other hand, it can be argued that the inflationary potential of cost pressures is less when output per head is rising than it is when output per head is static. At the very least, if prices are not likely to rise *much* faster under the stimulus of increased demand than if output is well below capacity, there is much to be said for combining a substantial increase in output with the inflation that is going to happen any way. The experience of 1950–3 suggests that under pressure of heavily increased demand substantial increases in output are possible without inordinate price increases, but so many special circumstances were present that it would be highly dangerous to generalize from this.[2]

The 'Right' or 'low pressure' approach is entirely different. In this view, the sources of economic growth are the resourcefulness, enterprise, initiative, and savings of the private sector, and not additional effective demand generated by the government. The role

[1] These terms were introduced by Professor H. Wallich. See *Review of Economics and Statistics*, 1956, p. 380; and *Yale Review*, Vol. XLVI, pp. 63–73.

[2] See J. P. Lewis, 'The Lull That Came to Stay', *Journal of Political Economy*, Vol. LXIII (1955), pp. 1–19; and Chapter IX, supra.

of the government in the process of growth is to promote economic efficiency by maintaining competition, to adjust the tax system so that it does not penalize enterprise, and to keep down the total weight of taxation so as not to interfere with incentives or to absorb funds which the private sector would use for investment. The other major contribution of the government is to prevent inflation, which is held to be inimical to sustained growth, as well as being a cause of social injustice and individual hardship and discontent. Great emphasis is typically placed on the prevention of inflation by supporters of the 'low pressure' approach.

While the individual hardships caused by creeping inflation are obvious enough, the adverse effect of 'creeping' inflation on economic growth is often asserted but seldom demonstrated. The principal contention is that inflation erodes the incentive to save, with the result that (assuming demand for investment, in real terms, to remain unaffected) the rate increase of the price level will accelerate and the reduced volume of savings (in real terms) will reduce the amount of investment carried out and so slow down the growth of capacity to produce. It is therefore held that the choice posed by supporters of the 'high pressure' approach between substantial growth accompanied by some inflation and price stability (or, more likely, slower inflation) accompanied by stagnation of real output is no genuine choice at all, in that creeping inflation, if tolerated, will accelerate, and in the end there will be ruinous inflation without any real growth greater than could have been had by non-inflationary means. But up to 1960 the changes in savings ratios in the U.S. have not been in accordance with the above hypothesis; the ratio of personal saving to disposable income was rather higher in 1957 than in 1929,[1] despite a rise of 89 per cent in the price level (measured by the implicit deflator for G.N.P.) or 70 per cent (if measured by the implicit deflator for personal consumption expenditure).[2] But the diverse price trends which since 1929 have added to a net increase of 70 per cent (or 89 per cent) are far removed from the continuous inflation being discussed above, so here too it is not possible to reach a verdict on evidence drawn from past experience.

The roles of public finance in the two sets of policies for economic

---

[1] According to the Department of Commerce's estimates the ratios were 5·0 per cent in 1929 and 6·8 per cent in 1957. *U.S. Income and Output*, 1959, Table II–1.

[2] Ibid., Table VII–2.

growth are thus in complete contrast. In the 'high pressure' system it is the principal method by which the stimulus is applied to the economy; in the 'low pressure' system its role is an anti-inflationary one, to be conducted in the classical way of keeping the budget as small as possible so as not to impede the private sector through heavy tax burdens. The 'low pressure' approach to public finance and the budget is really the orthodox classical approach in a new context, modified by the acceptance of deficits induced by automatic stabilization in recessions.

This 'low pressure' approach to growth is discernible in the statements of policy by members of the Eisenhower Administration and the Federal Reserve System, and in the policies pursued in 1955–60. It has the support of most of the business organizations, which is natural since it looks on the business executive as the driving force of economic growth and not the government. The 'high pressure' approach is discernible in the views of economists such as Dr. Keyserling, one of the most prominent exponents of the programme, in statements of trade unions' views on economic policy, in the report by the staff of the Joint Economic Committee's enquiry into economic growth and price stability, and in a statement of policy issued by the Democratic Advisory Council.[1] Whether a Democratic Administration would follow the 'high pressure' policy was far from clear, despite the Advisory Council's pronouncement and statements by prominent Democrats during the Eisenhower years. The way in which the Truman Administration struck the balance between running inflationary and deflationary risks did not differ much from the Eisenhower Administration's record in this respect. The effect of the doctrine of the self-equilibrating private economy is entirely in favour of the 'low pressure' approach, which would increase the difficulties of an Administration trying to follow the opposite policy. While complaint about the rate of growth achieved under the Eisenhower Administration was widespread it was also diffuse and did not, at the time, amount to a solid body of support for the specific measures which, taken together, would make up the 'high pressure' policy.

The differences between the two approaches to policy for the achievement of maximum growth in the long run have important implications for policies to maintain stability in the short run.

[1] It was issued on 6 December 1959, and its text is printed in the *New York Times*, 7 December 1959.

Because supporters of the 'low pressure' approach attach so much importance to the prevention of inflation, both for its own sake and because inflation is considered inimical to growth in the long run, they tend to a more cautious approach to anti-recession policy than do supporters of the 'high pressure' approach. Energetic measures to deal with a short-run deficiency of demand, it is held, may do more harm than good in the long run through strengthening inflation. Drastic measures could have inflationary effects through being too powerful for the deficiency of demand actually occurring, or not being reversible in time before recovery turns into boom. Likewise, when demand for Government securities is influenced by expectations of further price increases, a situation not envisaged in most discussions during the 1930's and the war years of deficit financing during deflation, the finance of a large deficit is likely to so increase the liquidity of the economy as to add to the difficulty of controlling demand when the recession is over. As a result, the low pressure approach tends to the view that fiscal policy in recession should be limited to the automatic stabilizers and small, quickly reversible increases in government expenditure.[1]

A fiscal policy of this type was recommended on several occasions by members of the Eisenhower Administration,[2] and is the policy which the Administration would have preferred, in retrospect, to have had the United States pursue in 1958. Such a policy can succeed in maintaining maximum employment only if the private economy is, in the words of Mr. Stans, 'vigorous and resilient enough to come out of a temporary recession and go on through a revival period to new prosperous peaks without any direct Federal interference'.[3] He went on to express the view, held by other members of the Administration as well, that the post-war experience, especially the recovery in 1958, demonstrated that the American economy did possess this 'inherent strength and resiliency'.[4]

But it is very doubtful whether experience in the three recessions following 1945 warrants so important a conclusion. The fluctuations

[1] For an example, see M. H. Stans (Director of the Bureau of the Budget), 'The Need for Balanced Federal Budgets' in *Inflation*, Vol. 326, of the *Annals* of the American Academy of Political and Social Sciences, November 1959.

[2] Stans, loc. cit.; and R. B. Anderson (Secretary of the Treasury) in U.S. Congress, Joint Economic Committee, *Hearings on the Economic Report of the President*, 1959, p. 400 ff.

[3] Op. cit., p. 23.

[4] The phrase is from *Economic Report of the President*, 1959, p. 2.

were indeed small compared with those experienced before 1939, but not solely because of the automatic stabilizers or of the inherent strength of the private economy. The action taken in each case went beyond what would be sanctioned by the principles just cited, especially in 1958. In each case the element of chance and good fortune worked in favour of stability. In both 1949 and 1958 an increase in defence expenditure, exogenous to the recession, added to demand when such an addition was needed, as did the payment of the service life insurance dividend in 1950. The promptness of the tax reduction in 1954 owed much to good fortune; and the tax reduction of 1948, however useful it turned out to be, was an instance of a measure which was 'right' (from the point of view of economic stability) for irrelevant reasons. Good fortune thus played some part in overcoming each of the recessions between 1945 and 1960.

Moreover, it is clearly possible that among the reasons for the strength of private investment in the United States after the Second World War was the effect on investors' expectations of the commitment of the government to a policy of maximum employment and production. Such a commitment, if regarded as genuine, strengthens the inducement to continue with investment plans despite declines in demand, for the expectation is that the government will take measures to ensure that the decline is only temporary. Such a commitment can thus exert a stabilizing influence without any specific measures at all, as was realized at the time of the passage of the Employment Act. It cannot be proved, of course, how important a source of stability this commitment was after 1946, but its loss is a hazard that would attend a policy of relying on the automatic stabilizers alone, renouncing in advance more drastic measures.

The case for the view that the American economy possesses the inherent strength and resilience claimed for it was thus not proven as of 1960; indeed, the recovery in 1954 is stronger evidence in its favour than the recovery of 1958, for the latter was promoted by measures which went far beyond reliance on the automatic stabilizers. To base policy on belief in the inherent strength and resilience of the private economy would be to run unnecessary risks. The length of the time lag before needed measures could be taken should the automatic stabilizers prove inadequate, as they might well do if the element of chance were unfavourable, would be much increased if the planning of anti-recession measures had been neglected because of confidence in the inherent resilience of the economy. It is not here suggested that inherent *in*stability is a characteristic of the American economy; but to base policy on an as yet unproven belief in its inherent stability is to run needless risks through introducing the likelihood of long delays in an area of policy where prompt action is all-important.

Among the features of the American economy which strengthened resistance to deflation in the 1950's was the magnitude of defence expenditure, a completely recession-proof sector of the economy. Government purchases of goods and services for civil purposes or transfer payments to recipients with a predictable propensity to consume would serve the same purpose, but support for placing as much as possible of the responsibility for social service expenditure on the state and local governments would place obstacles in the way of a large increase in Federal civil expenditure should a disarmament agreement make possible substantial cuts in military expenditure. The weakening of the automatic stabilizers that would probably result from disarmament (through reducing the size of the Federal budget in relation to G.N.P. unless the progressivity of the tax structure were steepened in a way which is politically unlikely) would increase the burden to be borne by positive counter-cyclical measures in the event of a recession and so would add to the hazards of relying on the automatic stabilizers alone. Keynes wrote in 1940: 'It is, it seems, politically impossible for a capitalistic democracy to organize expenditure on the scale necessary to prove my case— except under war conditions'.[1] The dilemma he posed might again trouble the United States in the event of a recession following near-disarmament. It is not suggested that disarmament would leave a permanent deficiency of demand that could not be filled by other means, but rather that the reduced size of the Federal budget in relation to G.N.P. would provide inadequate scope for the working of the automatic stabilizers or for tax reduction during recessions; whole categories of taxation cannot, for administrative reasons, be abandoned during the recession if they will be needed again after recovery has been achieved. Part of the problem here is again one of delays; in face of urgent necessity there is little doubt that Federal expenditures would be increased, but the frictions created by political views about 'capitalism' and 'States' rights' would in all probability slow this down. In the last resort, the extent to which higher unemployment is a lesser evil than a growth in the power and functions

[1] *New Republic*, 20 July 1940, p. 158.

of the Federal government is a matter of political value judgements, of course. How long the Right's suspensory veto would last if the circumstances envisaged above actually came to pass is a matter of speculation; it is discussed here only because it is a potentially important question which experience in the years considered in this book leaves unanswered.

In the late 1950's there were many signs of a growing readiness in the Administration and the Federal Reserve System, and in some sections of Congressional opinion, to accept a greater amount of short-run under-employment in order to restrain inflation more effectively. The proposal to amend the Employment Act to make price stability an explicit goal of public policy on par with maximum employment and production can only be construed as a move to persuade the interested public of the justification for doing so. In his State of the Union Message in January 1960 President Eisenhower said: 'We must fight inflation as we would a fire that imperils our home. Only by doing so can we prevent it from destroying our salaries, savings, pensions, and insurance, and from gnawing away the very roots of a free, healthy economy and the nation's security'.[1] Previously the Chairman of the Board of Governors of the Federal Reserve System had spoken about 'the battle against debasement of the currency and all its perils to free institutions'.[2] Such an emphasis on inflation is probably the result of the 'creeping inflation' of 1956–58, which had a strong impact on American official thinking. The difficulty of controlling that inflation led to an increased willingness to take risks and to forego other aims of policy in order to check inflation more effectively. As of 1960, it remained an open question whether this would be a continuing trend in American economic policy or whether it was just the position of the Eisenhower Administration of the late 1950's. There was no positive evidence of such a shift of opinion among the electorate; the Congressional elections of 1958 showed that the electors' aversion to recessions and unemployment was as strong as ever.

In 1958 and onwards the choice between the risks or evils, between inflation and lower output in the short run and (perhaps) slower growth in the long run became subject to a constraint familiar to Britain, though new to the United States. The rise in imports relative

---

[1] Text in *New York Times*, 8 January 1960.
[2] Joint Economic Committee, *Hearings on the Economic Report of the President*, 1959, p. 468.

to exports and the accumulation of short-term foreign claims on the United States added the prospect of balance of payments trouble to the other consequences of inflation. Both the effect of rising prices on the balance of trade and the impact of inflation and budget deficits on 'confidence in the dollar' appeared as limits to the extent to which the United States could risk inflation in order to pursue expansionary policies. The very size of the American gold reserve[1] compared with imports and short term liabilities made the problem less urgent for the United States than for most European countries. But the United States could no longer strike the balance between the risks of inflation and deflation solely according to domestic preferences and the sense of the obligations of a 'good creditor' towards her neighbours.

Several unresolved problems of general economic policy thus remained as the United States entered the 1960's. The above discussion has admittedly focused on the dangers of deflation involved in these problems; for notwithstanding the growth in the strength of the European economies, serious deflation in the United States would still wreak more harm on the outside world than anything less than catastrophic inflation. It is in the interest of the outside world that the United States should over-insure against deflation rather than against inflation, and *a fortiori* that the prevention of deflation should not have to yield to political principles which accord a higher priority to keeping the public sector small, especially the Federal part of it. It is not to be expected that majority opinion in the United States will always take the same view; hence an overseas observer's assessment of the problems facing American economic policy may differ in emphasis from the assessment an American would make.

The emphasis on the need to be watchful for future deflationary dangers must not lead to disregard of the encouraging features of the 1940's and 1950's. During these years familiarity with the general notions of the proper way to handle the problem of deflation spread, and the danger, a real one as of 1945, of mistaken measures which would make the situation worse became very remote. The difficulties of taking prompt action within the existing structure of government,

---

[1] At the end of 1959 the gold stock of the United States amounted to $19,456 million. Of this, some $11,960 million was legally required as reserves against the liabilities (deposits and notes) of the Federal Reserve System. The reserves should be compared with foreign short-term claims on the United States, which at the end of 1959 totalled $19,536 million, and the current deficit in 1959 (goods and services plus unilateral transfers) of $2,498 million. (*Federal Reserve Bulletin*, February 1960, pp. 168 and 242; and July 1960, pp. 816, 829.

granted the will, appeared to be less than some observers in the 1940's had thought, for legislation to increase expenditures was passed very promptly in 1958. Delay in taking action was caused less by any lag in the legislative process than by the lag between the onset of deflation and the abandonment, for the time being, of the struggle against inflation. Democratic countries appear to have difficulties in executing reversals of policy, even when changes in circumstances justify it, in economic affairs just as in foreign affairs. Shortening this lag is partly a matter for economists in the provision of accurate diagnoses of economic trends at an early stage, but it is equally a matter for politicians and ultimately for electorates, who must accustom themselves to more frequent changes in the direction of economic policy. The response which the restrictive monetary and fiscal measures in Britain in the spring of 1960 showed the widespread opposition to changes in the direction of policy, even though it was the first change of direction for eighteen months. The political obstacles to a flexible fiscal policy in a democratic country are not to be minimized.

It is probable that a fiscal policy more flexible than that achieved in the 1940's and 1950's will be needed in the United States to maintain adequate control over aggregate demand if the difficulties envisaged above come to pass. The progress made in the conduct of general economic policy in the 1940's and 1950's provides grounds for confidence that those problems which really turn on the control of aggregate demand will be handled in a reasonable way through political attitudes being adaptable enough when it comes to the point. The more general problem of structural features of the economy making for a long run tendency for the price level to rise was faced in the 1950's, but no real solution was found. Assuming that those contingencies, where a deficiency of effective demand is likely, are properly dealt with as they occur, the handling of the inflationary tendency appears to be the main economic problem facing the United States in the 1960's. The part to be played in this by conventional stabilizing fiscal policy appears limited; its function is the control of aggregate demand. Control of demand in particular sectors of the economy appears to be a useful role that fiscal policy could play in dealing with a 'structural' inflation; but like all the suggested measures to deal with the problem that go beyond the exercise of self-restraint by the various groups in the economy, it raises difficult questions of political acceptability. The experience of the 1940's and

1950's showed that stabilizing fiscal policy could be used in the United States, and as of 1960 there was every reason to expect its use in the future when circumstances so required. But for reasons that were economic, political, and administrative, this did not seem enough to ensure the desired combination of full employment, steady economic growth, and a stable price level.

SELECT BIBLIOGRAPHY

General Notes:

A COMPREHENSIVE bibliography on the theory and principles of fiscal policy is included in *Readings in Fiscal Policy* (selected by a Committee of the American Economic Association: London, 1955). This select bibliography has therefore been limited to the application of fiscal policy in the United States since 1945, including the economic situation to which that fiscal policy was directed and the background of politics and public administration which was relevant to the conduct of American economic policy during the period.

The bibliography is organized in the following way: annual, semi-annual, and monthly official publications; unofficial publications; the political and administrative framework within which American fiscal policy has had to be applied; the background of the 1930's and the Second World War; plans and forecasts for the post-war period, including the passage of the Employment Act; the economic situation and fiscal policies in the years 1945 to 1959, divided for analytical convenience into seven phases; and general discussion of American fiscal policy which relates to the whole period or a large part of it rather than primarily to one or two phases.

I. Official Publications

Annual Report of the Secretary of the Treasury.

Budget of the United States. Annual.

Economic Report of the President. Semi-annual (appearing in January and July) from January 1947 to July 1952; annual from 1953 onwards. From January 1949 to January 1953 (inclusive) included an *Economic Review* by the Council of Economic Advisers.

U.S. Congress, Joint Committee on the Economic Report (after 1956 known as the Joint Economic Committee), *Hearings on the Economic Report of the President.* Annual, 1949–52 and 1954 onwards.

U.S. Congress, Joint Committee on the Economic Report (and Joint Economic Committee), *Report on the Economic Report of the President.* Annual, 1948–52 and from 1954 onwards.

Congressional Record. (References are to the permanent bound edition except for 1947, when they are to the daily edition).

Federal Reserve Bulletin. Monthly.

Monthly Labor Review. Published by the Bureau of Labor Statistics.

Survey of Current Business. Monthly, published by the Office of Business Economics of the Department of Commerce.

II. Daily Press

New York Times.

III. Periodicals

Business Week.
CIO News.
Fortune.
Nation.
NAM News.

National City Bank Monthly Letter.
New Republic.
U.S. News and World Report.

IV. *The Institutions of Public Finance in the United States and their Relation to Fiscal Policy and Economic Stabilization*

S. K. BAILEY, 'Political Elements in Full Employment Policy', *American Economic Review,* Vol. XLV Supplement (1955), pp. 341–50.

R. BLOUGH, *The Federal Taxing Process* (New York, 1952).

—— 'Political and Administrative Requisites for Achieving Economic Stability, *American Economic Review,* Vol. XL Supplement (1950) pp. 165–78.

—— 'The Role of the Economist in Federal Policy Making', *University of Illinios Bulletin,* Vol. LI, No. 28, 1953.

P. F. BRUNDAGE, 'A Critical Look at the Budget Process', *Public Administration Review,* Vol. XIV (1954), pp. 247–52.

J. BURKHEAD, 'Budget Classification and Fiscal Planning', *Public Administration Review,* Vol. VII (1947), pp. 228–36.

—— *Government Budgeting* (New York, 1956).

S. M. COHN, 'Problems in Estimating Federal Government Expenditures', *Journal of the American Statistical Association,* Vol. LIV (1959), pp. 717–29.

G. COLM, 'The Federal Budget and the National Economy', (Washington, 1955).

Commission on Intergovernmental Relations, *Report to the President* (Washington, 1955).

J. P. CROCKETT, *The Federal Tax System of the United States* (New York, 1955).

R. E. FLANDERS, 'Administering the Employment Act—The First Year', *Public Administration Review,* Vol. VII (1947), pp. 221–7.

B. M. GROSS and J. P. LEWIS, 'The President's Economic Staff During the Truman Administration', *American Political Science Review,* Vol. XLVIII (1954), pp. 114–30.

A. H. HANSEN and H. S. PERLOFF, *State and Local Finance in the National Economy* (New York, 1944).

F. M. MARX, P. H. APPLEBY, E. G. NOURSE, H. W. DAVEY, C. CANNON, M. FAINSOD and N. E. LONG, 'Formulating the Federal Government's Economic Programme: A Symposium', *American Political Science Review,* Vol. XLII (1948), pp. 272–336.

J. A. MAXWELL, *Fiscal Policy: Its Techniques and Institutional Setting* (New York, 1956).

E. G. NOURSE, *Economics in the Public Service* (New York, 1953).

—— 'Public Administration and Economic Stabilization', *Public Administration Review,* Vol. VII (1947), pp. 85–92.

R. E. PAUL, *Taxation in the United States* (Boston, 1954).

A. SMITHIES, 'Federal Budgeting and Fiscal Policy' in *Survey of Contemporary Economics* (Philadelphia, 1948).

—— *The Budgetary Process in the United States* (New York, 1955).

P. J. STRAYER, *Fiscal Policy and Politics* (New York, 1958).

—— 'The Council of Economic Advisers: Political Economy on Trial', *American Economic Review,* Vol. XL Supplement (1950), pp. 144–54.

V. *Fiscal Developments in the 1930's and the Break with Previously Accepted Principles*

E. C. BROWN, 'Fiscal Policies in the 1930's: A Reappraisal', *American Economic Review,* Vol. XLVI (1956), pp. 857–79.

J. McG. BURNS, *Roosevelt: The Lion and the Fox* (New York, 1956).

F. B. FREIDEL, *Franklin D. Roosevelt—The Triumph* (Boston, 1956).

D. R. FUSFELD, *The Economic Thought of Franklin D. Roosevelt and the Origins of the New Deal* (New York, 1955).

F. E. GANNETT, 'Dangers to the Free Enterprise System' in B. BATCHELOR, (ed.) *The New Outlook in Business* (New York, 1940).

H. HOOVER, *Memoirs*, Vol. III (London, 1953).

S. LUBELL, *The Future of American Politics* (London, 1952).

Public Papers and Addresses of Franklin D. Roosevelt, Vol. I–VIII (New York, 1938–41.)

A. M. SCHLESINGER Jr., *The Age of Roosevelt—The Crisis of the Old Order*, Houghton Mifflin, Boston (1957).

—— *The Age of Roosevelt—The Coming of the New Deal* (Boston, 1959).

A. SMITHIES, 'The American Economy in the Thirties', *American Economic Review*, Vol. XXXVI Supplement (1946), pp. 11–27.

U. S. Congress, Senate, Committee on Finance, *Hearings on the Investigation of Economic Problems*, 72nd Cong., 2nd Sess. (1933).

R. L. WEISSMAN (ed.), *Economic Balance and a Balanced Budget, The Public Papers of Marriner S. Eccles* (New York, 1940).

VI. Political Attitudes to Fiscal Policy

S. S. ALEXANDER, 'Opposition to Deficit Financing for the Prevention of Un-employment' in *Income, Employment, and Public Policy: Essays in Honor of Alvin H. Hansen* (New York, 1948).

T. ARNOLD, *The Folklore of Capitalism* (New Haven, 1937).

D. BELL, (ed.), *The New American Right* (New York, 1955).

C. BOWLES *American Politics in a Revolutionary World* (Cambridge, Mass., 1956).

F. CHODOROV, *The Income Tax Root of All Evil* (New York, 1954).

J. T. FLYNN, *Decline of the American Republic* (New York, 1955).

—— *The Road Ahead* (New York, 1949).

J. K. GALBRAITH, *American Capitalism* (New York, 1952).

—— *Economics and the Art of Controversy* (New Brunswick, N. J., 1955).

—— *The Affluent Society* (New York, 1958).

M. KALECKI, 'Political Aspects of Full Employment', *Political Quarterly*, Vol. XIV (1943), pp. 322–30.

A. LARSON, *A Republican Looks at His Party* (New York, 1956).

S. LUBELL, *Revolt of the Moderates* (New York 1956).

H. L. LUTZ, *A Platform for the American Way* (New York, 1952).

National Association of Manufacturers, Economic Principles Commission, *The American Individual Enterprise System* (New York, 1946).

E. G. NOURSE, *The 1950's Come First* (New York, 1951).

F. X. SUTTON, S. E. HARRIS, C. KAYSEN, and J. TOBIN, *The American Business Creed* (Cambridge, Mass., 1956).

U.S. Congress, Joint Committee on the Economic Report, *Constitutional Limitation on the Federal Income, Estate, and Gift Tax Rates* (Washington, 1952).

U.S. Congress, Senate, Committee on the Judiciary, *Hearings on the Proposed Constitutional Amendment to Limit the Rates of the Federal Income, Estate, and Gift Taxes* (S. J. Res. 233, 83rd Cong., 1st Sess.), (1954).

VII. Fiscal Developments During the Second World War

E. D. ALLEN, 'Treasury Tax Politicies in 1943' *American Economic Review*, Vol XXXIV (1944), pp. 707–33.

L. V. CHANDLER, *Inflation in the United States* 1940–48 (New York, 1951).

S. E. HARRIS, *Inflation and the American Economy* (New York, 1945).

H. C. MURPHY, *The National Debt in War and Transition* (New York, 1950).

M. NEWCOMER, 'Congressional Tax Policies in 1943', *American Economic Review*, Vol. XXXIV (1944), pp. 734–56.

F. L. NUSSBAUM and A. SCHMEITZER, 'The Professors Versus The People', *American Economic Review*, Vol. XXXIII (1943), pp. 906–7.

VIII. Forecasts of Post-War Economic Trends and Plans Recommended to Promote Post-War Economic Stability

Committee for Economic Development, Research Committee, *Postwar Federal Tax Plan for High Employment* (New York, 1944).

Committee on Postwar Tax Policy, *A Tax Program for a Solvent America* (New York, 1945).

M. G. DE CHAZEAU, A. G. HART, G. C. MEANS, H. C. MYERS, H. STEIN, T. O. YNTEMA, *Jobs and Markets* (New York, 1946).

H. M. GROVES, *Production, Jobs, and Taxes* (New York, 1943).

E. E. HAGEN and N. KIRKPATRICK, 'Forecasting Gross National Product and Employment during the Transition Period', in *Studies in Income and Wealth*, Vol. X (New York, 1947).

S. E. HARRIS, *Postwar Reconstruction* (New York, 1945).

P. T. HOMAN, (ed.), *Financing America's Prosperity* (New York, 1945).

R. A. MUSGRAVE, 'Three Plans for Postwar Taxation', *Federal Reserve Bulletin*, Vol. XXX (1944), pp. 1163–76.

R. A. MUSGRAVE and E. D. DOMAR, *Public Finance and Full Employment* (Washington, 1945).

R. R. NATHAN, *Mobilizing for Abundance* (New York, 1944).

National Planning Association, *National Budgets for Full Employment* (Washington, 1945).

National Resources Planning Board, *After the War—Full Employment* (Washington 1943).

National Resources Planning Board, *National Resources Development*, Report for 1943, Part I (Washington, 1942).

National Resources Planing Board, *Postwar Agenda* (Washington, 1942).

R. E. PAUL, *Taxation for Prosperity* (Indianapolis, 1947).

B. RUML and H. C. SONNE, *Fiscal and Monetary Policy* (Washington, 1944).

C. SHOUP, 'Three Plans for Postwar Taxation', *American Economic Review*, Vol. XXXIV (1944), pp. 757–70.

Twin Cities Research Bureau, *The Twin Cities Plan for Postwar Taxes* (St. Paul, 1944).

A. J. ZURCHER and R. PAGE, (eds.), *Postwar Goals and Economic Reconstruction* (New York, 1944).

IX. The Passage of the Employment Act

S. K. BAILEY, *Congress Makes a Law* (New York, 1950).

A. H. HANSEN, *Economic Policy and Full Employment* (New York, 1949).

A. H. HANSEN, S. E. HARRIS, S. SLICHTER and M. P. McNAIR, 'Comments on the Murray Bill', *Review of Economics and Statistics*, Vol. XXVII (1945), pp. 102–16.

S. E. HARRIS, *Economic Planning* (New York, 1949).

U.S. Congress, House of Representatives, Committee on Expenditures in the Executive Departments, *Hearings on the Full Employment Bill* (Washington, 1945).

U.S. Congress, *H. Rept. No. 1334*, 79th Cong., 1st Sess.

U.S. Congress, Senate Committee on Banking and the Currency, *Hearings on S.380* (Washington, 1945).

U.S. Congress, *S. Rept. No.* 583, 79th Cong., 1st Sess.

J. H. WILLIAMS, 'The Employment Act of 1946' in *Postwar Monetary Plans and Other Essays* (Oxford, 1949).

X. The Transition Period, 1945–6

E. E. HAGEN, 'The Reconversion Period: Reflections of a Forecaster', *Review of Economic Statistics*, Vol. XXIX (1947), pp. 95–101.

C. HITCH, S. M. LIVINGSTONE, A. SMITHIES, J. C. HUBBARD, E. B. GEORGE and R. J. LANDRY, 'The American Economy in Transition', *Review of Economic Statistics*, Vol. XXIX (1947), pp. 16–38.

L. R. KLEIN, 'A Post Mortem on Transition Predictions of National Product', *Journal of Political Economy*, Vol. LIV (1946), pp. 289–308.

M. SAPIR, 'Review of Economic Forecasts for the Transition Period', in *Studies in Income and Wealth*, Vol. XI (New York, 1949), pp. 275–367.

U.S. Congress, *H. Rept. No.* 1106, 79th Cong., 1st Sess.

U.S. Congress, Senate, Committee on Finance, *Hearings on H.R.4309* (Washington, 1945).

U.S. Congress, *S. Rept. No. 655*, 79th Cong., 1st Sess.

W. S. Woytinsky, "What Was Wrong in Forecasts of Postwar Depression', *Journal of Political Economy*, Vol. LV (1947), pp. 142–51.

XI. Inflation and the Struggle over Tax Reduction, 1946–8

M. BRONFENBRENNER, 'Postwar Political Economy: The President's Economic Reports', *Journal of Political Economy*, Vol. LVI (1948), pp. 373–91.

Council of Economic Advisers, *Business and Government*, Annual Report to the President (Washington, 1949).

F. W. FETTER, 'The Economic Reports of the President and the Problem of Inflation', *Quarterly Journal of Economics*, Vol. LXIII (1949), pp. 273–81.

A. H. HANSEN, 'The First Reports Under the Employment Act of 1946', *Review of Economic Statistics*, Vol. XXIX (1947), pp. 69–74.

S. E. HARRIS, 'The Inflation Process in Theory and Recent History', *Review of Economics and Statistics*, Vol. XXXI (1949), pp. 200–10.

S. E. HARRIS, S. H. SLICHTER, F. C. MILLS, J. S. DAVIS, G. HABERLER, K. E. BOULDING, F. MACHLUP, M. KALECKI, A. P. LERNER and R. B. HEFLEBOWER, 'Ten Economists on Inflation: A Symposium', *Review of Economics and Statistics*, Vol. XXX (1948), pp. 1–29.

U.S. Congress, House of Representatives, Committee on Ways and Means, *Hearings on H.R.I* (Washington, 1947).

U.S. Congress, House of Representatives, Committee on Ways and Means, *Hearings on H.R.4790* (Washington, 1948).

U.S. Congress, *H. Rept. No. 6*, 80th Cong., 1st Sess.

U.S. Congress, *H. Rept. No. 35*, 80th Cong., 1st Sess.

U.S. Congress, *H. Rept. No. 180*, 80th Cong., 1st Sess.

U.S. Congress, *H. Rept. No. 1274*, 80th Cong., 2nd Sess.

U.S. Congress, Joint Committee on the Economic Report, *Hearings on Current Price Developments and the Problems of Economic Stabilization* (Washington, 1947).

U.S. Congress, Joint Committee on the Economic Report, *Hearings on the Anti-Inflation Program as Recommended in the President's Message of November 17 1947* (Washington, 1947).

U.S. Congress, Joint Committee on the Economic Report, *Hearings on Profits* (Washington, 1948).

U.S. Congress, Senate, Committee on Finance, *Hearings on H.R.1* (Washington, 1947).

U.S. Congress, Senate, Committee on Finance, *Hearings on H.R.4790* (Washington, 1948).

U.S. Congress, *S. Rept. No. 21*, 80th Cong., 1st Sess.

U.S. Congress, *S. Rept. No. 173*, 80th Cong., 1st Sess.

U.S. Congress, *S. Rept. No. 795*, 80th Cong., 1st Sess.

U.S. Congress, *S. Rept. No. 1013*, 80th Cong., 2nd Sess.

J. VINER, 'The Employment Act of 1946 in Operation', *Review of Economic Statistics*, Vol. XXIX (1947), pp. 74–9.

H. WORKING, 'Reflections on the President's Economic Report', *American Economic Review*, Vol. XXXVII (1947), pp. 383–6.

XII. Recession and Recovery, 1949–50

E. C. BRATT and J. P. ONDRECHEN, '1948–9 Recession Re-examined', *Economic Journal*, Vol. LXIII (1953), p. 98–104.

H. F. BYRD, *Now the Fiscal Crisis* (New York, 1949).

B. CAPLAN, 'A Case Study: The 1948–9 Recession', in *Policies to Combat Depression* (Princeton, 1956).

R. FELS, 'Theoretical Significance of the 1949 Recession', *American Economic Review*, Vol. XLV Supplement (1955), pp. 358–66.

E. A. GOLDENWEISER, 'The Douglas Committee Report', *American Economic Review*, Vol. XL (1950), pp. 389–96.

D. HAMBERG, 'The Recession of 1948–9 in the United States', *Economic Journal*, Vol. LXII (1952), pp. 1–14.

S. E. HARRIS, T. WILSON, F. W. PAISH, H. S. ELLIS, G. TERBORGH and E. E. HAGEN, 'The January 1949 Economic Report of the President', *Review of Economics and Statistics*, Vol. XXXI (1949), pp. 165–81.

R. R. NATHAN, *A National Economic Policy for 1949* (New York, 1949).

Statement of Republican Principles and Objectives, adopted by the Republican Members of Congress, and published by the Republican, National Committee, (Washington, 1950).

H. S. TRUMAN, *Memoirs*, Vol. II (London, 1956).

U.S. Congress, *H. Doc. No. 451*, 81st Cong., 2nd Sess.

U.S. Congress, Joint Committee on the Economic Report, Subcommittee on Monetary, Credit, and Fiscal Policies, *Compendium of Materials on Monetary Credit and Fiscal Policies* (Washington, 1949).

U.S. Congress, Joint Committee on the Economic Report, Subcommittee on Monetary, Credit, and Fiscal Policies, *Hearings on Monetary, Credit, and Fiscal Policies* (Washington, 1949–50).

U.S. Congress, Joint Committee on the Economic Report, Subcommittee on Monetary, Credit, and Fiscal Policies, *Report on Monetary, Credit, and Fiscal Policies* (*S. Doc. No. 129*, 81st Cong., 2nd Sess.).

U.S. Congress, *S. Rept. No. 498*, 81st Cong., 1st Sess.

H. H. VILLARD, 'The Council of Economic Advisers and Depression Policy', *American Economic Review*, Vol. XL (1950), pp. 600–4.

XIII. Fiscal Policy and the Korean War and Rearmament, 1950–52

L. V. CHANDLER and D. H. WALLACE, (eds.), *Economic Mobilization and Stabilization* (New York, 1951).

Committee for Economic Development, *Paying for Defense* (New York, 1950).

Committee for Economic Development, *An Emergency Tax Program for 1951* (New York, 1951).

P. H. DOUGLAS, *Economy in the National Government* (Chicago, 1952).

S. E. HARRIS, M. FRIEDMAN, A. P. LERNER, L. V. CHANDLER, A. H. HANSEN and J. TOBIN, 'The Controversy Over Monetary Policy', *Review of Economics and Statistics*, Vol. XXXIII (1951), pp. 179–200.

A. G. HART, *Defense Without Inflation* (New York, 1951).

A. G. HART and E. C. BROWN, *Financing Defense* (New York, 1951).

B. G. HICKMAN, *The Korean War and U.S. Economic Activity, 1950–52* (New York, 1955).

G. G. JOHNSON, 'Reflections on a Year of Price Controls', *American Economic Review*, Vol. XLII Supplement (1952), pp. 289–300.

J. P. LEWIS, 'The Lull That Came to Stay', *Journal of Political Economy*, Vol. LXIII (1955), pp. 1–19.

R. V. ROOSA, 'The Revival of Monetary Policy', *Review of Economics and Statistics*, Vol. XXXIII (1951), pp. 29–37.

W. THOMAS, 'Recent Experience with Monetary Fiscal Measures to Combat Inflation', *American Economic Review*, Vol. XLII Supplement (1952), pp. 273–88.

U.S. Congress, House of Representatives, Committee on Ways and Means, *Hearings on Excess Profits Taxation* (Washington, 1950).

U.S. Congress, House of Representatives, *Hearings on Revenue Revision* (Washington, 1951).

U.S. Congress, *H. Doc. No. 53*, 82nd Cong., 1st Sess.

U.S. Congress, *H. Rept. No. 3142*, 81st Cong., 2nd Sess.

U.S. Congress, *H. Rept. No. 586*, 82 Cong., 1st Sess.

U.S. Congress, Joint Committee on the Economic Report, Subcommittee on General Credit Control and Debt Management, *Monetary Policy and the Management of the Debt: replies to questions and other material for the use of the Subcommittee* (Washington, 1952).

U.S. Congress, Joint Committee on the Economic Report, Subcommittee on General Credit Control and Debt Management, *Hearings* (Washington, 1952).

U.S. Congress, Joint Committee on the Economic Report, Subcommittee on General Credit Control and Debt Management, *Report: Monetary Policy and the Management of the Public Debt (S. Doc. No. 162,* 82nd Cong., 2nd Sess.) (Washington, 1952).

U.S. Congress, Senate, Committee on Finance, *Hearings on H.R.9827* (Washington, 1950).

U.S. Congress, Senate, Committee on Finance, *Hearings on H.R.4473* (Washington, 1951).

U.S. Congress, *S. Rept. No. 2679,* 81st Cong., 2nd Sess.

U.S. Congress, *S. Rept. No. 644,* 82nd Cong., 1st Sess.

U.S. Congress, *S. Rept. No. 781,* 82nd Cong., 1st Sess.

H. C. WALLICH, 'Recent Monetary Policies in the United States'. *American Economic Review*, Vol. XLII Supplement (1953), pp. 27–42.

XIV. Recession and Recovery, 1953–55

E. C. BROWN, 'The New Depreciation Policy under Income Tax: An Economic Appraisal', *National Tax Journal*, Vol. VIII (1955), pp. 82–94.

A. F. BURNS, *Prosperity Without Inflation* (New York, 1957).

Committee on Tax Policy, *Federal Finances* (New York, 1954).

R. J. Donovan, *Eisenhower: The Inside Story* (New York, 1956).

A. H. HANSEN, 'Brief Note on the Role of Consumption in the 1954–55 Recovery', *Review of Economics and Statistics*, Vol. XXXVII (1955), pp. 424–5.

S. E. HARRIS, H. S. ELLIS, G. COLM, A. H. HANSEN, and M. BRONFENBRENNER, 'Symposium on the Economic Report of the President and Related Documents', *Review of Economics and Statistics*, Vol. XXXVI (1954), pp. 249–66.

B. HICKMAN, 'Postwar Cyclical Experience and Economic Stability', *American Economic Review*, Vol. XLVII Supplement (1957), pp. 117–34.

D. M. HOLLAND, *The Income Tax Burden on Shareholders* (Princeton, 1958).

N. H. JACOBY, *Can Prosperity Be Sustained* (New York, 1946).

K. D. ROOSE, 'Business Fluctuations in the United States Since 1951: Selected Developments', *American Economic Review*, Vol. XLV Supplement (1955), pp. 367–74.

D. T. SMITH, 'Two Years of Republican Tax Policy', *National Tax Journal*, Vol. VIII (1955), pp. 1–8.

B. W. SPRINKEL, 'The 1955 Economic Report of the President', *Journal of the American Statistical Association*, Vol. L (1955), pp. 240–8.

P. J. STRAYER, 'Full Employment—1954 Model', *American Economic Review*, Vol. XLIV (1954), pp. 884–93.

U.S. Congress, *H. Rept. No. 1307*, 83rd Cong., 2nd Sess.

U.S. Congress *H. Rept. No. 1337*, 83rd Cong., 2nd Sess.

U.S. Congress, Joint Committee on the Economic Report, Subcommittee on Economic Stabilization, *U.S. Monetary Policy: Recent Thinking and Experience* (Washington, 1954).

U.S. Congress, Senate, Committee on Finance, *Hearings on H.R.8223* (Washington, 1954).

U.S. Congress, Senate, Committee on Finance, *Hearings on H.R.8300* (Washington, 1954).

U.S. Congress, *S. Rept. No. 1085*, 83rd Cong., 2nd Sess.

U.S. Congress, *S. Rept. No. 1622*, 83rd Cong., 2nd Sess.

R. YOUNGDAHL, 'Monetary Policy in Recent Years', *American Economic Review*, Vol. XLV Supplement (1955), pp. 402–8.

XV. Boom and Inflation, 1955–7

American Assembly, *Wages, Prices, Profits, and Productivity* (New York, 1959).

S. E. HARRIS, S. H. SLICHTER, E. S. SHAW, P. A. SAMUELSON, W. FELLNER, H. M. GROVES, H. C. WALLICH, A. C. HARBERGER, and N. GOLDFINGER, 'The Economics of Eisenhower: A Symposium', *Review of Economics and Statistics*, Vol. XXXVIII (1956), pp. 357–85.

M. SINGER, 'Inflation Without Full Employment', *Social Research*, Vol. XXVI (1959), p. 1–17.

R. T. SELDEN, 'Cost Push versus Demand Pull Inflation, 1955–7' *Journal of Political Economy*, Vol. LXVII (1959), pp. 1–21.

C. SCHULTZE, *Recent Inflation in the United States*; *Study Paper No. 1 for the Joint Economic Committee* (Washington, 1959).

U.S. Congress, *H. Rept. No. 647*, 85th Cong., 1st Sess.

U.S. Congress, Joint Committee on the Economic Report, Sub-committee on Economic Stabilization, *Conflicting Official Views on Monetary Policy: April 1956* (Washington, 1956).

U.S. Congress, Joint Economic Committee, Subcommittee on Fiscal Policy, *Fiscal Policy Implications of the Economic Outlook and Budget Developments* (Washington, 1957).

U.S. Congress, Joint Economic Committee, *The Relationship of Prices to Economic Stability and Growth* (Washington, 1958).

U.S. Congress, Senate, Committee on Finance, *Hearings on the Investigation of the Financial Conditions of the United States* (Washington, 1957).

XVI. Recession and Recovery, 1957–9

E. BLOCH, 'Automatic Fiscal Stabilizers in the 1957–8 Business Contraction', *Review of Economics and Statistics*, Vol. XLI (1959), p. 312.

G. HABERLER, J. S. DUESENBERRY, S. E. HARRIS, and J. R. MEYER, 'Brief Comments on the Recession', *Review of Economics and Statistics*, Vol. XL (1958), pp. 309–18.

U.S. Congress, *H. Rept. No. 1409*, 85th Cong., 2nd Sess.

U.S. Congress, Joint Economic Committee, Subcommittee on Fiscal Policy, *Fiscal Policy Implications of the Current Economic Outlook* (Washington, 1958).

U.S. Congress, Senate, Committee on Finance, *Hearings on the Investigation of the Financial Condition of the United States* (Washington, 1958).

American Academy of Political and Social Science, *Inflation* (Philadelphia, 1959).

XVII. Assessments of Fiscal Policy in the United States Since 1945.

G. COLM (ed.), *The Employment Act: Past and Future* (Washington, 1956).

A. H. HANSEN, *The American Economy* (New York, 1957).

W. W. HELLER, 'C.E.D.'s Stabilizing Budget Policy After Ten Years', *American Economic Review*, Vol. XLVII (1957), pp. 634–51.

L. H. KIMMEL, *Federal Budget and Fiscal Policy, 1789–1958* (Washington, 1959).

W. L. SMITH, *Debt Management in the United States: Study Paper No. 19 for Joint Economic Committee* (Washington, 1960).

P. J. STRAYER, *Fiscal Policy and Politics* (New York, 1958).

INDEX

Rep. = Representative.   Sen. = Senator.   [D] = Democrat.   [R] = Republican.

Council of Economic Advisers—*cont.*
concern at level of investment 1950, 130; Congressional investigation demanded by Senator Byrd, 131; on government expenditures 1951, 155–6; views on higher interest rates 1952, 183; survival in question 1953, 199–203; see possibility of recession 1953, 211; Eisenhower's confidence in, 242; forecast for 1957, 271

Curtis, Carol T., Rep., later Sen., from Nebraska, [R], 58

Defence expenditure: limit imposed by President Truman 1948, 96; increase 1949, 106; contribution to economic stability, 129; during Korean War, 135, 148, 151–3, 180, 182, 188; cuts imposed by Eisenhower Administration, 204–5; and the recession of 1954, 215, 217–18, 224; increase in 1955; 251, Air Force appropriation 1956, 256; cut in 1957, 263; increase after 'Sputnik', 277; limits scope of fiscal policy, 301, 306; consequences of large reduction, 317

DeLacy, Hugh, Rep. from Washington, [D], 48 n

Dewey, Thomas E., 101, 197

Dingell, John D., Rep. from Michigan, [D], 86, 88, 169 n

Dirksen, Everett McK., Rep., later Sen., from Illinois, [R], 34, 143

Direct Controls—Prices: during World War II, 30; abandonment of in 1946, 46, 53–54; recommended by President 1949, 105; during Korean War, 134, 184–5, 203

Direct Controls—Wages: during Korean War, 134, 184–5, 203

Dodge, Joseph M., 199

Domar, E. D., 37

Donovan, R. J., 216 n, 237 n, 242

Doughton, Robert, Rep. from North Carolina, [D]: attitude to tax reduction in 1947, 79–80; opposes President's tax policy in 1948, 88–89; supports Revenue Act 1948, 95; attitude to tax increase 1949, 109; supports tax reform bill 1950, 126; opposes excess profits tax amendment 1950, 139; hearings on Excess Profits Tax Bill 1950; 145; rejects quick tax increase 1951, 158; and tax increases 1951, 160, 164–5, 168–9

Douglas, Paul H., Sen. from Illinois, [D]: opposes tax increase 1949, 109;

Douglas, Paul H.—*cont.*
supports cuts in government expenditure in 1949, 115, and in 1951, 1954; on fiscal policy in 1951, 155; supports larger tax increases 1951, 173; supports measures to close tax 'loopholes' 1952, 180; criticizes conduct of monetary policy 1953, 208 n, 209; supports tax reduction in recession of 1954, 222–3, 233; criticises Administration's handling of recession, 240; proposes tax reductions 1958, 279, 286

Durham, Carl T., Rep. from North Carolina, [D], 80

Dulles, John Foster, 304 n

Eastland, James O., Sen. from Mississippi, [D], 94

Eberharter, Herman P., Rep. from Pennsylvania, [D], 139, 162, 177

Eccles, Marriner S., 36

Eckstein, Otto, 246 n

Ecton, Zales N., Sen. from Montana, [R], 59, 199 n

Eden, Sir Anthony, 310 n

Edmonds, William J., 234

Education, Federal finance of, 35, 103, 108, 152, 153, 251, 257, 261, 264

Eisenhower, Dwight D., President: views on fiscal policy and economic affairs generally, 196–9, 305; orders cuts in expenditure 1953, 206; vetoes bill to reduce tax on admission to cinemas 1953, 206; economic policy in early months of his Administration, 209–10; accepts excise tax reduction 1954, 223; opposes general reduction in income tax 1954, 231; opposes tax reduction 1955, 237; handling of the recession of 1954, 217, 235, 241–2; programme of government expenditures 1955, 252–3; exhortation to responsible price and wage policies 1957, 259; and the budget 1957, 261–3, 265 n; budget recommendations 1958, 277–8; and the recession of 1958, 278, 281–2, 293–4, 297; vetoes bills to increase expenditure, 283; opposes tax reduction 1958, 285; denounces 'spenders' in election campaign 1958, 289–90; comparison of policies in dealing with recessions with those of President Truman, 299; and policies relating to economic growth, 315–16; on perils of inflation, 319